DIVERSITIES IN EDUCATION

Diversities in Education is a challenging text that will help educators, teacher educators and trainee teachers to be more effective in teaching a range of diverse learners. It covers five major categories of difference: sex and gender; social class and socio-economic status; race, ethnicity and culture; beliefs and religion; and different abilities and asks the urgent questions all policy-makers, educators and students should consider:

- Why should we value diversity and human rights?
- How can inclusive education accommodate diversity?
- How do society's aspirations for cohesion and harmony impact on people who are different?
- What meanings are given to differences, culturally and historically?
- Should educators seek to accentuate, eliminate, reduce or ignore differences?

By drawing attention to the latest research into the most effective educational policies and practices, this insightful book suggests strategies for meeting the challenges being posed in an era of superdiversity. It's a crucial read for any training or practising educator who wants to address the issue of diversity, learn effective ways to reach all learners and create more inclusive and harmonious societies.

David Mitchell is an Adjunct Professor at the University of Canterbury, Christchurch, New Zealand, and is an international consultant in inclusive education and evidence-based teaching. He is the author of *What Really Works in Special and Inclusive Education*, 2nd edition (Routledge), which has been translated into several languages.

DIVERSITIES IN EDUCATION

Effective ways to reach all learners

David Mitchell

 Routledge
Taylor & Francis Group

LONDON AND NEW YORK

First published 2017
by Routledge
2 Park Square, Milton Park, Abingdon, Oxon OX14 4RN

and by Routledge
711 Third Avenue, New York, NY 10017

Routledge is an imprint of the Taylor & Francis Group, an informa business

British Library Cataloguing in Publication Data
A catalogue record for this book is available from the British Library

Library of Congress Cataloging in Publication Data
Names: Mitchell, David R., author.
Title: Diversities in education : effective ways to reach all learners / David Mitchell.
Description: Abingdon, Oxon ; New York, NY : Routledge is an imprint of the Taylor & Francis Group, an Informa Business, [2017]
Identifiers: LCCN 2016015483| ISBN 9781138924680 (hardback) | ISBN 9781138924703 (pbk.) | ISBN 9781315684208 (ebook)
Subjects: LCSH: Culturally relevant pedagogy.
Classification: LCC LC1099 .M584 2017 | DDC 370.11/5-dc23
LC record available at https://lccn.loc.gov/2016015483

ISBN: 978-1-138-92468-0 (hbk)
ISBN: 978-1-138-92470-3 (pbk)
ISBN: 978-1-315-68420-8 (ebk)

Typeset in Interstate
by Cenveo Publisher Services

MIX
Paper from
responsible sources
FSC   FSC® C013056
www.fsc.org

Printed and bound in Great Britain by
TJ International Ltd, Padstow, Cornwall

For my family in all its diversity:

Jill
Grant, Mina, Kiki, Conrad, Zenji and Titus
Janet, Bevan, Ayaka and Tane

CONTENTS

PREFACE

I am different; I am unique; I am different today from yesterday and will be different tomorrow. I have a unique set of markers comprising my identity. While I undoubtedly share some of these markers with you, my reader, it is extremely unlikely that I share them all with you or any other person on the planet. And the same is true for you: we are both unique creatures. Some of our differences are immutable (e.g., our age and, for most, our gender), while others can be changed (e.g., our socio-economic status, our family structure, our religion and our political context). Children's options are rather more limited than adults' as they must subscribe to their parents'/caregivers' circumstances, but here education comes into play by providing children with the skills to make their own choices.

We live in increasingly diverse societies and you, as an educator, need to be able to respond appropriately and sensitively to this diversity. Your challenge is threefold: With reference to each domain of difference, should you seek to celebrate and accentuate it, eliminate or reduce it, or tolerate or ignore it?

In writing this book, my primary aim is to help educators (practising and trainee teachers, principals and the professionals who prepare and advise them, e.g., teacher educators and school psychologists) to become more effective in teaching diverse learners. I also intend that the book will provide guidance to those responsible for formulating legislation and policies relating to societies' diverse peoples. I hope that the book will go some way towards helping all my readers to bridge the growing gap between research and practice. I hope, too, that it will help to familiarize them with some of the cutting-edge research on effective educational policies and practices that has been, and is being, carried out around the world in the education of diverse children. As you will see, I consider that there is much more that can and should be done to improve their lives.

I have found writing the book to be a challenge – but an absorbing one – as I have had to traverse many disciplines: psychology, sociology, philosophy, economics, genetics, neurology, political science, theology, as well as education, of course. I have also sought to give the book an international scope by drawing upon United Nations conventions and reports, as well as publications issued by bodies such as the World Bank, the OECD and the Council of Europe. I am conscious that each of the topics I cover has generated many books. I saw my task as being to select and synthesize a wide body of literature on the 'big five' diversities: sex and gender, social class/socio-economic status, race/ethnicity/culture, beliefs/religion and ability/disability, and to explore commonalities among them.

By now, you will have noted that I have chosen to write often in the first person, a somewhat unusual style for someone steeped in academic traditions! My reason for this is simply that I want to connect with you the reader on a personal level as far as it is possible via the printed word. In keeping with this commitment, I will be sharing my personal experiences with diversity as I grew up. From the outset, I believe you have a right to know something of who

I am. As James Banks put it, 'the biographical journeys of researchers greatly influence their values, their research questions, and the knowledge they construct'.[1] Several markers of my biographical journey shape my present identity: I am a white, middle class, non-religious, heterosexual male of above average intelligence, living in a small, multi-cultural, social democracy, a former colony of Great Britain, located in the South Pacific. At any one time any one of these features may shape my thoughts and actions; but mostly these are shaped by various combinations of my identity markers. This, I believe, is also true of you, my reader.

Finally, let me introduce myself. I am David Mitchell, a New Zealander who has worked as a consultant in inclusive and special education in many countries. My education career commenced as a primary school teacher, with a particular focus on gifted and talented children, from which I moved to become an educational psychologist assisting educators to work with learners with special educational needs in a community with a large number of Māori families. My next career step was to work in as a teacher educator in universities, mainly in New Zealand, but also as a visiting professor and UNESCO consultant in countries as diverse as the United States, Canada, the United Kingdom, Japan, Singapore, Kazakhstan, South Africa, Ethiopia and Uzbekistan. My recent publications (all published with Routledge) include a four-volume series, *Special education needs and inclusive education* (2004), *Contextualizing inclusive education: Evaluating old and new international perspectives* (2005 and 2009), two editions of *What really works in special and inclusive education* (2008 and 2014) and a book I co-edited with Valerie Karr: *Crises, conflict and disability* (2014).

David Mitchell
Pegasus, New Zealand

Note

1   Banks, J. (2013). 'Educating citizens for tomorrow's diverse world.' In M.L. Kysilka & O.L. Davis (eds), *Schooling for tomorrow's America* (pp. 43-64). Charlotte, NC: Information Age Publishing, p. 44.

ACKNOWLEDGEMENTS

I should like to acknowledge the great support and editorial guidance provided by my wife, Jill Mitchell, in the two years in which this book was being brought to fruition.

I also acknowledge with gratitude the helpful feedback I obtained from Graeme Pratley, Derek Browne and Roger Rule on the religion chapter (5) and Vicki Carpenter on the socio-economic status chapter (3).

My granddaughter, Ayaka Archer, provided me with skilled assistance in preparing several of the graphics.

And finally, I am grateful for the encouragement and professionalism of the team at Routledge, particularly Alison Foyle, Sarah Tuckwell, Hannah Slater and Graeme Leonard.

1 Differences and samenesses

An introduction

Always remember that you are absolutely unique. Just like everyone else.
(Margaret Mead)

1.1 Introduction

Human beings have many features in common, some they share with some others, and many are specific to themselves. It is this diversity that enriches our lives in countless ways every day. Yet, to some, diversity elicits contempt, even fear, and challenges their acceptance to the point where they may discriminate against those who are different, marginalize and even persecute them.

At least in western countries, populations are becoming increasingly diverse. This reflects a range of factors, including the impact of globalization with the attendant mobility of labour; the upsurge of refugees fleeing conflict or the consequences of global warming, or seeking better economic futures; changing demographic profiles resulting from such factors as differential fertility rates among various groups; and independent choices of identity exercised by free citizens. With reference to Britain (but with wider application), Steven Vertovec, Professor of Transnational Anthropology at the University of Oxford, has termed this trend 'superdiversity', which he defined as

> a dynamic interplay of variables among an increased number of new, small and scattered, multiple-origin, transnationally connected, socio-economically differentiated and legally stratified immigrants who have arrived over the last decade.[1]

Unfortunately, diversity – and superdiversity – often creates intolerance and conflict at macro (societal) and micro (individual) levels, creating vulnerabilities in children. By addressing issues to do with diversity, schools can and should do much to create more peaceful, just and equitable societies (and world) based on mutual respect and tolerance. I hope this book contributes to this goal.

1.2 What we mean by 'different' and 'diverse'

Typical dictionary definitions of *different* are *not the same as another or each other; unlike in nature, form, or quality*. According to the Oxford English Dictionary, 'different' has its origins in Middle English *differren*, meaning *to distinguish*, and Latin *differre*, meaning *to bear apart, put off*. The definition of *diversity* is *a range of many people or things that are very different from each other.* It is derived from Old French *diversite,* from Latin *diversitas,* and *diversus.* *Diverse* is the past participle of *divertere, meaning 'to* turn aside'.

With respect to human beings, 'difference' and 'diversity' both typically refer to the dimensions of sex and gender; socio-economic status; race, ethnicity and culture; beliefs and religion; and special needs. These constitute the 'big five', which are the focus of this book.

In a challenging paper, Nicholas Burbules itemized several different ways of thinking about differences, in what he referred to as 'a grammar of difference'.[2] Briefly, these include: (1) difference of variety, as in different kinds within a particular category, e.g., different national identities; (2) difference in degree, as in differences along a continuum of qualities, e.g., skin colour; (3) difference as variation, as in different combinations of and emphases upon certain elements, e.g., different body types or different states of ability or disability; (4) difference as a version, as in a familiar standard that is altered through interpretation, but, unlike a variation, it leaves the key elements of the standard unchanged, simply giving to them a different sense of meaning and tone; e.g., differences of sexual identity; and (5) difference as an analogy, when differences are identified as relative, not to common standards, but to comparable, parallel standards, e.g., different moral distinctions.

1.3 Differences fascinate us

The media and, presumably, we, its consumers, are attracted to stories portraying human differences. Some differences we admire, even envy; others repulse us or engender fear; all seem to fascinate us. This range is illustrated in a selection of stories I have seen in newspapers in the course of a week:

- Gender differences: An item discusses civil unions and same sex marriage; a columnist stated that it was 'quite hard being a woman', as there are 'lots of rules' that 'turn up implicitly in editorials, popular commentary and casual conversation'.
- Socio-economic status differences: A report indicated that the 85 richest people on the planet have accumulated as much wealth between them as half of the world's population. Another report noted that the richest 1% currently own 48% of all global wealth.
- The International Organization for Migration was reported as saying that more than 1 million migrants and refugees had crossed into Europe in 2015, amid the fallout of war, poverty and persecution in Africa and the Middle East. This represented more than a four-fold increase from 2014.
- Religious differences: The European Court of Human Rights has upheld France's law banning face-covering Muslim veils from the streets, in a case brought by a woman who claimed her freedom of religion was violated; forces from the Islamic State of Iraq and Syria (ISIS) in Mosul warned Christians to leave, convert to Islam or face execution; in my city of Christchurch, New Zealand, a mother protested about the law that permits the teaching of religion in state schools under some circumstances.
- Intellectual differences: An item described how outstanding creative design formed the basis of sustainable business opportunities.
- Physical differences: An Australian study showed that children as young as eight are dissatisfied with their bodies and that the majority of 10- and 11-year-olds are trying to

control their weight; under a provocative headline, 'Talking about an awkward issue', an article raises the question – should disabled athletes be competing at the Commonwealth Games in Glasgow?

- Personality differences: A woman in an abusive relationship is found guilty of stabbing her partner; a man with the intriguing name of All Means All in prison for threatening to kill the prime minister, gave up his hunger strike.
- Age differences: A research report showed that first-born children are more likely to be the most ambitious and well-qualified of their siblings.
- Family structure differences: A correspondent's column described her experiences with a woman who had 11 children.

1.4 Differences can have serious consequences

Throughout the centuries and across the world, many people who are different have suffered from the effects of xenophobia, discrimination, segregation and marginalization. In the most serious of circumstances, their differences have led to them losing their lives in wars and other conflicts. According to the United Nations, during the 1990s a total of 53 armed conflicts resulted in 3.9 million deaths, nearly 90% of whom were civilians,[3] numbers that equate roughly to the entire populations of the city of Los Angeles or to the countries of Ireland and New Zealand. In addition, in 2002, there were approximately 22 million international refugees in the world and another 20-25 million internally displaced people.[4]

Being different has led to many individuals or groups being excluded from meaningful participation in education and society more generally. In its most extreme form, difference has resulted in attempts to exterminate whole classes of people, for example in Nazi Germany and, more recently, in Rwanda and Iraq/Syria. Even in modern, 'advanced' societies children who don't conform to dominant discourses are vulnerable to stigmatization and alienation.

1.5 Some education systems discriminate against those who are different

Unfortunately, education systems, both historically and contemporaneously, are replete with examples of active or passive discrimination against various groups of people – those of colour, those with disabilities, those with certain religious beliefs, immigrants, the poor, females ... Sometimes this discrimination has been benevolent and motivated by a wish to do the best for children as, for example, in the setting up of special schools or special classes for children with disabilities; at other times, the discrimination is overt and hostile, reflecting broader social values as, for example, apartheid-era education of blacks and coloured children in South Africa.

1.6 Goals and perspectives

This book is underpinned by two goals and 19 cross-cutting perspectives relating to how education and society should respond to diversity. The two goals are:

A.   to respect and enhance the human rights of diverse people, and
B.   to develop an inclusive society and global community.

The cross-cutting perspectives comprise the following:

1   Theories of distributive justice should underpin our approach to diversity
2   Diversities must be seen from an ecological perspective
3   Perceptions of diversity vary across time and space
4   Finding the right balance between sameness and diversity is a challenge
5   Interest convergence helps to explain shifts in behaviour and policies
6   Diversities intersect with each other
7   There are multiple causes of diversities
8   Human beings are genetically similar
9   Consideration should be given to an evolutionary perspective on diversity
10   Many differences are quite small, even if they are statistically significant
11   Economics play a major role in catering for diversities
12   Education is multi-level and multi-faceted
13   There can be a mismatch between children's and schools' cultural and social capital
14   Reason and evidence should determine educational policies and practices
15   Account should be taken of the impact of disruptive technologies on job prospects
16   Technology has the potential to transform education
17   The focus should be on the uniqueness of individuals
18   Universal design for learning provides fair opportunities for learning
19   Early prevention and intervention programmes should be developed.

1.7 Goal A: To respect and enhance the human rights of diverse people

Quite simply, it is important that we recognize that people who are different have human rights. Consideration of society's responsibilities towards children who are disadvantaged for whatever reason must be predicated on the broad concept of human rights.[5] These rights inform us as to what we may, must, and must not do to others and what we may expect of others in their behaviours towards us.

In 1948, the United Nations agreed to the *Universal Declaration of Human Rights* (UDHR). Adopted by the UN General Assembly on 10 December 1948, it was the result of the experience of World War II. With the end of that war, the international community vowed never again to allow atrocities like those of that conflict to happen again. The preamble to the UDHR thus included the following:

> Whereas recognition of the inherent dignity and of the equal and inalienable rights of all members of the human family is the foundation of freedom, justice and peace in the world, [and]
>
> Whereas disregard and contempt for human rights have resulted in barbarous acts which have outraged the conscience of mankind, and the advent of a world in which human beings shall enjoy freedom of speech and belief and freedom from fear and want has been proclaimed as the highest aspiration of the common people.

In terms of the theme of this book, three Articles are of particular relevance:

> Article 1: All human beings are born free and equal in dignity and rights. They are endowed with reason and conscience and should act towards one another in a spirit of brotherhood.

Article 2: Everyone is entitled to all the rights and freedoms set forth in this Declaration, without distinction of any kind, such as race, colour, sex, language, religion, political or other opinion, national or social origin, property, birth or other status ...

Article 7: All are equal before the law and are entitled without any discrimination to equal protection of the law. All are entitled to equal protection against any discrimination in violation of this Declaration and against any incitement to such discrimination.

According to Israeli scholar, Frances Raday,[6] the rights articulated in the UDHR had their origins in the shift from a religious to a secular state culture at the time of the eighteenth-century European Enlightenment. This was accompanied by the replacement of communitarianism by individualism, by the shift from status to contract, and by rationalism instead of faith. As we shall see in Chapters 3 and 5, although these shifts have been universally accepted, they are not always honoured and continue to give rise to conflict. While human rights covenants set normative frameworks, they don't provide answers as to how conflicts should be resolved.[7]

Since 1948, the commitment articulated in the UDHR has been translated into law – whether in the forms of treaties, customary international law, general principles, regional agreements and domestic law – through which human rights are expressed and guaranteed. As we shall see in subsequent chapters, it has formed the basis of a wide range of Conventions or other instruments relating to the rights of women; children; indigenous people; people with mental illness; national or ethnic, religious and linguistic minorities; migrant workers and their families; refugees; and, recently, people with disabilities.

The right to education is explicitly defined in three international instruments. The first of these is the 1989 *Convention on the Rights of the Child*. This Convention included Article 29, which requires that education should be directed to:

(a) The development of the child's personality, talents and mental and physical abilities to their fullest potential;

(b) The development of respect for human rights and fundamental freedoms, and for the principles enshrined in the Charter of the United Nations;

(c) The development of respect for the child's parents, his or her own cultural identity, language and values, for the national values of the country in which the child is living, the country from which he or she may originate, and for civilizations different from his or her own;

(d) The preparation of the child for responsible life in a free society, in the spirit of understanding, peace, tolerance, equality of sexes, and friendship among all peoples, ethnic, national and religious groups and persons of indigenous origin.

Even though every country except Somalia and the United States has ratified this Convention, at least 57.8 million children of primary school age around the world were out of school in 2012.[8] Although this is a striking improvement on the 2000 figure of 99.7 million, it is still a cause for major concern.

The second instrument is the 1999 *International Covenant on Economic, Social and Cultural Rights*.[9] The preamble to Article 13, which is concerned with the right to education, included the following:

> Education is both a human right in itself and an indispensable means of realizing other human rights. As an empowerment right, education is the primary vehicle by which economically and socially marginalized adults and children can lift themselves out of poverty and obtain the means to participate fully in their communities ... But the importance of education is not just practical: a well-educated, enlightened and active mind, able to wander freely and widely, is one of the joys and rewards of human existence.

In keeping with the last point, Article 13(1) of the *Covenant* asserts that 'education shall be directed to the full development of the human personality'. Article 13(2) goes on to specify that

> education in all its forms and at all levels shall exhibit the following interrelated and essential features: *availability* of functioning educational institutions and programmes in sufficient quantity; *accessibility* of educational institutions and programmes to all, without discrimination, and including physical and economic accessibility; *acceptability* of the form and substance of education, including curricula, teaching methods and cultural appropriateness; and *adaptability* of education to the needs of changing societies and communities, and to the needs of students within their diverse social and cultural settings.

The third international instrument concerning the right to education is UNESCO's 1960 *Convention against Discrimination in Education*. It included the following articles:

> 3(b) To ensure, by legislation where necessary, that there is no discrimination in the admission of pupils to educational institutions;
>
> 4(a) To make primary education free and compulsory; make secondary education in its different forms generally available and accessible to all; make higher education equally accessible to all on the basis of individual capacity; assure compliance by all with the obligation to attend school prescribed by law;
>
> 4(b) To ensure that the standards of education are equivalent in all public educational institutions of the same level, and that the conditions relating to the quality of the education provided are also equivalent;
>
> 5(a) Education shall be directed to the full development of the human personality and to the strengthening of respect for human rights and fundamental freedoms; it shall promote understanding, tolerance and friendship among all nations, racial or religious groups, and shall further the activities of the United Nations.
>
> 5(b) It is essential to respect the liberty of parents and, where applicable, of legal guardians, firstly to choose for their children institutions other than those maintained by the public authorities but conforming to such minimum educational standards as may be laid down or approved by the competent authorities ...

Many countries and regional entities have taken the lead from the UDHR and its associated covenants and committed themselves to their principles. For example, in my own country, New Zealand, it is against the law to discriminate against individuals in many areas of public life, including in work, education, official practice and policy and the provision of goods and services. The prohibited grounds of discrimination are set out in section 21 of the *Human Rights Act* of 1993. They are: age (from age 16), colour, disability, employment status, ethical belief (including lack of religious belief), ethnic or national origins, family status, marital status, political opinion, race, religious belief, sex and sexual orientation.

Similarly, the Canadian *Human Rights Act* of 1977 has the express goal of ensuring equal opportunity to individuals who may be victims of discriminatory practices based on a set of prohibited grounds such as sex, disability or religion. This Act applies throughout Canada, but only to federally regulated activities; each province and territory has its own anti-discrimination law that applies to activities that are not federally regulated. In one such province, Alberta, it is recognized that all persons are 'equal in dignity, rights and responsibilities without regard to race, religious beliefs, colour, gender, physical disability, mental disability, age, ancestry, place of origin, marital status, source of income, family status or sexual orientation'.

In the United Kingdom, the *Human Rights Act* prohibits discrimination on a wide range of grounds including 'sex, race, colour, language, religion, political or other opinion, national or social origin, association with a national minority, property, birth or other status'.

The European *Convention on Human Rights*, which came into force in 1953, prohibits discrimination based on 'sex, race, colour, language, religion, political or other opinion, national or social origin, association with a national minority, property, birth or other status'.

A final example is the *American Convention on Human Rights* (the Pact of San Jose, Costa Rica). This Convention, which covers the Organization of American States, came into force in 1978. Its preamble includes the recognition that states will recognize specified rights and freedoms 'without any discrimination for reasons of race, color, sex, language, religion, political or other opinion, national or social origin, economic status, birth, or any other social condition'.

For the most part these human rights Acts or Conventions aim at proscribing discrimination; as such, they focus on the negative claims rights that I outline below.

The school curricula in many countries' education systems reflect human rights principles, frequently including strong references to diversity. For example, the New Zealand Curriculum requires schools to, *inter alia*: (a) acknowledge the bicultural foundations of New Zealand, (b) reflect New Zealand's cultural diversity and value the histories and traditions of all its people, and (c) be non-sexist, non-racist and non-discriminatory, ensuring that students' identities, languages, abilities and talents are recognized and affirmed and that their learning needs are addressed. Similarly, in the United Kingdom, in an attempt to encourage diversity, the National Curriculum in 1999 identified 'diversity' as including: boys and girls, pupils with special educational needs, pupils with disabilities, pupils from all social and cultural backgrounds, pupils of different ethnic groups including Travellers, refugees and asylum seekers and those from diverse linguistic, religious backgrounds.[10] Essential elements in valuing pupil diversity were to ensure that pupils learned to appreciate and view positively differences in others, whether arising from race, gender, ability or disability, and that all forms of bullying, harassment and stereotypical views are challenged. At a wider level, teachers were encouraged to use materials and images in their teaching that reflect social, religious and cultural diversity.[11] At an international level, UNESCO has done much to promote the valuing of diversity through its advocacy of an inclusive curriculum. For example, in the Foreword to its influential publication, *Policy guidelines on inclusion in education*,[12] Nicholas Burnett emphasized that

> Inclusive education is a process that involves the transformation of schools and other centres of learning to cater for all children – including boys and girls, students from ethnic and linguistic minorities, rural populations, those affected by HIV and AIDS, and those with disabilities and difficulties in learning ... Its aim is to eliminate exclusion that is a consequence of negative attitudes and a lack of response to diversity in race, economic status, social class, ethnicity, language, religion, gender, sexual orientation and ability.[13]

In this book, I shall also address the problem of how to reconcile competing rights, for example in Chapter 5, I will discuss children's vs their parents' rights with regard to freedom of religion and females' rights to be treated equally vs religious norms and cultural practices which might argue otherwise. These dilemmas draw attention to the distinction between individual and group rights.

Why should we value diversity and respect human rights? At a biological level, Charles Darwin saw in the diversity of species the principles of evolution that operated to generate the species. This occurs through genetic diversity serving as a way for populations to adapt to changing environments. With more variation, it is more likely that some individuals will possess genes that are suited to particular environments if they come under stress. Such individuals are more likely to survive to produce offspring bearing those genes. This is what has occurred as modern humans evolved in Africa and spread across the world, adapting locally to the selective pressures of the climates, food sources and pathogens that they encountered. Thus, diversity evolved.

At a social level, there is an instrumental argument for valuing diversity. If societies in general and schools in particular value diversity, this can bring about several desirable outcomes. These include: (a) enhancing social development by expanding the pool of people with whom individuals can associate and develop relationships; (b) preparing students for future career success by becoming sensitive to human differences and able to relate to people of different abilities, nationalities and cultural backgrounds; (c) increasing individuals' knowledge base and creative thinking by interacting with a diverse group of people; (d) enhancing self-awareness by students comparing and contrasting their life experiences with others who differ sharply. Respect for diversity includes knowing how to relate to qualities and conditions that are different from our own and outside the groups to which we belong, yet are present in other individuals and groups.[14] This is the challenge facing educators at all levels of the education system in all countries.

Morally, there is a strong argument for valuing diversity, arising from the doctrine of human rights.[15] In a nutshell, it aims at identifying the fundamental prerequisites for each human being to lead a minimally good life and to enjoy the full rights of citizenship. It rests upon belief in the existence of a truly universal moral community comprising all human beings. Within Europe, the origins of moral universalism as a basis for human rights are typically associated with the writings of Aristotle. The contemporary idea of human rights most clearly emerged during the seventeenth and eighteenth centuries with the so-called 'doctrine of natural law', which argued that individuals possess rights independently of society or polity. The seventeenth-century philosopher, John Locke, argued that natural rights flowed from natural law, which originated from God. However, the eighteenth-century German philosopher, Immanuel Kant, argued that an appeal to the authority of some super-human entity was not necessary in justifying human beings' claims to certain, fundamental rights. Instead, he argued for the ideal of a potentially universal community of rational individuals autonomously determining the moral principles for securing rights. For him, the basis of moral reasoning must rest upon a condition to which all rational individuals are bound to assent. A related position on human rights argues that each individual owes a basic and general duty to respect the rights of every other individual because, by doing so, one's individual self-interest is furthered. From this perspective, individuals accept and comply with human rights because this is the best means for protecting one's interests against actions and omissions that might endanger themselves.

When considering human rights, it is useful to distinguish between 'positive claims rights' and 'negative claims rights'.[16] The former enjoins us to treat individuals in a positive manner by, for example, providing medical treatment in the case of illness or injury and providing appropriate education, irrespective of an individual's degree of disability. Negative claims rights evoke the second part of the Hippocratic Oath, namely that 'I will use treatments for the benefit of the ill in accordance with my ability and my judgment, but from what is to their harm and injustice I will keep them.' In other words, the guiding principle is that we should do no harm to people who are different.

Another distinction can be made between 'absolute rights' and 'conditional rights'. Elsewhere, I discussed this distinction with respect to providing medical treatment for seriously ill persons with disabilities.[17] I noted that although one of the fundamental moral and legal principles held by western societies is that human life has a value that exceeds all other considerations (i.e., an absolute right), there are exceptions, for example, killing in self defence and sacrificing one's life to save the lives of others (i.e., a conditional right). The sanctity of life position has been justified from several perspectives. A theistic view argues that since all humans are created in God's image, or that since all humans are God's property, or that since life is the gift of God, it would be contrary to divine will to take our own or someone's life. As I noted above, this would be the position of John Locke. In contrast, a Kantian view would have us believe that, from a natural law perspective, comes the obligation that, quite apart from any religious consideration, the duty to respect life rises from human beings' natural ends as entities. This view was argued by Thomas Aquinas, the thirteenth-century Italian philosopher and theologian and, more recently, by the twentieth-century French philosopher, Jacques Maritain, who held that, according to natural law, when a thing is looked at in terms of 'the normality of its functioning', it 'should achieve fullness of being either in its growth or in its behaviour'.[18] While I will not be considering issues to do with capital punishment and warfare in this book, the distinction between absolute and conditional rights is worth bearing in mind when we come to consider the individuals whose behaviours may jeopardize the welfare and rights of others.

In considering the rights of children, a question arises as to what extent should parents/ caregivers have a right to determine what kind of education their child should receive? Is this an absolute right or a conditional right? Are parents the sole arbiter in determining what is in their children's interests or does the state, too, have an interest in the development of its citizenry? How can these interests be reconciled when they come into conflict? These questions come into prominence when it comes to school choice: single-sex vs coeducational schools (see Chapter 2), the local school vs any other school, public (state) schools vs private vs charter schools vs home schooling (see Chapter 3), schools catering for particular cultural/ethnic groups vs multicultural schools (see Chapter 4), faith-based schools vs secular schools (see Chapter 5) and inclusive education vs segregated education for children with special needs (see Chapter 6).

1.8 Goal B: To develop inclusivist societies and global community

With the impetus of the UN Convention on the Rights of People with Disabilities, inclusive education is an idea whose time has arrived around the world. In almost every country, inclusive education has emerged as one of the most dominant issues in the education of students with disabilities/special educational needs. In the past 40-50 years this field has moved from a segregation paradigm through integration to a point where inclusion is central to contemporary discourse.

In this book, however, I wish to extend the scope of inclusive education from its focus on special educational needs arising from disabilities to encompass *all* learners. In particular, I will be giving consideration to other potential sources of disadvantage and marginalization, such as gender (in some countries), poverty, language, ethnicity and religious minority status. The complex inter-relationships that exist among these factors will also be a focus of attention. I first broached this broadened interpretation of inclusive education in *Contextualizing Inclusive Education*, a book I edited in 2005, when I stated:

> Inclusive education extends beyond special needs arising from disabilities, and includes consideration of other sources of disadvantage and marginalization, such as gender, poverty, language, ethnicity, and geographic isolation. The complex inter-relationships that exist among these factors and their interactions with disability must also be the focus of attention.[19]

This broadened conceptualization of inclusive education was articulated in the meeting at the 48th session of the UNESCO International Conference on Education, held in Geneva in November 2008, where it was acknowledged that 'inclusive education is an ongoing process aimed at offering quality education for all while respecting diversity and the different needs and abilities, characteristics and learning expectations of the students and communities, eliminating all forms of discrimination'.[20] A broadened definition has also been advocated in the United States by Susan Baglieri and her colleagues[21] and by Shelley Zion and Wanda Blanchett.[22]

By taking this track, it is necessary to examine such questions as the following: Is there any justification for single-sex schools? Can faith-based schools be justified? Should schools for particular cultural groups/races be tolerated? What should be done about schools that are *de facto* special schools catering for low socio-economic students? More widely, we must give consideration to how societies and the global community can be made more inclusive.

So, why is inclusiveness important? Advocacy for inclusive education revolves around four main arguments. First, some writers claim that any exclusion or segregation of students with special needs is a violation of their human rights and represents an unfair distribution of educational resources.[23] Second, others see inclusive education as contributing significantly to a democratic society.[24] The third argument revolves around the Intergroup Contact Theory, advanced by US psychologist, Gordon Allport, who suggested that contact between members of different groups can work to reduce prejudice and intergroup conflict.[25] He claimed that prejudice is a direct result of generalizations and oversimplifications made about an entire group of people based on incomplete or mistaken information. Such prejudice may be reduced if there is greater contact, enabling one to learn more about a category of people different from oneself. Ideally, such contact situations should be characterized by four key conditions: equal status, intergroup cooperation, common goals, and support by social and institutional authorities. The fourth argument has to do with the important role played by social interconnectivity, which is seen by many writers as being one of human beings' basic human needs – an orientation that likely can be traced to its survival benefit.[26]

In 2008, the Council of Europe put forward a persuasive approach to managing Europe's increasing cultural diversity that builds on the concept of inclusion.[27] A White Paper asked, 'how shall we respond to diversity and what is our vision of the society of the future?' It suggested two alternatives, favouring the one focusing on inclusion:

> Is it a society of segregated communities, marked at best by the coexistence of majorities and minorities with differentiated rights and responsibilities, loosely bound together by mutual ignorance and stereotypes? Or is it a vibrant and open society without discrimination, benefiting us all, marked by the inclusion of all residents in full respect of their human rights?[28]

In keeping with its inclusivist approach, the White Paper further argued that Europe's common future depends on its ability to safeguard and develop human rights, democracy and the rule of law and to promote mutual understanding. To achieve these goals, it reasoned that an 'intercultural approach', as distinct from a 'multicultural approach', offered the best model for managing ethnic, religious, linguistic and cultural diversity.[29] I will elaborate on this model in Chapters 4 and 5, but at this point it is worth mentioning what is involved in intercultural dialogue. Briefly, it is understood as 'an open and respectful exchange of views between individuals, groups with different ethnic, cultural, religious and linguistic backgrounds and heritage on the basis of mutual understanding and respect'.[30]

What do we mean by inclusive education? Quite simply, I define inclusive education as 'education that fits', i.e., education that fits the abilities, interests, values and experiences of learners – and their needs to relate to their peers in all their diversity. As I have written elsewhere,[31] it is no longer appropriate for policy-makers and researchers to define inclusive education solely, or even mainly, in terms of placement – although that, too, is important. Rather, I see it as being a multi-faceted concept that requires educators at all levels of a system to attend to vision, placement, curriculum, assessment, teaching, acceptance, access, support, resources and leadership.

1.9 Perspective 1: Theories of distributive justice should underpin our approach to diversity

In understanding the basis of human rights, we must also consider arguments about which economic framework and which resulting distribution of wealth is morally preferable. Deciding on the principles of 'distributive justice' that should apply is extremely significant for determining how societies respond to differences among its citizens, particularly how they behave towards those who are disadvantaged – and especially towards children.

Various notions of distributive justice have been advanced. This issue is a complex one to explore, involving the intersection of philosophy and economics. Nevertheless, it is one that underpins our approach to the education of people who are different and must be addressed. The following is but a brief summary of what I consider to be the five main approaches to distributive justice.[32]

Strict egalitarianism

This is perhaps the simplest idea of distributive justice. It calls for the allocation of equal material goods to all members of society, on the grounds that people are morally equal. As noted by Harvard philosopher Michael Sandel,[33] Kurt Vonnegut portrayed an extreme interpretation of this principle in his short story, 'Harrison Bergeron'. In the year 2081, goes the story, 'everybody was finally equal … Nobody was smarter than anybody else. Nobody was better looking than anybody else. Nobody was stronger and quicker than anybody else.' To enforce this equality, a 'United States Handicapper General' had wide powers to penalize individuals who did not conform to reduce them to the desired norm.

Two matters need to be resolved in egalitarianism: how to index any distribution and the time frame for any distribution. Using money is the most common way of indexing distributive principles. The timeframe problem cannot be solved as simply. One version requires that all people should have the same wealth at some initial point, after which they would be free to use it in whatever way they choose, with the consequence that future outcomes are bound to be unequal. The most common form of strict equality principle specifies that *income* should be equal in *successive* timeframes, though even this may lead to significant disparities in wealth if variations in savings are permitted. It is not surprising, perhaps, that the strict egalitarian principle of distributive justice has been criticized as being untenable and that it conflicts, for example, with what people might deserve and their freedom rights (see below). Partly as an attempt to avoid some of the pitfalls of strict egalitarianism, some economists design distributive principles that are sensitive to considerations of responsibility and luck in economic life; unsurprisingly, this approach is known as *luck egalitarianism*.

Although it is superficially attractive, I am not advancing strict egalitarianism as the moral basis for educating children from diverse backgrounds. I do recognize, however, that the current trend in many countries to move away from the principles of egalitarianism carries risks for people from disadvantaged backgrounds.

Libertarianism

This approach centres on the moral demands of liberty or self-ownership. Advocates of such *libertarian* principles argue for unrestricted markets and limited government regulation or interference, not in pursuit of economic efficiency, but in the name of human freedom. We have a right to do whatever we want with what we own (including our own bodies, our own self), provided we respect the rights of others to do the same. Just distribution of wealth arises in the free exchange of goods and services in an unfettered market. Persons should not be required to ensure the welfare of others for this would violate their right of self-ownership. Libertarians such as Robert Nozick,[34] thus believe in a minimal state, which is restricted to enforcing contracts, protecting private property and keeping the peace. Consequently, they reject any interference by the state to achieve any egalitarian redistribution of wealth, as outlined above. This view was promulgated, for example, by Milton Friedman, the American economist.[35] However, Nozick does concede that if it can be shown that one's advantages have been derived from past injustices (e.g., through the enslavement of others or the illegal confiscation of property), then some redistribution of one's wealth is acceptable. As well, libertarians reject paternalism (e.g., requiring people in vehicles to wear seatbelts or cyclists to wear helmets) and morals legislation (e.g., laws controlling prostitution).

Libertarianism, I believe, is part of the problem, not the solution, in addressing the needs of disadvantaged children. Neoliberalism, with its emphasis upon individualism, managerialism and competition within education, is not a strong philosophical basis for achieving equity for such children.

Utilitarianism

Classical utilitarianism's two most influential contributors are Jeremy Bentham, an eighteenth- to nineteenth-century British philosopher and social reformer, and, later, John Stuart Mill, another nineteenth-century British philosopher. The doctrine they promulgated was that actions are right if they are useful or for the benefit of a majority. In other words, actions are to be judged according to their consequences.[36] Only those actions that maximize utility (i.e., produce pleasure or happiness and prevent pain or suffering) are deemed to be morally right. Further, the greatest happiness of the greatest number of people should guide our conduct. This principle has led to utilitarianism being described as a welfare-based credo since distributive justice rests on determining what will maximize the welfare, or the collective happiness, of society as a whole. To quote Bentham, 'it is the greatest happiness of the greatest number that is the measure of right and wrong'.[37]

In subsequent revisions of Bentham's theory by John Stuart Mill, he mounted the classic defence of individual freedom, arguing that people should be free to do whatever they wanted, provided they did no harm to others. As he wrote, 'Independence is, of right, absolute. Over himself, over his own body and mind, the individual is sovereign.'[38] Mill couched this notion in utilitarian terms, arguing that, over time, respecting individual liberty will lead to the greatest human happiness overall. For example, a dissenting view may turn out to be true and so offer some correction to the prevailing view.

At first glance, utilitarianism, applied to disadvantaged children is inappropriate simply because these children constitute a minority and are not part of the 'greatest number of people'. However, I do concede that it could be argued that by allocating extra resources to such children and reducing the gaps I will be describing later in this chapter, the collective happiness of society as a whole could result. If equalization policies succeed, we could well see improved educational, social and health outcomes – to the benefit of all members of society.

Kant's view of rationally determined moral principles

Immanuel Kant, an eighteenth-century German philosopher, argued for the ideal of a potentially universal community of rational individuals autonomously determining the moral principles for securing rights. Michael Sandel describes Kant as providing 'one of the most powerful and influential accounts [of duties and rights] any philosopher has produced'[39] and that Kant's emphasis on human dignity 'informs present-day notions of universal human rights'.[40]

Kant saw people as having three essential qualities. First, we are rational beings, capable of reason. Second, we are each of us worthy of dignity and respect. Third, we are autonomous beings, capable of acting freely. Together, these features set us apart from a mere animal existence.

For Kant, the basis of moral reasoning must rest upon a condition to which all rational individuals are bound to assent. He believed that we can arrive at such principles of morality through 'pure practical reason' and through acting autonomously. This means acting according to laws we give ourselves, not according to the dictates of nature or social convention. When we act in this way, we do something for its own sake, as an end in itself, or, in the case of others, treating persons as ends in themselves. As Michael Sandel expresses it: 'What matters is doing the right thing because it is right, not for some ulterior motive.'[41] This is Kant's 'motive of duty'. While it may also bring one pleasure, this should not be the prime motive for an action toward others. As Kant expressed it, 'Act in such a way that you always treat humanity, whether in your own person or in the person of any other, never simply as a means, but always at the same time as an end.'[42] Moral law, he asserted, can rest neither on the interests and desires of individuals, nor on the interests or desires of a community. It can readily be seen how this principle underpins the modern-day concept of universal human rights and of our obligations towards those who are disadvantaged.

Kant also referred to a 'universal law' which, briefly, refers to the principle that one should 'Act only on that maxim whereby you can at the same time will that it should become a universal law.'[43] In a nutshell: what if everyone did or did not do something? This is a good test of whether one's actions put one's own interests ahead of everyone else's.

Rawls's difference principle

I turn now to a theory of distributive justice that is most pertinent to defining our obligations towards those who are disadvantaged. American philosopher, John Rawls,[44] suggested that we should determine principles of justice by choosing behind 'a veil of ignorance', in which we imagine we don't know anything about who we are – whether we are rich or poor, what our gender or ethnicity is and so on. He asserted that if no one knew any of those things, we would make choices from an original position of equality and the principles we would agree to would be just. Rawls claimed that this process would lead to two essential principles of justice. The first is that each person has equal basic rights and liberties, such as freedom of speech and religion. The second he referred to as the *difference principle*, in which he argued that divergence from strict equality is permitted so long as the inequalities in question would make the least advantaged in society materially better off than they would be under strict equality. If these two rules conflict in practice, however, Rawls argued that basic liberties should not be sacrificed in order to generate greater equality of opportunity or a higher level of material goods, even for the worst off.

Rawls was not opposed in principle to a system of strict equality *per se*, but nor was he arguing that he was seeking it; rather his concern was about the *absolute* position of the least advantaged group rather than their *relative* position. Further, Rawls believed that it was possible to correct for the unequal distribution of talents without handicapping the talented, as in the case of Kurt Vonnegut's 'Harrison Bergeron'. How to do this is rather controversial and, some would say, unrealistic. For example, he argued that gifts and talents should be allowed, even encouraged, to flourish, but the rewards accruing to those who possess them should belong to the community as a whole, with some redistribution to the least advantaged. As he stated: 'Those who have been favored by nature, whoever they are, may gain from their good fortune only on terms that improve the situation of those who have lost out.'[45]

Libertarians, of course, object to the difference principle on the grounds that it involves unacceptable infringements on liberty, property rights or self-ownership. It is also criticized on the grounds that it ignores claims that people deserve certain economic benefits because of their hard work or contributions. Utilitarians object to it because it is does not maximize utility. And, finally, advocates of luck egalitarianism argue that the principle does not fully capture the moral roles they believe luck and responsibility should play in principles of distributive justice.

Overall, in his review of theories of justice, Michael Sandel concluded that even when all criticisms have been taken into account, Rawls's theory 'represents the most compelling case for a more equal society that American political philosophy has yet produced'.[46] I see no reason to disagree with this summation. It forms a substantial basis for determining our obligations towards children who are disadvantaged by their SES or cultural backgrounds, level of ability, and, in some circumstances, by their gender or religion.

1.10 Perspective 2: Diversities must be seen from an ecological perspective

All living creatures live in environments, or ecosystems, of varying degrees of complexity. The diversities outlined in this book will be considered from a behavioural ecology perspective by focusing on how the child is influenced by complex interactions among societal, community, family, school and classroom factors. This means giving consideration to how human behaviour varies with, and adapts to, ecological contexts.[47] It also involves understanding what Mel Ainscow and his Manchester University colleagues refer to as the 'ecology of equity'. By this they mean that:

> the extent to which students' experiences and outcomes are equitable is not dependent only on the educational practices of their teachers, or even their schools. Instead, it depends on a whole range of interacting processes that reach into the school from outside. These include the demographics of the area served by the schools, the histories and cultures of the populations who send (or fail to send) their children to the school, and the economic realities faced by those populations. Beyond this, they involve the underlying socio-economic processes that make some areas poor and others affluent, and that draw different migrant groups into some places rather than others.[48]

Elsewhere, I have presented a comprehensive, ecological, 'wraparound' model for portraying the relationships among the various elements that impinge on children.[49] I portrayed this model in the form of a spiral system embracing both macro and micro components (Figure 1.1). In part, it is based on Urie Bronfenbrenner's 'ecological systems theory'.[50] Here are the main principles underlying the model:

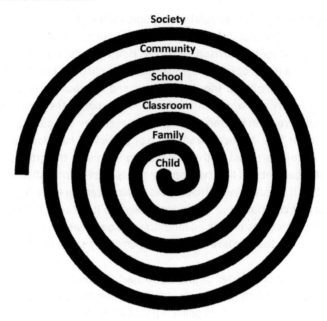

Figure 1.1 A comprehensive ecological model

- Individual children are at the heart of the system.
- Children are embedded in families, which, in turn, interact with a series of other systems – classrooms, schools, communities and the broader society. Family factors include interaction patterns, language, cultural capital and perceptions of the value of education. Classroom factors include the curriculum, assessment, pedagogy, peer group influences and classroom climate. School factors include policies, leadership, school culture and the deployment of human and capital resources. Community factors include demographic features, economic resources and cultural values. Societal factors include educational policies, resourcing and accountability mechanisms.
- Such systems should be 'joined up', which involves both horizontal and vertical integration. Horizontal integration requires linking systems at the same level to ensure consistency and compatibility of approach (e.g., among teachers in a school). Vertical integration requires linking more immediate, or proximal, systems with the more distal systems in which they are embedded (e.g., schools, communities and the wider society).
- Influences between systems are bi-directional. Just as families influence children, so too do children influence their families and just as schools influence families, so too do families influence schools and so on. In particular, I believe that children themselves significantly contribute to their own learning processes. They learn from their experiences, select what they attend to, and work out their own 'rules of the game'. Increasingly, with the ubiquitous Internet, children are independently choosing what, how and from whom to learn. They are active participants in their own development and are not mere clay being shaped by forces around them.

- Complexity theory draws attention to wholes rather than parts, multi-dimensional rela-tionships and dynamic interactions among components of a system, rather than linear models of cause and effect. With complex systems such as we are dealing with in this book, wholes are much more than the sums of their parts. Further, they change and de-velop through feedback loops that exist among their components.[51]

1.11 Perspective 3: Perceptions of diversity vary across time and space

Although I am writing this book in 2015-2016 from my New Zealand base, I am acutely aware that differences are perceived differently in different countries and at different times in his-tory. Contexts of time and space matter for how various domains of difference are socially constructed and the nature of the competing social forces that may operate in such struggles.

1.12 Perspective 4: Finding the right balance between sameness and diversity is a challenge

Striking a balance between recognizing the rights of diverse peoples and the need to estab-lish social cohesion constitutes a major challenge to societies around the globe. Inevitably, this challenge falls to a significant extent upon educators. When does tolerating or encour-aging diversity threaten the fabric of a cohesive society? Conversely, does the aspiration for social cohesion have the intended or unintended consequence of marginalizing those who are different? To what extent should educators seek to achieve homogeneity of values, achievement and behaviour among students? To what extent should they attempt to assimi-late those who are perceived to differ from the mainstream of society? What differences should they celebrate and enhance? Which ones should they seek to reduce, even eliminate? I hope this book goes some way towards answering these questions.

Clearly, all differences are not of equal value. Some, such as exceptional intelligence and physical prowess, would receive widespread approval and are deemed worthy of encourage-ment. Others, such as deviant personality traits resulting in criminal behaviour, are generally seen as repugnant and should be eliminated or reduced. However, even these two categories are not universally defined and different societies have different perceptions of giftedness and criminality, both contemporaneously and in the past. Indeed, each of the categories of difference I explore in this book probably elicits different reactions in different societies and at different times in their history. The challenge to educators is to interpret the value their society places on various categories of difference. This challenge becomes a dilemma when a particular society might be oppressive, as in Nazi Germany, for example: how should teachers there have handled critical thinking in their students in the 1930s?

At the broad political level, these questions are framed by the ongoing tensions that exist between what political geographer, Richard Hartshorne, described as *centrifugal and centripetal forces*.[52] He argued that the integration of a state's territory involves the equilibrium achieved at any one time between *centrifugal forces* that push populations apart, and *centripetal forces* that pull populations together. If centrifugal forces are stronger than centripetal forces, there may be fragmentation, instability, internal discord and challenges to the state's authority - to the extent that its very existence may be threatened. These two forces are portrayed in Figure 1.2.

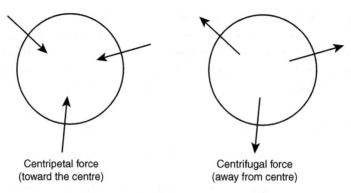

Centripetal force
(toward the centre)

Centrifugal force
(away from centre)

Figure 1.2 Centrifugal and centripetal forces

Examples of the centrifugal forces include wide differences in religious belief, culture, language and economic activity. These forces can limit interactions, produce regionalism and create dissimilarity among groups of citizens within a state. Instances here include (a) religious tensions (e.g., between Catholics and Protestants in Northern Ireland, between Buddhists and Hindus in Sri Lanka and Myanmar, and between Sunnis and Shiites in many Middle East countries); (b) ethnic tensions (e.g., between various groups in the Balkans around the time of World War I and, more recently, when Yugoslavia broke into seven separate countries); (c) class differences (e.g., in the events leading up to the French revolution and the Russian working class overthrowing the monarchy); and (d) language differences (e.g., Francophones in Quebec wanting independence from the rest of predominantly English-speaking Canada, and Russian speakers in eastern Ukraine wanting to secede from the rest of the country).

Centripetal forces are those that tend to unify people and create solidarity, thus enhancing support for the state. These include (a) similarities in religion (e.g., Hinduism in Nepal and India, Islam in Bangladesh, Buddhism in Thailand, Roman Catholicism in Mexico and the Republic of Ireland), (b) a common language (e.g., Indonesia created a national language, Bahasa Indonesia; Israel made Hebrew its official language; and nineteenth- and twentieth-century immigrants to the United States were expected to learn American English); (c) nationalism, i.e. the acceptance of national goals based on allegiance to a single country and the ideals and ways of life it represents, sometimes accompanied by a common enemy (e.g., Israel); and (d) unifying institutions (e.g., schools – the focus of this book).

How to reconcile the tension between sameness and diversity is an ongoing challenge to educational policy-makers and practitioners around the globe. Educational philosopher, Nicholas Burbules, whom I have already cited, has eloquently addressed this issue in a thoughtful essay.[53] He suggested that his own country, the United States, seemed to be

> fundamentally torn between, on the one hand, a desire to use education to make people more alike (whether this is in regards to a 'melting pot' of citizenship values and beliefs; the essential texts of 'cultural literacy'; the factual knowledge and skills that can be measured by standardized tests; or the establishment of uniform national standards across the curriculum) – and, on the other hand, a desire to serve the different learning

styles and needs, the different cultural orientations, and the different aspirations toward work and living represented by the diverse population of students in public schools.

Burbules went on to argue that, until relatively recently, the dominant discourse of educational policy in the United States has emphasized the common: what every educated person should learn, should know, and should be able to do. He felt that the kind of community that has typically been promoted is one either based on explicit homogeneity, or on a tolerant pluralism across a range of differences, under which it is assumed that people are all basically the same. In recent years, however, Burbules observed the development of powerful reactions against these traditional emphases. He stated that 'From feminist, multicultural, postcolonial, and generally postmodern theoretical positions, the postulates of a universal human nature, of canonical texts, of generalizable norms, of a common knowledge base, of shared traditions, of a common standard of citizenship, have all been challenged.' He pointed to the potential for harm when differences are defined from within the perspective of a given framework of understanding, without due regard to the very different meaning of those differences from within the perspective of those being talked about. Further, when these judgments are wrapped up with a high-stakes endeavour such as education, the choice presented to those who are different is to abandon or suppress their differences for the sake of conformity and 'fitting in'; or to accept the characterization of one's own differences from the dominant perspective, becoming alienated from one's self; or to reject the standards and norms others have set, and so lose out on the opportunity education represents. Finally, Burbules pointed out that tolerance of difference, or celebrations of difference, are not the ultimate educational outcomes we should be after; rather, what matters is 'the critical re-examination of difference, the questioning of our own systems of difference, and what they mean for ourselves and for other people'. Importantly, he asserts that 'education should not simply be about transmitting an existing system of belief and value, unchanged, from one generation to the next; there must be some room for questioning, re-interpreting, and modifying that system in light of a broadened understanding of where it fits in the context of a diverse, rapidly changing world'.

1.13 Perspective 5: Interest convergence helps to explain shifts in behaviour and policies

In 1980, Derek Bell, late of New York University Law School, put forward the principle of 'interest convergence'. He explained it with reference to the US situation regarding racial equality, claiming that 'the interest of Blacks in achieving racial equality will be accommodated only when it converges with the interests of Whites'.[54] An example of the application of this principle is the 1954 decision in *Brown v. Board of Education* which struck down the earlier ruling of 'separate but equal' school segregation. Bell argued that this occurred because it served the United States' cold war agenda of supporting human rights. Another more recent example can be found in German Chancellor, Angela Merkel's decision to accept up to 800,000 asylum seekers in 2015. In part at least, this was driven by economic considerations in a country experiencing labour shortages and low fertility levels. Thus, the interests of refugees and German society converged. In the remaining chapters, I will present other examples of this 'enormously influential'[55] interest convergence principle and how it can be used to increase equality for various categories of diversity.

Questions that arise when applying this principle include the following: (1) Whose interests are served by perpetuating inequalities? (2) What are those interests? (3) Where are there opportunities to seek convergence? (4) What do we need to do to get to convergence?[56]

Before leaving the interest convergence perspective, some criticisms that have been levelled at it by Justin Driver should be noted. First, he argued that the theory's overly broad conceptualization of 'black interests' and 'white interests' obscures the intensely contested disputes regarding what those terms actually mean. Second, the interest-convergence theory incorrectly suggests that the racial status of blacks and whites over the course of US history is notable more for continuity than for change. Third, the interest-convergence theory accords insufficient agency to two groups of actors – black citizens and white judges – who have played, and continue to play, significant roles in shaping racial realities.[57]

Three other caveats regarding interest convergence should be considered. The first one is that policies and practices arising from interest convergence can be reversed. This occurred, for example, when women's services in the workforce were needed during World War II, but were no longer required when men returned from the war. The second caveat is that while interest convergence might be perceived at the macro political level, it might not be so accepted at the grassroots of a society. At the time of writing, for example, we are seeing resistance to Angela Merkel's open door approach to asylum seekers. Third, since interest convergence depends largely on those with power relinquishing some or much of it, this will have repercussions not only at the personal level but also at the institutional level as schools and education systems adjust to new realities.

Nevertheless, as Driver concluded, the theory 'contains at least some persuasive force'.[58] As he said,

> The interest-convergence theory can offer valuable and formidable insights into the way that change occurs; it should not, however, be viewed as either flawless or all-encompassing. Instead of adhering to any unified theory, reformers seeking change would do better to think of the interest-convergence thesis as but one weapon in the fight for progress rather than as the entire arsenal.[59]

1.14 Perspective 6: Diversities intersect with each other

While I will be dealing with five major diversities in this book, it is essential to note that each one interacts with several others. This means that individuals' identities are composed of various combinations and permutations of these major categories, a situation which becomes even more complex when we throw other diversities such as age, family background, location and so on into the mix. For example, there is clear evidence of intersections between ethnicity, gender and class in influencing achievement (see Chapter 3). Similarly, abilities/disabilities interact with gender, class and ethnicity (Chapters 2, 3, 4 and 6) and so it goes on ...This 'intersectional approach' arose from feminist scholarship, which recognized that since there were important differences among women and men rather than simply between them, gender, race and class were interconnected as 'intersecting oppressions'.[60]

In a similar vein, Amartya Sen, the Nobel prize-winning economist, pointed out that while religion is important to a person's identity, it is never more than one aspect of it. There are serious problems created by the assumption that religion is, for everyone, the single most important aspect that overrides all others. I would take this a step further and argue that, just like religion, gender, ability (and disability), culture and social class should not become sole markers of a person's identity. As Sen insisted,

> we are *diversely different*. The hope of harmony in the contemporary world lies to a great extent in a clearer understanding of the pluralities of human identity, and in the appreciation that they cut across each other and work against a sharp separation along one single hardened line of impenetrable division.[61]

1.15 *Perspective 7: There are multiple causes of diversities*

In all of the chapters in this book, I will be drawing attention to low achievement and social problems experienced by various groups of children. To what or whom should we attribute these occurrences? The child? The parents/caregivers? The school? Society? Globalization? Often, the debate hinges on efforts to determine the relative influence of schools vs societal structural features such as socio-economic constraints. My compatriot, Martin Thrupp, has presented a good analysis of this debate, pointing out that those who 'blame' the latter are often accused of engaging in 'deficit thinking' and would, instead, want to put the responsibility for student achievement and behaviour on schools and teachers.[62] He claims that 'the problem with this kind of blanket, anti-deficit thinking stance is that, naively or knowingly, it contributes to teachers and schools becoming scapegoats for the effects on student achievement of an unequal society'.[63]

The position I take in this book is that it is unprofitable to look for causation solely among societal or school factors. Rather, I believe that there are multiple causes of differences among human beings. These include, singly and in combination, such factors as: evolution, globalization, poverty, geographic location, genetics, neuroscience, environmental degradation, cultural values, conflict, disasters, socialization, politics, neo-liberalism, technology, resources, parenting, diet, xenophobia and education.

1.16 *Perspective 8: Human beings are genetically similar across major identity markers, but genetically divergent individually*

What genetic variation does the human population actually possess? Across groups of people, it is surprisingly small, according to Richard Dawkins.[64] For example, only 6–15% of genetic variation can be accounted for by race. Thus, if the total variation in the human species is partitioned into between-race and within-race components, the former is a very small fraction of the total. Further, notes Dawkins, 'People are individually different, far more different from other members of their group than their groups are from each other.'[65] Somewhat provocatively, he also notes that 'If you take blood and compare protein molecules, or if you sequence genes themselves, you will find there is less difference between two human beings living anywhere in the world than there is between two African chimpanzees.'[66] This within-human species similarity Dawkins explains by our ancestors passing through a genetic bottleneck some 70,000 years ago, when the population of the world was perhaps only 15,000 people, caused by a volcanic winter and a thousand-year ice age. Even though the relatively recent worldwide diaspora out of Africa has taken us to an extraordinarily wide variety of habitats, climates and ways of life, where 'different conditions have exerted strong selection pressures, particularly on externally visible parts, such as the skin, which has to bear the brunt of the sun and the cold', most of our genomes have remained intact and uniform.[67]

However, culture seems to over-ride genomes. As Dawkins pointed out,

> because our mating decisions are so heavily influenced by cultural traditions, and because our cultures, and sometimes our religions, encourage us to discriminate against outsiders, especially in choosing mates, these superficial differences that helped our ancestors to prefer insiders over outsiders have been enhanced out of all proportion to the real genetic differences between us.[68]

Even though we may differ in trivial, superficial features, these may be conspicuous enough to serve as discrimination fodder, not just in mate choice but also in choice of enemies and leading to individuals becoming victims of xenophobic or religious prejudice.

But there are somewhat contrary views of the contribution of genetics to human behaviour, including educational attainment. For example, estimates suggest that around 40% of the variance in educational attainment is explained by genetic factors.[69] Furthermore, educational attainment is moderately correlated with other heritable characteristics including cognitive functioning.[70]

Recent developments in this field reflect the rapid and far-reaching advances in the Human Genome Project, which have yielded tools to investigate human DNA and its relationships to various human traits and diseases. For example, a US study by Cornelius Rietveld and his colleagues analyzed data from more than 100,000 individuals. It identified several genome-wide factors that were associated with educational attainment even when other factors were controlled for.[71] More specifically, the researchers reported on a genome-wide 'polygenic score' that predicted how far individuals were likely to progress in their educational careers.[72]

A second US study, carried out by Benjamin Domingue and his colleagues, took Rietveld et al.'s study further by investigating polygenic influences on length of schooling among pairs of siblings.[73] By focusing on siblings, the researchers were able to control for circumstances into which children are born (e.g., socio-economic status). In brief, these researchers showed that individuals with higher polygenic scores went on to complete more years of schooling than their lower-scored siblings. However, these effects were quite small, comprising 0.41 years of additional schooling for every standard deviation in polygenic scores. This compared with an additional 1.7 years of schooling if their mother graduated from college.

Although the research holds out promise for improving our understanding of the genetic influences on educational attainment, it is important to recognize that, as I have just noted, polygenic scores have only a small level of predictive power apropos educational attainment. Certainly, they do not have the precision of, say, predicting human height, where polygenic scores have predicted nearly 30% of population variance.[74] However, future studies with larger samples and developments in the specification of polygenic factors may well see improvements in their predictive power. For example, Rietveld et al. estimated that 15% of the variance in educational attainment might eventually be predicted from polygenic scores derived from one million respondents.[75]

As Daniel Belsky and Salomon Israel said, 'now is the time for social scientists to bring genetics into their research programs'.[76] They pointed out that 'the sequencing of the human genome and the advent of low-cost genome-wide assays that generate millions of observations of individual genomes in a matter of hours constitute a disruptive innovation for social science'. As an example of research already carried out, Belsky and Israel noted findings that children at high-genetic risk for obesity were born at similar weights to their low-genetic risk peers but subsequently grew more rapidly. In turn, this rapid growth mediated genetic influence on obesity during adolescence through midlife. Building on this finding, other researchers then showed that increased appetite beginning early in childhood was one path through which genetic influences contributed to accelerated weight gain, suggesting a potential intervention target.[77]

1.17 Perspective 9: Consideration should be given to an evolutionary perspective on diversity

In 1859, Charles Darwin, arguably the father of evolutionary psychology, claimed that 'Psychology will be based on a new foundation, that of the necessary acquirement of each mental power and capacity by gradation.'[78] Adaptation and natural selection, he suggested, would become the foundation for the field of psychology.[79] In a nutshell, evolutionary psychology argues that much human behaviour is the result of psychological adaptations that evolved to solve recurrent problems in past environments. According to American psychologist, David Buss,[80] it is based on a series of premises: (1) evolutionary processes have influenced not merely the body, but also the brain, the psychological mechanisms it houses, and the behaviour it produces; (2) many of those mechanisms are best conceptualized as psychological adaptations designed to solve problems that historically contributed to survival and reproduction; (3) psychological adaptations are activated in modern environments that differ in some important ways from ancestral environments; and (4) critically, the notion that psychological mechanisms have adaptive functions is a necessary, not an optional, ingredient for a comprehensive psychological science. Further, as noted by another evolutionary psychologist, Stephen Pinker, 'In the study of humans, there are major spheres of human experience – beauty, motherhood, kinship, morality, cooperation, sexuality, violence – in which evolutionary psychology provides the only coherent theory.'[81] In a nutshell, evolutionary psychology argues that much human behaviour is the result of psychological adaptations that evolved to solve recurrent problems in past environments. According to some writers, evolution by selection is the only known causal process capable of creating such complex adaptations.[82] Human variation is, at least in part, accounted for by the fact that as a species, we have colonized nearly every land area on the surface of the earth, and that each of these diverse ecologies has and is shaping our psychological design.

I will return to this evolutionary psychology explanation of behaviour in several of the subsequent chapters as I continue to explore human diversity and, ultimately, what it means to be human.

1.18 Perspective 10: Many differences are quite small, even if they are statistically significant

While many of the findings I will be presenting in this book refer to *statistically significant* differences within the various categories, it is important that we bear in mind the *practical significance* of any such differences. Here, I must describe what happens when *meta-analyses* are carried out. This relatively recent statistical procedure collates the results from multiple studies and measures the distance between means of two groups (for example, between males and females), to arrive at what is referred to as a *d statistic*. The convention is that *d* values from 0.11 to 0.35 are considered to be small, while 0.36 to 0.65 are moderate and 0.66 to 1.00 are large. When I refer to research on gender differences in Chapter 2, for example, most of them are small, often no more than 0.20. What does this mean? Quite simply, in the case of *d* = 0.20, for example, only 54% of one gender exceeds the 50th percentile of the other. In other words, the two genders show an 85.3% overlap.[83] In this case, it is much more likely that there is more variability *within* the two genders than there is *between* them. So one has to be very cautious in basing educational policies and practices on presumed gender differences of such low magnitude as reported in the literature and often exaggerated in the media. Certainly, we must not ascribe characteristics that might occur more often in a particular gender to all members of that gender (e.g., 'all girls are poor at mathematics', or 'all girls are good at reading'). Stereotyping must be avoided.

1.19 Perspective 11: Economics play a major role in catering for diversities

In his successful 1992 presidential campaign, Bill Clinton coined the phrase 'it's the economy, stupid'. Without wishing to insult the intelligence of my readers, I would agree with Clinton that the economy plays a large role in almost everything we do – and vice versa. Thus, in most of the chapters in this book, I will be drawing attention to the economic benefits of achieving greater equality for disadvantaged groups and I will examine various funding models aimed at redressing various perceived disadvantages. And, of course, one whole chapter (Chapter 3) centres on socio-economic status. Particular attention needs to be paid to those countries that rely heavily on local property taxes for financing their schools. This is the case in the United States, where, a recent Commission bemoaned 'the broken system of education funding', with funding levels ranging from a low of $6,454 per student in Utah to $18,167 per student in New York in 2010.[84]

1.20 Perspective 12: Education is multi-level and multi-faceted

In this book I will be examining education through the various prisms of human diversity. This involves giving consideration to education at multiple levels: national and district systems, schools and classrooms. In doing so, I recognize that education is multi-faceted, comprising such features as the following:

Control: To what extent does state vs private control influence how education systems accommodate to differences? What effects does central vs devolved control of education influence accommodation to differences? Are there differences in the ways in which non-formal vs formal education systems take account of children's differences?

Goals: To what extent do the goals of education systems recognize differences? Are the goals sufficiently comprehensive to reflect what schools should be teaching, beyond emphasizing student test scores? For example, do they incorporate such goals as 'civic responsibility, democratic values, cultural competency and awareness, economic self sufficiency and social and economic mobility'?[85]

Organization: To what extent are education systems organized to take account of differences such as age, ability, gender, religion and language?

Collaboration with other social agencies and support services: To what extent does the education system cooperate with other social agencies such as health and social welfare to better accommodate to differences in children and their families?

Funding: Is there differential funding to take account of children's differences?

Choice: Do parents have a choice in the type of school they enrol their children in, for example through zoning policies? (See next section.)

Curricula and materials: Do curricula and associated materials give consideration to differences?

Assessment, examinations: Do assessment and examinations give consideration to differences?

Pedagogy: How can/should pedagogy give consideration to differences?

Parent involvement: What policies and practices are in place for involving parents in their children's education?

Teachers: How can teachers be prepared through initial teacher education and professional development to meet the needs of different students?

Technology: How can technology enhance the education of children who are different?

I also recognize that education systems are complex entities that reflect a host of different influences, both historically and contemporaneously: economic, philosophical, cultural and political. As a consequence, one approach to education cannot possibly fit all contexts. Therefore, while I shall take the bold step of recommending various approaches to accommodating to diverse students in this book, I should like to emphasize that they should be examined critically to determine their degree of fit within given situations.

In the course of the book, I will be focusing on the period of compulsory schooling, i.e. primary/elementary education and secondary/high school education, although I will be making some references to early childhood/pre-school education and to higher/tertiary education.

1.21 Perspective 13: There can be a mismatch between children's and schools' cultural and social capital

Children who come from class, gender, cultural and religious backgrounds that differ from the prevailing norms and expectations of schools can be seriously disadvantaged. This disjunction leads us to consideration of 'cultural capital', a concept had its origins with French sociologist Pierre Bourdieu, the idea of 'hegemony', given prominence by the Italian philosopher, Antonio Gramsci, and 'critical pedagogy', as put forward by Paulo Freire, the Brazilian educator and philosopher. Space permits only brief summaries of their contributions.

First, let's turn to Pierre Bourdieu. In 1979, he argued that children learn from their parents a 'habitus', which is an unconscious orientation towards ways of life that are appropriate to their class: it comprises deeply ingrained habits, skills and dispositions.[86] Such learning comprises the accumulated cultural knowledge and skills that confer varying degrees of power and status in society. More broadly, cultural capital is made up of non-financial social elements such as education, intellect, style of speech, tastes in food and art, posture, clothing, mannerisms, material belongings, credentials, dress and physical appearance. Collectively, these elements form a person's identity and group position and serve to reproduce social stratification. By providing their children with differing types of cultural capital, parents transmit different attitudes and knowledge, which are not always that which is needed to succeed in educational systems. According to Bourdieu, those who inherit the cultural capital of the education system, which is generally that of the middle class, begin their schooling with an advantage they are likely to maintain.[87] In other words, the culture of the home and the school correspond, while for other children there may be a disjunction of cultures.

Certain forms of cultural capital are valued over others, and can help or hinder one's social mobility just as much as financial capital. It can be a major source of social inequality. Teachers, too, have absorbed the cultural capital of their own backgrounds and may not understand or be sympathetic to those of their students who come to school with different cultural capital. As with other groups who hold positions of power in society, such as employers, teachers epitomize what is culturally valued and may consciously or unconsciously act to 'reaffirm and reproduce social class and privilege by valuing the preferences, behaviours, and attitudes of the dominant class over those of the non-dominant groups'.[88] In other words, there is often a disconnect between the cultural capital valued by schools and the cultural capital valued by many in their communities.

This leads me to give consideration to the distinction between 'single loop' and 'double-loop learning', put forward by US business theorists, Chris Azgyris and Donald Schon, in the 1970s.[89] In their analysis of 'learning organizations', these two writers described single-loop learning as what occurs when individuals, groups, or organizations modify their actions according to the difference between expected and obtained outcomes. In double-loop learning, these entities question the values, assumptions and policies that led to the actions in the first place and modify them accordingly. The link with cultural capital that I would like to draw here is that by engaging in double-loop learning, we come to question our own habitus and examine our (often unconscious) biases and prejudices. Schon expressed this process as one involving 'reflective practice', which he defined as 'the capacity to reflect on action so as to engage in a process of continuous learning'.[90] I believe that this is not always an easy or comfortable process, but is necessary if we are fully to understand our and others' perception of differences.

A related concept to 'cultural capital' is the concept of 'social capital', which has extended the notion of an individual asset to communities and even nations. For example, writing from a US perspective, Robert Putnam argued that 'what many high achieving school districts have in abundance is social capital, which is educationally more important than financial capital'.[91] Putnam defined social capital as different kinds of connectedness, such as informal links to relatives, friends and acquaintances, as well as participation in communal functions such as churches, sports and volunteer activities. These bonds, he wrote, 'have powerful affects on health, happiness, educational success, public safety, and child welfare'.[92] However, like financial capital and human capital, social capital is distributed unevenly, and differences in social connections contribute to the opportunity gaps.

The concept of social capital has been given prominence in the writings of James Coleman,[93] Alejandro Portes,[94] and, recently, Bill Mulford.[95] The latter defined it in terms of the groups, networks, norms and trust that people have available to them. With reference to education systems, he identifies three types of social capital: (a) 'bonding social capital', which concerns relationships among personnel within a school; (b) 'bridging social capital', which occurs between schools through collaboration; and (c) 'linking social capital', which relates to relationships between a school and the wider community. My recommendations will take account of all three levels of social capital.

In my discussion of cultural capital, above, I referenced it to social class, but, as we shall see in this book, the concept is equally valid when applied to gender, culture, religion and, to a certain extent, variations in physical, intellectual and personality attributes. In general, those occupying minority positions are at risk for being marginalized, sometimes deliberately, at other times quite unconsciously. Many of them may well come to school with cultural capital that differs from their teachers. The challenge to schools (and to education systems more broadly) is to determine how far they can and should go in accommodating the cultural capital of diverse groups, those with different worldviews from their own.[96] This will involve engaging in double-loop learning. At stake here is the comfort, even the feelings of safety, that children will experience in the school environments that they are (usually) compelled to attend. In turn, this will impact on their self-esteem, identities, sense of empowerment and, ultimately, their behaviour and achievement.

Second, mention must be made of Antonio Gramsci. In the 1930s, Gramsci used the term *hegemony* to denote the dominance of one social class over others. He argued that hegemony represents not only political and economic control, but also the ability of the dominant class to project its own ways of seeing the world so that those who are subordinated by them accept them as 'common sense' and 'natural'.[97] Gramsci saw hegemony as the permeation *throughout* society of an entire system of values, attitudes, beliefs and morality that has the effect of supporting the status quo in power relations.[98] He described this as a form of 'consensual control', as distinct from 'coercive control' through domination. He further argued that ruling groups devise educational structures aimed at reproducing society. For lower-class students, he claimed, this meant gearing their education toward technical and vocational training, thus denying them access to general or universal education necessary to attain positions of power in society. To address such imbalances, Gramsci introduced the notion of a 'counter-hegemonic' struggle aimed at advancing alternatives to the dominant ideas of what is normal and legitimate. This takes place through consciousness-raising aimed at changing the minds and hearts of people.[99] Since hegemony is never stable, it is possible to disrupt it and to put forward alternative ways of looking at the world.

Third, we turn to the challenging work of Paulo Freire. In his highly influential 1972 book, *Pedagogy of the Oppressed*, Freire examined the balance of power between the colonizer (the oppressor) and the colonized (the oppressed), arguing that it remains relatively stable.[100] To disrupt this homeostasis, Freire stated that freedom 'must be pursued constantly and responsibly' for it is 'the indispensable condition for the quest for human completion'. Further, freedom will be the result of 'praxis' – informed action – when a balance between theory and practice is achieved.[101] To bring this about, according to Freire, requires respect, or, as he put it:

One cannot expect positive results from an educational or political action program which fails to respect the particular view of the world held by the people. Such a program constitutes cultural invasion, good intentions notwithstanding.

According people respect may not always be a comfortable process for oppressors, 'whose tranquillity rests on how well people fit the world the oppressors have created, and how little they question it'.

In pursuing a liberation objective, Freire was critical of the 'banking' approach to education in which students are seen as empty bank accounts into which teachers make deposits – a process that he sees as dehumanizing both students and teachers and which stimulates oppressive attitudes and practices in society. Instead, he argued for a more 'authentic' approach to education through a process of 'conscientization'. He also proposed 'dialogics' as a means of freeing the colonized through the use of cooperation, respect, unity, building social capital and cultural synthesis, thus leading to social justice. This is in contrast to 'antidialogics', which use conquest, manipulation, cultural invasion and the concept of divide and rule. According to one commentator, Freire consistently argued that a thorough understanding of oppression must always take a detour through some form of class analysis. However, he resisted any approach that reduced all analysis to one monolithic entity.

1.22 Perspective 14: Reason and evidence should determine educational policies and practices

As I have pointed out in my recent book, *What really works in special and inclusive education*,[102] increasingly around the world, educators are being expected to draw upon research-based evidence in planning, implementing and evaluating their teaching. In Europe, for example, since 2010 there has been a project, Evidence-informed Policy and Practice in Education in Europe, with 34 partner organizations from 24 countries, together with four affiliates from outside Europe.[103] This project aims to broker knowledge using common reference tools and approaches, as well as exchanging good practices, data and evidence from relevant European agencies and national-level resources.

In the United States, the 2001 No Child Left Behind (NCLB) law required teachers to use 'scientific, research-based programs', defined as: '(1) grounded in theory; (2) evaluated by third parties; (3) published in peer-reviewed journals; (4) sustainable; (5) replicable in schools with diverse settings; and (6) able to demonstrate evidence of effectiveness'. In 2015, the Every Student Succeeds Act (ESSA) replaced the NCLB Act and the Elementary and Secondary Education Act. Like the NCLB Act, ESSA emphasized the role of evidence, defining four categories of evidence based on their relative strength. Further, the recent establishment of centres specializing in gathering and disseminating evidence-based education policies and practices provides further support for the growing commitment to evidence-based education in the United States.[104]

Given this book's focus on diversity, I should like to address the critical question of whether different categories of learners require distinctive teaching strategies? As I pointed out elsewhere,[105] the answer to this question is both 'Yes' and a qualified 'No'. First, *yes*: some students – especially those with severe disabilities – do require some significantly different teaching strategies from those that educators in regular classes might usually employ.

For example, some students with visual impairments are reliant on their tactile and auditory senses for learning and will require specialized techniques such as Braille and orientation and mobility training. Similarly, those with major language difficulties may require augmented and alternative communication. Second, *no*: for the most part, all students, irrespective of their category of diversity, simply require good teaching. For example, some writers argue that there is little evidence to support the notion of disability-specific teaching strategies, but rather that all learners benefit from a common set of strategies, even if they have to be adapted to take account of varying cognitive, emotional and social capabilities and cultural backgrounds.[106] In subsequent chapters, I will argue that this not only applies to learners with special educational needs, but also to those from different socio-economic backgrounds, genders, cultures and religions. What is required is the systematic, explicit and intensive application of a wide range of effective teaching strategies.[107]

As well as empirical, research-based evidence, educationists should also be basing their policies and practices on reasoning derived from philosophical and theoretical analyses. For example, in all of the chapters I will discuss the application of human rights, while in the chapter on religion (Chapter 5) I will be referring to philosophical analyses of indoctrination and in the chapter on abilities/disabilities (Chapter 6) I will discuss arguments in favour of inclusion.

1.23 Perspective 15: Account should be taken of the impact of disruptive technologies on job prospects

Given that high proportions of children who are the focus of this book leave school with minimal or no qualifications, we should give consideration to their future job prospects. In a word, these are not very promising. Advances in computerization and other technology areas mean that, at best, some jobs will continue to be available but will undergo significant transformations, whereas, at worst, some will disappear altogether. On the plus side, technological change also brings direct and indirect job creation as machines require building and maintenance, more wealth is created and new markets are opened.[108]

We now live in a world of 'disruptive technologies', defined by Harvard Business School professor, Clayton Christensen, as new emerging technologies that unexpectedly displace an established one.[109] According to the McKinsey Global Institute, there are 12 technologies that can produce great disruptions in our near future as they transform the economy and our lives.[110] These comprise: the mobile Internet, the automation of knowledge work, the Internet of things, advanced robotics, the cloud, autonomous or near-autonomous vehicles, next generation storage, 3D printing, advanced materials, advanced oil and gas exploration and recovery, and renewable electricity. The OECD has pointed out that the impact of technological change on employment and jobs is biased towards certain types of skills:

> routine tasks that are easily programmable and non-person-to-person interactions are most affected. Person-to-person services and occupations relying more on creativity, context adaptability, task discretion, social skills and tacit cognitive capacities have been less affected.[111]

The OECD has also claimed that more than half of adults in the United States do not have the skills to fulfil simple problem-solving tasks in technology-rich environments.

In a recent seminal paper, Oxford academics Carl Frey and Michael Osborne addressed the question: how susceptible are jobs to computerization?[112] In making their case, they pointed to recent employment growth in occupations involving cognitive tasks, originality, negotiation, persuasion, social perceptiveness, and assisting and caring for others.[113] As well, certain low-income manual occupations fall into the low risk category. Against these trends, whole swathes of jobs have either disappeared or have been substantially reduced.[114] These include middle-income routine jobs such as most manufacturing jobs, but also bookkeepers, cashiers, bank tellers, typists, airline reservation clerks and telephone operators. The result has been a 'hollowing-out' of occupational opportunities, a shift that is resulting in many high-skilled workers moving down the occupational ladder, taking on jobs that were traditionally performed by low-skilled workers, thus 'pushing low-skilled workers even further down the occupational ladder and, to some extent, even out of the labour force'.[115] Frey and Osborne predict that these trends will continue. Drawing upon recent advances in machine learning, mobile robotics and artificial intelligence, they categorized occupations according to their susceptibility to computerization in the future. They estimated that 47% of US jobs (39% in Germany, 35% in the United Kingdom) were at risk of being automated in the next 20 or so years through the cost-effective application of existing and foreseeable technologies. For example, autonomous driverless cars, developed by Google, will soon lead to increasing automation of manual tasks in transport and logistics. Other instances of automatization include diagnostic tasks in health care, legal research and, surprisingly, service occupations. One recent estimate suggested that sophisticated algorithms could substitute for approximately 140 million full-time knowledge workers worldwide.[116]

Unlike in past eras of technologization, Frey and Osborne are pessimistic as to whether sufficient new jobs will be created to compensate for the losses resulting from computerization. Compounding this problem (at least for developed countries) is the increasing proportion of jobs that are predicted to be 'offshorable': 22-29% of US jobs by about 2020, according to one estimate.[117]

While disruptive technologies are by no means a new phenomenon, their impact appears to be accelerating. Klaus Schwab, the Founder and Executive Chairman of the World Economic Forum, has written about what he termed the Fourth Industrial Revolution, which is characterized by a fusion of technologies that is blurring the lines between the physical, digital and biological spheres.[118] Compared with the preceding revolutions, this one is evolving at an exponential rather than a linear rate, according to Schwab. For example, a recent article in *The Atlantic* pointed out that the share of prime-age Americans (25-54 years old) who are working has been trending down since 2000.[119] Among men, the decline began even earlier, with the proportion of men out of work doubling since the late 1970s. In the United States, one of the prime factors in this decline of participation in the workforce is the loss of manufacturing jobs, which reduced by about 30% between 2000 and 2015. Further, *The Economist* points out that the share of American employment in manufacturing has declined from almost 30% in the 1950s to less than 10% in 2014, while, at the same time, service jobs increased from less than 50% to almost 70%.[120] Schwab's Fourth Industrial Revolution, then, could yield greater inequality. As he argued, the displacement of workers by machines might increase the gap between returns to capital and returns to labour (thus exacerbating existing trends noted by Thomas Piketty, whose views I will outline in Chapter 3). As well as constituting an economic concern, these inequalities also constitute societal concerns with the potential to build up centrifugal forces I described in section 1.12.

These technological trends will impact most heavily on those who leave school with minimal or low qualifications. As we shall see in this book, those who are most at risk in the changing work environments are children from low socio-economic homes, ethnic minorities and those with disabilities, and, in some countries, religious minorities and girls. As noted in *The Atlantic* article, work as a central feature of adult identity may well 'dissipate for a significant portion of society'. This may well be the case for many of those who are the focus of this book.

1.24 Perspective 16: Technology has the potential to transform education

Technology also has an upside. We live in changing times, when technology permeates almost everything we do – in our workplaces, in our interactions with businesses, in our entertainment. And now, information and communication technology (ICT) is increasingly influencing what, where and how we teach. However, as we shall see in this book, not all children are in a position to benefit from ICT. Many children are on the wrong side of the 'digital divide', whether it is because their families or schools cannot afford modern technologies or their parents and teachers are unfamiliar with its use.

This is to be regretted, for there is increasing evidence that technology-based learning and assessment systems have the potential to enable and motivate all students, regardless of their backgrounds, to achieve. Already, the vast majority of students access technology in their daily lives 24/7 creating multimedia content and participating in social networks. The time is surely come when ICT has to be utilized skilfully in our classrooms. As a US report put it, 'The challenge to our education system is to leverage the learning sciences and modern technology to create engaging, relevant, and personalized learning experiences for all learners that mirror students' daily lives and the reality of their futures.'[121]

1.25 Perspective 17: The focus should be on the uniqueness of individuals

Throughout this book, I will be emphasizing the importance of looking at diversity in terms of individual differences rather than exclusively in terms of group membership. I will be referring to the heterogeneity of children who fit within the categories of diversity and suggesting that rather than trying to accommodate education programmes to such broad categories, the best way forward is individualization or, as some put it, 'personalization'.

Perhaps the best-known and most widely publicized definition of personalization is the one included in the US Department of Education's National Education Technology Plan, referred to above:

> Personalization refers to instruction that is paced to learning needs, tailored to learning preferences, and tailored to the specific interests of different learners. In an environment that is fully personalized, the learning objectives and content as well as the method and pace may all vary (so personalization encompasses differentiation and individualization).[122]

1.26 Perspective 18: Universal design for learning provides fair opportunities for learning

In recent years, the importance of universal design for learning (UDL) has been increasingly emphasized in education. UDL is a multi-component strategy that involves planning and delivering programmes with the needs of *all* students in mind. It applies to all facets of education: from curriculum, assessment and pedagogy to classroom and school design. In the United States, UDL means a scientifically valid framework for guiding educational practice that

- provides flexibility in the ways information is presented, in the ways students respond or demonstrate knowledge and skills, and in the ways students are engaged; and
- reduces barriers in instruction, provides appropriate accommodations, supports, and challenges, and maintains high achievement expectations for all students, including students with disabilities and students who are limited English proficient.[123]

In other words, UDL focuses on ways to provide cognitive, as well as physical, access to the curriculum, assessment and pedagogy for all students. The US Center for Applied Special Technology provides a useful definition:

> the design of instructional materials and activities that allows the learning goals to be achievable by individuals with wide differences in their abilities to see, hear, speak, move, read, write, understand English, attend, organize, engage and remember. It is achieved by means of flexible curricular materials and activities that provide alternatives for students with disparities in abilities and background as well as those with no visible disabilities. [It] applies not only to the content, but also to goals, methods, and manner of assessment.[124]

1.27 Perspective 19: Early prevention and intervention programmes should be developed

With the possible exception of religion, it is important to develop early programmes to prevent disadvantages from occurring and to intervene as soon as possible. The latter has two meanings: (a) pre-school provisions and (b) the early identification and remediation of children's lack of progress and behaviour difficulties whenever they occur at school.

According to a UK review, there is abundant evidence of the effectiveness of practices around early intervention and prevention.[125] For example, in England, the Effective Pre-school and Primary Education 3-11 Project studied the developmental trajectories of approximately 2,800 children from age 3 to 11 years.[126] It found that the benefits of pre-school education largely persisted through to the end of Key Stage 2 (age 11). Attendance at pre-school was beneficial for both academic and social/behavioural outcomes, as well as pupils' self-perceptions. Importantly the quality of the pre-school predicted pupils' developmental outcomes, net of all other influences. For all social outcomes, the benefits of pre-school were greater for boys, for pupils with special educational needs, and for pupils from disadvantaged backgrounds. However, for some of the outcomes, notably English, Mathematics and 'Hyperactivity', only pre-schools of medium or high quality had lasting effects. The higher the academic effectiveness of the pre-school attended, the better the longer-term outcomes for children.

Children who did not attend pre-school and those who attended low quality pre-school showed a range of poorer outcomes at age 11.

Just as early intervention with a focus on preventing problems is important, so, too, is early identification and remediation of behaviour problems. One example of a study will suffice. In a review, James Buckley from the US Department of Education's Institute of Education Science concluded that 'a substantial body of research has shown that the early onset of behavioral and mental health problems during elementary school is associated with an increased risk for subsequent severe behavior and academic problems'.[127] He went on to note research that shows that 'in the absence of effective intervention, many students who exhibit serious behavior problems in the early elementary grades … develop more significant anti-social and disruptive behavior patterns by the upper elementary or middle school grades'.[128]

1.28 Structure of the book

What follows is a taxonomy of what I consider to be the markers of diversities and questions that arise regarding their educational significance (see Figure 1.3). This is followed by a summary of the key questions I will address in the five main areas of diversity discussed in this book: sex and gender; socio-economic status; race, ethnicity and culture; beliefs and religion; and ability.

Sex and gender

While it has always been recognized that there are two sexes, in recent years people have had to revise their thinking to accommodate differences in sexual orientation and gender identity, i.e., lesbian, gay, bisexual and transgender (LGBT). While males and females are more alike than they are different in their underlying psychological makeup, they demonstrate many differences in their behaviours. I will address three main questions: (1) What are the sex/gender ratios across the world? (2) How are genders different? (3) What causes gender differences? (4) How should education respond to gender differences? I will refer to research into gender gaps in general, especially in developing countries in the present and in developed countries in the past.

Social class/socio-economic status

Most societies historically and contemporaneously are stratified, usually on the basis of the relative socio-economic status of their members. I will explore such issues as the following: (1) What is the relationship between socio-economic factors and educational achievement and behaviour? (2) How do socio-economic factors impact on students? (3) How should education accommodate to any socio-economic differences in its student body? (4) In cases of extreme poverty in societies with limited resources, how can education best be provided?

Race/ethnicity/culture

Often within a society there exist groups of people who share systems of values, beliefs, meanings and ways of life that are transmitted from one generation to another. Sometimes these groups may comprise a majority in the country in which they live;

sometimes they are in a minority. Increasingly, societies around the world are becoming multi-ethnic and multi-cultural, often as a result of an acceleration of migration. I will be asking such questions as: (1) What is meant by race, ethnicity and culture? (2) What is the evidence of the relationship between race/ethnicity/culture and educational performance? (3) Can race/ethnicity/culture be separated from socio-economic status? (4) What are the educational implications of race/ethnicity/culture? In particular, (a) what does it mean to provide a culturally sensitive or culturally responsive education? (b) what is required in multicultural or bicultural education? (c) are there any universal values that transcend cultures that educators should seek to inculcate through, for example, education for global citizenship? (d) what language policies should be adopted?

Beliefs/religion

Many people believe in a god or in a group of gods or have interests or beliefs that are very important to them. In this chapter, I will examine the relationship between religion/beliefs and education, in particular: (1) To what extent do different countries separate church and state in education and how does that impact on requirements to respect the personal religious views of students? (2) How does such a separation affect students' orientation to and engagement with school practices and curricula? (3) Can a case be made for dissolving dualisms between the sacred and the secular in education?

Ability

As can be seen in Figure 1.3, ability spans three main domains:

Health and physical ability   Human beings vary in their health and physical ability, with some excelling and others having disabilities. Questions to arise here include: (1) What variations are there in individuals' health and physical ability? (2) What effects do such variations have on education and employment? (3) How should schools accommodate to physical differences that range from those with exceptional sporting prowess to those with physical disabilities? In particular, (a) what purposes are served through physical education and physical therapy? (b) what is the relationship between physical education/therapy and cognitive development? (c) should schools play a role in developing physical skills such as sporting excellence? (d) how can various sports be adapted to take account of physical disabilities? (e) is there a place for the Special Olympics? (e) what role does education play in reducing or eradicating such diseases as HIV/AIDS?

Personality   Personality plays an important role in children's relationships with peers and teachers, influencing classroom behaviour and contributing to academic achievement. Dysfunctional personalities pose particular challenges to teachers and families, sometimes creating risks to the children themselves and to their peers. In this chapter, I will focus on broad domains such as temperament, attachment, motivation, anxiety, conduct disorders, aggression and depression. Questions here include: (1) What are the variations in personality? (2) What are the origins of various personality traits? (3) How should and can schools

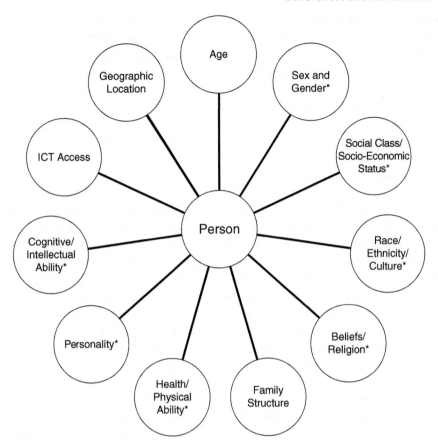

Figure 1.3 A taxonomy of diversities

Note: * = the focus of this book

accommodate to personality variations? (4) Should and can schools intervene to change children's personalities?

   Cognitive/intellectual ability Cognitive/intellectual development involves the construction of thought processes, including remembering, reasoning, problem solving and information processing, and the application of these abilities to achieve major developmental tasks. Such development varies from individual to individual and spans a range from giftedness to intellectual disabilities, including autistic spectrum disorder, dyslexia and ADHD. Questions to be considered here are: (1) What are the variations in intellectual/cognitive functioning? (2) Do people with intellectual disabilities or who are gifted learn differently from other people? (3) What kind of education best suits children with diverse intellectual/cognitive functioning?
   As well as the above 'big five', there are another four areas of diversity that space limitations preclude me from addressing, although I will make brief references to them in the appropriate chapters. These comprise age, family structure, geographic location and access to ICT:

Age   After our birth, we typically develop through the cycle of infancy, childhood, adolescence, adulthood and old age, until our death. Age is an ascribed status that provides a basis for much of the social differentiation and stratification that takes place in all societies, not least in education. It raises several questions: (1) How do humans change biologically, psychologically, socially and emotionally with age? (2) What does brain development tell us about age-based differences? (3) Does ageism exist with children? (4) What are the educational implications of age-related factors? In particular, (a) what is the justification for age-stratified education, particularly in light of the growing development of web-based learning opportunities? (b) at what age should children commence school? (c) should there be grade retention or social promotion of students who cannot reach certain standards for their age group?

Family structure   Families are changing in many ways across most countries, and most have seen a decline in the fertility rate since the past 1980s. As a result, the average household size has also declined. While the picture of the nuclear or extended family that stays together through life is still the norm in most nations, it is changing in many countries around the world. In western countries, the family unit is increasingly taking a variety of forms, reflecting higher rates of divorce, remarriage, blended and step-family relations, and adults who have never married or are voluntarily childless/childfree. Questions such as the following arise: (1) What changes in family structures are occurring? (2) What effects do family changes have on child outcomes? (3) What are the mechanisms that link family structure and family change to child outcomes? (4) What is the educational significance of changes in the structures of families?

Geographic location   While there is a growing trend towards urbanization, the fact remains that many people live in rural areas, some of which are quite isolated. Currently, more than half (54%) of the world's population lives in towns and cities, but it is predicted that by 2050 about 64% of the developing world and 86% of the developed world will be urbanized.[129] The United Nations has also recently projected that nearly all global population growth from 2015 to 2030 will be absorbed by cities. Migration is driving much of this increase in urbanization, making cities increasingly more diverse places in which to live.[130]

There are often distinct differences between urban and rural populations. On the one hand, rural settlements have low population densities, are typically culturally homogeneous, and have low levels of education. On the other hand, urban settlements are characterized by the presence of a great number of very different people in a very limited space – most of them strangers to each other, making it possible to build up a vast array of subcultures close to each other, exposed to each other's influence. Urban areas provide opportunities for improved standards of living, higher life expectancy and higher literacy levels. For women, urbanization is associated with greater access to employment opportunities, lower fertility levels and increased independence. However, cities are also home to high concentrations of poverty.[131] Nowhere is the rise of inequality clearer than in urban areas, where wealthy communities coexist alongside, and separate from, slums and informal settlements.[132]

Information and communication technology   Recent years have seen rapid advances in the development of computers, which enable users to access, store, transmit and manipulate information. Information and communication technology (ICT) is increasingly influencing the

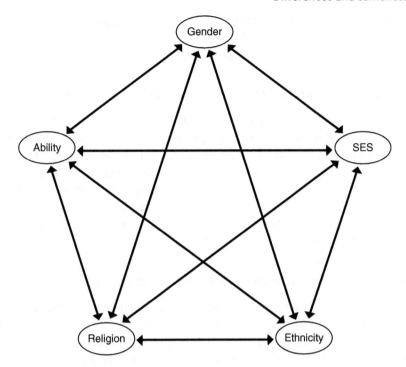

Figure 1.4 Areas of diversity and their intersections

content of curricula and pedagogy. Unfortunately, not all children have access to high quality ICT, for a variety of reasons, including poverty or low incomes in families, and parents or
teachers who are unfamiliar with its use. The result is what some refer to as a 'digital divide',
which can impede social inclusion in today's era. Questions such as the following are important:
(1) To what extent do people have access to modern ICT? (2) What factors govern this access?
(3) What are the educational implications of differential access to ICT?

As mentioned above, this book is focused on five main areas of diversity and their intersections with each other, as portrayed in Figure 1.4.

1.29 Conclusion

Human diversity both attracts and repels, depending on time and place – and the person.
Historically and contemporaneously, various categories of diversity have elicited, and continue to elicit, discrimination, even persecution. Equally, some categories are valued and are
sought after.

Given the increasing diversity of many western countries, there is a compelling need to
understand the phenomenon and to develop public policies to accommodate to those who are
different from the 'mainstream' in an equitable and just manner. This challenge is one of the
greatest confronting societies, education systems, schools and classrooms around the world.
Failure to develop appropriate policies and practices to deal with it risks exacerbating conflict
between nations and groups, creating disaffection which may threaten the stability of societies,
as well as jeopardizing the human rights and well-being of those who are 'different'. I hope that

this book contributes to developing a better understanding of human diversity and how education may successfully address the challenges it poses.

In writing this book, I have two intersecting goals in mind:

A To respect and enhance the human rights of diverse people

The human rights of different groups must be understood and protected. These rights inform us as to what we may, must, and must not do to others and, correspondingly, what we may expect of others in their behaviours towards us. A challenge arises with respect to reconciling competing rights, for example children's vs their parents' rights with regard to freedom of religion. A related point involves deciding on the principles of distributive justice that should apply. This is extremely significant for determining how societies respond to differences among its citizens, particularly how they behave towards those who are disadvantaged – and especially towards children.

B To develop inclusivist societies and global community

In this book, I wish to extend the scope of inclusive education from its focus on special educational needs arising from disabilities to encompass *all* learners. In particular, I will be giving consideration to other potential sources of disadvantage and marginalization, such as gender (in some countries), poverty, language, ethnicity and religious minority status.

In pursuing these two goals, throughout the book I will consider 19 interlocking principles:

1   Deciding on the principles of distributive justice that should apply is extremely significant for determining how societies respond to differences among their citizens, particularly how they behave towards those who are disadvantaged – and especially towards children.
2   Diversities must be seen from an ecological perspective. The child is influenced by complex interactions among societal, community, family, school and classroom factors. Correspondingly, interventions must address these factors and how they can be 'joined-up'. A related point to take into account is that while society and its instruments, including schools, have a major responsibility for what children learn, they themselves also significantly contribute to this process. Children are active constructors of knowledge and, by-and-large, are capable of driving their own learning.
3   Perceptions of diversity vary across time and space. Differences are perceived differently in different countries and at different times in history. Contexts of time and space matter for how various domains of difference are socially constructed and the nature of the competing social forces that may operate in such struggles.
4   There is a need to strike a balance between sameness and diversity. When does tolerating or encouraging diversity threaten the fabric of a cohesive society – or a cohesive school or classroom? Conversely, could the aspiration for social cohesion have the intended or unintended consequence of marginalizing those who are different? Resolving this tension between centrifugal (away from the centre) and centripetal (toward the centre) forces is a continuing challenge to governments, school administrators and teachers.

5   The theory of interest convergence helps to explain shifts in behaviour and policies. Although it offers valuable insights into the way that change occurs, it should not be viewed as either flawless or all-encompassing.

6   Consideration must be given to the intersection of different categories of difference. Individuals' identities are composed of various combinations and permutations of categories. For example, there is clear evidence of intersections between ethnicity, gender and class in influencing achievement. Similarly, abilities/disabilities interact with gender, class and ethnicity.

7   Consideration must be given to the multiple factors that, singly or in combination, give rise to human differences. These include such factors as: evolution, globalization, poverty, geographic location, genetics, neuroscience, environmental degradation, cultural values, conflict, disasters, socialization, politics, neo-liberalism, technology, resources, parenting, diet, xenophobia and even education.

8   Human beings are genetically similar. Although genetic variation across groups of people is quite small, considerable variance in educational attainment is explained by genetic factors.

9   An evolutionary perspective on diversity must be considered. Human variation is, at least in part, accounted for by the fact that as a species, we have colonized nearly every land area on the surface of the earth, and that each of these diverse environments has shaped our psychological design and continues to do so.

10 Many differences are small, even if they are statistically significant. While many of the findings I will be presenting in this book refer to statistically significant differences within the various categories, it is important that we bear in mind the practical significance of any such differences. A related point to remember is that there is considerable diversity within the various categories of difference discussed.

11 Economic considerations come into play when seeking to understand various disadvantages, both in ascertaining how they arise and in determining how to redress them.

12 Education should be perceived as a multi-level and multi-faceted concept that requires consideration of such issues as parental choice, an ecological perspective on diversity, inclusive education and evidence-based pedagogy.

13 Children who come from class, gender, cultural and religious backgrounds that differ from the prevailing norms and expectations of schools can be seriously disadvantaged. This disjunction leads us to consideration of cultural and social capital, hegemony and critical pedagogy.

14 Educators should draw upon evidence-based pedagogy. Increasingly around the world, educators are being expected to draw upon research-based evidence in planning, implementing and evaluating their teaching. This book will rely heavily in gathering and interpreting both empirical and theoretical evidence relating to the various categories of diversity.

15 In planning for the futures of disadvantaged learners (and others), we must take account of the fact that we live in a world of 'disruptive technologies'. Advances in computerization and in other areas mean that, at best, some jobs will continue to be available but will undergo significant transformations, whereas, at worst, some will disappear altogether.

16 Information and communication technology (ICT) is increasingly influencing what, where and how we teach, but not all children are in a position to benefit from it. This is to be regretted,

for there is increasing evidence that technology-based learning and assessment systems has the potential to enable and motivate all students, regardless of their backgrounds, to achieve.

17   Rather than trying to accommodate education programmes to broad categories of diversity, the best way forward is individualization or, as some put it, 'personalization'. Thus, the focus should be on the uniqueness of individuals.

18   Universal design for learning focuses on ways to provide cognitive, as well as physical, access to the curriculum, assessment and pedagogy for all students. It applies to all facets of education: from curriculum, assessment and pedagogy to classroom and school design.

19   It is important to develop early programmes to prevent disadvantages from occurring and to intervene as soon as possible. The latter has two meanings: (a) pre-school provisions and (b) the early identification and remediation of children's lack of progress and behaviour difficulties whenever they occur at school.

Notes

1   Vertovec, S. (2007). 'Superdiversity and its implications.' *Ethnic and Racial Studies*, 30(6), 1024–1054.
2   Burbules, N.C. (1997). 'A grammar of difference: Some ways of rethinking difference and diversity as educational topics.' *Australian Education Researcher*, 24(1), 97–116.
3   United Nations Development Programme (UNDP) (2004). *A global report: Reducing disaster risk: A challenge for development*. New York: Author. URL: http://www.undp.org.lb/WhatWeDo/Docs/Reducing%20Disaster%20Risk%20-%20A%20Challenge%20for%20Development.pdf (accessed 20 August 2014).
4   Ibid.
5   This section is drawn mainly from Sandel, M.J. (2009). *Justice: What's the right thing to do?* New York, NY: Farrar, Strauss and Giroux; but also from Fagan, A. (2014). 'Human rights.' *Internet Encyclopedia of Philosophy*. URL: http://www.iep.utm.edu/hum-rts/ (accessed 1 July 2014); and Wenar, L. (2011). 'Rights'. *The Stanford Encyclopedia of Philosophy* (Fall 2011 edn), Edward N. Zalta (ed.). URL: http://plato.stanford.edu/archives/fall2011/entries/rights/ (accessed 15 October 2014).
6   Raday, F. (2003). 'Culture, religion, and gender.' *International Journal of Constitutional Law*, 1(4), 663–715.
7   Harris, N. (2007). *Education, law and diversity*. Oxford: Hart Publishing; and Lundy, L. (2012). 'Children's rights and educational policy in Europe: The implementation of the United Nations Convention on the Rights of the Child.' *Oxford Review of Education*, 38, 393–411.
8   UNESCO Institute for Statistics, 'Fixing the broken promise of Education for All'. August 2014, Montreal.
9   Office of the High Commissioner for Human Rights (1999). *CESCR General Comment No. 13: The Right to Education (Art 13)*. Adopted at the Twenty-first Session of the Committee on Economic, Social and Cultural Rights, on 8 December 1999. URL: http://www.refworld.org/publisher,CESCR,GENERAL,,4538838c22,0.html (accessed 1 November 2015).
10 DfEE (1999). *Social inclusion: Pupil support*. London: DfEE Circular 10/1999.
11 See Maylor, U., Read, B., Mendick, H., Ross, A. & Rollock, N. (2007). *Diversity and citizenship in the curriculum: Research review*. London: The Institute for Policy Studies in Education, London Metropolitan University. URL: http://webarchive.nationalarchives.gov.uk/20130401151715/https://www.education.gov.uk/publications/eorderingdownload/rr819.pdf (accessed 1 July 2014).
12 UNESCO (2009). *Policy guidelines on inclusion in education*. Paris: Author. URL: http://unesdoc.unesco.org/images/0017/001778/177849e.pdf (accessed 3 July 2014).
13 Ibid., p. 4.
14 Hyman, J.S. & Jacobs, L.S. (2009). 'Why does diversity matter at College anyway?' *Professors' Guide*. URL: http://www.usnews.com/education/blogs/professors-guide/2009/08/12/why-does-diversity-matter-at-college-anyway (accessed 30 June 2014).

15 This section is drawn from Fagan, A. (2014). 'Human rights.' *Internet Encyclopedia of Philosophy.* URL: http://www.iep.utm.edu/hum-rts/ (accessed 1 July 2014).

16 Houlgate, L.D. (1980). *The child and the state.* Baltimore, MD: Johns Hopkins University Press.

17 Mitchell, D.R. (1985). 'Ethical and legal issues in providing medical treatment for seriously ill handicapped persons.' *Australia and New Zealand Journal of Developmental Disabilities,* 11(4), 245-256.

18 Maritain, J. (1951). *Man and the state.* Chicago: University of Chicago Press.

19 Mitchell, D. (2005). 'Introduction: Sixteen propositions on the contexts of inclusive education.' In D. Mitchell (ed.), *Contextualizing inclusive education: Evaluating old and new international perspectives* (pp. 1-21). London: Routledge.

20 UNESCO/IBE (2009). *Defining an inclusive education agenda: Reflections around the 48th session of the International Conference on Education.* Geneva: Author, p. 126.

21 Baglieri, S., Bejoian, L.M., Broderick, A.A., Connor, D.J. & Valle, J. (2011). '[Re]claiming "inclusive education" toward cohesion in educational reform: Disability studies unravels the myth of the normal child.' *Teachers College Record,* 113(10), 2122-2154.

22 Zion, S. & Blanchett, W. (2011). '[Re]conceptualizing inclusion: Can critical race theory and interest convergence be utilized to achieve inclusion and equity for African American students?' *Teachers College Record,* 113(10), 2186-2205.

23 Christensen, C. (1996). 'Disabled, handicapped or disordered: What's in a name?' In C. Christensen & F. Rizvi (eds), *Disability and the dilemmas of education and justice* (pp. 63-78). Buckingham: Open University Press.

24 Lipsky, D.K. & Gartner, A. (1999). 'Inclusive education: A requirement of a democratic society.' In H. Daniels & P. Garner (eds), *World yearbook of education 1999: Inclusive education* (pp. 12-23). London: Kogan Page.

25 Allport, G.W. (1954). *The nature of prejudice.* Cambridge/Reading, MA: Addison-Wesley.

26 Allman, D. (2013). 'The sociology of social inclusion.' *Sage Open,* 3(1), doi:1177/2158244012471957.

27 Council of Europe (2008). *Living together as equals in dignity. White Paper on intercultural dialogue.* Strasbourg: Author.

28 Ibid., item 1.

29 For an advocacy of intercultural approach, see also UNESCO (2005). *Convention on the Protection and Promotion of the Diversity of Cultural Expressions.* Paris: Author.

30 Ibid., item 22.

31 Mitchell, D. (2015). 'Inclusive education is a multi-faceted concept.' *Center for Educational Policy Studies Journal* (Slovenia), 5(1), 9-30.

32 See Sandel, op. cit.

33 Ibid.

34 Nozick, R. (1974). *Anarchy, state and utopia.* New York, NY: Basic Books.

35 Friedman, M. (1962). *Capitalism and freedom.* Chicago: University of Chicago Press.

36 Hence, utilitarianism is sometimes referred to as *consequentialism.*

37 Bentham, J. (1776). *A fragment on government.* R. Harrison (ed.). Cambridge: Cambridge University Press, 1988.

38 Mill, J.S. (1859). *On liberty.* S. Collini (ed.). Cambridge: Cambridge University Press, 1989. Chapter 1.

39 Sandel, op. cit., p. 104.

40 Ibid., p. 105.

41 Ibid., p. 111.

42 Kant, I. (1785). *Groundwork for the metaphysics of morals.* New York: Harper Torchbooks. As cited by Sandel, op. cit., p. 122.

43 Ibid., p. 421. As cited by Sandel, op. cit., p. 120.

44 Rawls, J. (1971). *A theory of justice.* Cambridge, MA: The Belknap Press of Harvard University Press.

45 Ibid., sec. 17.

46 Sandel, op. cit., p. 166.

47 Nettle, D., Gibson, M.A., Lawson, D.W. & Sear, R. (2013). 'Human behavioral ecology: Current research and future prospects.' *Behavioral Ecology,* doi: 101093/beheco/ars222.

48 Ainscow, M., Dyson, A., Goldrick, S. & West, M. (2012). *Developing equitable education systems.* London: Routledge, pp. 10, 11.

49 See Mitchell, D. (2012). *Joined-up: A comprehensive ecological model for working with children with complex needs and their families. A review of the literature carried out for the New Zealand Ministry*

of Education. Wellington, New Zealand: Ministry of Education. URL: http://www.minedu.govt.nz/~/media/MinEdu/Files/TheMinistry/Consultation/JoinedUp.pdf (accessed 19 May 2016).

50 Bronfenbrenner, U. (1979). *The ecology of human development: Experiments by nature and design*. Cambridge, MA: Harvard University Press.

51 For detailed descriptions of complex systems, see Cochrane-Smith, M., Ell, F., Ludlow, L., Grudnoff, L. & Aitken, G. (2014). 'The challenge and promise of complexity theory for teacher education research.' *Teachers College Review*, 116(5), 1-38; and Byrne, D. (1998). *Complexity theory and the social sciences*. New York, NY: Routledge.

52 Hartshorne, R. (1950). 'The functional approach in political geography.' *Annals of the Association of American Geographers*, 40(2), 95-130.

53 Burbules, op. cit.

54 Bell, D. (1980). '*Brown v. Board of Education* and the interest convergence dilemma.' *Harvard Law Review*, 93(3), 518-533, p. 523.

55 See Driver, J. (2011). 'Rethinking the interest-convergence thesis.' *Northwestern University Law Review*, 105(1), 149-197, p. 152.

56 After Zion, S. & Blanchett, W. (2011). '[Re]conceptualizing inclusion: Can critical race theory and interest convergence be utilized to achieve inclusion and equity for African American students?' *Teachers College Record*, 113(10), 2186-2205.

57 Driver, op. cit.

58 Ibid., p. 157.

59 Ibid., p. 197.

60 Crenshaw, K. (1989). 'Demarginalizing the intersection of race and sex: A black feminist critique of antidiscrimination doctrine, feminist theory and antiracist politics.' *University of Chicago Legal Forum*, 140, 139-167.

61 Sen, A. (2006). *Identity and violence: The illusion of destiny*. London: Allen Lane, pp. xiii-xiv.

62 Thrupp, M. (2015). 'Deficit thinking and the politics of blame.' In V.M. Carpenter & S. Osborne (eds), *Twelve thousand hours: Education, and poverty in Aotearoa New Zealand* (pp. 88-101). Auckland, New Zealand: Dunmore Publishing.

63 Ibid., p. 89.

64 Dawkins, R. (2004). *The ancestor's tale: A pilgrimage to the dawn of life*. London: Phoenix.

65 Ibid., p. 421.

66 Ibid., p. 416.

67 Ibid., p. 422.

68 Ibid., pp. 422-423.

69 Rietveld, C.A., et al. (2013). 'GWAS of 126,559 individuals identifies genetic variants associated with educational attainment.' *Science*, 340(6139), 1467-1471.

70 Deary, J., Strand, S., Smith, P. & Fernandes, C. (2007). 'Intelligence and educational achievement.' *Intelligence*, 35(1), 13-21.

71 Rietveld et al., op. cit.

72 Polygenic scores are made up of variations in the entire human genome that summarize an individual's cumulative genetic predisposition to a particular disease or trait. Of most interest are 'single-nucleotide polymorphisms' (SNPs) defined as 'single-letter changes in the human DNA sequence that are present in < 1% of the population' (Domingue, B.W., Belsky, D.W., Conley, D., Harris, K.M. & Boardman, J.D. (2015). 'Polygenic influence on educational attainment: New evidence from the National Longitudinal Study of Adolescent to Adult Health'. *AERA Open*, 1(3), doi: 10.1177/2332858415599972 (accessed 19 August 2015).

73 Domingue et al., op. cit.

74 Wood, A.R. et al. (2014). 'Defining the role of common variation in the genomic and biological architecture of adult human height.' *Nature Genetics*, 46(11), 1173-1186.

75 Rietveld et al., op. cit.

76 Belsky, D.W. & Israel, S. (2014). 'Integrating genetics and social science: Genetic risk scores.' *Biodemography and Social Biology*, 60(2), 137-155.

77 Belsky, D.W., Moffitt, T.E., Houts, R., Bennett, G.G., Biddle, A.J., Blumenthal, J.A. & Evans, J.P. (2012). 'Polygenic risk, rapid childhood growth, and the development of obesity: Evidence from a 4-decade longitudinal study.' *Archives of Pediatrics and Adolescent Medicine*, 166(6), 515-521.

78 Darwin, C. (1859). *The origin of species*. London: Murray, p. 399.

79 For an argument that evolutionary psychology provides a cogent meta-theory for psychologi-
    cal science, and how it accounts for many behaviours, including sex differences, see Buss, D.M. &
    Reeve, H.K. (2003). 'Evolutionary psychology and developmental dynamics: Comment on Lickliter
    and Honeycutt (2003).' *Psychological Bulletin*, 129(6), 848-853.

80 Buss, D.M (2009). 'Darwin's influence on modern psychological science.' *Psychological Science
    Agenda*, May 2009, 2-3. *See also* Buss, D.M. (2009). 'The great struggles of life: Darwin and the
    emergence of evolutionary psychology.' *American Psychologist*, 64, 140-148.

81 Pinker, S. (2002). *The blank slate: The modern denial of human nature.* New York: Viking, p. 135.

82 Buss, D.M. & Schmitt, D.P. (2011). 'Evolutionary psychology and feminism.' *Sex Roles*, published on-
    line 26 April 2011.

83 Hyde, J.S. & Linn, M.C. (2006). 'Gender similarities in mathematics and science.' *Science*, 314, 599-600.

84 US Department of Education (2013). *For each and every child: A strategy for educational equity and
    excellence.* Washington, DC: Author, p. 17.

85 Rice, J.K. (2015). *Investing in equal opportunity: What would it take to build the balance wheel?* Boul-
    der, CO: National Education Policy Center, School of Education, University of Colorado Boulder, p. 3.

86 Bourdieu, P. (1984). *Distinction.* London: Routledge.

87 Bourdieu, P. & Passeron, J.C. (1977). *Reproduction in education, society and culture.* London: Sage.

88 Hampden-Thompson G., Guzman, L. & Lippman, L. (2008). 'Cultural capital: What does it offer
    schools?' In J. Zajda, K. Biraimah & W. Gandelli (eds), *Education and social inequality in the global
    culture* (pp. 155-180, p. 158). New York: Springer.

89 Argyris, C. & Schön, D.A. (1978). *Organizational learning: A theory of action perspective.* Reading,
    MA: Addison-Wesley.

90 Schon, D. (1983). *The reflective practitioner: How professionals think in action.* New York, NY: Basic
    Books, p. 102.

91 Putnam, R.D. (2000). *Bowling alone.* New York, NY: Simon and Schuster, p. 306.

92 Putnam, R. (2015). 'Why mentors matter.' *The Rotarian*, October 2015. URL: https://www.
    rotary.org/myrotary/en/news-media/why-mentors-matter (accessed 14 November 2015).

93 Coleman, J. (1988). 'Social capital in the creation of human capital.' *American Journal of Sociology*,
    94(1), S95-S120.

94 Portes, A. (1998). 'Social capital: Its origins and applications in modern sociology.' *Annual Review of
    Sociology*, 24, 1-24.

95 Mulford. B. (2007). 'The challenge of building social capital in professional learning communities.' In
    L. Stoll & K. Seashore Louis (eds), *Professional learning communities: Divergence, depth and dilem-
    mas* (pp. 166-180). London: Open University Press/McGraw Hill.

96 Corson, D. (1998). *Changing education for diversity.* Buckingham: Open University Press.

97 Chandler, D. (1995). *Marxist media theory.* URL: http://visual-memory.co.uk/daniel/Documents/
    marxism/marxism.html (accessed 6 November 2014).

98 Boggs, C. (1976). *Gramsci's Marxism.* London: Pluto Press.

99 See also, Freire, P. (1970). *Pedagogy of the oppressed.* Harmondsworth, UK: Penguin.

100 Freire, op. cit.

101 Smith, M.K. (1997, 2002) 'Paulo Freire and informal education', *The Encyclopaedia of Informal
     Education.* URL: http://infed.org/mobi/paulo-freire-dialogue-praxis-and-education/ (accessed 21
     October 2015).

102 Mitchell, D. (2014). *What really works in special and inclusive education.* Second edition. London:
     Routledge.

103 *Evidence informed policy in education in Europe.* URL: http://www.eipee.eu/ (accessed 10
     December 2014).

104 See, for example, the *Best Evidence Encyclopedia.* URL: http://www.bestevidence.org/index.cfm
     (accessed 15 November 2014); What Works Clearinghouse. URL: www.whatworks.ed.gov (accessed
     14 November 2014); and The Coalition for Evidence-Based Policy (URL: http://coalition4evidence.
     org (accessed 15 November 2014).

105 Mitchell (2014), op. cit.

106 Kavale, K.M. (2007). 'Quantitative research synthesis: Meta-analysis of research on meeting special edu-
     cation needs'. In L. Florian (ed.), *The Sage handbook of special education* (pp. 207-221). London: Sage.

107 Lewis, A. & Norwich, B. (eds) (2005). *Special teaching for special children? Pedagogies for inclusion.*
     Maidenhead: Open University Press.

108   OECD (2016). *Future of work in figures.* Paris: Author. URL: http://www.oecd.org/employment/ministerial/future-of-work-in-figures.htm (accessed 20 January 2016).

109   Christensen, C. (1997). *The innovator's dilemma: When new technologies cause great firms to fail.* Cambridge, MA: Harvard Business Review Press.

110   Manyika, J., Chui, M., Bughin, J., Dobbs, R., Bisson, P. & Marrs, A. (2013). *Disruptive technologies: Advances that will transform life, business, and the global economy.* Tech. Rep., McKinsey Global Institute. URL: http://www.mckinsey.com/insights/business_technology/disruptive_technologies (accessed 22 October 2015).

111   OECD, op. cit.

112   Frey, C.B. & Osborne, M.A. (2013). *The future of employment: How susceptible are jobs to computerization?* Oxford: Oxford Martin School, Programme on the Impacts of Future Technology, University of Oxford. URL: http://www.futuretech.ox.ac.uk/sites/futuretech.ox.ac.uk/files/The_Future_of_Employment_OMS_Working_Paper_1.pdf (accessed 19 May 2016).

113   These trends may well favour women since they consistently score higher on tests of emotional intelligence.

114   A somewhat different perspective has been offered by McKinsey and Company, who suggested that a more accurate way to think about the impact of automation is not in terms of entire jobs, but in terms of activities within jobs, although there is also some truth in the former. They claim that as many as 45% of the activities individuals are paid to perform can be automated by adapting current technologies. See Chui, M., Manyika, J. & Miremadi, M. (2015). *Four fundamentals of workplace automation.* McKinsey and Company. URL: http://www.mckinsey.com/insights/business_technology/four_fundamentals_of_workplace_automation (accessed 12 November 2015).

115   Ibid., p. 13.

116   Manyika et al., op. cit.

117   Blinder, A.S. (2009). 'How many US jobs might be offshorable?' *World Economics*, 10(2), 41-78.

118   Schwab, K. (2015). 'The fourth Industrial Revolution: What it means and how to respond.' *Foreign Affairs*, 15 December 2015.

119   Thompson, D. (2015). 'A world without work.' *The Atlantic*, July/August 2015.

120   'The future of jobs: The onrushing wave.' *The Economist*, 18 January 2014.

121   US Department of Education, Office of Educational Technology (2010). *Transforming American education: Learning powered by technology. National Technology Plan 2010.* Washington, DC: Author, p. x.

122   US Department of Education, Office of Educational Technology, op. cit., p. 12.

123   Higher Education Opportunity Act of 2008 (PL 110-315) §103(a)(24).

124   Center for Applied Special Education Technology (2012). URL: http://www.cast.org/research/faq/index.html (accessed 25 October 2012).

125   For a review, see Springate, I., Atkinson, M., Straw, S., Lamont, E. & Grayson, H. (2008). *Narrowing the gap in outcomes: Early years (0-5).* Slough: NFER.

126   Sylva, K., Melhuish, E.C., Sammons, P., Siraj-Blatchford, I. & Taggart, B. (2004). *The Effective Provision of Pre-School Education (EPPE) Project: Final report.* London: DfES/Institute of Education, University of London.

127   Buckley, J.A. (2009). 'Introduction to this special issue: Implementing evidence-based interventions in elementary schools for students at risk for severe behavior disorders.' *Journal of Emotional and Behavioral Disorders*, 17(4), 195-196, p. 195.

128   Ibid.

129   'Urban life: Open-air computers.' *The Economist*, 27 October 2012.

130   International Organization for Migration (2015). *World migration report 2015 – Migrants and cities: New partnerships to manage mobility.* Geneva: Author.

131   United Nations Population Fund (2015). *Urbanization.* New York, NY: Author. URL: http://www.unfpa.org/urbanization (accessed 23 October 2015).

132   Tacoli, C. (2012). *Urbanization, gender and urban poverty: Paid work and unpaid carework in the city.* New York, NY: International Institute For Environment and Development, United Nations Population Fund.

2 Sex and gender differences

From an early age, I was aware that there were two sexes and only in recent years have I had to revise my thinking to accommodate differences in sexual orientation and gender identity. Like all members of my species – and many others – I was aware that I had a mother and a father and that they played different roles in my life, as did my grandparents and many aunts and uncles. I, and both of my children, received all of our schooling in coeducational schools, as are my six grandchildren. Only my wife attended a single-sex school for her secondary education. Although most of my lessons were delivered to both boys and girls, it was in the playing fields that the sexes were differentiated. Apart from occasional mixed-sex games, there was a clear divergence of interest and opportunity for both organized and unorganized games. Boys played rugby, hockey, cricket, marbles and various chasing games, while girls played basketball (an earlier term for modern netball), skipping rope ('jump rope', in America), knucklebones and hopscotch. Some activities, like swimming and athletics, were mixed, although the competition was exclusively gender-based. The closest we came to physical activities that combined boys and girls was dancing, which, at high school involved boys selecting partners to learn the foxtrot, the waltz, the schottische and square dances. And, of course, this legitimate close contact with the opposite sex was something most of us eagerly looked forward to, particularly when we approached adolescence.

At high school, I took some pride in learning that, in 1893, New Zealand was the first country in modern times to introduce women's suffrage. But the significance of this event was somewhat lost on me and it wasn't until I experienced the debates arising from the feminist movement of the 1960s and 1970s, that I became aware of wider issues concerning women's rights. I recall, for example, learning with some embarrassment that some of my language was sexist (e.g., using the pronoun 'he' to refer to both males and females). More recently, I have had to adjust my thinking to recognize not only the existence of people of different sexual and gender orientations, but also their rights to equal treatment, for example, in same-sex marriage, which became legal in New Zealand in August 2013.[1]

In this chapter, I will attempt to answer four key questions:

A   What do we mean by sex/gender?
B   How are genders different?
C   What causes gender differences?
D   How should education respond to gender differences?

A What do we mean by sex/gender?

2.1 Gender and sex are not synonymous

In this chapter, I will be referring to both sex and gender. While they are often used interchangeably, they are different concepts. One source distinguished between the two as follows:

> Sex is usually understood as relating to the biological and physiological body. Gender is often understood as the cultural interpretation of sexed bodies, embedded in the whole apparatus of a society's roles and norms.[2]

According to the *Publication Manual* of the American Psychological Association, '*Gender* is cultural and is the term to use when referring to women and men as social groups. *Sex* is biological; use it when the biological distinction is predominant.' Similarly, the World Health Organization described the distinction as follows:

> *Sex* refers to the biological and physiological characteristics that define men and women. *Gender* refers to the socially constructed roles, behaviours, activities, and attributes that a given society considers appropriate for men and women.

To make matters more complicated, some writers point out that there are more than two sexes and genders, referring, in addition to males and females, to transsexuals and people with congenitally ambiguous sex organs. As well, according to one writer, there are many ways of 'performing' gender: 'gay, lesbian and trans-genders fluidity of these performances and their capacity to change over time and across societies'.[3] Another writer has referred to five genders recognized in Sulawesi (Indonesia).[4] According to a recent paper from the authoritative Williams Institute of the UCLA School of Law,[5] an increasing number of population-based surveys in the United States and across the world include questions designed to measure sexual orientation and gender identity. In a review of findings from such surveys in the United States, it was estimated that 3.5% of adults identified as lesbian, gay or bisexual (LGB), while an estimated 0.3% of adults were transgender. Among adults who identified as LGB, bisexuals comprised a slight majority (1.8% compared with 1.7% who identified as lesbian or gay). Women were substantially more likely than men to identify as bisexual. In addition, 8.2% reported that they had engaged in same-sex sexual behaviour at some stage in their lives. Another recent US survey[6] found that 12 was the median age at which lesbian, gay and bisexual adults first felt they might be something other than heterosexual, or straight. For those who say they now know for sure that they are lesbian, gay, bisexual or transgender, that realization came at a median age of 17.

Recently, there have been two well-publicized cases involving athletes whose sex has been challenged. The first of these was the South African runner, Caster Semenya, who, in 2009, was barred from and then reinstated into athletic competitions, but only after she was required to undergo gender testing. The second was the Indian athlete, Dutee Chand, whose gender was challenged in 2014. Apparently, she has a condition called 'hyperandrogenism', which means that her body produces natural levels of testosterone that place her in the male range in the eyes of athletics officials. In order for her to compete as a woman, she would have to lower her levels of testosterone through drugs or surgery.[7] A more recent development appeared in a January 2016 news item from the International Olympic Committee which stated that surgery will no longer be required, with female-to-male transgender athletes eligible to take part in men's competitions 'without restriction' while male-to-female transgender athletes will need to demonstrate that their testosterone level has been below a certain cutoff point for at least one year before their first competition.

For the sake of simplicity, I will use the term *gender* throughout, with its meaning being synonymous with *sex*. At the risk of offending the purists, I will use gender to refer simply to 'boy' and 'girl', 'male' and 'female' in the sense these are generally understood.

2.2 Sex ratios vary across the world

Whether you are a male or female, you are different from half the population. Well, this is not quite true, as in humans, indeed in all mammals, male births invariably occur slightly in excess of female births. The male to female ratio of live births is generally expressed as the ratio of male live births divided by total live births (stated as M/F). In humans, this is expected to be 0.515, which translates into approximately 3% more males born than females.

However, this M/F of 103% is not universally present when we look at population statistics. For example, if you live in Latvia, Estonia, the Russian Federation, Armenia, Belarus or Georgia, the gender ratio is in the 80s. If you live in China and India, however, the ratio is heavily weighted in favour of males (M/Fs of 108% and 107%, respectively), while, at the extreme, UAE and Qatar, with their large populations of foreign, mainly male, workers, have ratios of 228% and 311%, respectively. (In comparison, the ratios for the United States and the United Kingdom are both 97%).[8]

The reason(s) for this M/F discrepancy is uncertain as testicles produce equal numbers of X-bearing and Y-bearing spermatozoa. Perhaps it is nature's way of taking into account the fact that, in utero, the male foetus is more prone to morbidity and mortality from external influences than the female foetus, as well as being at slightly greater risk for obstetric complications.

Climate has also been implicated in attempts to unravel the M/F discrepancy. In January 2014, I visited the Georgia Sea Turtle Center in St Simons Island in United States. There, I was surprised to learn that the sex of the turtles depends on the ambient temperature experienced by the eggs in the nest: those in the centre being more likely to be females and those towards the outside being more likely to be males. As the sign said, 'Girls are hot, boys are cool'! Apparently, this phenomenon of temperature-dependent sex-determination has been known since the 1960s and has been shown to exist not only in turtles, but also in crocodiles and a few species of lizards. But what about humans? Does temperature also have an effect on the sex ratios in our species? Apparently so, even though sex is determined at conception, as distinct from during embryogenesis as in the case of the turtles. One recent study found a strong relationship between sex ratios and latitude, with significantly more females being produced at tropical latitudes. This relationship emerged despite enormous lifestyle and socio-economic variation among countries and continents.[9] Another study found a similar latitude gradient. However, it's by no means a straightforward matter as there is evidence that the gradients differ between Europe and North America. In the former, more males are born towards the south of Europe, whereas in the latter more males are born towards the north.[10] South American data are in accordance with the latitude gradient observed in North

America.[11] Thus, the evidence on latitudinal influences on M/F ratios is not clear-cut and would-be parents are not advised to manipulate their thermostats to increase the chances of having a baby boy or baby girl!

We have to look beyond nature for other explanations of the M/F discrepancy. We have to ask if there are societal factors that influence it? A clear example is afforded by China, where there are more males than females. Many years of the one-child-per-family law and an overwhelming preference for sons have led to abortion and infanticide of baby girls.[12] Similar preferences for boys are also present in India.

Conversely, some countries have more females than males. Consider for a moment the situation in the Russian Federation, where there are around 11 million more women than men. Multiple reasons have been put forward for this imbalance. Historically, the country has been through a century or more of revolutions, gulags and wars that drained its male population. More recently, we must also take account of the fact that male life expectancy in the Russian Federation is only 64 years, as opposed to females' 73 years, the largest gap of any country in the world. Overall, a quarter of Russian men die before reaching 55, compared with 7% of men in the United Kingdom and about 10% in the United States.[13] This has been attributed to higher rates of smoking, heart disease, accidents and the consumption of vodka among males. The gender imbalance in general has also been related to the higher levels of testosterone in males, contributing to elevated aggression and risk-taking.[14]

Further support for the effects of societal factors on M/F ratios can be found when we look at the impact of adverse environmental factors. For example, a declining M/F has been observed in many industrialized countries since 1950.[15] This has been attributed to the more fragile male foetuses being spontaneously aborted at a higher rate than the more robust female foetuses when exposed to deleterious environmental factors.[16] Similarly, there is evidence that M/Fs decline as a result of warfare, earthquakes and environmental disasters. Such events, it would seem, promote stressed pregnant women to spontaneously abort male foetuses to a greater extent than female foetuses.[17]

B How are genders different?

In this section I will review a sample of the myriad literature on gender differences in educationally significant domains. I will refer to research into gender gaps in general, especially in developing countries in the present and in developed countries in the past; differences in physical strength, sexual attitudes and behaviours, interest in computer science, mental health, HIV/AIDS, sexual violence and abuse, mathematics achievement, verbal ability, special educational needs, aggression, rates of offending, suicide, accidents and disability; and disproportionate rates of bullying of LGBT students.

2.3 Females live longer than males

Worldwide, over the period 2010–2013, the average life expectancy at birth was 68.5 years for males and 73.5 years for females.[18] According to the World Health Organization, women on average live longer than men in all countries, with the exception of Cameroon, Chad, Somalia and Sudan, where values were equal between the genders, and in Central

African Republic, Tonga and Tuvalu, where values were greater for males than females.[19] The longevity prize for males goes to Monaco at 85.3 years and for females to Japan at 87.3 years.

2.4 'Males and females are more alike than they are different on most, but not all, psychological variables'[20]

This quote, taken from John Hattie's analysis of the influence of gender on student achievement, is a good starting point for a review of gender differences. Hattie presented a mega-analysis of some 41 separate meta-analyses of nearly 3,000 studies involving over five and a half million participants and arrives at a very low effect size of 0.12. He cited an earlier study which found gender similarities in such variables as communication, social and personality variables and well-being, but with larger differences in motor performance and aggression (higher in boys) and agreeableness (higher in girls).[21]

You may recall reading in Chapter 1 (section 1.18) my comment on statistics, with particular reference to the meaning of effect sizes in meta-analyses. It is important that you understand this as in the period 1987 to 2013, some 370 meta-analyses comparing the sexes have appeared in the research literature,[22] some of which I will be presenting in this chapter.

2.5 In a growing number of countries, women are more educated than men

Whereas in 1950, women had more years of education than men in only 11 out of 146 countries (Canada, the United Kingdom and the United States among them), in 2010 this figure had grown to 43 countries. These included all Nordic countries as well as Australia, the United States, Canada and the United Kingdom. Overall, in 9 out of 24 advanced economies, the overall female population was, on average, more educated than the male population. Also, females were in a clear majority among secondary school graduates, among students enrolled in tertiary education, and among tertiary graduates.[23] According to UNESCO data for 2008, female enrolments in tertiary education were higher than the male enrolments in 81 out of 119 countries. This was true for all OECD countries with the exception of Japan, South Korea, Switzerland and Turkey. Furthermore, female enrolments in tertiary education were also higher in some large non-OECD countries such as the Philippines, Iran and Thailand.[24]

Judging from recent trends, it seems likely that the gender gap in educational attainment will keep on widening in favour of women in the future.[25] This trend reflects two factors in most industrialized countries: the growth in male educational attainment is stalling or starting to decline, whereas female educational attainment is keeping on growing.[26]

These gender differences in educational attainment are having far-reaching labour market implications in industrialized countries. According to one writer, 'highly rewarded high-skill workers will be predominantly female and increasingly disadvantaged low-skill workers will be predominantly male'.[27]

However, contrary to these current global trends, until relatively recently in developed countries, females had less access to education than males and they continue to remain disadvantaged in many developing countries.

2.6 Females had less access to education than males in developed countries in the past

Access to formal education is a relatively recent arrival in world history, especially for females. Since space limitations permit only a brief coverage of this theme, I have selected the recent history of differential approaches to boys' and girls' education in Great Britain as an illustration of changes in societal perceptions. In particular, I will focus on the reports of two influential commissions.

In Great Britain, one of the earliest official documents to focus on the education of girls and women was the report of the *Schools Inquiry Commission,* of 1867-1868. It painted a bleak picture:

> We have had much evidence, showing the general indifference of parents to girls' education, both in itself and as compared to that of boys ... there is a long-established and inveterate prejudice, though it may not often be distinctly expressed, that girls are less capable of mental cultivation, and less in need of it, than boys; that accomplishments, and what is showy and superficially attractive, are what is really essential for them; and in particular, that as regards their relations to the other sex and the probabilities of marriage, more solid attainments are actually disadvantageous rather than the reverse. [28]

However, while still maintaining the woman's role as a wife, the Commission's report goes on to observe that this was not incompatible with her receiving a more liberal education:

> The most material service may be rendered to the husband, in the conduct of his business and the most serious branches of his domestic affairs, by a wife trained and habituated to a life altogether different from that of mere gentleness and amiability ... a life of no slight intellectual proficiency, and capacity for many functions too commonly thought to be reserved for the male sex.[29]

The Commission felt that a major impediment to the education of girls was the poor quality of 'female teachers in girls schools', who 'must be pronounced not fully equal to their task'. This arose from their comparative isolation and the fact that 'hardly any women take teaching up as a profession, meaning to stick to it', marriage 'almost always causing a schoolmistress to give it up'. As well, 'they have not themselves been well taught, and they do not know how to teach'. This was especially so in the case of subjects 'which rest on scientific principles, which females at present cannot teach'.

The next milestone in the education of girls and women in Great Britain occurred in 1923 with the publication of *Report of the Consultative Committee on Differentiation of the Curriculum for Boys and Girls Respectively in Secondary Schools* (known as the Hadow Report).[30]

This progressive Committee thought there was weighty evidence to show that the essential capacity for learning was the same, or nearly the same, in the two sexes. They cited with approval the conclusions of Columbia University educational psychologist, E.L. Thorndike, who had noted that

> The most important characteristic of ... differences between the sexes is their small amount. The individual differences within one sex so enormously outweigh the differences between the sexes in these intellectual and semi-intellectual traits that for practical purposes the sex difference may be disregarded.[31]

The Committee was thus inclined to believe that 'the foundation, the main and leading elements of instruction, should be the same in the two cases, and further, that ample facilities and encouragement, and far more than now exist, should be given to women who may be able and willing to prosecute these studies to a higher point'. However, it went on to conclude that 'the complete assimilation of the education of the sexes, such as prevails in America, should not be attempted'.

The Committee further observed that while there is 'equal intellectual capacity of the sexes', many differences exist:

> such as the tendency to abstract principles in boys contrasted with the greater readiness to lay hold of facts in girls – the greater quickness to acquire in the latter with the greater retentiveness in the former – the greater eagerness of girls to learn – their acuter susceptibility to praise and blame – their lesser inductive faculty – and others.

Finally, the Committee expressed concern that many girls in day schools were 'expected to do a considerable amount of fairly heavy house work in their homes, with the result that they are often seriously overworked physically and mentally'. It was considered, too, that 'girls in general were more inclined than boys to worry over their work'. As one witness expressed it, 'If you give a girl too much to do she breaks down; if you give a boy too much to do, he doesn't do it.' The Committee considered, too, that 'girls were physically less strong than boys, and were probably less capable of severe and prolonged mental effort, especially from the age of 13 or 14 upwards'. 'Moreover, many girls were more highly strung than boys, and consequently more liable to nervous strain.' 'This tendency to overstrain was often intensified by home duties ...The daughter in many middle class families, while still at school, was expected to help her mother in household duties and in cases of sickness to act as nurse.' While not going so far as the medieval scholar, St Thomas Aquinas, who asserted that 'The woman is subject to man on account of the weakness of her nature', the Committee did feel some sympathy for the idea that girls were physically unable to cope with their workloads. Thus, it recommended that they might with advantage generally postpone examinations for entry to higher education 'to an age rather later than that which was usual for boys, and thus escape the risk of overstrain during the period of adolescence'.

This belief in the fragility of girls and women had earlier been expressed in New Zealand when a prominent ophthalmologist, Dr Lindo Ferguson, expressing concern at the overburdened syllabus and excessive homework, recommended reducing girls' workloads. This, he argued, would reduce undue stress on the mothers of the next generation and would not upset the nervous balance of their heirs.[32]

2.7 Gender gaps vary considerably from country to country

The *Global Gender Gap Index*, introduced by the World Economic Forum in 2006, is a framework for capturing the magnitude and scope of gender-based disparities and tracking their progress. It benchmarks national gender gaps on economic, political, education and health criteria. It measures the relative difference between males and females in outcomes, not inputs, and focuses on access to resources and opportunities rather than on the actual levels of resources and opportunities that exist in particular countries. The education component looks at access to primary, secondary and tertiary education and on literacy rates. Taking all four domains into account, the top 10 rankings in 2013 were as follows: Iceland (1), Finland (2), Norway (3), Sweden (4), Philippines (5), Ireland (6), New Zealand (7), Denmark (8), Switzerland (9) and Nicaragua (10). The bottom 10 comprised Saudi Arabia (127), Mali (128), Morocco (129), Iran (130), Cote d'Ivoire (131), Mauritania (132), Syria (133), Pakistan (135) and Yemen (136). The United Kingdom was ranked 18th and the United States 23rd.[33]

According to the World Economic Forum, the *Index* tracks the strong correlation between a country's gender gap and its national competitiveness. Because women account for one-half of a country's potential talent base, a nation's competitiveness in the long term depends significantly on whether and how it educates and utilizes its women. Quite apart from respecting the rights of women to be treated equally, their active participation in the workforce has a strong economic imperative. For example, a recent report from the McKinsey Global Institute found that advancing women's equality could add $US12-28 trillion to global growth, depending on their degree of participation in the workforce.[34] The report pointed to huge contrasts between countries, with women accounting for about 40% of GDP in the United States and western Europe, compared with only 17% in India and 18% in the Middle East and North Africa. Another way to interpret these statistics is through the lens of interest convergence that I explained in section 1.13 in Chapter 1: by furthering the interests of females, the interests of society are also furthered.

Data collated by the OECD provide a good picture of the variable status of women in the workforce.[35] Two sets of data are instructive. First, comparisons of the employment status of women in 2015 showed that women aged 25-54 were less likely then men to be in employment, the respective OECD averages being 67.4% and 88.5%. There was considerable variation among countries with the highest figures for women's employment being recorded in Kazakhstan (85.8%), Sweden (83.3%), Iceland (83.2%) and Lithuania (82.3%). The lowest figures were for Saudi Arabia (23.5%), India (33.0%), Turkey (35.6%) and South Africa (50.9%). The United States recorded 70.2% and the United Kingdom 76.6%. Second, data on the wage gap for fulltime workers showed a mean difference of 15.3% in favour of men across the OECD. Again, there was wide variation among countries, with the smallest gaps being recorded in New Zealand (5.6%), Belgium (5.9%), Luxembourg (6.5%) and Denmark (6.8%). The largest gaps were in Korea (36.6%), Estonia (26.6%), Japan (26.6%) and Israel (21.8%). The US gap was 17.9% and the UK gap was 17.5%.

2.8 Females currently have less access to education than males in some developing countries

Of the nearly one billion people around the world who receive little or no formal education, the majority are women and girls.[36] The ratio of girls-and-boys in primary, secondary and tertiary education differs from region to region across the world. If we take an enrolment ratio of 1 to mean that there is gender parity and anything less than 1 to mean a male advantage, and more than 1 to mean a female advantage, then we find that girls are most under-represented in South Asia and Africa. In contrast, gender equality features in high-income countries and Eastern European countries, South America and Central Asia.[37]

Women remain disadvantaged in terms of access to tertiary education in sub-Saharan Africa, as well as South and West Asia. For example, in 2009, the tertiary gross enrolment rate in sub-Saharan Africa for women was 4.8%, compared with 7.3% for men. Women face significant barriers to tertiary education in countries with the lowest levels of national wealth. Seven countries with a GDP per capita of less than US$1,000 have fairly low Gender Parity Indices (GPI), ranging from 0.17 to 0.51. They include Chad (0.17), Ethiopia (0.31), Niger (0.34), Democratic Republic of the Congo (0.35), Central Africa Republic (0.43) and Malawi (0.51).[38]

UNICEF has drawn our attention to a range of other statistics showing the disadvantageous position of girls and women in education. Thus, for every 100 boys not attending school, there are 117 girls in the same situation, with some 67 countries having primary school enrolment rates for girls below 85%. Further, two-thirds of the world's 799 million illiterate adults aged 15 and over are female.[39] Almost half of the world's school-aged girls who are not in school live in sub-Saharan Africa, with another quarter living in South Asia.[40] UNICEF considers that gender discrimination in accessing education is affected less by political institutions than by culture and religion. Thus, Muslim-dominated countries stand out as having less gender equality than most other countries.[41]

According to a recent report from UNESCO's EFA Global Monitoring Report Team, gender disparity patterns varied between countries in different income groups.[42] Thus, among low-income countries, disparities were commonly at the expense of girls: 20% achieve gender parity in primary education, 10% in lower secondary education and 8% in upper secondary education. However, among middle- and high-income countries, where more countries achieve parity at any level, the disparities were increasingly at the expense of boys as one moves up to the lower and upper secondary levels. For example, 2% of upper-middle income countries had disparities at the expense of boys in primary school, 23% in lower secondary school and 62% in upper secondary school.

This Team was at pains to emphasize that gender parity – equal enrolment ratios for girls and boys – is just the first step towards the goal of full gender equality in education. Other starting points include making sure the school environment is safe, improving facilities to provide, for example, separate latrines for girls and boys, training teachers in gender sensitivity, achieving gender balance among teachers and rewriting curricula and textbooks to remove gender stereotypes.[43]

In many developing countries, gender intersects with other inequalities, particularly those associated with poverty, rural life, conflict, threats associated with climate change, inadequate distribution of resources, violence against girls and women, HIV/AIDS,[44] refugee status,[45] and, as noted above, religion.

2.9 Gender differences in mathematics and related skills are small and quite complex

Despite the widespread assumption that boys are better at mathematics than girls, the evidence is quite equivocal – and complex. Many studies show no differences, while others indicate either a small male or even a female advantage. When there is a mathematics gap in favour of boys, it tends to be declining with time, suggesting that efforts to close it might be succeeding.[46] It might also suggest that biological differences are not playing an important role or that they can be easily overcome by intervention.[47]

Variability in mathematics achievement may well reflect differences in the age of the students and the way such performance is assessed. In an analysis of a nationally representative data set from the United States, no differences were found between boys' and girls' mathematics performance upon entry to school, but girls lost one-quarter of a standard deviation relative to boys over the first six years of school.[48] This finding found some support in a recent meta-analysis, which found no sex differences among elementary and middle school students and a small, but significant, male advantage in high school and college students.[49] However, recent data from England showed that 73.6% of boys reached at least the expected level of achievement in early arithmetic goals, but 81.4% of girls achieved that standard. (As noted below, a similar gender discrepancy was noted for reading and writing.)[50]

Mathematics assessment can be of two types: instruments based on the taught curriculum and those using non-curricular measures. On the one hand, evidence from curriculum-based assessment tends to indicate no sex differences or is in favour of girls. On the other hand, assessments not based on the taught curriculum (e.g., the Programme for International Student Assessment (PISA) and the Trends in International Mathematics and Science Study (TIMMS)) show only small sex differences in favour of boys, which become more pronounced in older students.[51] More detailed analyses of the performances on different types of items throw up sex differences, with boys tending to do better on complex problem solving, while girls do better on conventional problems that can be solved using taught procedures.[52]

Notwithstanding the inconsistency of evidence relating to sex differences in mathematics performance, there is quite a strong indication that males have the edge in spatial skills. This clearly emerged in a meta-analysis of studies carried out in 49 countries.[53] Boys seem to have a particular advantage in what is referred to as 'mental rotation ability', which involves holding images in one's mind while mentally manipulating them. For example, students might be asked to mentally rotate a figure by 180 degrees and choose the resulting image from a display. On such tasks, males tend to be more accurate and faster than females, particularly with tasks involving 3-D stimuli.[54] These differences first appear in quite young children, but become greater in middle school and increase through college and university years. Further research shows that differences in spatial reasoning predict mathematics performance for boys, but not for girls.[55]

2.10 Gender differences in verbal ability favour girls, but are small and quite complex

In general, females perform better than males in verbal tests, but, just as with mathematics, the differences are small and variable. Research has found that girls score better than boys on such topics as capitalization, punctuation, the generation of synonyms, writing proficiency, language usage and reading comprehension. However, at some ages and on some tasks, there are male advantages.[56]

According to a 2006 meta-analysis of gender differences in reading at the secondary school level, girls performed 0.19 standard deviation units above their male peers, regardless of age, or language of instruction.[57] This gender gap was even more pronounced for the assessment programmes conducted by the National Assessment Program for Education in the United States, for assessment programmes in Australia and the OECD's PISA.

These results were also reflected in a recent meta-analysis of academic self-efficacy (i.e., the strength of belief in one's own ability to complete tasks and reach goals).[58] Here, females displayed higher language arts self-efficacy than males (the latter exhibiting higher self-efficacy in mathematics, computer studies and social sciences).

There is some evidence that age plays a role in gender differences in verbal ability. Thus, recent data from England showed that 63.6% of boys reached at least the expected level of achievement in early writing goals, but 78.3% of girls achieved that standard. The comparable figures for reading were 70.6% and 81.9%, respectively.[59] These findings have led at least one writer (Tom Loveless) to suggest that the sexes are 'hardwired' differently for literacy.[60] Loveless also observed that the gender gaps in reading are narrower among elementary students and wider among middle and high school students, suggesting different maturation rates for boys and girls. This explanation finds some support in findings of reading in adulthood, when scores for men and women were statistically indistinguishable up to the age of 35, but were in favour of men all the way to the age group of 55 and older.[61]

There is also some evidence of geographic variation in the gender gap in reading achievement in schools. Thus, on the 2012 PISA tests, while all countries exhibited a gap in favour of girls, the size of the gap varied from 62 points to 23 points. The largest gaps were present in Northern European countries, with Finland 'leading' the way, followed by Slovenia, Sweden, Iceland, Greece and Norway. The smallest gaps were present in Chile, Korea, Mexico, Japan, United Kingdom and Netherlands.[62]

2.11 Females are not attracted to computer science

In the United States, women earn 57% of bachelor's degrees, but only slightly over one-quarter of computer science degrees, according to a 2009 report by the National Science Foundation.[63] This is occurring at the same time as technology industries rank among the fastest growing in the nation.

2.12 Males are stronger; females are physically more flexible

The physical makeup of human beings generally means that males are stronger than females, but that females are more flexible. Males' superior strength reflects differences in at least three areas. First, testosterone and other hormones contribute to them having a greater percentage of lean muscle, especially in the upper body, resulting in more physical strength. Second, they have larger hearts, resulting in more blood – and hence oxygen – per heartbeat being sent to muscles. The resultant aerobic capacity is typically 15-25% greater in males than in females. This translates into greater endurance. Third, body fat ranges from 20-32% in females, whereas the range for males is 10-22%, meaning that males are stronger per kilogram/pound. In most sports, the top male athletes outperform top female athletes by 10% plus or minus 2.94%, and this is consistent among most cycling, swimming, and running and jumping events. The gender gap ranges from 5.5% (800-m freestyle, swimming) to 18.8% (long jump). The mean gap is 10.7% for running performances, 17.5% for jumps, 8.9% for swimming races, 7.0% for speed skating and 8.7% in cycling.[64]

The superior physical flexibility of females reflects their joints having a greater range of motion and their pelvises being shallower than males' pelvises.[65]

2.13 *Women are more likely to be obese than men, but more boys than girls are obese in some countries*

In all WHO regions, women are more likely to be obese than men, with the exception of high-income countries where they are similar. In the WHO regions of Africa, Eastern Mediterranean and South East Asia, women had roughly double the obesity prevalence of men.[66] Among young people aged 2 to 19 in the United States, 18.6% of boys and 15% of girls are considered to be obese.[67] A recent international study of obesity rates for people under the age of 20 years showed considerable variation, not only in the overall rates, but also in gender differences. Here are some of the results: North America: boys 12.1%, girls 13.0%; Western Europe: boys 7.2%, girls: 6.4%; Australasia: boys 7.5%, girls 7.6%; East Asia: boys 6.8%, girls 2.8%; and South East Asia: boys: 4.6%, girls 4.3%. One of the highest rates for both genders, but especially for girls, was recorded in Samoa (boys: 23.7%, girls: 29.6%).[68]

2.14 *Gender differences in sexual attitudes and behaviours are small and diminishing*

In two recent meta-analyses, small to medium gender differences were found on 11 of 14 sexual behaviours and 15 of 16 sexual attitudes. In general, men reported more sexual behaviours and more liberal sexual attitudes than women.[69] Nations and ethnic groups with greater gender equity had smaller gender differences for some reported sexual behaviours than nations and ethnic groups with less gender equity. Compared with an earlier (1993) meta-analysis by the same authors, it seems that men and women are becoming more similar in sexual attitudes and behaviours. These studies are largely limited to western countries.

2.15 *There are major gender differences in mental health*

According to the World Health Organization,[70] overall rates of psychiatric disorder are almost identical for men and women, there being no marked gender differences in the rates of severe mental disorders like schizophrenia and bipolar disorder. However, across a range of different countries, there are striking gender differences in the patterns of mental illness. On the one hand, women predominate in the rates of depression, anxiety and somatic complaints. Unipolar depression, for example, which is predicted to be the second leading cause of global disability burden by 2020, is twice as common in women. Further, an estimated 80% of 50 million people affected by violent conflicts, civil wars, disasters and displacement are women and children. These events are frequently accompanied by a high prevalence of sexual violence directed at women and girls with a correspondingly high rate of post traumatic stress disorder.

Men are more than three times more likely to be diagnosed with antisocial personality disorder than women.

2.16 *Males drink more alcohol and smoke more than females*

The prevalence rate for alcohol dependence is more than twice as high in men than women. In developed countries, approximately 1 in 5 men and 1 in 12 women develop alcohol dependence during their lives.

According to a World Health Organization paper,[71] worldwide it is estimated that men smoke nearly five times as much as women, but the ratios of female-to-male smoking preva-lence rates varies across countries. In high-income countries, women smoke at nearly the same rate as men, but in many low- and middle-income countries women smoke much less than men. In China, for example, 61% of men are reported to be smokers, compared with only 4.2% of women. However, while women's smoking prevalence rates are currently lower than men's, they are projected to rise in many low- and- middle-income countries. Data from the Global Youth Tobacco Survey show that worldwide smoking rates among boys and girls resemble each other more than smoking rates among adult women and men, with boys between the ages of 13 and 15 years smoking only 2 to 3 times more than girls.[72]

2.17 Boys and girls express aggression in different ways

According to meta-analytic reviews, boys are more physically aggressive than girls, while girls show more relational aggression than boys,[73] often expressing it verbally and in covert ways.[74] Respectively, these two forms of aggression may be defined as harm through damage (or threat of damage) to another's physical well-being,[75] and behaviour that harms others through damage (or threat of damage) to their relationships.[76] Taken together, boys and girls are almost equally aggressive.[77]

2.18 Males commit more offences than females

Throughout the world, men offend at much higher rates than women for all crimes, except prostitution (when it is defined as a crime). The greatest gender gap is for serious crime such as murder and assault, the least being for milder crimes such as those involving property.[78]

This gender difference in offending rates occurs early in life. For example, some 10,000 children in England, Wales and Scotland were permanently excluded from school in 2005/06. Of these, around 8,000 were boys and 2,000 were girls. Crimes committed by children and youth also show gender differences. While theft accounted for two-thirds of all crimes com-mitted by girls, by contrast, although still the largest single category, theft accounted for just a third of the crimes committed by boys.[79]

2.19 Girls are better than boys in inhibiting their impulses

A possible explanation for the preceding finding relates to gender differences in tempera-ment. In a meta-analysis of this topic, a group of US researchers noted that temperament reflects biologically based emotional and behavioural consistencies that appear early in life and predict patterns and outcomes in numerous other domains in personality.[80] Using meta-analytical techniques, they found that 'effortful control' showed a large difference favour-ing girls and the dimensions within that factor (e.g., inhibitory control: d = −0.41, perceptual sensitivity: d = −0.38) showed moderate gender differences favouring girls. These findings were considered to be consistent with boys' greater incidence of externalizing disorders. 'Surgency' – an emotional dimension that is characterized by high levels of activity and pos-itive emotion, impulsivity and engagement with their environment – showed a difference that favoured boys, as did some of the dimensions within that factor (e.g., activity: d = 0.33, high-intensity pleasure: d = 0.30). These were considered to be consistent with boys' greater involvement in active rough-and-tumble play.

2.20 Girls are subject to more sexual violence than boys

According to the United Nations Girls' Education Initiative, gender-based violence dispropor-tionately affects girls and women and is a major obstacle to the achievement of gender equal-ity. It is a global phenomenon that knows no geographical, cultural, social, economic, ethnic or other boundaries.[81] For example, National Violence Against Children surveys in Swaziland, Tan-zania, Zimbabwe and Kenya revealed that 28-38% of girls and 9-18% of boys were subjected to unwanted sexual experiences before the age of 18,[82] which placed them at greater risk of contracting HIV. According to a US survey of adults, as many as one in three girls and one in seven boys were sexually abused at some point in their childhood. Most perpetrators were acquaintances, but as many as 47% were family or extended family members.[83] In another US survey, it was found that 75% of the juvenile victims of Internet predators were girls. [84]

There has been growing awareness of the impact of school-related gender-based violence on the achievement of quality education for all.[85] Evidence suggests that girls are at greater risk for sexual violence, while boys are at risk for physical violence in schools. For example, data from 40 low- and middle-income countries showed that up to 10% of adolescent girls aged 15-19 reported incidents of forced sexual intercourse or other sexual acts in the previous year.[86] Even more concerning was a finding by the Cote d'Ivoire Ministry of National Educa-tion that 47% of teachers reported having elicited sexual relations with students.[87] Sexual violence in schools is not limited to low-income countries. For example, in the United Kingdom one in three 16- to 18-year-olds have experienced unwanted sexual touching in schools.[88] As well as unwanted pregnancies, the experience or even the threat of school-related gender-based violence often results in irregular attendance, dropout, truancy, poor school perfor-mance and low self-esteem, which may follow into their adult lives.[89]

2.21 More females attempt suicide, but more males complete suicide

Across the age span females attempt suicide at four times the rate of males, whereas males complete suicide at four times the rate of females. The latter rates are reflected, for example, in Australia where the overall rates have remained fairly constant over the past hundred years at about 21 deaths per 100,000 for males and 5.5 deaths per 100,000 for females. These gender differences also apply or are even greater for adolescents, with females constituting 90% of suicide attempts in that age group and males making up 80% of suicide completions.[90]

Account must be taken of ethnicity, too. For example, there is evidence from England that Asian women between the ages of 15-35 are two to three times more vulnerable to suicide and self-harm than their non-Asian counterparts.[91]

2.22 Males dominate motor vehicle accidents

Motor vehicle crash fatalities are generally higher for males than females in all age groups, even when the male population is equal to or less than the female population in all age groups.

For example, in the United States for the period 1996-2006, in the age group 16-20 years, 68% of crash fatalities were male. This figure grew to 76% for 21- to 25-year-olds.[92] A related statistic is that males are about 1.5 times as likely as females to sustain a traumatic brain injury.[93]

2.23 Boys do less well at school than girls

There is an extensive literature on boys' underachievement at school. An excellent review of this literature can be found in a 2005 Cambridge University report.[94] In their survey of the international literature on boys' academic underachievement, the authors included the following points: In the United Kingdom, national performance data have shown a 'gender gap' between the levels of boys' and girls' performance, whether at the age of 7 in reading and writing or at the age of 16, in virtually all GCSE subjects. For example, since the late 1980s girls in England have out-performed boys at age 16, scoring on average 10% higher than boys in terms of the proportion achieving five or more A*-C grades at GCSE, the gap being particularly large in relation to English and language subjects.[95]

Gender differences between English and mathematics are apparent among students from low socio-economic backgrounds in England. According to the Joseph Rowntree Foundation, boys receiving free school meals do worse than girls in English by around ten percentage points. By contrast, in mathematics, there is no difference between boys and girls.[96]

Educationalists in many countries have expressed concern about boys' educational performances.[97] In Australia, for example, there are references to 'underachieving and under privileged' boys and of boys as the 'new disadvantaged'. In the United States, too, there are concerns around the theme of how to 'protect' boys, and on how teachers and therapists might identify and respond to boys' hidden despondency and depression. In mainland Europe, there are similar concerns. Belgian research suggests that boys' culture is less study-oriented than girls' and that this impacts upon achievement levels in secondary schooling; in Sweden, there has been a concern with the need to develop boys' social competence and democratic understanding; while in Germany girls have been obtaining better school marks than boys, repeating classes less often and gaining school certificates more successfully.

2.24 Boys are over-represented in special education (or, conversely, girls are under-represented)[98]

Abundant evidence from many countries shows significant gender differences in access to special education. For example, in the United States, since the 1960s, the overall male to female ratio in special education has been between 2:1 and 3:1.[99] In Norwegian elementary schools, boys receive 70% of special education resources, and there is some evidence that their over-representation in special education is due to behavioural problems.[100] In England there is clear evidence of a gender imbalance in special education statistics.[101] According to recent studies, 68% of the 88,000 students in special schools were boys and, of students with formal statements, 72% were boys. Further, almost five times as many boys as girls are expelled from school.

The OECD, too, has reported gender imbalances in special education enrolments across a range of countries. Using a three-way categorization, it found that the median percentages for boys were: 61.3% in category A (disabilities), 66.78% in category B (difficulties), and with a typical range for category C (disadvantages) of between 50 and 60%. It also noted that the gender imbalance for Category A was most marked for autistic spectrum disorders, emotional and behavioural difficulties and learning difficulties, and was the least marked for hearing impairments.[102]

Some writers argue that these gender imbalances in special education enrolments reflect either or both an over-identification of males and an under-identification of girls.[103] Also, at least one writer has interpreted the gender imbalance to mean that boys receive more resources than girls and thus unfairly gain more access to the curriculum.[104] According to this argument, it is therefore ironic if over-representation of boys is considered to be a problem for them.

2.25 More boys than girls have disabilities

At least part of the over-representation of boys in special education can be attributed to the preponderance of boys over girls in the incidence of disabilities.[105] For only a few childhood disorders are prevalence rates higher for girls than boys. These include separation anxiety, selective mutism, neural tube defects (NTD) and translocation Down syndrome. With respect to NTD, females are affected 3-7 times as frequently as males, except for sacral-level NTDs, which are about equal.[106] Translocation Down syndrome in females occurs at three times the rate than in males.[107] Only for deaf/blindness are boys identified at about the same rate as girls.

For all other impairments or disabilities, males predominate: (a) hearing impairments (52%), (b) orthopedic impairments (54%), (c) deafness (54%), (d) other health impairments (56%), (e) visual impairments (56%), (f) mental retardation (secondary school) (58%), (g) trisomic Down syndrome (59%),[108] (h) speech impairments (60%), (i) multiple disabilities (65%), (j) learning disabilities (73%) and (k) emotional disorders (76%).[109] Studies of cerebral palsy report a ratio between 1.1:1 and 1.5:1).

In several studies of gender ratios in autism,[110] the M/F ratio varied from 1.33:1 to 16:1, with a mean ratio of 4.3:1. Gender differences were more pronounced when not associated with mental retardation. In 13 studies where the sex ratio was available within the normal band of intellectual functioning, the median sex ratio was 5.5:1. Conversely, in 12 studies, the sex ratio was 1.95:1 in the group with autism and moderate to severe mental retardation.

There is evidence that boys are more likely to be diagnosed with Attention Deficit and Hyperactivity Disorder (ADHD) than girls, a male/female ratio of around 2:1 to 3:1 for children being reported.[111] The latter figure is reflected in Norwegian data where four-fifths of children with ADHD were reported to be boys.[112] However, it is important to probe beneath the overall statistics, for ADHD comprises three subtypes: hyperactivity/impulsivity, inattentiveness and a combination of the two. Girls were more often diagnosed with the predominantly inattentive type,[113] while boys had higher rates of impulsivity.[114] As well, girls were less prone to coexisting conditions such as conduct disorders and oppositional defiance disorders and were less likely to have an associated learning disability.[115]

2.26 More women than men are classified as disabled

Notwithstanding the fact that boys outnumber girls in special education and disability statistics, when we look at adults, there is clear evidence that more women than men are classified as disabled. This arises from several factors, including the following:

- With differential ageing, women live longer than men and are consequently more prone to age-related impairments and disabilities.
- While disabled people are much more likely to live in poverty than non-disabled people, disabled women are even more likely to be poorer than disabled men, especially in developing countries where there are rigid patriarchal property ownership structures.
- Related to the previous point, disabled women achieve lower educational outcomes and are less likely to be in the paid workforce than either men with disabilities or non-disabled women, and therefore have lower incomes from employment and consequent higher rates of dependence.
- Especially in developing countries, women are more likely to experience public spaces as intimidating and dangerous; are less likely to have access to rehabilitation and have less access to employment when they do receive rehabilitation; are less able to compete in situations of scarcity; are less likely to be accepted as refugees by industrially advanced countries; and, when sexually abused, are likely to have few if any social supports or options.[116]

2.27 The prevalence rate of HIV/AIDS is higher among females than males in some countries

In low- and middle-income countries worldwide, HIV/AIDS is the leading cause of death and disease in women and girls of reproductive age. According to UNICEF, Eastern and Southern Africa continues to be the epicentre of the HIV/AIDS epidemic and has the highest number of young HIV-infected people between the ages of 15 and 24 out of all regions. The total number of infected girls and young women of that age is more than twice as high as among their male counterparts – 1.9 million compared with 780,000.[117] In some countries, the prevalence rates among young women aged 15–24 years is three to four times higher than men and boys of the same age.[118] In Swaziland and Lesotho, for example, the HIV prevalence among adolescent girls aged 15–17 years is more than four times higher than among their male peers (6.2% and 1.4%, respectively). Many of these girls have been infected by young men, who are at least five years older, which corresponds to the fact that age-disparate relationships are very common in the region.[119] Women with disabilities are particularly disadvantaged, having lower levels of HIV knowledge than men with disabilities.[120]

2.28 Students who are LGBT are disproportionately bullied at school

Students who are lesbian, gay, bisexual or transgender (LGBT) tend to be disproportionately bullied at school[121] and are more likely to attempt suicide and experience significant depressive symptoms than their heterosexual peers.[122] In the United States, for example, gay and lesbian teens are two to three times as more likely to commit teen suicide than other youths. About 30% of all completed suicides have been related to sexual identity crisis. LGBT students report being five times more likely to miss school because they feel unsafe after being bullied due to their sexual orientation. About 28% of those groups feel forced to drop out of school altogether.[123]

In a study conducted in Thailand, 55.7% of self-identified LGBT students reported having been bullied within the past month because they were LGBT. Nearly one-third of self-identified LGBT students (30.9%) experienced physical abuse, 29.3% reported verbal abuse, 36.2% stated social abuse, and 24.4% reported being victims of sexual harassment specifically because they were LGBT. Even among students who did not indicate they were LGBT, 24.5% reported having been bullied in some way because they were perceived to be transgender or attracted to the same sex.[124]

A recent US study of high school students found that the use of homophobic epithets was significantly associated with the primary bully role and the supportive roles of reinforcing and assisting the bully for both boys and girls.[125] Some writers go so far as to argue that most bullying is primarily a problem of the performance of masculine identity, or what is referred to a 'heteronormativity', which is premised on the belief that heterosexuality is normal, while all other expressions of sexuality are abnormal.[126]

C What causes gender differences?

Why can't a woman be more like a man?
(Henry Higgins in My Fair Lady*)*

Why, indeed? Or perhaps the question should be 'why can't a man be more like a woman?' Is it in our natures to be different or does our environment lead to differences? The debate centring on nature–nurture explanations of gender differences has been with us for some time and shows no sign of abating. Since around the late 1980s, the weighting on nature or nurture has ebbed and flowed.[127] Historically, nature-related explanations were pre-eminent, with widespread assertions that females were the 'weaker sex' and more fragile. Then, in the 1960s, the feminist movement argued that the social contexts of females' lives determined much of their behaviour. This view has continued, but was challenged in the 1980s, and since then, by evolutionary psychologists and neuroscientists, who reasserted nature as an explanation of gender differences. At present, it seems likely that explanatory models that take an interactive approach will replace the either-or situation.

In this section, I will present evidence relating to both nature and nurture, with the former referring to biological structures and processes and the latter to socio-cultural influences. I will conclude with a brief description of an interactive model.

I *Nature-related explanations*

The case for a biological explanation of gender differences centres on such factors as genetics, hormones, maturation and brain function. Before reviewing such biological explanations, I must sound a note of caution: they have been used to imply determinism and to justify gender inequality. While those risks still attend such explanations, current biological approaches emphasize the ways in which they interact with social factors to produce behaviours. I will take up this point when I describe the interactive model.

2.29 *X chromosome-linked factors are implicated in sexuality and some disorders*

As noted in an earlier section, several reports document higher rates among boys for foetal mortality, postnatal mortality, complications during pregnancy and childbirth, and congenital malformations.[128] These findings have led some writers to note that males are at increased risk for X-linked disorders because they receive only one copy of the X chromosome from their parents, whereas females receive two, thus having a better chance of receiving at least one unaffected copy of the X chromosome.

As well, recent, so far unpublished, research has suggested that male sexual orientation may be influenced by genetics. In tests of the DNA of 409 gay men, Michael Bailey of Northwestern University in the United States, reported that at least two chromosomes may affect a man's sexual orientation.[129] These comprised an area on the X chromosome, known as Xq28, and another stretch of DNA on chromosome 8 that were found to have some impact on sexual orientation. He noted, however, that a man's sexual orientation depends on about 30-40% of genetic factors, while environmental factors, including the hormones a foetus is exposed to in the womb, may also influence a male's sexuality. Bailey reported that no genes had been discovered that influenced female sexuality.

2.30 Boys mature more slowly than girls

Some studies suggest that the overrepresentation of males in special education and the male predominance in childhood psychiatric disorders and learning disabilities are related to boys maturing more slowly than girls.[130]

2.31 The presence or absence of testosterone influences neural development prenatally

Sex development begins at conception with the union of two X chromosomes (genetic female) or an X and a Y chromosome (genetic male). The main role of these sex chromosomes in human sexual differentiation is to determine whether the gonads become testes or ovaries. The testes begin to produce testosterone prenatally, and the ovaries do not. Consequently, male and female foetuses differ in the amount of testosterone to which they are exposed. According to some writers, the effects of testosterone on neural development provide powerful mechanisms for influencing behaviour across the lifespan.[131]

Some writers hypothesize that hormones have pervasive effects on behaviour that extend well beyond sexual and reproductive behaviours.[132] A group of researchers took up this latter point when they linked brain differences between girls and boys to the latter's testosterone.[133] Similarly, they cited researchers who have argued for a biological construction of masculinity, with studies showing behavioural sex differences at a very early age, before children are able to form any notions of socially constructed gender.

However, while sex hormones - typically *oestrogen* - are crucial for many sex differences, they cannot explain all of them.[134]

2.32 There are sex differences at all levels of the nervous system

It is becoming increasingly clear that sex matters in the development and functioning of the brain. As one researcher put it, 'The picture of brain organization ... is of two complex mosaics - one male and one female - that are similar in many respects but very different in others.'[135] As expressed by another writer, this is not surprising:

It seems incontrovertible that males and females evolved under some similar, and some very different pressures. We should therefore expect a priori that their brain organization will be both similar in some respects, and markedly different in others.[136]

Much has been learned about the brain as a result of the development of brain imaging techniques such as positron emission tomography (PET) and Magnetic Resonance Imaging (MRI). Much, too, has been learned from experiments on animals, especially rats.

This is a complex, but promising – and controversial – topic. Let me summarize some of the key research findings:

- *Total brain size* is often reported to be 8–10% larger in males.[137] However, at this stage of our knowledge, this difference should not be interpreted as implying any sort of functional advantage or disadvantage.[138]
- There is evidence that women have a larger *corpus collosum* – the area of the brain responsible for the transfer of information from one brain hemisphere to the other – relative to cranial capacity than do men. (Note that this and other studies of the relative sizes of regions of the brain adjust for total brain size).[139]
- Extensive evidence shows sex differences in the anatomical structure, neurochemical makeup and reactivity to stress of the *hippocampus*, a region of the brain associated with learning and memory. MRI studies show that the hippocampus is larger in women than in men. As well, there is evidence for sex differences in many of the *neurotransmitter systems* within the hippocampus.[140]
- The *amygdala* – which plays a significant role in memory for emotional events – is significantly larger in men than women. The left amygdala seems to play the more important role in women and the right amygdala in men.[141]
- A recent – controversial – study carried out at the University of Pennsylvania investigated connections in the brain among 949 8- to 22-year-old individuals. The researchers found greater neural connectivity from front to back and within one *hemisphere* in males. To the researchers, this suggested that male brains are structured to facilitate connectivity between perception and coordinated action. In contrast, in females, the connectivity between the left and right hemispheres was stronger, suggesting that their brains facilitate emotional processing and the ability to infer others' intentions in social interactions. These differences first became apparent at about the age of 13 years and became more pronounced in adolescence and young adults.[142] According to some writers, too much should not be made of this research. Some point out that although the differences are statistically significant, they are actually not substantive and that they portray average differences with a lot of overlap. Also, the Pennsylvania researchers did not in fact look at behavioural differences between the sexes – but only guessed at how any wiring differences might be related to behavioural differences between the sexes.[143]
- Using MRI, a team of researchers in the United States and Canada have found robust male/female differences in the shapes of brain development trajectories, with total *cerebral volume* peaking at age 10.5 years in females and 14.5 years in males.[144] A recent study carried out by these researchers at the United States' National Institutes of Health (NIH) concluded that the most profound difference between girls and boys is not in their

brain structures, *per se*, but rather in the trajectories of development of the various brain regions.[145] While the differences between the brains of adult women compared with adult men are small, this is not the case among children. In fact, differences between girls and boys, in terms of brain development, are much larger than differences between them in terms of height. Thus, the NIH study found that different regions of the brain develop in a different sequence, and at a different tempo, in girls compared with boys. When the 'inflection point' (roughly the halfway point in brain development) is considered, girls reach it just before the age of 11 years, while boys do not reach it until just before age 15 years. Thus, in terms of brain development, a young woman reaches full maturity between 21 and 22 years of age. In contrast, a young man does not reach full maturity until nearly 30 years of age.

- A University of Iowa study shows just how complex the relationships between brain structure, behaviour and sex/gender can be. These researchers compared the *straight gyrus* (SG) component of the *ventral frontal cortex* region of 30 adult males and 30 adult females matched for age and IQ. They found that the SGs were proportionately larger in the women than in the men. Since this region of the brain is known to be involved in social cognition and interpersonal judgment, which many studies have shown to be at higher levels in females than males, it was argued that there must be a connection between the SG and these social skills.

  To investigate the relationship between the SG structure and social cognition in *children*, the Iowa researchers studied 37 boys and 37 girls aged 7–17, matched by age and IQ. In contrast to the findings in adults, the SG was slightly smaller in girls than boys. Further, in girls, but not boys, smaller SG volumes significantly correlated with better social perception and higher identification with feminine traits. In both studies, the researchers added another complication. Instead of dividing their subjects by *biological sex*, they also classified them in a test of *psychological gender* in a questionnaire that assesses a person's degree of masculinity vs femininity. They found that in both adults and children, this measure of gender identity also correlated with the SG size. Not surprisingly, the researchers concluded that there is a complex relationship between sex, femininity, social cognition and SG morphology.[146]

  The majority of the regions in the brain that show sex differences also show differences associated with such neuropsychiatric conditions. These regions include the amygdala, hippocampus and the insula. In other words, it is quite possible that the factors leading to the development of sex differences in the brain also play a role in sex-biased neuropsychiatric conditions. Future research could well help us to understand how male and female brains have different predispositions for risk or resilience to such conditions.[147]

- Caution must be exercised in interpreting brain differences such as those I have just described. For example, it is not yet possible to establish whether there is a direct link between gender differences in various cognitive domains and particular brain differences. It could be argued that the direction of the effect could be either way: brain differences cause the cognitive differences or greater participation in various activities cause the brain differences. Perhaps both explanations have merit and gender differences reflect the interaction between biology and psychosocial influences.[148]

2.33 Students' ages influence gender ratios

There is some evidence that gender ratios are influenced by students' age. One writer, for example, found that disproportionality was greatest among children aged 5-11, during which time referral rates to special education for boys appear to surge. Before and after that, identification rates for boys and girls were much more similar.[149]

II Nurture-related explanations

Socio-cultural influences on gender roles include those arising from broad cultural values at the societal level, ethnicity, socio-economic status, parenting patterns, schooling and the peer group.

2.34 Socio-cultural stereotypes can influences performances

Teachers and parents may hold various stereotypes regarding gender differences and explicitly or implicitly convey these to children in their care. Thus, messages are conveyed that 'Boys are good at mathematics' or, conversely, that 'Girls are bad at mathematics'. Such messages that a particular subject is not important, useful, doable or part of their identity can easily become internalized. In turn, they can have the effect of becoming self-fulfilling prophecies that influence the way children perform on particular tasks. Such stereotypes can work both negatively and positively, but they seem to be more likely to have a negative effect on girls' performances and a positive effect on boys' performances.[150] This has led some writers to argue that socially constructed gender roles are based on a male-advantaged gender hierarchy.[151] As Virginia Woolf expressed it in her 1929 novel, *A room of one's own*, 'It is obvious that the values of women differ very often from the values which have been made by the other sex. Yet it is the masculine values that prevail.'[152]

2.35 Parents often create a 'gender trap'

In her recent book, *The gender trap*, sociologist Emily Kane described how families teach children about gender through the selection of toys, clothes, and activities and the styles of play and emotional expression they encourage.[153] She pointed out that despite recent awareness that girls are not too fragile to play sports and that boys can benefit from learning to cook, we still find ourselves surrounded by limited gender expectations and persistent gender inequalities. She showed how most parents make efforts to loosen gendered constraints for their children, while paradoxically also engaging in a variety of behaviours that reproduce traditionally gendered childhoods. Kane concluded that conventional gender expectations are deeply entrenched and that there is great tension in attempting to undo them while letting 'boys be boys' and 'girls be girls'.

In her research with 42 parents, Kane found five types of parents. *Naturalizers* are those who are primarily committed to biological accounts of gender and who discourage gender-atypical behaviour in their children. *Cultivators* are also interested in having traditionally gendered children. Yet, unlike Naturalizers, Cultivators understand gender as fairly social and think parents figure prominently in the development of children's gendered identities. Kane called parents who adhere equally to biology and society for explanations for gender, *Refiners*. These parents are interested in modest change to gender categories and practices, but not in significant shifts in the gender structure. Innovators and Resisters are the groups most interested in change. Kane described *Innovators* as an optimistic group who believe they can raise children in less gendered ways. Finally, *Resisters,* the smallest group, are similar to Innovators. They not only accept gender-non-normative behaviour, but they also most actively reject traditional gender behaviour.

2.36 Schools vary in their identification of problem behaviours

Writing from an English perspective, researchers have noted that overall patterns of gender imbalance obscured considerable inter-school variability in the identification of problem behaviours, with the ratios of girls to boys varying from 1:1 to 1:8.[154] The authors argued that there is thus a need to investigate what aspects of schools give rise to such disparities.

2.37 Teachers define what are unacceptable behaviour patterns

Several writers have referred to the tendency for more boys than girls to exhibit behaviour patterns (such as externalizing their feelings) that are considered by teachers and other professionals to be socially unacceptable and thus are more likely to lead to special education referrals.[155] Thus, there may be a gender bias in special education referrals and admissions. A related point, advanced by some writers, is that schooling is becoming feminized and, possibly a corollary, that masculine behaviours exhibited by boys are less acceptable.[156] Related points have been made by writers citing studies indicating boys' disregard for authority, academic work and formal achievement and the formation of concepts of masculinity that are in direct conflict with the ethos of the school.[157]

The relationship between classroom behaviour and educational achievement has been explored in a New Zealand study of a cohort of 1265 individuals studied from birth to age 25. The authors found a small, but significant, tendency for females to score better than males on standardized tests of achievement and to achieve more school and post-school qualifications. These differences could not be explained by differences in cognitive ability as both genders had similar IQ scores. However, from age 6 to age 12, boys were described by their teachers as displaying significantly higher levels of distractible, restless, inattentive, aggressive, anti-social and oppositional behaviour than girls. When the scores were adjusted for gender differences in these behaviours, most of the achievement differences were eliminated.[158]

2.38 Girls' problems may be under-identified

A corollary of the previous point may occur because current definitions of emotional disorders mean that school personnel do not adequately recognize the problems presented by girls. Commonly used measures for assessing these in schools may not capture the emotional and behavioural problems that are relatively more common in girls (e.g., adolescent depression and relational aggression).[159]

2.39 The significance of modelling of male gender roles by male teachers is not supported by research

This explanation seems counter-intuitive. Isn't it obvious that male teachers should play an important role in helping boys to assume the identity of males in a given culture, especially when women dominate the teaching profession in elementary schools? Not so, according to Canadian researchers Wayne Martino and Goli Rezai-Rashti, who criticized 'unsubstantiated claims about the influence of male teachers and the politics of role modelling in boys' lives'.[160] They pointed out various weaknesses in the argument that boys learn to be males from male teachers.[161] First, it exaggerates differences between men and women teachers. Second, it obscures the fact that gender identity is culturally, politically and socially defined. Third, it assumes that a teacher's gender identity is a singular social marker, when the reality is that teachers embody a wide range of identities arising from such features as their race, sexuality, generation, and class, in addition to their gender.

In their own research, Martino and Rezai-Rashti interviewed and observed elementary teachers (74 in Canada and 10 in Australia) and interviewed 51 students. They found that the overwhelming majority of students did not express a preference for male or female teachers and did not consider their teachers to be role models. The authors rejected 'the simplistic matching of teacher and students on the basis of their gender and/or race', arguing that 'policy-makers should focus more attention on the importance of teachers' pedagogical capacities … in determining teacher effectiveness'.[162] This point particularly resonates with me as I have recently published a book directed at educators, which outlines evidence-based teaching strategies.[163]

2.40 Gender interacts with ethnicity and socio-economic status

Here, findings from the United States and the United Kingdom need to be considered. A US study noted a similarity of gender disproportionality across racial/ethnic groups, regardless of disability condition.[164] The authors interpreted this finding to suggest that, whatever the forces are that influence gender disproportionality, they act on all racial/ethnic groups in a similar fashion. However, this finding was contradicted in a 1999 UK study that found gender differences were much greater among whites than among blacks, suggesting that both gender and race should be considered simultaneously.[165]

In a recent major study, UK author, Steve Strand, extended this point. He argued that equity researchers 'need to develop more nuanced accounts of educational success or failure, focused on the intersections between ethnicity, gender and class'.[166] In his analysis of the achievement levels of over 15,000 students aged 11, 14 and 16 in England, Strand found substantial interactions between ethnicity and gender. For example, at age 16, White British girls did better than White British boys, a gender gap that was significantly larger among Bangladeshi and Black Caribbean students. When socio-economic status (SES) is added to the mix, the situation becomes even more complex. For example, among low SES boys, White British and Black Caribbean boys were jointly the lowest scoring groups. For low SES girls, Black Caribbean girls joined other minority groups in scoring significantly higher than White British girls. When high SES students were compared, few ethnic contrasts were significant, with only Indian boys scoring higher than White British boys and only Black Caribbean boys scoring lower than White British boys. In absolute terms, the lowest achieving groups were the low SES Black Caribbean boys, low SES White British Boys and low SES White British girls. Results also indicated that middle and high SES Black Caribbean boys (but not Black Caribbean girls) achieved significantly lower scores than their White British peers. Strand suggested that the underachievement of average and high SES Black Caribbean boys may reflect factors within the school system such as teachers' low educational expectations or pervasive racism within the educational process. However, he pointed out that such explanations also need to be able to account for the lack of a significant Black Caribbean–White British gap in achievement among low SES boys and why Black Caribbean girls do as well as or better than White British girls. As Strand said, 'there is something about the particular combination of ethnicity, SES and gender that is uniquely related to attainment'[167] – a theme I will return to in subsequent chapters.

2.41 Peers influence boys' approaches to education

One of the crucial factors leading to boys' underachievement is the importance for many of them to be accepted by other boys, to enable them to identify with and act in line with peer group norms, so that they are seen as belonging, rather than as different.[168] In many western countries, such acceptance is often dependent on showing behaviours, speech, dress and body language that incorporate aspects of 'laddishness' and risk-taking to gain and protect a macho image. Such laddishness often runs counter to the expectations of the school.

2.42 Countries vary in the extent to which they have gender-equal cultures

Making use of the *Global Gender Gap Index*[169] and the 2003 PISA scores, a 2008 study found that while girls generally underperformed boys in mathematics, they had higher mean performances in countries with more gender-equal cultures.[170] Also, in such countries, girls' advantage in reading was enhanced. With particular reference to Spain, this has been explained in terms of mothers' greater participation in the labour market, leading to the transmission of gender role attitudes from mothers to daughters – but not, it appears, to sons.[171] However, a recent, and more comprehensive, analysis of PISA data reveals a more nuanced picture of the relationship between sex differences in achievement and national differences in gender equality in economic and political participation.[172] After their analysis of four sets of PISA results (2000, 2003, 2006 and 2009), the authors found the following: (a) there was no reliable relation between gender equality measures and sex differences in mathematics achievement or in overall achievement; (b) there was a surprisingly large number of countries, including some highly developed countries with progressive gender equality policies, in which boys fell considerably below girls in overall achievement (for example, this was true of 70% of OECD and partner countries in the 2009 PISA tests); (c) even though boys fell behind on average, the pattern was different among the top performers, especially in OECD countries, where top performing boys had higher achievement levels than did top performing girls; and (d) individual boys, on average, have better mathematics skills than reading skills, whereas individual girls have, on average better reading skills than mathematics skills.

The between-country differences on the *Global Gender Gap Index* can obscure within-country differences in enrolment patterns. The latter often occur in developing countries.

In China, for example, while there is nearly no significant gender inequality in urban areas or in the case of the nine years of compulsory education, girls still face inequality in rural areas, especially if they belong to minority groups, and when they reach high school and beyond. However, there is a downward trend for both inequalities over time.[173]

2.43 Some societies place women at a socio-economic disadvantage

According to the World Health Organization,[174] 'macrosocial' risk factors for common mental disorders disproportionately affect women. These include gender-based violence; discrimination; hunger, malnutrition, overwork and limited access to resources; low or subordinate social status and rank; and unremitting responsibility for the care of others.

2.44 Some societies discriminate against women and girls with disabilities

There is clear evidence that, in some countries, women and girls with disabilities face significantly more difficulties than males in attaining access to adequate education and vocational training, are more likely to be institutionalized, and are often at greater risk, both within and outside the home, of violence, injury or abuse, neglect or negligent treatment, and maltreatment or exploitation. These factors undoubtedly contribute to the global literacy rate of 1% for women with disabilities.[175] The gravity of this situation is recognized in the UN Convention on the Rights of Persons with Disabilities.[176]

2.45 Educational levels influence women's traditional vs modern role perceptions, but not men's

A recent Ghanaian study examined the extent to which men and women will adopt traditional, vs modern (i.e., egalitarian), attitudes towards gender roles and if age and education moderate these attitudes. A total of 476 respondents, made up of high and low education groups, were selected for this study. The researchers found that education seemed to minimize females' perceptions of traditional roles, but not males' perceptions. The results seemed to support the notion that males are less likely to change from socialization practices that encourage male hegemony.[177] Clearly, males relinquishing power is a much harder prospect than females aspiring for greater power.

2.46 LGBT children and young people are subject to teasing and physical abuse

A very comprehensive, recent US study[178] questioned 10,030 participants aged 13-17 who self-identified as LGBT and compared them with 510 non-LGBTs of similar ages. Here are some of the important findings:

- LGBT youth were more than twice as likely as non-LGBT youth to say they have been verbally harassed and called names at school (51% vs 25%).
- Among LGBT youth, 17% reported they have been physically attacked often while 10% of their peers say the same.

- Among LGBT youth, 48% said they have been excluded often while 26% of their non-LGBT peers said the same.
- Compared with their non-LGBT peers, LGBT youth reported much lower levels of happiness (37% vs 67%), a higher incidence of alcohol and drug use (52% vs 22%), and less connection to adult support during personal problems.
- LGBT youth were much more likely than their non-LGBT peers to say they can be more honest about themselves online than in real life (73% vs 43%).
- Fewer LGBT youth had an adult in their community to talk with if they feel worried or sad, compared with their peers.
- On a positive note, three-quarters of LGBT youth said that most of their peers do not have a problem with their identity as LGBT – but that also meant that one-quarter felt otherwise.

2.47 Schools may be exacerbating the problems experienced by LGBT students

According to some writers, the above problems facing LGBT students may well be exacerbated by schools which can operate as 'heteronormalizing institutions' because of their 'use of silence, the pathologization of (homo)sexuality and the policing of gender through adherence to binary frameworks which define appropriate and normal gender and sexual behaviours'.[179] Further, the pervasive silence of schools concerning LGBT people's experience, feelings and perceptions of their sexuality can have disempowering effects by contributing to the isolation and invisibility of LGBT youth within the school environment.[180]

2.48 Attitudes towards LGBT individuals are becoming more accepting (at least in western countries)

According to a recent Pew Research Center report, an overwhelming share of America's LGBT adults (92%) say society has become more accepting of them since the early 2000s and an equal number expect it to grow even more accepting in the future.[181] The authors attributed the changes to a variety of factors, from people knowing and interacting with someone who is LGBT, to advocacy on their behalf by high-profile public figures, to LGBT adults raising families.

Such acceptance is by no means universal, as can be seen in anti-gay laws passed in 2013 in Russia and Uganda, for example.[182]

2.49 Girls suffer violence associated with attending school in some countries

In some countries, violence in, on the way to, or associated with school is an important reason why girls do not enrol in or attend school.[183] In recent times, there have been episodes of Taliban groups coercing girls not to attend school. For example, in 2009, the Taliban in Pakistan barred girls from attending school and when teenager Malala Yousafzai won international attention for speaking out against the ban, Islamic fundamentalists tried to make an example of her. In October 2012 a gunman shot her in the face as she rode the bus to school. More recently, in 2014, the Islamist group Boko Haram (translated as 'Western education is sinful') kidnapped 270 schoolgirls in Nigeria.

2.50 Girls and boys have different learning strategies

Studies show gender differences in attitudes to work, goals and aspirations and learning strategies. With respect to the last point, girls place more emphasis on collaboration, talk and sharing, while boys are less likely to collaborate to learn, and are less inclined to use coopera-tive talk and discussion to aid and support their own learning.[184]

2.51 There is no strong evidence favouring single-sex schooling over coeducational schooling

In their attempts to increase the performances of both boys' and girls' achievement and academic interest, some countries are expanding the establishment of single-sex school-ing. This is particularly the case in the United States where, for example, there were 233 public schools offering gender-separate education in 2006, whereas in 1998 there were just four.[185]

Three theoretical models underpin this shift.[186] First, there is the *expectancy-value the-ory*, which is based on the idea that people decide to pursue a challenge if they (a) have some expectation of success and (b) perceive the value of the task. It is thus argued that, on both counts, girls are dissuaded from pursuing success in science, technology, engineering and mathematics (STEM). This could have two contradictory outcomes as far as single-sex schooling is concerned: it may increase girls' expectations for success or it may increase their belief that STEM is not for them. A second model is known as the *developmental inter-group theory*. This attempts to explain how gender becomes the basis of stereotyping and prejudice, which could become accentuated in single-sex schools. A third model is based on the argument that there are large *biologically based differences* between boys and girls and that these lead to differences in their learning styles that warrant targeted instruction based on these presumed differences. Further, it is argued that in co-educational classrooms boys are domineering, seeking out and receiving the majority of teachers' attention. This, it is argued, is a sufficient reason for separating boys and girls.

So where does the evidence lead us? Much of the earlier research has been marred by methodological weaknesses in which there has not been random assignment into the two conditions of single-sex and coeducational schooling. Also, selection to single-sex schooling is often confounded with other factors such as religious values, financial privilege, small class size and highly motivated teachers. Fortunately, a recent meta-analysis has been able to throw light on the question.[187] This examined 184 studies from 21 countries involving Grades K–12. Uncontrolled studies showed some modest advantages for single-sex schooling for both boys and girls, for outcomes such as mathematics achievement, but not for science. Con-trolled studies, however, showed only trivial differences between students in mathematics performance ($d = 0.10$ for girls, 0.06 for boys) and science performance ($d = 0.06$ for girls 0.04 for boys) in favour of single-sex schooling. In some cases, there were small differences favouring coeducational schooling (e.g. for girls' educational aspirations). The authors noted the lack of comparisons of the impact of single-sex and coeducational schools on low-income students and ethnic minorities. There was some evidence that girls in coeducational class-rooms were more gender stereotyped than those in single-sex classrooms, but there were insufficient controlled studies to compute an effect size for boys.

Other studies on the effect of the gender composition of the peer groups suggest that single-sex schooling exacerbates gender differences in attainment rather than reducing them. According to an Israeli study, the achievement of both boys and girls appears to increase according to the fraction of females in their peer groups. Students who have more female peers report a lower level of classroom violence and disruption and better relationships with other students and with teachers.[188]

A New Zealand study contrasts with the above. It examined the effects of single-sex and coeducational schooling on the gender gap in educational achievement to age 25. Data were drawn from the Christchurch Health and Development Study, a longitudinal study of a birth cohort of 1,265 individuals born in 1977 in Christchurch, New Zealand. After adjustment for a series of covariates related to school choice, there were significant differences between single-sex and coeducational schools in the size and direction of the gender gap. At coeducational schools, there was a statistically significant gap favouring females, while at single-sex schools there was a non-significant gap favouring males. This pattern was apparent for educational achievement both at high school and in tertiary education. The authors interpreted the results as indicating that single-sex schooling may mitigate male disadvantages in educational achievement.[189]

Some writers have argued that gender-segregated schooling (within, as well as between, schools) can have negative effects, including increased gender stereotyping.[190]

III An interactive approach

In recent years, there has been a rapprochement of the nature vs nurture explanations of gender differences. The focus is now shifting to addressing the interactive processes by which they work together, interacting with each other to produce sex/gender differences and similarities.[191] As one writer so succinctly put it:

> Genes do not specify behaviors or cognitive processes; they make regulatory factors, signaling molecules, receptor enzymes and so on, that interact in highly complex networks, modulated by environmental influences, in order to build and maintain the brain.[192]

Some proponents of the interactive approach cite the timing of menarche in adolescent girls as an example.[193] They point out that the maturation of the adrenal glands and the regulatory effects of the hypothalamus–pituitary–gonadal axis regulate the age of onset of the menarche. However, this sequence is modulated by environmental factors, so that girls begin menstruation as young as 12 years in some settings and as late as 18 in others. One source of this variance can be found in the quality of family life, according to some writers.[194] They point out that in girls (but not boys), families characterized by high stress levels accelerate pubertal maturation. These researchers suggest that in such environments the release of stress hormones (cortisol and epinephrine) activates the adrenal androgens that initiate pubertal development.

Another example of the interactive approach is afforded by what is referred to as a 'developmental intergroup theory of social stereotypes and prejudice'.[195] This theory is based on the premise that children have a drive to understand the world, and that this drive is shown in their tendency to classify objects (including people) into categories and to search their environments for cues as to which categories are important. Thus, children come to perceive that their world is inhabited by two genders, a perception that is reinforced by adults (and peers) who use gender-based labels, provide gender-based clothes and toys, and even employ gender-based segregation. Gender comes to be a powerful organizing category in children's lives. In such a manner, they come to form gender stereotypes and even prejudices of varying degrees of strength.

2.52 A developmental evolutionary model is a good fit

Earlier in this chapter I described research indicating that boys perform somewhat better than girls on visuo-spatial skills. Some writers ascribe this difference to evolution, suggesting that, in the past, selection pressures favoured these skills in men as hunters.[196]

This developmental evolutionary model posits that environmental factors have an impact on gene expression, on the brain and, in turn, on behaviour.[197] In 1859, Charles Darwin, arguably the father of evolutionary psychology, claimed that 'Psychology will be based on a new foundation, that of the necessary acquirement of each mental power and capacity by gradation.'[198] Adaptation and natural selection, he suggested, would become the foundation for the field of psychology.[199] Further, as rather controversially noted by a more recent evolutionary psychologist, Stephen Pinker, 'In the study of humans, there are major spheres of human experience – beauty, motherhood, kinship, morality, cooperation, sexuality, violence – in which evolutionary psychology provides the only coherent theory.'[200] In a nutshell, evolutionary psychology argues that much human behaviour is the result of psychological adaptations that evolved to solve recurrent problems in past environments. For example, in hunter-gatherer societies, the need to take care of young children limited females' freedom to hunt and to assume certain positions of power. According to some writers, evolution by selection is the only known causal process capable of creating such complex adaptations.[201] In terms of the theme of this chapter:

> Women and men are expected to differ in domains in which they have faced recurrently different adaptive problems over human evolutionary history. They are expected to be similar in all domains in which they have faced similar adaptive problems over human evolutionary history.[202]

D How should education respond to gender differences?

Clearly, educationalists must take account of the nature of sex/gender differences and the factors that contribute to them, as outlined in this chapter. As suggested in the ecological perspective I take in this book, some of these implications are at the broad societal level (e.g., addressing gender inequalities in all facets of society); some are at education policy level (e.g., single-sex vs coeducational schools, academic and vocational tracking); some are at the school level (e.g., avoiding gender stereotypes, involving women in school governance and management); while some are at the classroom level (e.g., making classrooms safe for all, avoiding gender stereo-types in curriculum materials).

I Society and system-level accommodations

2.53 Recognize that the genders overlap

When considering the role of education in responding to gender differences, it must be recognized that, although there are clear gender differences in the incidence of many dis-abilities and that, on the whole, boys are at greater risk for underachievement and special education referral, there are considerable overlaps between the genders. By no means are all boys underachievers or identified as having special educational needs, nor are all girls outside these categories. Remember, there is more diversity *within* genders than *between* genders.

2.54 Recognize that gender intersects with ethnicity and social class

One should not consider gender in isolation from other factors, particularly ethnicity and social class. Rather, the situation is much more nuanced and requires one to consider the intersections between gender, ethnicity, social class and religion.[203]

2.55 Recognize that there is no strong evidence favouring single-sex schooling

At best, single-sex schooling shows only modest advantages for both boys and girls, with small gains in favour of the former.

2.56 Recognize that different genders have equal rights

As I outlined in Chapter 1, Article 2 of the *Universal Declaration of Human Rights* (UDHR) states that, irrespective of a person's sex, everyone is entitled to all the rights and freedoms set forth in the Declaration, Also, as I discussed in Chapter 5, when women's rights clash with cultural practices and religious norms, UN conventions give precedence to gender equality. I noted, however, that this situation is more honoured in the breach than in its observance in some countries.

2.57 Promote gender equity in HIV/AIDS programmes and services[204]

UNICEF, in partnership with UNESCO and the World Health Organization, aims to empower adolescent girls and boys to take informed decision about their sexuality through compre-hensive life skills programmes, in many cases integrated into education curricula. These interventions offer young people gender-specific, age-appropriate information on HIV and the steps they can take to prevent infection, including delayed sexual debut, correct and con-sistent condom use, mutual faithfulness, the reduction in age difference between partners as well as in the number of partners, and the use of testing and counselling services for HIV and other sexually transmitted illnesses.[205]

2.58   *Globally, take major, coordinated efforts to address gender inequality*

At a more global level, promoting gender equality and the empowerment of women has been well recognized in international law since the adoption by the United Nations of the Universal Declaration of Human Rights in 1948. This was given impetus by the UN Decade for Women 1975-1985 and by the 2012 World Development Report.[206] Gender equality is now considered to be essential to the achievement of the internationally agreed development goals. For example, one of the UN's Millennium Development Goals is to 'Promote gender equality and empower women', with targets that include the elimination of gender disparity in primary and secondary education at all levels by 2015.[207] Unfortunately, it seems that this date will not be achieved in at least 40 countries, mostly in Africa. In 2005, only 59 of 181 countries had achieved gender parity in the gross enrolment rates for both primary and secondary education.[208] In 2009, two regions in particular had low ratios of girls to boys completing the last grade of primary school: Arab States and sub-Saharan Africa (0.94 and 0.95, respectively).[209] Within country variations in completion rates are also apparent, with the poorest and those living most distant from power centres having the least adequate educational provisions.

International organizations have begun to focus on accelerating secondary education for girls. A recent report noted that there remain significant challenges to progressing this goal. These include cultural norms that do not recognize the value of girls' education, early marriage and childbearing, security concerns and long distances to school, among others. The report outlined five strategies at the school level that can benefit girls' completion of primary school and their transition to secondary education:

- ensuring reasonable travel distance to school;
- making available private, safe latrines/acceptable menstrual hygiene management facilities, as well as basic reproductive health education;
- ensuring a safe and secure school environment;
- ensuring the presence of female teachers in the school; and
- making the curriculum relevant to life skills and the labour market.[210]

Quite apart from a rights argument, it must be recognized that educating girls increases human capital and has a positive influence on economic growth and development, both directly and indirectly through the positive influences mothers have on their children.[211] According to UNICEF, study after study show that educating girls (for at least six years) is the single most effective policy in lowering infant and maternal mortality, improving family nutrition, protecting women from HIV/AIDS, and ensuring that they immunize their children.[212]

2.59   *Prevent and respond to gender-based violence*

Governments should establish a monitoring framework with standardized indicators to establish the extent of school-related gender-based violence.[213] Addressing such violence requires a multi-sectoral approach with collaboration across education, health, social welfare and youth sectors.[214] School authorities should be vigilant in detecting, preventing and dealing with gender-based violence, both in school precincts and on students' travel to and from school.[215] Although girls are more likely than boys to be victims of violence, both should be attended to.

2.60 *Include women in decision-making at all levels of educational policy-making*[216]

In most western countries, women have significant roles at all levels of educational leadership. Where this does not occur, steps should be taken to ensure that women are equitably represented in leadership roles in the governance and management of education.

II School-level strategies

2.61 *Monitor students' progress by gender*

Schools should regularly monitor students' progress, behaviour, attendance and exclusion by gender.[217] Where patterns emerge that indicate one gender is causing concern, steps should be taken to investigate further and take remedial action.

2.62 *Avoid over-identifying boys with certain special needs*

In the case of students whose special educational needs are more clearly associated with environmental factors, schools should carefully evaluate their policies and procedures to deal with these factors. For example, the school and classroom disciplinary procedures may be biased against boys and there may be insufficient attempts to deal with aspects of boys' culture that are inimical to them acquiring more socially acceptable behaviour or more appropriate academic motivation. In other words, there may be a discrepancy between the cultural capital that boys bring to school and that which is valued by the school.

2.63 *Avoid under-identifying girls with certain special needs*

Turning to the possibility of girls being unidentified as having special educational needs, schools and those responsible for assessing students' needs for special support should re-examine their criteria to ensure that problems girls may have are not overlooked. For example, girls with ADHD may not be detected in school because they are more likely to display inattentiveness rather than the disruptive behaviours often associated with boys' ADHD. Also, girls are more likely than boys to employ relational aggression. This can often go unnoticed in schools because of its subtlety and its deployment in social media sites. Teachers should be alert to relational aggression and work with parents to deal appropriately with those who direct and receive it.

2.64 *Examine what kind of masculinities and femininities are being promoted*[218]

Schools should examine their policies and teachers their behaviours to determine to extent they consciously or unconsciously promote stereotyped images of what it is to be a male or a female and how they should interact. This means, for example, dealing with such masculin-ized issues as 'laddish' behaviour, bullying of gays and attention-seeking. As well, support should be given to those boys who do *not* conform to such 'norms'.

2.65 Recognize that children and young people have a right to an education that prepares them for adult life, and that includes their sexuality

The World Health Organization articulates this right in the following terms: all persons, free of coercion, discrimination and violence have the right to:

> the highest attainable standard of health in relation to sexuality, including access to sexual and reproductive health care services; seek, receive and impart information in relation to sexuality; sexuality education; respect for bodily integrity; choice of partner; decide to be sexually active or not; consensual sexual relations; consensual marriage; decide whether or not, and when to have children; and to pursue a satisfying, safe and pleasurable sexual life.[219]

III Classroom-level strategies

2.66 Recognize that boys are biologically at greater risk for certain disabilities

Educators should recognize that, in general, boys are biologically at higher risk than girls for certain disabilities. Apart from recognizing such causation of disabilities, and not search-ing for environmental explanations, teachers must accommodate their teaching to take any associated learning difficulties into account. This might mean, for example, allowing for the fact that boys tend to mature more slowly than girls by making appropriate adjustments to the curriculum and teaching strategies.

2.67 Make classrooms safe and inclusive for both genders and all sexual orientations

Teachers set the tone in their classrooms and principals influence the climate throughout a school. In fulfilling these responsibilities, educators should particularly note that since many LGBT youth are afraid to 'come out' at school because they fear being bullied, it is important that they make their classrooms and schools safe and inclusive for all. They should also con-sider ways to include LGBT issues and themes in the curriculum.[220]

With respect to the latter point, it is pertinent to draw attention to Andrew Solomon's 2012 book, *Far from the tree*.[221] He drew a distinction between *vertical identities* and *horizontal identities*. In the former, attributes and values are passed down from parent to child through DNA and shared cultural norms, for example ethnicity. In the latter, a child may have an inher-ited or an acquired trait that is different from his or her parent and therefore must acquire an identity from a peer group. Solomon cited being gay as an example of this horizontal identity and argued that many parents in that situation experience their child's identity as an affront and may make attempts to change it. Such children are 'apples that have fallen far from the tree'. Teachers should be aware of such circumstances when they arise and understand the stresses that many LGBT children may be experiencing in their families, as well as at school.

As well, schools catering for pre-adolescents and adolescents should consider instituting sexuality-diversity workshops, possibly as part of the health curriculum. In a New Zealand study of the impact of such workshops targeting 12- to 15-year-olds, more than three-quarters of the participants thought they would help reduce bullying in schools.[222]

It is relevant here to mention that there is no evidence to suggest that the children of lesbian women and gay men are disadvantaged relative to children of heterosexual parents. Admittedly, though, research in this area is limited in extent and longitudinal studies that follow lesbian and gay families over time are needed.[223]

2.68 Avoid stereotyped gendered behaviour patterns

Danish writer, Anne-Marie Kruse,[224] has argued that 'boys need the opportunity to explore and change their ambivalent views of women, to be confronted with the effects of the misuse of power'. Girls, as well as boys, should be helped to arrive at equitable perceptions of male and female identities.

There may well be debate, however, as to whether countries would want to go as far as Sweden. Based on the assumption that language reflects gender stereotypes, Sweden has introduced the word *hen*, as a gender-neutral pronoun that can be applied to objects and people who have been traditionally identified as male or female. This is intended to replace *han* (he in English) and *hon* (she).[225] This move is a near equivalent to the widespread use of *Ms* in English to avoid the reference to marital status embodied in the terms *Miss* and *Mrs*. It reflects Sweden's designation as the fourth most gender-equal country in the world and its growing aspiration to be a gender-neutral society.[226]

2.69 Avoid raising negative gender stereotypes

Teachers and parents should be aware of the dangers of conveying to either sex any indication that they cannot do certain tasks because of their gender. In the first place, as we have seen in this chapter, many of the gender differences are quite small, with considerable overlaps. Second, there is a risk of exacerbating any such differences by extrapolating from population statistics to individuals. Third, there is a risk that stereotypes come to be believed and not challenged. Schools represent the most direct policy levers with which to address negative gender stereotypes through individual guidance and encouragement, teacher expectations and teacher-student interactions.[227]

2.70 Ensure that curriculum materials are free of gender-stereotyped imagery

Since the 1980s, educational publishers in western countries have taken pains to remove gender bias from school texts. Prior to that time, various analyses by feminists and others have concluded that women were largely invisible or were portrayed in domestic contexts or in low status and marginal roles.[228] The need for vigilance remains.

The way ahead, surely, is for educators to commit to the principles of a curriculum based on universal design for learning. This means making it accessible to all students including, in this case, boys and girls, and LGBT students.

E Conclusions

It is clear that while males and females are more alike than they are different in their under-lying psychological makeup, they demonstrate many differences in their behaviours. As I have shown in this chapter, compared with females, males are less well educated (in western countries, but not in the past); are stronger; are more physically aggressive; have more liberal sexual attitudes; are more likely to have alcohol dependence; commit more offences, especially serious crimes; do less well in inhibiting their impulses; dominate motor vehicle accidents; are more likely to succeed in suicide attempts; do less well in school; are over-represented in special education; and are more likely to have disabilities as children. As well as the reciprocals of the foregoing, compared with males, females have higher life expec-tancies (in most parts of the world); show more relational aggression; have higher rates of depression, anxiety and somatic complaints; are more subject to sexual violence; make more attempts to commit suicide; are more likely to have disabilities as adults; and have higher rates of HIV/AIDS.

As I have shown in this chapter, gender cannot be taken in isolation. It must be considered alongside ethnicity and class (and, as I will point out in later chapters, religion and disability). As Strand emphasizes, 'there is something about the particular combination of ethnicity, SES and gender that is uniquely related to attainment'.[229] Further, gender must be considered in the contexts of time and place. Although multi-country studies show high levels of gender similarity in many of the above comparisons, there is considerable variation globally in edu-cational equality and attitudes toward gender. Many of these arise from countries' religion, cultural beliefs, economic resources and their histories. As well as such macrosocial factors, other nurture-related explanations of gender differences include socio-cultural stereotypes held by parents, teachers and peers; schools' definitions and tolerance of certain behav-iours; the interactions of gender with ethnicity and socio-economic factors; and societies' approaches to gender issues, including towards persons identifying as LGBT. In contrast to these nurture-related explanations, one must take into account a range of nature-related explanations. This involves considering the role of X-linked genetic factors, the slower matu-ration rates of males, the influence of testosterone and other hormones, sex differences in the nervous system, and the age of individuals. In recent years, there has been a rapproche-ment of the nature vs nurture explanations, with an increasing emphasis on the interactions between the two. A related explanation involves considering developmental evolutionary models, which draws attention to the way in which environmental factors in the distant past have impacted on gene expression, the brain and, in turn, behaviour.

When we consider the educational implications of the above, we must take into account three main principles. First, although there are many examples of gender differences, for almost every variable there is a high degree of overlap. Since there is more diversity within genders than between them, it behoves educators not to impose gender stereotypes on their students. Second, educators should respect the overarching principle that individuals should enjoy equal rights, irrespective of their gender or sexual orientation. Third, as with all of the differences explored in this book, educators should strive to implement inclusive educa-tion, i.e., education that best fits the needs of individual students. These three principles require policies and practices to be designed and implemented at three levels of an education

Table 2.1 Summary of proposed actions regarding gender in education

Society (government)	Education system	Schools	Classrooms
• Accept and promote obligations to different genders and sexual orientations under the *Universal Declaration of Human Rights* and other UN instruments. • Respect individuals' rights to pursue their sexual orientations. • Promote understanding and tolerance of different genders and sexual orientations. • Recognize that there is no strong evidence favouring single-sex schooling. • Take major, coordinated efforts to address gender inequality in all aspects of living, including employment. • Include women in decision-making at all levels of educational policy-making. • Prevent and respond to gender-based violence.	• Respect the freedom of individuals to pursue their own gender identity and sexual orientation. • Give due weight to the views of the child 'in accordance with their age and maturity'. • Formulate and promote policies of inclusive education that embrace all forms of diversity, including gender diversity. • Develop a curriculum that includes consideration of gender issues. • Ensure that teacher education and professional development programmes include consideration of gender issues. • Recognize that gender intersects with ethnicity and social class. • Recognize that while boys are at greater risk for certain disabilities, care should be taken not to over-identify boys or under-identify girls as having special needs. • Promote gender equity in HIV/AIDS programmes and services. • Monitor students' progress by gender.	• Ensure that textbooks do not contain stereotypes of different genders. • Ensure that students are taught about their rights and responsibilities under international human rights conventions and their own country's human rights legislation with regard to gender. • Recognize that genders overlap on most variables and that there is more diversity within than between genders. • Prevent and respond to gender-based violence.	• Employ the principles of universal design for learning to accommodate to all students' ways of learning and expressing their knowledge and skills. • Accept that students may well have gender identities or sexual orientations different from those held by the teacher and respond to these identities with tolerance and understanding. • Make the development of tolerance and the avoidance of prejudice and discrimination part of the everyday classroom life. • Avoid negative gender stereotyping. • Ensure that curriculum materials are free of gender-stereotyped imagery.

system: nationally in legislation and regulations; at the school level in policies, governance and management; and at the classroom level in the creation of positive and productive learning environments, free of gender discrimination. These are summarized in Table 2.1.

Notes

1   As of May 2014, 16 countries (Argentina, Belgium, Brazil, Canada, Denmark, France, Iceland, Netherlands, New Zealand, Norway, Portugal, Spain, South Africa, Sweden, United Kingdom and Uruguay) and several sub-national jurisdictions (parts of Mexico and the United States) allow same-sex couples to marry. URL: http://en.wikipedia.org/wiki/Same-sex_marriage (accessed 20 May 2014).

2   Meekosha, H. (2006). 'Gender international.' In G. Albrecht (ed.), *Sage encyclopaedia of disability*, Volume 2 (pp. 764-769). Thousand Oaks, CA: Sage.

3   Ibid., p. 764.

4   Graham, S. (2001). *Sulawesi's fifth gender*. URL: http://www.insideindonesia.org/weekly-articles/sulawesis-fifth-gender (accessed 20 May 2014).

5   Gates, G.J. (2011). *How many people are lesbian, gay, bisexual and transgender?* Los Angeles: Williams Institute, UCLA School of Law. URL: http://williamsinstitute.law.ucla.edu/wp-content/uploads/Gates-How-Many-People-LGBT-Apr-2011.pdf (accessed 20 May 2014).

6   Pew Research Center (2013). *A survey of LGBT Americans: Attitudes, experiences and values in changing times*. Washington, DC: Author. URL: http://www.pewsocialtrends.org/2013/06/13/a-survey-of-lgbt-americans/ (accessed 20 May 2014).

7   Macur, J. (2014). 'Indian sprinter seeks right to compete in the body she was born with.' *International New York Times*, 8 September 2014.

8   UN Statistics Division, Department of Economic and Social Affairs (2011). *World population prospects: The 2010 revision*. URL: http://www.geohive.com/earth/pop_gender.aspx (accessed 10 January 2014).

9   Navara, K.J. (2009). 'Humans at tropical latitudes produce more females.' *Biology Letters*, 5(4), 524-527.

10 Grech, V., Vassallo-Agius, P. & Savona-Ventura, C. (2003). 'Secular trends in sex ratios at birth in North America and Europe over the second half of the 20th century.' *Journal of Epidemiology and Community Health*, 57(8), 612-615.

11 Grech, V. (2013). 'Secular trends in sex ratios at birth in South America over the second half of the 20th century.' *Journal of Pediatrics*, 89(5), 505-509.

12 In November 2015, this policy was rescinded.

13 *The Guardian*, 31 January 2014. URL: http://www.theguardian.com/world/2014/jan/31/russian-men-losing-years-to-vodka (accessed 30 May 2014).

14 URL: http://curiosity.discovery.com/question/women-live-longer-men (accessed 10 January 2014).

15 Davis, G.L., Gottlieb, M.B. & Stampnitzky, J.R. (1998). 'Reduced ratio of male to female births in several industrial countries: a sentinel health indicator?' *Journal of American Medical Association*, 279(13), 1018-1023.

16 James, W.H. (2008). 'Evidence that mammalian sex ratios at birth are partially controlled by parental hormone levels around the time of conception.' *Journal of Endocrinology*, 198, 3-15.

17 Byrne, J. & Warburton, D. (1987). 'Male excess among anatomically normal fetuses in spontaneous abortions.' *American Journal of Medical Genetics*, 26, 605-611.

18 United Nations, Department of Economic and Social Affairs, Population Division (2013). *World population prospects 2012 revision*. New York, NY: Author.

19 World Health Organization (2012). *World health statistics 2012*. URL: http://www.who.int/gho/publications/world_health_statistics/2012/en/ (accessed 25 May 2014).

20 Hattie, J. (2009). *Visible learning: A synthesis of over 800 meta-analyses relating to achievement*. London: Routledge, p. 55.

21 Hyde, J.S. (2005). 'The gender similarities hypothesis.' *American Psychologist*, 60(6), 581-592.

22 Eagly, A.H. & Wood, W. (2013). 'The nature-nurture debates: 25 years of challenges in understanding the psychology of gender.' *Perspectives in Psychological Science*, 8, 340-357.

23 Barro, R.J. & Lee, J.-W. (2010), *A new data set of educational attainment in the world, 1950-2010.* NBER Working Paper 15902. Cambridge, MA: National Bureau of Economic Research.

24 Pekkarinen, T. (2012). *Gender differences in education.* Discussion paper No. 6390. Bonn, Germany: Institute for Study of Labor (IZA). URL: http://ftp.iza.org/dp6390.pdf (accessed 12 February 2016).

25 Pekkarinen, T. (2012). 'Gender differences in education.' *Nordic Economic Policy Review*, 1/2012, 1-31.

26 Ibid.

27 Ibid., p. 2.

28 *Schools Inquiry Commission Report*, Volume 1, Chapter 6 (1867-1868). Reprinted as Chapter 1 in *Reports issued by the Schools' Inquiry Commission on the education of girls*, by D. Beale, Principal of the Ladies' College, Cheltenham. London: David Nutt, 1870, p. 1.

29 Ibid., p. 2.

30 Hadow, W.H. (Chairman) (1923). *Report of the Consultative Committee on Differentiation of the Curriculum for Boys and Girls Respectively in Secondary Schools.* London: HM Stationery Office (The Hadow Report).

31 Thorndike, E.L. (1914). *Educational psychology*, Volume III. New York, NY: Teachers College, Columbia University, p. 184.

32 Fry, R. (1985). *It's different for daughters.* Wellington: New Zealand Council for Educational Research.

33 World Economic Forum (2013). *The global gender gap report 2013.* Geneva: Author.

34 Woetzel, J., Madgavkar, A., Ellingrud, K., Labaye, E., Kutcher, E., Manyika, J., Dobbs, R. & Krishnan, M. (2015). *The power of parity: How advancing women's equality can add $12 trillion to global growth.* McKinsey Global Institute.

35 OECD (2016). *Policy forum on the future of work.* URL: http://www.oecd.org/employment/ministerial/employment-in-figures.htm (accessed 20 January 2016).

36 UNESCO (2009). *Global monitoring report 2009: Overcoming inequality: Why governance matters.* Paris: Author.

37 Cooray, A. & Potrafke, N. (2010). 'Gender inequality in education: Political institutions or culture and religion.' *European Journal of Political Economy*, 27, 268-280.

38 UNESCO Institute for Statistics (2010). *Trends in tertiary education: Sub-Saharan Africa.* URL: http://www.uis.unesco.org/FactSheets/Documents/fs10-2010-en.pdf (accessed 22 April 2014).

39 UNICEF. URL: http://www.unicef.org/mdg/gender.html (accessed 10 March 2014).

40 World Bank (2011). *The World Bank Education Statistics Newsletter*, August, 2011, V(1).

41 Ibid.. See also Norris, P. & Inglehart, R. (2004). *Sacred and secular: Religion and politics worldwide.* Cambridge, UK: Cambridge University Press.

42 The EFA Global Monitoring Report Team (2014). *Teaching and learning: Achieving quality for all.* Paris: UNESCO Publishing.

43 Ibid., p. 77.

44 Unterhalter, E.E. (2010). *Partnership, participation and power for gender equality in education.* Prepared for The E4 Conference: Engendering Empowerment: Education and Equality. Dakar, Senegal, May 2010.

45 Owiny, E. & Nagujja, Y. (2014). 'Caught between a rock and a hard place: Challenges of refugees with disabilities and their families in Uganda.' In D. Mitchell & V. Karr (eds), *Crises, conflict and disability: Ensuring equality* (pp. 202-209). London: Routledge.

46 This is not the case with physics and earth sciences, where the gaps in favour of boys are more consistent or increasing over time, and with reading and writing, where the gap in favour of girls persists. The latter is shown up, for example, in the OECD PISA results. Lauzon, D. (2001). 'Gender differences in large scale, quantitative assessments of mathematics and science achievement.' Paper prepared for the Statistics Canada-John Deutsch Institute WRNET Conference on Empirical Issues in Canadian Education, Ottawa, November 2001.

47 Ibid. and Friedman, L. (1989). 'Mathematics and the gender gap: A meta-analysis of recent studies on sex differences in mathematical tasks.' *Review of Educational Research*, 59(2), 185-213.

48 Fryer, R.G. & Levitt, S.D. (2009). *An empirical analysis of the gender gap in mathematics.* Cambridge, MA: National Bureau of Economic Research.

49 For reviews, see Lindberg, S.M., Hyde, J.S., Petersen, J.L. & Linn, M.C. (2010). 'New trends in gender and mathematics performance: A meta-analysis.' *Psychological Bulletin*, 136, 1123-1135; and Cassidy, K.W. (2007). 'Gender differences in cognitive ability, attitudes, and behavior.' In D. Sadker & E.S. Silber (eds), *Gender in the classroom* (pp. 33-72). Mahwah, NJ: Lawrence Erlbaum Associates.

50 Department for Education (2015). *Early Years Foundation Stage Profile results in England, 2013/14.* URL: https://www.gov.uk/government/uploads/system/uploads/attachment_data/file/364021/SFR39_2014_Text.pdf (accessed 18 November 2015).

51 For reviews, see Ganley, C.M. & Vasilyeva, M. (2011). 'Sex differences in the relation between math performance, spatial skills, and attitudes.' *Journal of Applied Developmental Psychology*, 32, 235-242.

52 See, for example, Lindberg et al., op. cit.

53 Else-Quest, N.M., Hyde, J.S. & Linn, M.C. (2010). 'Cross-national patterns of gender differences in mathematics: A meta-analysis.' *Psychological Bulletin*, 136, 103-127.

54 Voyer, D., Voyer, S. & Bryden,, M.P. (1995). 'Magnitude of sex differences in spatial abilities: A meta-analysis and consideration of critical variables.' *Psychological Bulletin*, 117, 250-270.

55 Ganley & Vasilyeva, op. cit.

56 Cassidy, op. cit.

57 Lietz, P. (2006). 'A meta-analysis of gender differences in reading achievement at the secondary school level.' *Studies in Educational Evaluation*, 32(4), 317-344.

58 Huang, C. (2013). 'Gender differences in academic self-efficacy: A meta-analysis.' *European Journal of Psychology of Education*, 28(1), 1-35.

59 Department for Education (2015), op. cit.

60 Loveless, T. (2015). 'How well are American students learning?' *Brown Center on Education Policy*, 3(4), 8-17.

61 Ibid.

62 OECD (2015). *Trends shaping education 2015 Spotlight 7*. URL: http://www.oecd.org/edu/ceri/Spotlight7-GenderEquality.pdf (accessed 17 November 2015).

63 URL: https://www.collegeboard.org/releases/2013/national-science-foundation-provides-52-million-grant-create-new-advanced-placement-compute (accessed 25 May 2014).

64 Thibault, V., Guillame, M., Berthelot, G., El Helou, N., Schaal, K., Quinquis, L. Nassif, H., Tafflet, M., Escalona, S., Hermine, O. & Toussaint, J.-F. (2010). 'Women and men in sport performance: The gender gap has not evolved since 1983.' *Journal of Sports Science and Medicine*, 9, 214-223.

65 Berkowitz, B. & Cuadra, A. (2014). *The Washington Post*, 25 February 2014.

66 World Health Organization (2014). *Global health observatory*. Geneva: Author. URL: http://www.who.int/gho/ncd/risk_factors/obesity_text/en/ (accessed 26 May 2014).

67 Ogden, C.L., Carroll, M.D., Kit, B.K., & Flegal K.M. (2012). 'Prevalence of obesity and trends in body mass index among US children and adolescents, 1999-2010.' *Journal of the American Medical Association*, 307(5), 483-490. URL: http://jama.jamanetwork.com/Mobile/article.aspx?articleid=1104932 (accessed 27 May 2014).

68 Ng, M. et al. (2014). 'Global, regional, and national prevalence of overweight and obesity in children and adults during 1980-2013: A systematic analysis for the Global Burden of Disease Study 2013'. *The Lancet*, Early Online Publication, 29 May 2014. URL: http://www.thelancet.com/journals/lancet/article/PIIS0140-6736%2814%2960460-8/abstract (accessed 19 May 2016).

69 Petersen, J.L. & Hyde, J.S. (2010). 'A meta-analytic review of research on gender differences in sexuality, 1993-2007.' *Psychological Bulletin*, 136(1), 21-38; and Petersen, J.L. & Hyde, J.S. (2011). 'Gender differences in sexual attitudes and behaviors: A review of meta-analytic results and large datasets.' *Journal of Sex Research*, 48(2/3), 149-165.

70 Department of Mental Health and Substance Dependence, World Health Organization (nd). *Gender disparities in mental health*. Geneva: Author. URL: http://www.who.int/mental_health/prevention/genderwomen/en/ (accessed 25 May 2014).

71 Hitchman, S.C. & Fong, G.T. (2011). 'Gender empowerment and female-to-male smoking prevalence ratios.' *Bulletin of the World Health Organization*, 89, 195-202.

72 Warren, C.W., Jones, N.R., Eriksen, M.P. & Asma, S. (Global Tobacco Surveillance System (GTSS) collaborative group). (2006). 'Patterns of global tobacco use in young people and implications for future chronic disease burden in adults.' *The Lancet*, 367, 749-753.

73 Knight, G.P., Fabes, R.A. & Higgins, D.A. (1996). 'Concerns about drawing causal inferences from meta-analyses: An example in the study of gender differences in aggression.' *Psychological Bulletin*, 119(3), 410-421; and Crick, N.R. & Grotpeter, J.K. (1995). 'Relational aggression, gender, and social-psychological adjustment.' *Child Development*, 66, 710-722.

74 Bjorkqvist, K., Lagerspetz, K.M. & Osterman, K. (2006). 'Sex differences in covert aggression.' *Aggressive Behavior*, 202(20), 27-33.

75 Crick & Grotpeter, op.cit.
76 Crick, N.R., Werner, N.E., Casas, J.F., O'Brien, K.M., Nelson, D.A., Grotpeter, J.K. & Markon, K. (1999). 'Childhood aggression and gender: A new look at an old problem.' In D. Bernstein (ed.), *Nebraska symposium on motivation* (pp. 75–114). Lincoln, NE: University of Nebraska Press.
77 Crick & Grotpeter, op. cit.
78 Steffensmeier, D. & Allan, E. (1996). 'Gender and crime: Toward a gendered theory of female offending.' *Annual Review of Sociology*, 22, 459–487.
79 Parker et al., op. cit.
80 Else-Quest, N.M., Hyde, J.S., Goldsmith, H.H.M. & Hulle, C.A.V. (2006). 'Gender differences in temperament: A meta-analysis.' *Psychological Bulletin*, 132(1), 33–72.
81 United Nations Girls' Education Initiative (2014). *School-related gender-based violence in the Asia-Pacific Region*. Bangkok: Asia and Pacific Regional Bureau for Education, UNESCO.
82 Ibid.
83 Briere, J. & Eliot, D.M. (2003). 'Prevalence and psychological sequelae of self-reported childhood physical and sexual abuse in a general population sample of men and women.' *Child Abuse and Neglect*, 27(10), 1205–1222.
84 Wolak, J., Finkelhor, D. & Mitchell, K.J. (2004). 'Internet-initiated sex crimes against minors: Implications for prevention based on findings from a national study.' *Journal of Adolescent Health*, 35(5), 11–20.
85 United Nations Girls' Education Initiative and UNESCO (2015). *School-related gender-based violence is preventing the achievement of quality education for all*. Policy Paper 17. Paris: EFA Global Monitoring Report, c/o UNESCO.
86 UNICEF (2014). *Hidden in plain sight: A statistical analysis of violence against children*. New York, NY: Author.
87 Dedy, S. (2010). *Analyse situationnelle des OEV et enquête des connaissances attitudes et pratiques des élèves et enseignants sur les IST, le VIH/Sida, et les grossesses en milieu scolaire*. C te d'Ivoire: Minist re de l' ducation Nationale.
88 End Violence Against Women Coalition (2010). *2010 poll on sexual harassment in schools*. London. URL: http://www.endviolenceagainstwomen.org.uk/2010-poll-on-sexual-harassment-in-schools (accessed 15 December 2015).
89 United Nations Girls' Education Initiative, op. cit.
90 Berman, A.L. & Carroll, T.A. (1984). 'Adolescent suicide: A critical review.' *Death Education*, 8(sup001), 53–64.
91 Soni-Raleigh, V. (1996). 'Suicide patterns and trends in people of Indian Subcontinent and Caribbean origin in England and Wales.' *Ethnicity and Health*, 1(1), 55–63.
92 Chang, D. (2008). *Comparison of crash fatalities by sex and age group*. Washington, DC: NHTSA's National Center for Statistics and Analysis. URL: http://www-nrd.nhtsa.dot.gov/Pubs/810853.pdf (accessed 20 May 2014).
93 Faul M., Xu L., Wald M.M., & Coronado V.G. (2010). *Traumatic brain injury in the United States: Emergency department visits, hospitalizations and deaths 2002–2006*. Atlanta, GA: Centers for Disease Control and Prevention, National Center for Injury Prevention and Control.
94 Younger, M., Warrington, M., Gray, J., Rudduck, J., McLellan, R., Bearne, E., Kershner, R. & Bricheno, P. (2005). *Raising boys' achievement: Research report RR636*. Annesley, Nottingham: Department for Education and Skills.
95 Strand, S. (2014). 'Ethnicity, gender, social class and achievement gaps at age 16: Intersectionality and "getting it" for the white working class.' *Research Papers in Education*, 29(2), 131–171.
96 Parker, G., MacInnes, T. & Kenway, P. (2007). *Monitoring poverty and social exclusion 2007*. Water End, York: Joseph Rowntree Foundation.
97 Younger et al., op. cit.
98 The principal sources of information for this section are Oswald, D.P., Best, D.P., Coutinho, M.J. & Nagle, H.A.L. (2003). 'Trends in the special education identification rates of boys and girls: A call for research and change.' *Exceptionality*, 11(4), 223–237; and Younger, et al., op. cit.
99 Oswald, et al., op. cit.
100 Haraldsvik, M. & Bonesrønning, H. (2014). *Peer effects on student achievement: does the educational level of your classmates' parents matter?* Trondheim, Norway: Department of Economics, NTNU. URL: http://www.svt.ntnu.no/iso/marianne.haraldsvik/Workshop%202014/Papers/haraldsvik.pdf (accessed 22 December 2015).

101   National Pupil Database Version 2.2 (combining 2003 PLASC data and final 2002 attainment data); Department for Children, Schools and Families (2007). *Statistical first release*; Daniels, H., Hey, V., Leonard, D. & Smith, M. (1999). 'Issues of equity in special needs education from a gender perspective.' *British Journal of Special Education*, 26(4), 189-195; and Eason, G. (2002). 'Boys dominate special needs.' *BBC News*, 29 November, 2002. URL: http://news.bbc.co.uk/2/hi/uk_news/education/2525017.stm (accessed 10 March 2014).

102   OECD (2005). *Students with disabilities, learning difficulties and disadvantages: statistics and indicators*. Paris: Author.

103   Wehmeyer, M.L. & Schwartz, M. (2001). 'Disproportionate representation of males in special education services: biology, behavior or bias?' *Education and Treatment of Children*, 24(1), 28-45.

104   Evans, P. (2000). 'Equity indicators based on the provision of supplemental resources for disabled and disadvantaged students.' In W. Hutmacher, D. Cochrane & N. Bottani (eds), *In pursuit of equity in education: Using international indicators to compare equity policies* (pp. 253-266). Dordrecht: Kluwer Academic.

105   Frombone, E. (2005). 'Epidemiological studies of pervasive developmental disorders.' In F.R Volkmar, R. Paul & D. Cohen (eds), *Handbook of autism and pervasive developmental disorders* (pp. 42- 69). Hoboken, NJ: John Wiley; Yeargin-Allsopp, M., Drews-Botsch, C. & Van Naarden-Brawn, K. (2007). 'Epidemiology of developmental disabilities.' In M.L. Batshaw, L. Pellegrino, & N.J. Roizen (eds), *Children with disabilities*. Sixth edition (pp. 231-243), Baltimore, MD: Paul H. Brookes; and Oswald et al., op. cit.

106   Liptak, G.S. (2007). 'Neural tube defects.' In Batshaw et al., op. cit.

107   Roizen, N. (2007). 'Down syndrome.' In Batshaw et al., op. cit.

108   Ibid.

109   Recent New Zealand data show that boys are almost twice as likely as girls to be diagnosed with emotional and behavioural problems: including: depression, anxiety disorder, attention deficit disorder (ADD) and/or attention deficit and hyperactivity disorder (ADHD). Ministry of Health (2013). *New Zealand Health survey: Annual update of key findings 2012/13*. Wellington: Author.

110   See, for example, Frombone, E. (2005). 'Epidemiological studies of pervasive developmental disorders.' In F.R Volkmar, R. Paul. & D. Cohen, D (eds), *Handbook of autism and pervasive developmental disorders* (pp. 42-69). Hoboken, NJ: John Wiley.

111   Purdie, N., Hattie, J. & Carroll, A. (2002). 'A review of the research on interventions for attention deficit hyperactivity disorder: What works best?' *Review of Educational Research*, 72(1), 61-99.

112   The Norwegian Institute of Public Health (2012). *Facts about ADHD*. URL: http://www.fhi.no/eway/default.aspx?pid=233&trg=MainLeft_5648&MainArea_5661=5648:0:15,2917:1:0:0:::0:0&MainLeft_5648=5544:60586:::1:5647:2:::0:0 (accessed 5 May 2014).

113   Biederman, J., Mick, E., Faraone, S.V., Braaten, E., Doyle, A., Spencer, T. & Johnson, M.A. (2002). 'Influence of gender on attention deficit hyperactivity disorder in children referred to a psychiatric clinic.' *American Journal of Psychiatry*, 159(1), 36-42; and Nussbaum, N.L. (2012). 'ADHD and female specific concerns: A review of the literature and clinical implications.' *Journal of Attention Disorders*, 16(2), 87-100.

114   Hasson, R. & Fine, J.G. (2012). 'Gender differences among children with ADHD on continuous performance tests: A meta-analytic review.' *Journal of Attention Disorders*, 16(3), 190-198.

115   Biederman et. al., op. cit.

116   Meekosha, H. (2006). 'Gender international.' In G. Albrecht (ed.), *Sage encyclopedia of disability* (pp. 765-770). Thousand Oaks, CA: Sage.

117   UNICEF (2008). *Gender and HIV/AIDS: Prevention among young people*. New York, NY: Author.

118   US President's Emergency Plan for AIDS Relief (PEPFAR) (2013). *Addressing gender and HIV/AIDS*. Washington, DC: Author.

119   UNICEF, op. cit.

120   Rohleder, P., Eide, A.H. & Swartz, L. (2014). 'Excluded from a health crisis? HIV and persons with disabilities.' In Mitchell & Karr, op. cit.

121   UNESCO (2012). *Education sector responses to homophobic bullying: Good policy and practice in HIV and health education*. Paris: Author. URL: http://unesdoc.unesco.org/images/0021/002164/216493e.pdf (accessed 20 May 2014).

122   Marshal M.P., Dietz L.J., & Friedman M.S. et al. (2011). 'Suicidality and depression disparities between sexual minority and heterosexual youth: A meta-analytic review.' *Journal of Adolescent Health*, 49, 115-123.

123 See URL: http://www.bullyingstatistics.org/content/gay-bullying-statistics.html (accessed 22 May 2014).

124 Mahidol University, Plan International Thailand, UNESCO Bangkok Office (2014). *Bullying targeting secondary school students who are or are perceived to be transgender or same-sex attracted: Types, prevalence, impact, motivation and preventive measures in 5 provinces of Thailand*. URL: http://www.unescobkk.org/ru/education/news/article/bullying-of-lesbian-gay-bisexual-and-transgender-young-people-in-thailand-risks-and-realities/ (accessed 20 May 2014).

125 Poteat, V.P. & Rivers, I. (2010). 'The use of homophobic language across bullying roles during adolescence.' *Journal of Applied Developmental Psychology*, 31(2), 166–172.

126 Carlson, D. (2013). 'Afterword.' In sj Miller, L.D. Burns & T.S. Johnson (eds). *Generation BULLIED 2.0: Prevention and intervention strategies for our most vulnerable students* (pp. 183–189). New York, NY: Peter Lang Publishing.

127 Eagley, A.H. & Wood, W. (2013). 'The nature-nurture debates: 25 years of challenges in understanding the psychology of gender.' *Perspectives on Psychological Science*, 8, 340–357; and Francis, B. (2006). 'The nature of gender.' In C. Skelton, B. Francis & L. Smulyan (eds), *The Sage handbook of gender and education* (pp. 7–17). London: Sage.

128 See Oswald et al., op. cit.

129 Knapton, S. (2014). 'Being homosexual is only partly due to gay gene, research finds.' *The Telegraph*, 14 February 2014. URL: http://www.telegraph.co.uk/news/science/science-news/10637532/Being-homosexual-is-only-partly-due-to-gay-gene-research-finds.html (accessed 19 May 2016).

130 Ibid.

131 Hines, M. (2011). 'Gender development and the human brain.' *Annual Review of Neuroscience*, 34, 69–88.

132 Ibid.

133 Younger et al., op. cit.

134 Cahill, L. (2006). 'Why sex matters for neuroscience.' *Nature Reviews Neuroscience*, 1–8. Published online 10 May 2006.

135 Witelson, S.F. (1991). 'Neural sexual mosaicism: sexual differentiation of the human temporo-parietal region for functional asymmetry.' *Psychoneuroendrocrinology*, 16, 131–153.

136 Cahill, op. cit., p. 4.

137 Goldstein, J.M., Seidman, L.J., Horton, N.J., Makris, N.K., Kennedy, D.N., Caviness Jr., V.S., Faraone, S.V. & Tsuang, M.T. (2001). 'Normal sexual dimorphism of the adult human brain assessed by in vivo magnetic resonance imaging.' *Cerebral Cortex*, 11, 490 –497.

138 Lenroot, R.K., Gogtay, N., Greenstein, D.K., Wells, E.M., Wallace, G.L., Clasen, L.S., Blumenthal, J.D., Lerch, J., Zigdenbos, A.P., Evans, A.C. Thompson, P.M. & Giedd, J.N. (2007). 'Sexual dimorphism of brain developmental trajectories during childhood and adolescence.' *NeuroImage*, 36(4), 1065–1073.

139 Johnson, S.C., Farnworth, T., Pinkston, J.B., Bigler, E.D., & Blatter, D.D. (1994). 'Corpus callosum surface area across the human adult life span: Effect of age and gender.' *Brain Research Bulletin*, 35, 373–377.

140 Cahill, op. cit.

141 Ibid.

142 Ingalhalikar, M., Smith, A., Parker, D., Satterthwaite, T.D., Elliott, M.A., Ruparel, K., Hakonarson, H., Gur, R.E. & Verma, R. (2013). 'Sex differences in the structural connectome of the human brain.' *Proceedings of the National Academy of Sciences*. Published online before print, 2 December 2013.

143 See URLs: http://www.wired.com/2013/12/getting-in-a-tangle-over-men-and-womens-brain-wiring/ and http://www.neogaf.com/forum/showthread.php?p=92615587 (accessed 20 April 2014).

144 Lenroot et al., op. cit.

145 Ibid.

146 Wood, J.L., Murko, V. & Nopoulos, P. (2008). 'Ventral frontal cortex in children: Morphology, social cognition and femininity/masculinity.' *Social Cognitive and Affective Neuroscience*, 3(2), 168–176.

147 Ibid. and Bao, A.M. & Swaab, D.F. (2010). 'Sex differences in the brain, behavior, and neuropsychiatric disorders.' *Neuroscientist*, 16, 550–565.

148 Cassidy, op. cit.

149 Phipps, P. M. (1982). 'The LD learner is often a boy – Why?' *Academic Therapy*, 17(4), 425–430.

150 Ibid.

151 Wood, W. & Eagly, A.H. (2002). 'A cross-cultural analysis of the behavior of women and men: Implications for the origins of sex differences.' *Psychological Bulletin*, 128, 699–727.

152   Woolf, V. (1989). *A room of one's own.* New York: Harcourt Brace and Co., p. 76.
153   Kane, E.W. (2012). *The gender trap: Parents and the pitfalls of raising boys and girls.* New York, NY: New York University Press.
154   Daniels et al., op. cit.
155   OECD, op. cit.; Oswald et al., op. cit..
156   OECD, op. cit., p. 140.
157   Younger et al., op. cit.
158   Gibb, S.J., Fergusson, D.M. & Horwood, L.J. (2008). 'Gender differences in educational achievement to age 25.' *Australian Journal of Education,* 52(1), 63-80.
159   Oswald et al., op.cit.
160   Martino, W. & Rezai-Rashti, G. (2012). *Gender, race, and the politics of role modeling.* London: Routledge, p. 242.
161   The same arguments apply to race-role modeling.
162   Ibid., p. 241.
163   Mitchell, D. (2014). *What really works in special and inclusive education: Using evidence-based teaching strategies.* Second edition. London: Routledge.
164   Oswald et al., op. cit.
165   Daniels et al., op. cit.
166   Strand, op.cit., p. 165.
167   Ibid, p. 133.
168   Younger et al., op. cit.
169   World Economic Forum (2013). *The global gender gap report 2013.* Geneva: Author.
170   Guiso, L., Monte, F., Sapienza, P. & Zingales, L. (2008). 'Culture, gender and math.' *Science,* 320(5880), 1164-1165.
171   De San Roman, A.G. & Goiricelaya, S. de la R. (2012). *Gender gaps in PISA test scores: The impact of social norms and the mother's transmission of role attitudes.* Bonn: Institute for the Study of Labor. URL: http://ftp.iza.org/dp6338.pdf (accessed 19 May 2016).
172   Stoet, G. & Geary, D. C. (2015). 'Sex differences in academic achievement are not related to political, economic, or social equality.' *Intelligence,* 48, 137-151.
173   Zeng, J., Pang, X., Zhang, L., Medina, A. & Rozelle, S. (2014). 'Gender inequality in education in China: A meta-regression analysis.' *Contemporary Economic Policy,* 32(2), 474-491.
174   Department of Mental Health and Substance Dependence, World Health Organization, op. cit.
175   UN Enable. United Nations (2006). *Some facts about persons with disabilities.* URL: http://www.un.org/disabilities/convention/facts.shtml (accessed 15 March 2016).
176   United Nations (2006). *Convention on the Rights of Persons with Disabilities.* New York: Author.
177   Akota, C.S. & Anum, A. (2012). 'The moderating effects of age and education on gender differences on gender role perceptions.' *Gender and Behaviour,* 10(2), 5022-5043.
178   Human Rights Campaign (2012). *Growing up LGBT in America HRC Youth Survey Report Key Findings.* URL: http://hrc-assets.s3-website-us-east-1.amazonaws.com//files/assets/resources/Growing-Up-LGBT-in-America_Report.pdf (accessed 20 May 2014).
179   Quinlivan, K. & Town, S. (1999). 'Queer pedagogy, educational practice and lesbian and gay youth.' *Qualitative Studies in Education,* 12(5), 509-524, p. 514.
180   Sears, J. (1992). 'Researching the other/searching for self: Qualitative research on (homo)sexuality in education.' *Theory into Practice,* 31(2), 147-156.
181   Pew Research Center, op. cit.
182   Silva, M. & Niquette, M. (2014). 'Gay rights gained in U.S. amid Russian, Ugandan reversals.' *Bloomberg,* 1 March 2014. URL: http://www.bloomberg.com/news/2014-02-27/gay-rights-gained-in-u-s-amid-russian-ugandan-reversals.html (accessed 27 May 2014).
183   Unterhalter, E. (2010). 'Partnership, participation and power for gender equality in education.' Paper prepared for UNGEI E4 Conference: Engendering Empowerment: Education and Equality, Dakar, Senegal, May 2010.
184   Younger et al., op. cit.
185   Buchmann, C., DiPrete, T.A. & McDaniel, A. (2008), 'Gender inequalities in education.' *Annual Review of Sociology,* 34, 319-337.
186   Pahlke, E., Hyde, J.S. & Allison, C.M. (2014).'The effects of single-sex compared with coeducational schooling on students' performance and attitudes: A meta-analysis.' *Psychological Bulletin,* 140(3), 911-920.

187 Ibid.

188 Lavy, V. & Schlosser, A. (2011). 'Mechanism and impacts of gender peer effects at school.' *American Economic Journal: Applied Economics*, 3, 1-33; and Hoxby, C. (2000). *Peer effects in the classroom: Learning from gender and race variation.* NBER Working Paper 7867. Cambridge, MA: National Bureau of Economic Research.

189 Gibb, S.J., Fergusson, D.M. & Horwood, L.J. (2008). 'Effects of single-sex and coeducational schooling on the gender gap in educational achievement.' *Australian Journal of Education*, 52(3), 301-317.

190 Fabes, R.A., Martin, C.L., Hanish, L.D., Galligan, K. & Pahike, E. (2013). 'Gender-segregated schooling: A problem disguised as a solution.' *Educational Policy*, 29(3), 431-447.

191 Eagly & Wood. op. cit.

192 Fisher, S.E. (2006). 'Tangled webs: Tracing the connection between genes and cognition.' *Cognition*, 101, 270-297, p. 270.

193 Eagley & Wood, op. cit.

194 James, J., Ellis, B.J., Schlomer, G.L. & Garber, J. (2012). 'Sex-specific pathways to early puberty, sexual debut, and sexual risk-taking. Tests of an integrated evolutionary-developmental model.' *Developmental Psychology*, 48, 687-702.

195 Bigler, R.S. & Liben, L.S. (2006). 'A developmental intergroup theory of social stereotypes and prejudice.' *Advances in Child Development and Behavior*, 34, 39-89.

196 Eagly & Wood, op. cit.

197 Lickliter, R. & Honeycutt, H. (2003). 'Developmental dynamics: Toward a biologically plausible evolutionary psychology.' *Psychological Bulletin*, 129, 819-835.

198 Darwin, C. (1859). *The origin of species.* London: Murray, p. 399.

199 For an argument that evolutionary psychology provides a cogent meta-theory for psychological science, and how it accounts for many behaviours, including sex differences, see Buss, D.M. & Reeve, H.K. (2003). 'Evolutionary psychology and developmental dynamics: Comment on Lickliter and Honeycutt (2003).' *Psychological Bulletin*, 129(6), 848-853.

200 Pinker, S. (2002). *The blank slate: The modern denial of human nature.* New York: Viking, p. 135.

201 Buss, D.M. & Schmitt, D.P. (2011). 'Evolutionary psychology and feminism.' *Sex Roles.* Published online 26 April 2011.

202 Ibid.

203 Strand, op. cit.

204 US President's Emergency Plan for AIDS Relief (PEPFAR), op. cit.

205 UNICEF, op. cit.

206 World Bank (2012). *World development report 2012: Gender and development.* Washington DC: Author.

207 URL: http://www.un.org/millenniumgoals/gender.shtml (accessed 10 March 2014).

208 UNESCO (2008). 'Education for All by 2015: Will we make it?' *EFA global monitoring report.* Paris: Author.

209 UNESCO (2012). *Global monitoring report.* Paris: Author.

210 United Nations Girls' Education Initiative and Global Partnership for Education (2014). *Accelerating secondary education for girls: Focusing on access and retention.* New York, NY: UNICEF.

211 Cooray & Potrafke, op. cit.; and Schultz, T. (2002). 'Why governments should invest more to educate girls.' *World Development*, 30(2), 207-225.

212 UNICEF, op. cit.

213 United Nations Girls' Education Initiative and UNESCO, op. cit.

214 Ibid.

215 Ibid.

216 Unterhalter, op. cit.

217 Arnot, M., Gray, J., James, M., Ruddock, J. & Duveen, G. (1998). *Recent research on gender and educational performance.* London: Office for Standards in Education.

218 Epstein, D. & Mac an Ghaill, M. (2001). 'Series editors' introduction.' In C. Skelton, *Schooling the boys: Masculinities and primary education* (pp. ix-xi). Buckingham: Open University Press; and Foster, V., Kimmel, M. & Skelton, C. 'What about the boys" An overview of the debates.' In Martino, W. & Meyenn, B. (eds), *What about the boys? Issues of masculinity in schools* (pp. 1-23). Buckingham: Open University Press.

219 World Health Organization (2003). *UN Commission on Human Rights Agenda item 6, Racism, Racial Discrimination, Xenophobia, and all Forms of Discrimination. Statement by the World Health*

Organization, Geneva, 24 March 2003. URL: http://www.who.int/reproductive-health/gender/sexual_health.html (accessed 20 July 2014). See also Forrest, S. (2012). 'Straight talking: Challenges in teaching and learning about sexuality and homophobia in schools'. In M. Cole (ed.), *Education, equality and human rights*. Third edition (pp. 138-158). London: Routledge.

220 Human Rights Campaign, op. cit., See also URLs: Gay, Lesbian & Straight Education Network, Gay-Straight Alliance Network, and Welcoming Schools (accessed 20 May 2014).

221 Solomon, A. (2012). *Far from the tree*. New York: Scribner.

222 Lucassen, M.F.J. & Burford, J. (2015). 'Educating for diversity: an evaluation of a sexuality diversity workshop to address secondary school bullying.' *Australasian Psychiatry*, 23, 544-549.

223 Patterson, C.J. (2005). 'Lesbian and gay parents and their children: Summary of research findings.' In Committee on Lesbian, Gay and Bisexual Concerns (eds), *Lesbian & gay parenting* (pp. 5-20). Washington, DC: American Psychological Association.

224 Kruse, A.-M. (1992). '"We have learnt not just to sit back, twiddle our thumbs and let them all take over." Single-sex settings and the development of pedagogy for girls and for boys in Danish schools.' *Gender and Education*, 4(1-2), 81-103.

225 Rothschild, N. (2012). 'Sweden's new gender-neutral pronoun: *Hen*.' *Slate*, 11 April 2012.

226 World Economic Forum, op. cit.

227 Lauzon, op. cit.

228 Arnot et al., op. cit.

229 Strand, op. cit.

3 Social class/socio-economic status differences

There are many pleasant fictions of the law in constant operation, but there is not one so pleasant or practically humorous as that which supposes every man to be of equal value in its impartial eye, and the benefits of all laws to be equally attainable by all men, without the smallest reference to the furniture of their pockets.
(Charles Dickens, Nicholas Nickleby)

For unto every one that hath shall be given,
and he shall have abundance;
but from him that hath not shall be taken away,
even that which he hath.
(Matthew 25:29)

As a child, I was aware that some people had more money in their pockets than others. My parents were not poor, but nor were they well off – a circumstance that first entered my consciousness when, as a four- or five-year-old, I noticed that two brothers who were my playmates possessed a wide range of sophisticated metal toys that dominated the sandpit in which we played. They also had much more elaborate birthday parties. Both my parents left school at the age of 13, my father to work as a 'bush-man' (i.e., forest worker) and my mother to work on her parents' farm. Neither were enthusiastic readers and there were few books in my home as I grew up. They were, however, ambitious to improve their lot, having lived through the Great Depression and World War II, and eventually bought their own dairy farm. My family's comparative poverty in my early years was one of the reasons that led me as a ten-year-old to seek some additional income through trapping possums, fishing, gardening for the local Presbyterian minister, and painting. It also meant that I chose to go to a teachers college rather than a university since the former paid an allowance that enabled me to enrol in both institutions. I was the first in my extended family to receive tertiary education. Looking back, I became aware that my parents were not so much poor as prudent and were saving to buy a farm. Nevertheless, as a child, and subsequently as a student, teacher and researcher, I have become increasingly aware of socio-economic differences.

Let me give an historical perspective. I am a fourth generation New Zealander, my great-grandparents having arrived here in the late nineteenth century from Great Britain and Germany. I was brought up to believe that they, and others like them, were motivated by a desire to escape from highly stratified, class-conscious societies and were determined to create an egalitarian utopia in the South Pacific. For much of my life, it seemed that this ambition of a *classless society was being met, with various social welfare programmes being introduced into New Zealand, sometimes as world-firsts. However, there is recent evidence that this ambition has been steadily eroded, with the gap between rich and poor increasing, some would argue as a result of the introduction of neo-liberal economic principles in the late 1980s.*

To further set the scene for this chapter, let me quote from a recent OECD document, which asserted that

> An equitable education system can redress the effect of broader social and economic inequalities. In the context of learning, it allows individuals to take full advantage of education and training irrespective of their background.[1]

In this chapter, I address four key questions relating to the OECD's desire for equitable education systems, while also considering Dickens's 'furniture of their pockets' and Matthew's notion of the rich getting richer and the poor getting poorer:

A   What do we mean by social class/socio-economic status (hereafter SES)?
B   How do students from different SES backgrounds differ in educational achievement?
C   What causes SES differences?
D   How should education accommodate to any SES differences?

A What do we mean by social class/socio-economic status?

3.1 Definitions of social class/socio-economic status

Although they are often used interchangeably, the terms 'social class' and 'socio-economic status' (SES) refer to different concepts, with the former referring to one's relatively stable socio-cultural background and the latter referring to one's *current* social and economic situation and, consequently, being more changeable over time.[2] More specifically, SES refers to an individual's or family's economic and social position in relation to others, based on income, education and occupation.[3] Poverty forms a subset of SES and is usually, but not always, highly correlated with SES.

Internationally, for the purposes of the PISA assessments of 15-year-old students, the OECD measures the socio-economic background of students from all participating countries, using an index of economic, social and cultural status. This index is based on students' responses to questions about their family and home background, including their parents' education and occupations and their home possessions, such as a desk to use for studying and the number of books in the home. Using this index, participating students are distributed into deciles of SES background representing a scale of relative disadvantage (bottom decile) through to relative advantage (top decile). It must be noted that the reliance on student reports on family background could lead to a considerable amount of measurement error, which needs to be taken into account when interpreting SES findings from PISA.[4]

Throughout this chapter, I will be referring to SES, except where the material I cite has social class or poverty as the referent. Specifically, my focus will be on children from low-SES families, i.e., the lowest 40%.

3.2 The aim should be to respect and enhance the human rights of children from low-SES backgrounds

As I noted in Chapter 1, consideration of society's responsibilities towards children from low-SES backgrounds must be predicated on the broad concept of human rights. These rights inform us as to what we may, must, and must not do to others and what we may expect of others in their behaviours towards us. Also, as noted, in understanding the basis of human rights, we must consider arguments about which economic framework and which resulting distribution of wealth is morally preferable. Deciding on the principles of 'distributive justice' that should apply is extremely significant for determining how societies respond to differences among its citizens, particularly how they behave towards those who are disadvantaged – and especially towards children. In this connection, I would remind you of the power of Kant's and Rawls's theories, summarized in Chapter 1.

3.3 A Marxist perspective bears consideration

Any discussion of social class necessarily involves mention of the Marxist perspective. According to Mike Cole, 'without social class exploitation, capitalism could not exist'.[5] Capitalism, he argues, is 'underpinned by and depends for its very existence on the exploitation of one class, the working class, by another, the capitalist class'. This argument was originally advanced by Marx and Engels, who pointed out that, according to the economic conditions of the time, class disparities have existed throughout history. Thus, slaves struggled with their owners and serfs struggled with their lords. Only the hunter-gatherers, with their primitive communism, were exceptions. The Marxist interpretation of class assumes that the interests of capitalists and workers are diametrically opposed since benefits to capitalists (profits) occur as costs to workers (their labour). This book is not the place to analyze Marxist thought in detail, nor do I have the skills to do so. Suffice to say that consideration should be given to this perspective if the issues I present in this chapter are to be addressed at a macro, societal, level.

3.4 Failure to improve the performance of students from low-income families has an economic and social cost

In 2012, Barbara Ischinger, Director for Education in the OECD, described how school failure penalizes a child for life. She stated that

> This can be seen in lower initial and lifetime earnings, more difficulties in adapting to rapidly changing knowledge-based economies, and higher risks of unemployment. The same child is also less likely to take up further learning opportunities and less able to participate fully in the civic and democratic aspects of modern societies.[6]

And, further, Ischinger pointed to the social costs of children failing in school:

> Poorly educated people limit economies' capacity to produce, grow and innovate. School failure damages social cohesion and mobility, and imposes additional costs on public budgets to deal with the consequences – higher spending on public health and social

support and greater criminality, among others. For all these reasons, improving equity in education and reducing school failure should be a high priority in all OECD education policy agendas.[7]

According to an analysis carried out by McKinsey Company in the United States, if the gap between low-income students and the rest had been narrowed, the GDP in 2008 would have been $400 billion to $670 billion higher, or 3 to 5% of GDP. Put another way, failing to provide a first-rate education to all students and, by implication, allowing socio-economic achievement gaps to persist, 'imposes on the United States the economic equivalent of a permanent national recession'. But the report also noted that the wide variation in performance among schools and school systems serving similar students 'suggests that the opportunity and output gaps related to today's achievement gap can be substantially closed'.[8]

The Boston Consulting Group made a similar claim with respect to the United Kingdom, arguing that by boosting the educational outcomes of children from less educated families so that their absolute test scores became in line with the UK average – but without reducing the scores of those from the most educated families – the result would result in a £14 billion a year increase in GDP by 2030.[9]

Thus, as well as moral imperatives, there are substantial economic and social reasons for equalizing educational opportunities for those who are disadvantaged by reason of their low-SES backgrounds. In other words, the principle of interest convergence that I outlined in section 1.13 in Chapter 1 applies: by improving the lot of children from low socio-economic status backgrounds, they gain better access to good jobs and have better health outcomes, while society as a whole benefits economically and in terms of social cohesion.

B How do students from different SES backgrounds differ in educational achievement?

3.5 Introduction

Given the almost universal concern with the impact of inequality and poverty on children's education, it is arguable that we have reached a 'tipping point', defined by Malcolm Gladwell in his book of the same name as 'that magic moment when an idea, trend, or social behavior crosses a threshold, tips, and spreads like wildfire' or 'the moment of critical mass, the threshold, the boiling point'.[10] This is particularly the case in the current era of globalization, in which governments are seeking to maximize the productivity of all its citizenry and to reduce welfare dependency, while at the same time pursuing their particular notions of distributive justice.

This chapter outlines how SES is a strong predictor of educational achievement, particularly when it interacts with ethnicity and gender, and how poverty has a negative impact on child development.

3.6 Social class/socio-economic status is a strong predictor of educational achievement

A consistent finding of educational research studies is the effect of the students' social class and SES backgrounds on their educational achievement. For example, across OECD countries, a more socio-economically advantaged student scored 39 points higher in the 2012 PISA mathematics test – the equivalent of nearly one year of schooling – than a less-advantaged student.[11] Writing from a UK perspective in 2010, Emma Perry and Becky Francis concluded that 'Social class remains the strongest predictor of educational achievement in the United Kingdom, where the social class gap for educational achievement is one of the most significant in the developed world.'[12]

An Australian report has noted that schools that enrol mainly children from low income and poorly educated families record reading scores that place the average child at about two years behind the average child in a school with mainly high SES students. This gap tends to grow over stages of schooling.[13] Similar patterns emerge elsewhere. For example, across all OECD countries, almost one of every five students does not reach a basic minimum level of skills to function in today's societies. Students from low SES backgrounds are twice as likely to be low performers, implying that personal or social circumstances are obstacles to achieving their educational potential.[14] Students from low SES backgrounds in Sweden are 2.61 times more likely to be low performers than their peers with high SES, as reflected in PISA 2009 results, which is above the OECD average of 2.37 times. Students whose parents have low educational attainment have twice as high a risk of low performance (2.10 times). Disadvantaged schools tend to reinforce students' SES inequalities since they do not mitigate the negative impact of the students' disadvantaged background on educational attainment. Northern European and Asian countries tend to have less variance in reading performance explained by socio-economic background, whereas in countries with highly selective systems (like Austria, Belgium, Germany and Hungary) about 20% is explained by SES background.[15] Also, in countries with comprehensive educational systems, most of the SES effects on achievement are typically found *within* schools, with only weak effects *between* schools. Conversely, in countries with selective or socially segregated educational systems, the reverse applies.

Finland is an example of a comprehensive system. Its low SES variance has been explained by the relative homogeneity of the Finnish society, but also by its success in implementing the equity goals of the basic school.[16] Between-school variances are also very small in the other Nordic countries: Iceland, Norway and Sweden.[17] These countries have in common an adherence to the principle of equality of educational opportunity, the task of the comprehensive school being to provide all children with equal opportunities for learning regardless of the school they attend, or their background or circumstance.

In his 2009 book, *Visible Learning*, John Hattie examined the results of four meta-analyses, involving 499 studies, on the contributions of SES on student achievement.[18] He found an effect size of 0.57, which he described as 'a notable influence'. According to one of the meta-analyses Hattie examined, the various sub-components of SES have similar influences.[19] For example, the effect size between student achievement and parental education was 0.60, parental occupation was 0.56 and parental income was 0.58. The same meta-analysis noted that there was little variability in the relation between SES and various types of achievement, with mathematics yielding an effect size of 0.70, verbal subjects 0.64 and science 0.54.

There is strong evidence to suggest that the SES gaps I have described above are worsening. In the United States, for example, Stanford University researcher Sean Reardon found that the achievement gap between high- and low-income families is roughly 30–40 % larger among children born in 2001 than among those born 25 years earlier.[20] In fact, it appears that the income achievement gap has been growing since around the 1960s. In the United States, according to Reardon, family income is now nearly as strong as parental education in predicting children's achievement. Reardon also noted that the income achievement gap (defined as the average achievement difference between a child from a family at the 90th percentile of the family income distribution and a child from a family at the 10th percentile) is now nearly twice as large as the black-white achievement gap. In the 1960s, in contrast, the black-white gap was one and a half to two times as large as the income gap. In other US research, reported by Greg Duncan and Katherine Magnuson, students in the bottom quintile of family SES score more than a standard deviation below those in the top quintile on stand-ardized tests of mathematics and reading when they enter kindergarten.[21] Moreover, this gap does not appear to grow (or narrow) appreciably as children progress through school.

However, it must be noted that some 6% of students across OECD countries – nearly one million students – are 'resilient', meaning that, in some countries, they beat the SES odds against them and exceed expectations, when compared with students in other countries. For example, in Hong Kong–China, Macao–China, Shanghai–China, Singapore and Vietnam, some 13% or more of low-SES students perform among the top 25% of students across all par-ticipating countries and economies. This ability of some children from low-SES backgrounds to 'succeed against the odds' has also been reported in England, where more than 20% of such children achieved benchmark levels of attainment at the end of statutory schooling and 13% proceeded on to higher education.[22] Future research could well seek to find reasons for the apparent resilience of such children. What are the factors in their environments or their personal attributes that could explain these findings? In the remainder of this chapter, I hope to unpack possible explanations.

Before doing so, a word of caution might be in order. According to Gregory Miller and his col-leagues, there is evidence that upward mobility in the United States may carry health risks.[23] In their study of resilient African American children (i.e., those who achieve positive outcomes in adverse circumstances), they found that academic success was not accompanied by improved health outcomes. In fact, the reverse was true: these students at 19 were more obese, had higher blood pressure and produced more stress hormones than their less resilient peers. Miller and his colleagues attributed these findings to the effects of internal pressures to suc-ceed, social isolation from peers, and their encountering of racism and discrimination. To the researchers these findings suggested the need for health education, screenings and checkups, as well as stress management programmes.

3.7   *SES interacts with ethnicity and gender to influence achievement*

Hattie's meta-analyses, referred to above, took SES as the single variable. It is important to recognize that SES interacts with gender and ethnicity as determinants of educational achievement. As I noted in Chapter 2, this point about intersectionality is emphasized by UK author, Steve Strand, who analyzed the achievement levels of over 15,000 students aged 11, 14 and 16.[24] Among low SES boys, White British and Black Caribbean boys were jointly the lowest scoring groups. For low SES girls, Black Caribbean girls joined other minority groups in scoring significantly higher than White British girls. As Strand said, 'there is something about the particular combination of ethnicity, SES and gender that is uniquely related to attainment'.

3.8 Poverty has a negative impact on child development

The deleterious effects of poverty on child development have been well established in research, with poverty identified as being among the most powerful risk factors for development.[25] For example, children exposed to poverty have poorer cognitive outcomes and they are at higher risk for antisocial behaviours and mental disorders.[26]

A recent US study carried out at the Washington University School of Medicine in St Louis showed that poverty in early childhood has a negative impact on brain development at school age.[27] Children were assessed annually for 3 to 6 years, during which they were evaluated on psychosocial, behavioural and other developmental dimensions. There were two major findings: first, poverty was shown to be associated with smaller white and cortical grey matter and hippocampal and amygdala volumes, and, second, the effects of poverty on hippocampal volume were mediated by caregiving support/hostility, as well as stressful life events. These brain regions, involved in memory, stress regulation and emotion processing, are known to be sensitive to environmental stimuli. The authors noted that poverty is strongly associated with a number of risk factors implicated in poor developmental outcomes, such as unsupportive parenting, poor nutrition and education, lack of caregiver education, and high levels of traumatic and stressful life events. This study is consistent with other research that found a smaller hippocampus and amygdala in 5- to 17-year-old children living in poverty.[28] Another study similarly found that lower SES was associated with smaller hippocampal grey matter volumes in a small sample of healthy 10-year-old children.[29]

These findings accentuate the importance of providing children from low-SES backgrounds with appropriate stimulation and acceptable levels of stress, particularly in their early development when they are most vulnerable to adverse environmental conditions.

C What causes social class/socio-economic status differences?

3.9 Introduction

The social class/SES differences outlined above, which impact on educational achievement, arise from a complex interaction among societal, family and school factors, which overlap with each other. In Chapter 1, section 1.10, I presented a comprehensive, ecological, 'wraparound' model for portraying how they impinge on children (see Figure 3.1).

These factors will be addressed in turn, but before doing so, I should like to acknowledge the similarity between my model and the arguments recently put forward in England by Alan Dyson and his colleagues at the University of Manchester, in association with Save the Children,[30] in their advocacy of 'children's zones'. Their work has been informed, in turn, by the Harlem Children's Zone in the United States.[31] Briefly, children's zones include the following characteristics:

- a 'doubly holistic' approach to improving outcomes and enhancing life chances by working with children and young people from birth to adulthood and across all aspects of their lives;

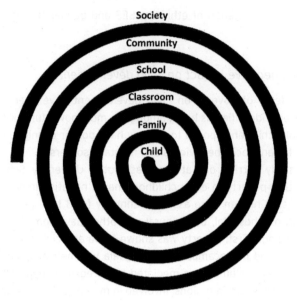

Figure 3.1 A comprehensive ecological model

- a focus on a geographic area where there is a common set of issues facing children and young people;
- involvement of a range of partners, with a strategy for joint action to be sustained over time;
- recognition that while stand-alone, single-issue interventions have a place, they suffer from serious limitations; and
- rejection of the notion that socio-economic disadvantage alone accounts for poor out-comes, but, instead, that there is a complex set of mediating factors linking the two, which should be addressed as a whole.

I Societal factors

SES has its origins in the broad features of a society, most notably its economy and its cultural values. In this section, I will examine two societal factors: income inequality and cultural capital.

3.10 Income inequality

One of the leading scholars of the relationship between poverty and educational achievement is the US academic, David Berliner. In a recent paper, he addressed the question of why so many school reform efforts have produced so little improvement in American schools.[32] The answer, he asserted, is that the sources of America's educational problems lie outside school and primarily result from income inequality. In support of this view, Berliner cited Richard Wilkinson and Kate Pickett's influential 2010 book, *The Spirit Level,* which makes it clear that the bigger the income gap in a nation or a state, the greater the number and degree of social problems encountered, including poor educational achievement.[33] This book contains analyses of inequality in relation to 29 health and social problems in 23 of the richest countries. It shows that problems that tend to be more common lower down the social ladder – such as violence, drug abuse and infant mortality – are worse in more unequal societies. Wilkinson and Pickett explained this by arguing that inequalities erode the cohesion of a society, the degree to which individual citizens are involved in their society, the strength of the social networks within it, and the degree of trust and empathy between citizens. Further, as individuals internalize inequality, their psyches becoming profoundly affected by it, and that in turn affects their physical as well as their mental health, leading to attitudes and behaviours that appear as a variety of social and health problems.[34] When these problems become widespread and those affected see no hope for the future, there is a risk, as I outlined in section 1.12 in Chapter 1, that centrifugal forces become stronger than centripetal forces, thus undermining the authority of the state.

In an earlier paper, Berliner argued that the American system of public education works extremely well for those living in middle class communities, attending middle class schools. He noted that the poorest students economically are also the poorest students in international assessments of achievement. Quite simply, he said, 'Money matters'. Berliner further asserted that 'Failing schools are not filled with lazy students, uncaring parents, and incompetent teachers'. Instead, they are 'filled with children from families who are in economic and social crises; located in neighborhoods of great poverty, crime, and drug use; staffed by the least prepared and the newest teachers, and greatly under-funded compared to suburban schools'.[35] He went on to argue that the design of better economic and social policies, such as providing families with living wages, can do more to improve US schools than continued work on educational policy independent of such concerns. Berliner's sentiments are echoed by other writers, as summarized by Mel Ainscow and his colleagues in the United Kingdom.[36]

The relationship between economic policies and poverty has been dramatically demonstrated by the French leftist economist Thomas Piketty who, in a recent book, *Capital in the Twenty-first Century*, purported to show that capitalism produces inexorably widening inequality. In his analysis of data from twenty countries, ranging as far back as the eighteenth century, Piketty concluded that the main driver of inequality is the tendency of returns on capital to exceed the rate of economic growth – and incomes.[37] He pointed out that capital is very unequally distributed. For example, in the United States, the top 10% own about 70% of all the capital, half of that belonging to the top 1%; the next 40% – who comprise the 'middle class' – own about a quarter of the total (much of that in the form of housing), and the remaining half of the population owns next to nothing, about 5% of total wealth. He noted that the typical European country is a little more egalitarian, with the top 1% owning 25% of the total capital, and the middle class 35%.

A recent report on economic inequality in the United Kingdom noted that the richest 10% of the population were more that 100 times as wealthy as the poorest 10%,[38] while another report found that 17% of all UK children lived in households below the poverty line.[39] Yet another UK report, this one by the Social Mobility and Child Poverty Commission, noted the growing social divide by income.[40] In terms of earnings, the income share of the top 10% had increased from 28% in 1979 to 39% in 2015 and the income share of the top 1% had more than doubled from 6% to 13% over the same time period.

As long as the rate of return exceeds the rate of economic growth, said Piketty, the income and wealth of the rich will grow faster than the typical income from work.[41] He concluded that if the ownership of wealth becomes even more concentrated during the rest of the twenty-first century, the outlook is pretty bleak unless one has a taste for oligarchy.[42] Capitalism, he argued, is not a tide that lifts all boats. At the heart of his book is the notion that inequality is 'potentially threatening to democratic societies and to the values of social justice on which they are based'. How to arrest this trend? In a nutshell, Piketty's strong preference is for an annual progressive tax on wealth.

Similar arguments were put forward by Lawrence Summers (former US Secretary of the Treasury) and Ed Balls (former Shadow Chancellor of the Exchequer in the British Parliament), in their capacity as co-chairs of an international Inclusive Prosperity Commission. Like Piketty, they argued that

> When democratic governments and market systems cannot deliver such prosperity to their citizens, the result is political alienation, a loss of social trust, and increasing conflict across the lines of race, class and ethnicity. Inclusive prosperity nurtures tolerance, harmony, social generosity, optimism, and international cooperation. And these are essential for democracy itself.[43]

Perhaps the most objective way of comparing the distribution of incomes in different countries is to refer to the work of Italian statistician Corrado Gini. In 1921, he introduced what is, unsurprisingly, known as the *Gini Coefficient*. This index quantifies the extent to which a country's income is equitably distributed, with 0 = total equality and 1 = total inequality. Table 3.1 presents a representative set of Gini Coefficients for 32 out of 141 countries[44]:

Recent data from the World Bank,[45] the international organization charged with reducing poverty, show that the proportion of people living on less than $US1.25 a day fell from 43.1% in 1990 to 20.6% in 2010 (see Table 3.2). Between 2005 and 2008, both the poverty rate and the number of people living in extreme poverty fell in all six developing country regions, the first time that had happened. Encouragingly, the global target of the Millennium Development Goals of halving world poverty was reached five years early. However, pockets of extreme poverty continue to exist, in countries such as the Congo Democratic Republic, where 87.7% of the population live on $US1.25 or less a day, Liberia (83.8%) and Madagascar (81.3%).

According to a recent report by The EFA Global Monitoring Report Team, education is a key way of helping individuals escape poverty and of preventing poverty from being passed down through the generations.[46] Its calculations showed that if all students in low-income countries left school with basic reading skills, 171 million people could be lifted out of poverty, which would be equivalent to a 12% cut in world poverty. Further, a one-year increase in the average educational attainment of a country's population would increase annual per capita GDP growth from 2% to 2.5%.[47]

The interaction of poverty, economics, education and disaffection is nowhere better illustrated than in northern Nigeria. In a recent article in the *Los Angeles Times*, a graphic description focused on groups of young boys, known as the *almajiri*, who have flooded the streets of Kano in recent years, trying to survive through begging, hawking and criminal pursuits.[48] Many of these children have been dislocated as a result of the displacement of hitherto thriving textile industries by cheap Chinese imports and by an erratic electrical system,

Table 3.1 Gini Coefficients in selected countries

OECD countries

Country	Gini	Rank
Australia	0.303	120
Canada	0.321	105
Denmark	0.248	137
Finland	0.268	131
France	0.306	117
Germany	0.270	130
Japan	0.376	76
Netherlands	0.309	115
New Zealand	0.362	86
Norway	0.250	135
Sweden	0.230	141 (most equal)
Switzerland	0.287	123
United Kingdom	0.323	104
United States	0.450	41

Non-OECD countries

Country	Gini	Rank
Argentina	0.458	36
Bangladesh	0.321	106
Botswana	0.630	3
Cambodia	0.379	73
Chile	0.521	14
China	0.473	27
Egypt	0.308	116
Guatemala	0.551	11
Hong Kong	0.537	12
India	0.368	80
Lithuania	0.355	88
Lesotho	0.632	1 (least equal)
Malaysia	0.462	33
Mexico	0.483	25
Russia	0.420	50
Singapore	0.463	32
Slovenia	0.237	140
South Africa	0.631	2

Table 3.2 Extreme poverty, by region (% of population living on $US1.25 or less per day)

Region	1990	2010
East Asia/Pacific	56.2	12.5
Europe/Central Asia	1.9	0.7
Latin America/Caribbean	12.2	5.5
Middle East/North Africa	5.8	2.4
South Asia	53.8	31.0
Sub-Sahara Africa	56.5	48.5
Global	43.1	20.6

while others have been affected by the collapse of fishing and agriculture sectors, the former through the shrinkage of Lake Chad caused by climate change and by overuse. Even if their parents could afford to send them to school, there is a reluctance to do so for secular education is associated with earlier British colonial rule and, more recently, with a corrupt western-educated elite. The result is that only 28% of children in northern Nigeria attend school, and there is a literacy rate of only 32%, compared with the national average of 68%. The situation often leads parents to enrol their children in rudimentary Islamic education centres run by clerics. Further, it sometimes leads the children to being enticed or coerced into the terrorist group, Boko Haram (which means 'Western education is sinful').

3.11 Mismatch of cultural and social capital

As I pointed out in section 1.21 in Chapter 1, children who come from class, gender, cultural and religious backgrounds that differ from the prevailing norms and expectations of schools can be seriously disadvantaged. I drew upon two notions: cultural capital and social capital.

First, let me remind you of Pierre Bourdieu's consideration of 'cultural capital'. He argued that those who inherit the cultural capital of the education system, which is generally that of the middle class, begin their schooling with an advantage they are likely to maintain.[49] In other words, the culture of the home and the school correspond, while for other children there may be a disjunction of cultures. These family background factors may be exacerbated by teachers who 'valorize middle-class rather than working-class cultural capital',[50] and who perceive the latter as deficient and their children thus deserving of lower expectations. Certain forms of cultural capital are valued over others, and can help or hinder one's social mobility just as much as financial capital. It can be a major source of social inequality. Teachers, too, have absorbed the cultural capital of their own backgrounds and may not understand or be sympathetic to those of their students who come to school with different cultural capital. As with other groups who hold positions of power in society, such as employers, teachers epitomize what is culturally valued and may consciously or unconciously act to 'reaffirm and reproduce social class and privilege by valuing the preferences, behaviors, and attitudes of the dominant class over those of the non-dominant groups'.[51] In other words, there is often a disconnect between the cultural capital valued by schools and the cultural capital valued by many in their communities. This can result in lower expectations and poorer achievement among those who feel marginalized in their schools. For example, in situations where children are placed in streams, these social class differences are often reflected in low SES students being disproportionately represented in low ability streams.[52]

Second, you will recall that I outlined Robert Putnam's notion of social capital. In his recent book, *Our Kids: The American Dream in Crisis*, Putnam claimed that the most important divide in America today is class, not race.[53] He pointed to the growing gulf between how the rich and the poor raise their children in the United States. For example, in 2007 fewer than 10% of all births to female graduates were outside marriage, compared with 65% of those with just a high school education. He also observed that educated parents engage in Socratic dialogue with their children, helping them to make up their own minds about right and wrong, true and false. Further, professional families have much wider circles of friends, extending beyond their immediate neighbourhood.

II Family factors

SES is highly correlated with what takes place in family environments, most notably the degree of stimulation afforded by families and nutrition levels.

3.12 Many low-SES families provide un-stimulating environments

While I recognize that I may be approaching this topic with a middle-class cultural capital perspective, I believe that there is universal agreement as to what constitutes an environment that optimizes cognitive and linguistic development in children. Equally, there is widespread agreement that many children from low-SES backgrounds are brought up in less than optimal developmental environments. For example, the United Kingdom's National Equality Panel found that in some disadvantaged areas up to 50% of children begin their primary education without the necessary language and communication skills.[54] A similar finding was reported by the Social Mobility and Child Poverty Commission who noted that less than half of the poorest children in England are ready for school by the age of five, compared with almost two-thirds of other children.[55] The Commission recommended that steps be taken to halve this gap by 2025 and, as part of this objective, developing a national definition of school readiness.

It has been estimated that a young child in a low-SES home hears less than one-third the number of words than in a professional home.[56] For example, in an influential study, University of Kansas researchers, Betty Hart and Todd Risley, found that the average child on welfare had half as much experience of words (616 per hour) as the average working-class child (1,251 per hour) and less than one-third that of the average child in a professional family (2,153 words per hour).[57] In the first four years of life, this would amount to an average child in a professional family experiencing almost 45 million words, an average child in a working-class family 26 million words, and an average child in a welfare family 13 million words. Other home factors include: differential access to books, broadband Internet and private tutoring;[58] low aspirations for children's achievement;[59] parents' inadequate provision of role models for their children;[60] parents' low involvement in school activities;[61] and parents' lack of knowledge of how to make their way around the educational system and negotiate with teachers and principals.[62]

In my very first academic paper, which was published in 1970, I attempted to answer the question of how SES manifests itself so as to have an influence on student achievement?[63] I noted that, in New Zealand, a significant number of children begin their school careers with learning and motivational problems arising from their contacts with environments characterized by a narrow range of stimuli and experiences and by restricted linguistic patterns. I noted the observation of English sociologist, Basil Bernstein, that when such children enter school they are faced with 'symbolic and social change', whereas their advantaged age-mates face 'symbolic and social development'.[64] I believe this to be still the case.

A recent article in *The Economist* attributes the differences between children from high- and low-SES families at least in part to 'assortative mating', a process in which the highly educated increasingly marry each other.[65] For example, in 1960 25% of men with university degrees married women with degrees, whereas in 2005, 48% did. People brought together by their education and values will deem such things important and will transfer them to their children both deliberately and by example. The result, according to *The Economist*, is 'an hereditary meritocracy'.

3.13 Many low-SES families provide inadequate meals

According to a recent review, a large body of epidemiologic data shows that diet quality follows a socio-economic gradient.[66] Whereas higher-quality diets are associated with greater affluence, persons of lower SES preferentially consume energy-dense diets that are nutrient-poor. For example, whole grains, lean meats, fish, low-fat dairy products and fresh vegetables and fruit are more likely to be consumed by groups of higher SES. In contrast, the consumption of refined grains and added fats has been associated with lower SES. New Zealand data obtained in 2007 found that around 12% of New Zealand children did not eat breakfast at home every day, and these children were significantly more likely to be Māori, Pasifika and from low-SES areas.[67] Moreover, they were also more likely to consume fizzy drink and fast food of limited nutritional value. Another New Zealand study found that 25% of children in 'deciles' 1 and 2 schools come to school with some degree of food need. [68]

3.14 Low-SES children are at greater risk for obesity

Obesity also seems to follow a socio-economic gradient. For example, a European study across 13 countries found that over 20% of the obesity found among men in Europe, and over 40% of the obesity found in women, was attributable to inequalities in SES. Obesity and overweight among children was also associated with the SES of their parents, especially their mothers. Furthermore, other cross-country comparisons show the prevalence of childhood overweight is linked to a country's degree of income inequality or relative poverty.[69] For example, US surveys have shown that obesity rates increased by 10% for all US children 10- to 17-years old between 2003 and 2007, but by 23% during the same period for low-income children.[70] This national study of more than 40,000 children also found that, in 2007, children from lower-income households were more than twice as likely to be obese than children from higher-income households. In another US study, rates of severe obesity were approximately 1.7 times higher among poor children and adolescents in a nationally representative sample of more than 12,000 children aged 2 to 19 years.[71]

III School and classroom factors

The societal and family disadvantages experienced by low-SES students can be exacerbated at the school level when there is a high proportion of such students enrolled, limited access to funds, widespread use of ability grouping, and limited Internet access.

3.15 Disadvantaged schools may exacerbate the negative effects of low SES

Children from low-SES family backgrounds may be in a minority (or be completely absent) in some schools, while in others they may constitute a majority, even an overwhelming one. The latter could be said to be functioning as quasi-special schools. There is considerable evidence that low-SES students' achievement is typically lower in schools where most of the students come from similar backgrounds, compared with the same students' achievement if they were to receive their education in more mixed SES school environments.[72] For example, in the Third International Mathematics and Science test, students from disadvantaged homes scored 50 points higher if they attended schools with few low-SES students, compared with similar students attending schools with predominantly low-SES students.[73] These results were echoed in an Australian study of 2003 PISA results carried out by Laura Perry and Andrew McConney.[74]

They found clear evidence that increases in the mean SES of a school were associated with consistent increases in students' academic achievement, regardless of their individual SES. For example, for the typical student in the first SES quintile, being part of a high-SES school group versus a low-SES school group was associated with a difference of about 57 points (0.6 of a standard deviation) in reading, with similar results for mathematics and science. Douglas Willms has further confirmed this relationship between schools' SES and student achievement.[75] He found that students in countries with low levels of 'horizontal segregation' (i.e., unequal distribution of students with differing SES) have the highest success rates, the correlation being −0.42.

In commenting on patterns such as these, the OECD had this to say:

> disadvantaged schools tend to reinforce students' socio-economic inequalities. This represents a double handicap for disadvantaged students, since schools do not mitigate the negative impact of the students' disadvantaged background and on the contrary amplify its negative effect on their performance.[76]

Why should this be the case? Perry and McConney attributed their findings in part, at least, to the better resourcing of high-SES schools and a more academically demanding curriculum. But there are other possible explanations, one of which has to do with the influence of school peers on student educational outcomes. For example, after reviewing several theories to account for this influence, US scholar, Douglas Harris, advanced a new hybrid theory – 'group-based contagion' – as being consistent with the evidence.[77] Briefly, he argued that students follow the leads of their classmates – especially those who belong to the same group, and that peers influence one another's beliefs and values. In addition, peers indirectly influence one another by affecting the school resources to which they have access, especially the qualifications of their teachers. (This latter point may be truer of the United States than other countries where resources are distributed more equitably.) Harris went on to suggest that if his theory is correct, it adds weight to the educational desirability of desegregation – a point I will return to in Chapter 4.

As well as the within-school factors I have just described, contextual factors also contribute to the low achievement of low-SES students. Thus, the OECD has noted that schools with higher proportions of disadvantaged students are at greater odds of suffering from a myriad of social and economic problems that can inhibit students' learning: higher levels of unemployment and lower income in their neighbourhoods, higher proportions of single-parent families, more health problems, higher crime rates and migration of better-qualified youth.

Even though there is clear evidence that disadvantaged schools may exacerbate the negative effects of low-SES, it is important to note that many schools located in disadvantaged neighbourhoods around the world do manage to provide high quality education by introducing targeted support strategies. Some of these will be reviewed later in this chapter.

3.16 Schools serving low-SES communities have less capacity for fundraising

Data from Canada show that family income has a powerful influence on children's chances for success.[78] For example, in Ontario's publicly funded schools, those with the highest average family income had an advantage when it comes to fundraising for enrichment and enhanced resources, raising five times as much as schools with the lowest family income. This puts children in lower-income schools at a double disadvantage with less access to learning-enhancing resources both at home and at school.

3.17 Ability grouping disadvantages low-SES students

Many educational jurisdictions practise various versions of selection/setting/tracking/grouping of students according to their presumed ability. Thus, most secondary schools in the United Kingdom employ some form of ability grouping, usually setting, for at least some subjects.[79] Similarly, in the United States, tracking in various forms has been among the predominant organizing practices in public schools for the last century.[80]

There is a high risk that such practices do not result in improved achievement of low-SES students and may even have a deleterious effect on them. Such students are often placed in lower streams or groups, thus constituting a form of de facto segregation. The OECD, for example, notes that early student selection has a negative impact on students assigned to lower tracks and exacerbates inequities, without raising average performance.[81]

A recent review concluded that 'much of the available evidence suggests that the effects of ability-grouping on pupil attainment is limited and no firm conclusions can be drawn from its use'.[82] This conclusion reflects the results of an earlier meta-analysis that reported on the impact on learners' achievement of within-class ability grouping and between-class ability grouping.[83] This showed a negligible overall effect size of less than 0.10, with a range of −0.03 to 0.22. A similar result was reported by John Hattie, whose meta-analysis yielded an effect size of 0.21 for ability grouping's impact on student achievement.[84] In other words, these two reviews showed that ability grouping had little or no significant impact on overall student achievement. A recent Dutch review of the literature, however, differentiated between its impact on high- and low-achieving learners.[85] It concluded that although the mean results of studies trended towards showing higher achievement in ability groups than in mixed-ability groups, this was mainly due to the fact that high-achieving students benefited more than low-achieving students. The authors cited several studies where low-achieving learners performed more poorly in between-class ability groups than in mixed-ability groups. Also of relevance is an early UK study that reported that in comprehensive schools with mixed ability grouping practices, a higher proportion of lower attaining students were entered for national examinations.[86]

Another drawback of ability grouping is that although the importance of students being able to move sets has been stressed in the United Kingdom, in practice there is very little movement, even when teachers become aware that students are wrongly allocated.[87] The same authors reported that among secondary school students studying mathematics in ability-grouped sets, 83% either wanted to return to mixed ability sets or to change their set. Their own research with over 8,000 students in 45 secondary schools also showed that a high proportion of them were unhappy with their set or class placement. For example, in mathematics, where there was the highest level of ability grouping, 38% were unhappy with their set or class placement; unsurprisingly, more students in the bottom set (62%) wished to change. Significantly, their reasons for wanting to change were more related to learning than status; for many of them they felt there was a mismatch between the work set and what they perceived was appropriate.

In a similar vein, US research points to evidence that, compared with 'high-track' classes, 'low-track' classes are much more likely to receive course content that focuses on below-grade level knowledge and skills.[88] This finding has recently been confirmed in an important international study reported by William Schmidt and his colleagues. They found that 'opportunity to learn' (OTL) was significantly related to SES and could well explain SES differences student outcomes – in this case mathematics.[89] The concept of OTL rests on the fairly obvious assumption that students' ability to learn a subject depends on whether and for how long they are exposed to it in school. The researchers drew upon PISA data on students' mathematics achievement, their SES, and the intensity of exposure to mathematics, as reported by the students (i.e., their OTL). In brief, Schmidt et al. found that, overall, 37% of the total SES inequalities were related to OTS inequalities.[90] (In the United States, this percentage was close to 50%). In all 62 PISA education systems, SES was significantly related to OTL, with the strongest relationship in Korea, Netherlands and Japan and the smallest in Sweden, Iceland and Estonia. In other words, there is strong evidence that students from low-SES backgrounds have less or weaker exposure to the mathematics curriculum than those from higher-SES backgrounds. Thus, OTL seems to be an important mediator for the effects of SES on achievement. These findings strongly suggest that 'any serious efforts to reduce educational inequalities must address unequal content coverage within schools'.[91]

3.18 Lack of Internet access disadvantages many low-SES students

In the modern era, the ability to access and create new knowledge using information and communication technologies is critical to formal and informal learning, as well as for social inclusion. According to UNESCO, Media and Information Literacy (MIL) is a prerequisite for individuals, communities and nations to enjoy and exercise their universal human rights and fundamental freedoms, as articulated in the Universal Declaration of Human Rights. MIL is equally important for the existence of good governance, accountability and transparency in any society, and for tackling poverty, economic and societal development.[92] Also, as I mentioned in Chapter 1, disruptive technology is leading to some jobs disappearing and others undergoing significant transformations. Students leaving school with no or low qualifications face a dim future.

Evidence points to disparities in ownership and Internet access across SES groups around the world. According to a recent US survey,[93] for example, low-income teens were noticeably less likely to own computers and use the Internet than high-income teens. In overall Internet use, youth aged 12-17 who were living in lower-income and lower-education households were somewhat less likely to use the Internet in any capacity – mobile or wired. (However, those who fall into lower SES groups were just as likely, and in some cases more likely, than those living in higher income and more highly educated households to use their cell phone as a primary point of access.) Teachers in high-poverty US schools were strikingly more likely than those in more affluent schools to say that the 'lack of resources or access to digital technologies among students' was a challenge in their classrooms (56% vs. 21%). Even more significantly, only 3% of teachers in high-poverty schools agreed that 'students have the digital tools they need to effectively complete assignments while at home', compared with 52% of teachers in more affluent schools.

Social inequalities in access to the Internet are present, too, in Europe, with better-off, more educated households more likely to provide their children with Internet access. A study found that in 2008, 76% of highly educated parents claimed their child used the Internet compared with 61% from the lowest educational group. Furthermore, low-SES children were more exposed to risk online, this being compounded by them being least likely to have parents who can support them in these situations, thus perpetuating cycles of disadvantage.[94]

D How should education accommodate to any SES differences?

3.19 Introduction

In this section I will present strategies that have been shown to be effective in improving the educational outcomes of low SES students. As outlined in the previous sections, I will be drawing upon empirical research, as well as best practices identified by such bodies as the OECD, Ofsted in the United Kingdom and the Education Review Office in New Zealand.

As in the previous section, the strategies are broadly grouped into three overlapping levels:

1   society and system-level accommodations, with a particular focus on international models for allocating educational resources with loadings for SES;
2   school-level accommodations; and
3   classroom-level accommodations.

Some important caveats

Before addressing educational approaches to addressing equity challenges posed by students from low SES backgrounds, it is necessary to take into account five caveats:

- Students from similar SES backgrounds are heterogeneous: as I noted in section 3.6, some are resilient.
- Schools serving low-SES communities are heterogeneous: as I noted in section 3.6, some succeed against the odds.
- Most educational programmes that are beneficial for students from low-SES backgrounds are beneficial for all students.
- SES interacts with ethnicity and gender as determinants of educational achievement.
- Some students from high-SES backgrounds may have educational needs similar to those from low-SES backgrounds.

I Society and system-level accommodations

This level of analysis includes the societal component of my ecological model, described in section 1.10 of Chapter 1. In particular, it considers the role of government in setting macro-economic and social priorities, as well as developing policies to mitigate the effects of low SES upon students from those backgrounds. Depending on the jurisdiction, system-level accommodations targeting low-SES students may be at the national, regional or district levels or some mix of all three.

In this section, I will pay particular attention to funding models, but also to such topics as reducing poverty, attracting and retaining high quality teachers, full service schools, inter-agency partnerships, managing school choice, social promotion policies, and early intervention.

3.20 Take steps to reduce poverty

As I noted in section 3.10, David Berliner claims that the sources of America's educational problems lie outside school and primarily result from income inequality. Further, he argues that the design of better economic and social policies, such as providing families with living wages, can do more to improve US schools than continued work on educational policy independent of such concerns. In the same section, I also noted Thomas Piketty's strong preference for an annual progressive tax on wealth to reduce the disparities in income.

Governments possess a range of instruments for reducing poverty. At the broadest level, they can enact policies to expand growth in their economies, relying on the indirect, 'trickle-down' effect of putting more money into the pockets of the poorer members of society, by putting more money in pockets of the richer members of society who, in turn, would be expected to invest in plant, equipment and labour. This approach has been criticized by Piketty, among others, on the grounds that it is often accompanied by growing income inequality. New OECD research shows that when income inequality rises, economic growth falls, one reason being that poorer members of society are less able to invest in their education.[95]

More directly, governments can adjust taxation rates, welfare benefits, housing subsidies, parental leave, child support arrangements, the costs of childcare and health care and so on, to mitigate the worst impacts of poverty.[96] Attention should be paid, too, to income levels. For example, a recent report from the United Kingdom's Social Mobility and Child Poverty Commission recommended that the government should set a clear objective for the country to become 'a Living Wage country' by 2025, having noted that 1.5 million children were in poverty because their working parents did not earn enough to secure a basic standard of living.[97] It is important to note that, according to a recent OECD analysis, redistribution *per se* does not lower economic growth, while at the same time recognizing that redistribution policies that are poorly targeted and do not focus on the most effective tools can lead to a waste of resources and generate inefficiencies.[98]

Some writers express caution in expecting too much from attempts to mitigate poverty. Looking at social class through an evolutionary lens, Daniel Nettle, from the University of Newcastle in the United Kingdom, is one such writer.[99] He observed that differences in behaviour between members of different social classes in Britain are not only very substantial, but they have failed to diminish despite decades of increases in the standard of living. He posed the question, Why should these differences persist, and why do they take the form that they do?

In taking an evolutionary approach to social class differences, Nettle began by assuming that individuals of different SES backgrounds experience different ecologies. He then argued that by examining the features of these ecologies, we can make predictions about what behavioural differences we should expect to see as people seek to preserve their fundamental interests given their local context. With regard to poverty, Nettle asserted that the different behaviours associated with it are not independent and constitute coherent parts of a way of trying to live. He therefore criticized public policies in which each component is treated piecemeal, as if they were unrelated to all of the others. From an evolutionary point of view, he argued that these behaviours may be adaptive responses to prevailing ecological conditions. For example, the greater anxiety in low-SES communities reflects the adaptive function of anxiety mechanisms, which is to detect threats; and these environments actually are more dangerous. Thus, however people in deprived areas behave, they will be exposed to a somewhat harsher ecology than people in more affluent neighbourhoods.

Nettle concluded that the lesson of behavioural ecology is that if you want to change an organism's behaviour, you need to change its environment, which means that actually reducing poverty in the most deprived areas of Britain is likely to be far more influential than superficial education or awareness-raising schemes. How quickly relief of poverty will affect behaviour will depend on the nature of the psychological mechanisms by which the environment 'gets under the skin'. Accordingly, behavioural responses to relief of poverty may follow quickly or may take a generation or more to work through. In other words, the cultural capital possessed by low-SES families may be resistant to change, whatever the incentives to do so. Put another way, such families may have reached a steady-state equilibrium.

3.21 Attract and retain high quality teachers

Improving the achievement and behaviours of low-SES students, indeed all students, critically depends on ensuring that high quality teachers teach them. Berliner, whose views I summarized earlier in this chapter, advocates providing pay scales and mentoring programmes to attract the best of newly certified teachers, and providing incentives and better working conditions to attract well-regarded, experienced teachers.[100] The OECD echoed these views when it emphasized the need to attract, support and retain high quality teachers as one of its five main recommendations in improving the achievement of low-SES students. It argued that policies must raise teacher quality for disadvantaged schools and students by:

- providing targeted teacher education to ensure that teachers receive the skills and knowledge they need for working in schools with disadvantaged students;
- providing mentoring programmes for novice teachers; developing supportive working conditions to improve teacher effectiveness and increase teacher retention; and
- developing adequate financial and career incentives to attract and retain high quality teachers in disadvantaged schools.[101]

In a similar vein, a recent report from the United Kingdom's Social Mobility and Child Poverty Commission recommended improving teaching by providing better pay to compete with other graduate professions and ending fees for initial teacher education.[102]

3.22 Provide funding to compensate for disadvantage

Since the 1990s, an increasing number of countries have introduced funding schools by formula.[103] Many of these formulae give consideration to the SES of schools and/or individual students. Thus, the OECD recommends that to ensure equity and quality across education systems, governments should 'use funding strategies, such as weighted funding formulae, that take into consideration that the instructional costs of disadvantaged students may be higher'.[104] As well, account needs to be taken of free school meals, which I will mention in comments on the relevant countries below.[105]

Many jurisdictions provide extra funding aimed at raising the achievement of low-SES students. As will be seen in the following examples of country systems (arranged alphabetically, apart from an overview of Europe), many different funding models are in place, with variations in factors such as:

- the specification of which children should receive the most direct or indirect assistance;
- how SES is determined, and at what level(s) in the education system;
- how the quantum of funding is determined;
- the proportion of schools/students in receipt of special funding;
- how often special funding is reviewed; and
- the strings attached to special funding.

I will conclude this section by presenting an analysis of the different funding models in terms of their transparency, adequacy, efficiency, equity, robustness and freedom from unintended consequences.

Europe

According to a 2014 report from the European Commission, the socio-economic background of students is taken into account in determining the level of funding for teaching and non-teaching staff in primary and secondary education only in Belgium, France, the Netherlands, Slovakia, and across all four parts of the United Kingdom.[106] However, as I shall point out with reference to particular European countries, several of them have instituted special programmes directed at low-SES students, often at the municipality level.

Australia

In Australia, education funding is very complex. Briefly, federal funding is passed onto state and territory governments, who then combine it with their own funding before passing it along to the relevant school system authority, be it a state Department of Education, a state's Catholic Education Commission, or individual independent schools. Each of these authorities then adds its own revenue before distributing it to schools, in allocation mechanisms that vary from state to state. Finally, individual schools add their own revenue – such as fees and donations. The federal government's funding is provided in lump sums and it is up to the states to use them as they see fit, according to their own funding model. The proportion of funding targeting low-SES varies from state to state, as does the formulae and the methods for calculating them. Funding for non-government schools largely comes from the federal government, which includes an SES component.

In 2011, the Gonski Review[107] (named after its chairperson) noted that Australia had one of the biggest gaps amongst developed nations between high and low performing students, and that educational performance was strongly linked to students' backgrounds - the more disadvantaged, the worse the students' outcomes.

The panel recommended new public funding arrangements based on a number of fundamental principles. For example, they should:

- be allocated in a fair, logical and practical way so that schools with similar characteristics and student populations have similar access to it;
- be allocated to schools and students on the basis of need, in particular to ensure that differences in educational outcomes are not the result of differences in wealth, income, power or possessions;
- contribute to improved educational outcomes of all students, particularly for students from disadvantaged backgrounds;
- provide demonstrable value for money and recipients should be accountable for its proper use;
- provide objectivity, simplicity and transparency in the derivation of the measure;
- be sensitive to changes in circumstances; and
- be economic in the administrative costs for schools, systems and governments.

The review recommended a model that gave every student a funding benchmark amount plus loadings, for specific disadvantages: low-SES background, indigenous background, limited English, rural or small schools and disability. The low-SES loading was to be applied to the lowest 50% of households, with higher amounts to the lowest 25%. It was to link a student's residential addresses to national census data at the Census Collection District level - the smallest spatial unit in Australia for statistical purposes - to obtain a socio-economic profile of the school community. The SES score of a school would apply for four years, unless the school or school system considers that the SES score has not been determined correctly, does not reflect the socio-economic circumstances of the school's community, or is no longer accurate because of a significant change in the school's circumstances. In these cases, review and appeals processes would be in place.

However, Gonski recognized that the area-based SES measure then being used was subject to potentially significant error due to variability in family SES within census Collection Districts. The panel therefore recommended that it should be replaced in time with a more precise measure that would reflect directly the circumstances and background of each student. One possible measure cited was the Index of Community Socio-Educational Advantage (ICSEA), which includes several components based on direct parent data, where it was available, from that already collected at enrolment and indirect area-based data from the census in other cases.

At the time of writing, the Gonski review has itself been subject to review and has come in for criticism by the current government.[108]

Canada

In Canada, since education is the responsibility of the provinces, there is some variation in the funding models that have been adopted. In *Alberta*, a low SES loading of 14% applies based on a SES measure that includes parental education, family status, home ownership and income. In *Manitoba*, an SES indicator is calculated according to the formula: $(0.75 \times C) + (0.25 \times D)$, where: C = the percentage of low-income families with school-aged children in the school catchment area (based on Census data) and D = the incidence of school migrancy. As well, $500 per pupil is allocated for those under the care of Child and Family Services. In *Québec*, the Ministry of Education's intervention *Agir autrement* (Act differently) programme aims at fostering large-scale transformation in the province's most disadvantaged schools, to improve both student success and equity. The Ministry gives these schools (189 in the year 2007-2008) access to a large database of effective practices for intervention so they can develop their expertise. School boards, through resources and especially through coordination, support the school leadership team in the implementation of practices that are adapted to their students' SES characteristics.[109]

Denmark

Municipalities receive their overall funds (including for education) from central government based in part on their 'socioeconomic expenditure need'. This is calculated on the basis of a number of criteria regarding the 'socioeconomic burden' in each municipality, calculated by using different weights for a range of criteria. These include: 20- to 59-year-olds without employment (19% weighting), 25- to 49-year-olds without vocational training (16%), children in families where parents have little or no education (8%), rented apartments (5%), number of mentally handicapped (5%), number of psychiatric patients (5%) and children with single parents (4%).

The weight of each criterion in the index is calculated by multiplying the population of the municipality within the criterion with its weight and dividing it by the total population in the municipality. The sum gives the total SES index. If the index is more than 100, the municipality has a relatively heavy SES burden compared with the national average. The SES expenditure need in a municipality is then calculated by multiplying the SES index with a unit amount per inhabitant and the population in the municipality.[110] It is then up to each municipality to determine how the SES expenditure need is translated into school funding each year.

Finland

Finnish schools are funded based on a formula guaranteeing equal allocation of resources to each school regardless of location or wealth of its community. Funding responsibilities are divided between the federal and municipal governments with the federal government assuming about 57% of the financial burden of schools and municipal authorities assuming the remaining 43%. There is no direct mechanism for providing additional resources to low-SES students at the national level. However, there may be such mechanisms at the municipal level, which in the end anyway decides how they use money they get from the Ministry. As well, there are some projects funded by the Ministry of Education, via the national Board of Education – which must specifically address any inequalities between schools – for which municipalities can apply.[111] Given the low variance in academic achievement explained by socio-economic background in Finland (noted in Section 3.6),[112] the lack of specific loadings for SES is not altogether surprising. Further, it must be recognized that, since 1957, free school meals have been available for *all* children, irrespective of their SES. Also, Finland has a philosophy of education for all in comprehensive schools, does not have streaming, enrols 23% of students in early part-time 'special education', and Finnish parents have a high level of education. Above all, perhaps, Finnish teacher are of high quality, only 10% of applicants for teacher education being accepted and most graduate with masters-level qualifications.[113]

Netherlands

Here, a system was developed with the aim of compensating disadvantaged groups in two ways: first, through 'weighted funding', whereby elementary schools receive more funding for students from underprivileged families, and, second, on top of this, additional subsidies for schools located in districts and regions with a high number of underprivileged families. Parental qualifications are used as a means of targeting this additional funding. Under this weighted funding system, those from lower SES backgrounds are awarded 1.25 times the basic amount per student.[114]

New Zealand

The New Zealand Ministry of Education calculates decile ranking to determine the amount of SES-related funding each school receives. Decile 1 schools comprise the 10% of schools with the highest proportion of students from low SES communities, whereas decile 10 schools are the 10% of schools with the lowest proportion of these students and so on. Census information, obtained every five years, is used to calculate the decile. A school provides its student addresses and these are used to determine which specific 'meshblocks' (containing about 50 households) its students come from. The meshblock is examined against five socio-economic factors: household income, parents' occupations, household crowding, parents' educational qualifications and parents' receipt of income support.

The number of students from each meshblock weights these five factors. Schools are ranked in relation to every other school for each of the five factors, receiving a score according to the percentile that they fall into. The five scores for each school are added together (without any weightings) to give a total.[115] This total gives the overall standing of a school in relation to all other schools in the country, enabling the ministry to place schools into ten groups called deciles, each having the same number of schools. Each decile attracts a different amount of money, referred to as Targeted Funding for Educational Achievement, which is allocated to individual school boards who determine how it is spent. In addition, schools' deciles also affect the allocation of other grants.

A major reassessment of all schools' deciles is undertaken following each five-yearly Census but, in intervening years, schools can apply for a review of their decile on the basis of perceived change in the SES of students in their catchments. Of the country's 2,406 state and state-integrated schools in 2014, roughly one-third moved to a lower decile rating, one-third moved up, and one-third remained the same. Transitional funding was provided to assist schools if their new decile rating resulted in a lower funding level.

Norway

The Norwegian public sector is divided between the central, county and municipal government levels. The municipalities are responsible for primary and lower secondary education and the counties are responsible for upper secondary education, but within the limits set by central government in the Education Act. Both municipalities and counties are mainly financed by taxes, user charges and grants from the central government. The main revenue sources at the local government level are taxes, with rates (45% of revenues), grants from the central government (33%) and user charges (16%), with interest and other revenues accounting for the rest. Block grants are intended to equalize economic opportunities across local governments. Local taxes are highly regulated by the centre. The main economic argument in favour of local discretion to set tax rates is that local tax rates and service provision can adjust to varying spending preferences and cost conditions. These constitute decentralization gains that can be achieved, compared with a situation with uniform service provision decided at the national level.[116] Norway also has a spending needs equalization scheme to compensate local governments with unfavourable cost conditions, expensive age structures and social problems. Notwithstanding these arrangements, while all students in Norway enjoy the same entitlement to education, regardless of where they live, the expenditure per student varies greatly between municipalities. Per-student costs range from around NOK 80,000 in the lowest-spending municipality, to more than NOK 230,000 per student in the highest-spending municipality.[117]

South Africa[118]

Post-Apartheid South Africa recognized the need to transform its education sector to rectify gross inequalities by introducing a redistributive, pro-poor system of allocating disproportionate benefits to the poorest and most vulnerable students. Four mechanisms were introduced. First, in 2000 a Norms and Standards for School Funding was put in place. This formula-driven financial policy determined financial allocations per institution and per student. It was done by assigning a poverty score to each school, based on census data, which was then used as a basis for sorting schools into five quintiles. Schools were then allocated 'non-personnel funding' which varied according to the quintile – the lowest quintile schools receiving six to seven times more per student than the highest quintile schools. In 2008, these allocations amounted to 11.8% of provincial education budgets (with a range from 7.4% to 19.2% in different provinces). Second, in 2006, the Minister of Education declared all schools in the lowest two quintiles as 'no-fee' schools, extending this to schools in the third quintile in 2009. Third, the National Schools Nutrition Programme feeds the poorest children in the three lowest quintiles. These provisions amounted to over nine million children, or half the school population, in 2009. Fourth, the Quids Up Programme provides ring-fenced funding for learning and teaching support materials, infrastructure upgrades etc. in the quintiles 1-3 schools.

Sweden

According to Chapter 1 of Sweden's Education Act (2010: 800), teaching in schools shall be equal in all parts of the country and be based on science and proven experience. However, a process of decentralization has left the national government with few policy levers at a national scale.[119] It establishes national goals and the National Agency for Education develops syllabi and criteria for grading, and has the main task of reviewing the quality and results of education, both at local authority and school level. Municipalities receive a lump sum and have freedom to decide where to spend it, how school education is to be organized and what resources to allocate for this purpose out of their budgets. A feature of the Swedish education policy is the overriding preference for universal and equal entitlements of citizenship, as opposed to targeting those in need. Thus, there exist very few education programmes that are targeted to special groups, or that pursue explicit 'affirmative action' on behalf of less privileged children, schools or communities. The underlying philosophy is that universalism is the most effective approach to promote social inclusion and equality of resources, in part because it helps sustain social solidarity and political support behind redistributive policies and, in part, because it minimizes social stigmatization and segmentation.[120] Although there is no automatic allocation of money to schools with low-SES from the state, municipalities are obliged to distribute resources in order to favour socially disadvantaged districts and schools. A formula of equalizing – though not earmarked – grants has been designed to redistribute resources from wealthy to poorer municipalities. As well, there is specially designated money that municipalities (schools) can apply for each year to support low-SES pupils. The Swedish National Audit Office, however, has recently concluded that this way of allocating money has gone totally wrong. Well-off municipalities can, according to the report, afford qualified people to write successful applications while this is not the case in poorer municipalities. Against this, it must be recognized that, since 1973, free school meals have been available for all children, irrespective of their SES.

United Kingdom

In 2011, the UK coalition government introduced a Pupil Premium.[121] This provided extra funding to publicly funded schools, paid by their Local Authority and with the express intention 'to raise the attainment of disadvantaged pupils and close the gap between them and their peers'. Initially, this was set at £430 per pupil per year, for those who were in receipt of free school meals (FSMs)[122] and those who had been 'looked after' (i.e., under the care of the Local Authority) for a minimum period of 6 months. In 2012-2013, the Pupil Premium was extended to all children who were eligible for FSMs, or who had been eligible for them since summer 2006. The rate per-pupil increased to £623. Approximately 27% of the school population was covered by these provisions in 2012-2013, but only a relatively small proportion of schools' total income was derived from them (ranging from 3.8% for primary schools with high levels of FSMs to 1% for secondary schools with low levels of FSMs).

In addition to the Pupil Premium, the government in 2014 announced a prize fund of £4m to be awarded to schools that best improve the performance of their disadvantaged pupils. It must also be noted that, in the United Kingdom, as of 2014, in excess of £6 billion was being spent on deprivation funding in schools, only £2.5 billion of which was the Pupil Premium. The other funding, distributed by local authorities, was based on the Income Deprivation Affecting Children Index (IDACI)[123] measures of deprivation and low prior attainment, and thus included children who were not eligible for the Pupil Premium but were still underachieving. Average IDACI scores per pupil for each school are derived using the post-codes from the school censuses. This average is then multiplied by the number of pupils attending a school to give a 'Pockets of Deprivation' score.

It is up to headteachers to decide how to spend Pupil Premium funds. A recent survey commissioned by the Department for Education[124] included the following findings:

- schools were using a wide range of criteria to define disadvantage, not just FSM and looked after children, preferring instead to use educational rather than economic criteria;
- they often combined funding from Pupil Premium with funding from other sources to target a wide range of disadvantaged pupils (this makes for some difficulties in assessing the impact of the Pupil Premium and holding schools to account for its expenditure);
- some schools used evidence-based systems for determining the needs of their students;
- all schools used a range of support, including one-to-one tutoring, small group teaching, additional staff (extra teachers, teaching assistants, learning mentors and family support workers), support from specialist services, school trips, provision of materials or resources and parental support.
- most schools were working with other schools and external providers to provide support for their disadvantaged students, many pooling their resources to enable this; and
- almost all schools were monitoring the impact of the support they were providing for their disadvantaged students.[125]

United States

In marked contrast to most developed countries, the US funding regimes perversely favour students from high-SES families since nearly half of school funding comes from local property taxes. This leads to wide funding differences between schools serving wealthy and poor communities, whether they be among states, among school districts within each state and even among schools within specific districts.[126] In 1998, for example, New Jersey schools received, on average, $8,801 per student, whereas in Utah the comparable amount was $3,804. Within-state disparities were also shown, for example, in Alaska where district-level funding of schools ranged from $16,546 per student to $7,379. Invariably, the poorest-funded schools were serving low-SES populations.

However, some federal correction takes place under Title I of the Elementary and Secondary Education Act of 1965 (20 U.S.C. 6301 et seq.): Improving the Academic Achievement of the Disadvantaged. The purpose of this legislation is 'to ensure that all children have a fair, equal, and significant opportunity to obtain a high-quality education and reach, at a minimum, proficiency on challenging State academic achievement standards and state academic assessments'. Nearly 14,000 of the 15,000 school districts in the United States conduct Title I programmes, accounting for over 51,000 schools and an expenditure of $15 billion per annum. In January 2002, Title I was reauthorized as the No Child Left Behind Act of 2001. As well, free school meals are available for some children.

Title I includes Targeted Assistance Schools that receive funds 'to provide services to eligible children identified by the school as failing, or most at risk of failing, to meet the state's academic standards' and 'to support methods and instructional strategies that are proven to be effective and that strengthen the core curriculum'. Records must be maintained to document that such funds are spent only on activities and services for eligible students.

Schoolwide programmes also operate under Title I. These comprise a comprehensive strategy designed to upgrade the entire educational programme in a Title I school. The primary goal of the schoolwide programme is to ensure that all students, particularly those who are low-achieving, demonstrate proficient and advanced levels of achievement on state tests. As with the Targeted Assistance component of Title I, there are requirements that schools use effective, scientifically based instructional strategies that:

- strengthen the core academic programme in the school;
- increase the amount and quality of learning time, by providing an extended school year, before- and after-school and summer programmes and opportunities, and an enriched and accelerated curriculum; and
- include strategies for meeting the educational needs of historically underserved populations.

Another Title I programme targeting students from low-income families is the School Improvement Grants (SIG) fund for very low-achieving schools. (In fiscal years 2009 and 2010, less than 10% of eligible schools received SIGs.) Until 2014, SIG schools had to choose among four school intervention models:

1   *Transformation*: This required that districts replace the principal of the school, develop an evaluation system for teachers and principals that incorporated student progress, institute comprehensive instructional reforms, increase learning time, create community-oriented schools, and provide operational flexibility and sustained support (for example, allowing the school to make decisions typically made at the district level in areas such as hiring and firing, length of school day and budgets).
2   *Turnaround*: This required that districts replace the principal of the school, re-hire no more than 50% of the staff, institute comprehensive instructional reforms, increase learning time, create community-oriented schools, and provide operational flexibility and sustained support.
3   *Restart*: This model required that districts convert the school into a charter school or close and reopen it under a charter school operator, charter management organization, or an education management organization selected through a rigorous review process.
4   *Closure*: This model required that districts close the school and enrol its students in higher-achieving schools in the district.

In 2014, the US Department of Education issued revised SIG rules.[127] These added three additional options, one of which was to implement a whole-school reform model with a strong evidence base, offered by an external agency with a track record of success. The standards were high: in order to qualify, programmes must have at least two studies that meet the rigorous standards of the What Works Clearinghouse[128] and show positive effects on important outcomes.

Earlier, in 2002, the United States introduced the Comprehensive School Reform (CSR) programme to provide grants to schools to adopt proven comprehensive reforms. It focused on reorganizing and revitalizing whole schools rather than implementing a number of specialized, and potentially uncoordinated, school improvement initiatives. In general, the funding targeted high-poverty schools with low student test scores. The Department of Education defined CSR on the basis of 11 components that were intended to constitute a scientifically based approach to school reform, including 'the employment of proven methods for student learning, teaching, and school management that are founded on scientifically based research and effective practices and have been replicated successfully in schools'.[129]

A 2003 meta-analysis reviewed research on the achievement effects of 29 widely implemented models of CSR, concluding that their overall effects appeared promising and that research-based models of educational improvement can be brought to scale across many schools and children from varying contexts. The researchers noted, however, that rather than approving programmes on the basis of input requirements, schools and policymakers pay even stronger attention to outputs.[130]

As well as the above federal programmes, each state in the United States has developed its own approach to funding schools, taking account of its particular demography. These are not reviewed here.

Analysis of funding models

According to English scholar, Rosalind Levačić, and her colleagues, school funding formulae may be assessed in relation to the four standard criteria of transparency, adequacy, efficiency and equity.[131] To these four criteria I would add two more: robustness and freedom from unintended consequences. I will deal with each of these six criteria in turn and briefly indicate how the above funding models conform to them.

Transparency   refers to the situation when stakeholders have easily available information on the amount of funding each administrative unit receives, the basis for this allocation and how these resources are used. Without exception, the funding models I have outlined meet the first two of these criteria, but only some jurisdictions spell out how the funds are to be used. For example, the US Department of Education defines the Comprehensive School Reform programme on the basis of several components that are intended to constitute a scientifically based approach to school reform. In a similar, but less prescriptive, vein, the province of Quebec in Canada provides schools with access to a large database of effective practices for intervention.

Adequacy   refers to resources being sufficient to achieve a specified standard of education for students. There are several problems in making such a determination. First, with few exceptions, countries have not linked their funding levels for low-SES students with their educational outcomes. Second, as noted under my comments on transparency, most jurisdictions do not specify the uses to which additional funding can be put. Third, since a number of countries that have introduced formula funding have done so nation-wide, there are no control schools with which to make comparisons. Fourth, comparisons of changes in attainment scores over time are unsatisfactory tests since other policies aimed at improving attainment, for example accountability and high stakes testing polices, have been implemented at the same time. Fifth, as I noted in the outline of the UK system, it is difficult to disentangle SES-related funding from other sources of grants to schools.

While Israel has reported a positive relationship between budgetary regimes and student outcomes, the evidence from research is generally not encouraging. It suggests that the effect of additional expenditure per student is sometimes positive but relatively small[132] or, according to other views, non-existent.[133] Thus, it is very difficult to link school funding formulae to education outcomes in a reliable and reasonably precise way.[134] For example, writing from a US perspective, W. Norton Grubb and his colleagues argued that money is a necessary, but not sufficient, determinant of educational outcomes.[135] They pointed out that debates about money within education typically overshadow debates concerning teaching and learning. They noted that while spending has increased per student in the United States, there are still problems and disparities within education. They recommended that new models of the link amongst educational revenues, resources and outcomes need to be developed.

I believe that funding models must give serious consideration to determining their adequacy. In other words, there is a need for rigorous cost–benefit analyses.[136] Here, a costing-out study carried out in Pennsylvania to determine the basic cost per student of providing an education to meet the state's academic standards and assessments, is a possible way forward. Also, the School Improvement Grants recently instituted in the United States, with their emphasis on funding having to show positive effects on important outcomes, provide a useful model. In a similar vein, Chile requires schools in receipt of supplementary funding to develop plans for educational improvement with specified educational outcomes.

Efficiency　While adequacy is judged in terms of the value of inputs needed to achieve a specified educational output, *efficiency* means achieving the highest feasible output from a given volume of resources. This requires selecting the least-cost combination of inputs for producing a given amount of educational output. Obviously, if it is difficult to ascertain the adequacy of funding, this sets limits on determining its efficiency. Furthermore, schools' efficiency is difficult to measure for they produce multiple outputs, ranging from cognitive attainment to socialization. Furthermore, the contribution of inputs that the school does not control, in particular pupils' prior attainment and/or family characteristics, must be taken into account in assessing efficiency. Arguments have been mounted that decentralized financing may lead to substantial efficiency gains.[137]

Economists distinguish two types of efficiency – internal and external. *Internal efficiency* is concerned only with the production of a given output (e.g., exam results) at a minimum feasible cost and makes no assumption about the social value of that output. *External efficiency* is concerned with using a given amount of resources to produce the combination of educational outputs, such as qualifications at different levels, specific skills, attitudes and behaviours that are most valued by society. Attempts to measure schools' efficiency are generally limited to internal efficiency – which considers only the relationship between inputs and schools' outputs (as far as these can be quantified). Israel has attempted to go down this track by by basing its funding model on an examination of the correlation between students' background characteristics and their achievement.

Equity　refers to the fairness with which resources in education are allocated and used. *Horizontal equity* is the equal resourcing of pupils with similar characteristics or learning needs, while *vertical equity* refers to differentially funding students according to differences in their needs.[138] In every jurisdiction reviewed above, vertical equity is the principal driver of differential funding related to SES. All of them seek to differentiate between students from high- and low-SES families, usually making a binary distinction, but, in the case of New Zealand, making a fine-grained distinction between deciles. Not all jurisdictions achieve horizontal equity. In the preceding country summaries, I drew attention to the wide locational disparities in per-student expenditure in, for example, the United States and Norway.

Horizontal equity is a problematic concept for it could well be the case that some children in the high-SES rankings have similar needs to those from low-SES rankings, and vice versa. In other words, SES is not the only driver of school performance. Other factors that can contribute to student achievement include (importantly) the quality of teachers, as well as the location of the school, the quality of school buildings and equipment, special educational needs unrelated to SES, ethnicity, cultural background and competence in the language of instruction. One way of addressing this issue might be to develop a funding formula that takes account of students' learning needs, irrespective of how these arise – a radical suggestion! This is occurring in the United Kingdom where, as I noted, schools are using a wide range of criteria to define disadvantage, preferring to use educational rather than economic criteria. Similarly, the Gonski review in Australia recommended a model that takes account not only of low-SES background, but also indigenous background, limited English, disability and rural or small schools. Israel, too, extended SES criteria to include immigrant status and periphery location status (i.e., schools located far from large cities).

Robustness   By *robustness* I mean that an allocation mechanism should not be open to distortions, in particular the possibility of 'gaming the system' by the deliberate falsification of information or by the employment of unreliable means of gathering data. A possible example of the former is when parents report on their occupations and income, knowing that their child's school would benefit financially from under-reporting. This is a possible risk in the Gonski proposal in Australia to ascertain SES from direct parent data collected at enrolment, although this may be mitigated by the employment of census data as well.

Moral hazard is another source of distortion to be avoided. This may occur when there is information asymmetry, i.e., where the risk-taking party to a transaction knows more about its intentions than the party paying the consequences of the risk. More broadly, moral hazard occurs when the party with more information about its actions or intentions has a tendency or incentive to behave inappropriately from the perspective of the party with less information. Moral hazard also arises in a principal–agent situation, where one party, the agent, usually has more information about his or her actions or intentions than the principal does, because the principal usually cannot completely monitor the agent.[139] This situation could arise in any SES-based funding arrangement that is conditional upon schools being required to implement certain programmes and to report on their outcomes, as in the case of the US School Improvement Grants.

Freedom from unintended consequences   refers to funding mechanisms that lead to erroneous or distorted messages regarding the quality of education in particular schools. This has occurred in New Zealand, where there have been concerns that a school's decile ranking is widely perceived as being a proxy indicator for its educational quality or status and thus may carry a stigma in the case of low decile rankings. There is evidence that parents are seeking to enrol their children in high decile schools: for example, a study found that 40% of parents elected to enrol their children in a secondary school that was not their closest one – usually in a higher decile one.[140] It is difficult to envisage any system of differential funding based on SES not being subject to such unintended consequences, even when they are based on erroneous assumptions.

3.23 Institute free school meals for low-SES students

As noted in the previous section, school meal programmes are very common in many countries, especially in Europe (including the United Kingdom), but also Russia, Hong Kong, Brazil and Chile.[141] These usually comprise school lunches (often cooked), but also include both breakfasts and lunches in some countries. Programmes vary in terms of targeting (by age and or income) or universality. There is no national school food programme in New Zealand, but there are non-government programmes operating in hundreds of schools.

According to a review carried out by the New Zealand Children's Commissioner, the provision of nutritious food to children has effects in a number of areas that might be reasonably expected to lead to better educational outcomes.[142] These include attendance at school, concentration, memory, mood and test scores in various subjects. Effects are consistently largest for nutritionally at-risk or undernourished children.[143] The Commissioner also noted that separate from the nutritional effects of lack of food, there is evidence that food insecurity and nutritional at-risk status has been found to have a negative effect on children's mental health and psychosocial functioning.[144] A review of school feeding programmes found only 18 studies conducted over 80 years that were rigorous enough to be included. From these studies it found mixed (but tending towards positive) results for high-income countries.[145]

An article compared the findings of three studies that explored the role of increased blood glucose in improving memory function for subjects who ate breakfast.[146] An initial improvement in memory function for these subjects was found to correlate with blood glucose concentrations. In subsequent studies, morning fasting was found to adversely affect the ability to recall a word list and a story read aloud. It was concluded that breakfast consumption preferentially influences tasks requiring aspects of memory. It appears that breakfast consumption influences cognition via several mechanisms, including an increase in blood glucose.

3.24 Explore Full-Service (or Extended) Schools

The traditional borders between schools and their communities are undergoing dramatic change. Nowhere is this better illustrated than with the development of Full-Service (or Extended) Schools (FSSs) in many jurisdictions around the world.[147] In a nutshell, a FSS is a 'one-stop' institution that integrates education, medical, social and/or human services to meet the needs of children and youth and their families in a school's campus. As described by Joy Dryfoos, the earliest, and most cited, of its proponents, a FSS:

> integrates education, medical, social and/or human services that are beneficial to meeting
> the needs of children and youth and their families on school grounds or in locations which

are easily accessible. A full-service school provides the types of prevention, intervention and support services children and families need to succeed ... services that are high quality and comprehensive and are built on interagency partnerships which have evolved from cooperative ventures to intensive collaborative arrangements among state and local and public and private entities.[148]

FSSs vary in character according to the nature of the communities they serve and the availability and commitment of various agencies. They have several features in common, including those enumerated by the Scottish Office in its description of 'new community schools': (a) focus on all the needs of all pupils at the school; (b) engagement with families; (c) engagement with the wider community; (d) integrated provision of school education, informal as well as formal education, social work and health education and promotion services; (e) integrated management; (f) arrangements for the delivery of these services according to a set of integrated objectives and measurable outcomes; (g) commitment and leadership; and (h) multidisciplinary training and staff development.[149]

In establishing FSSs, careful consideration has to be given to a range of issues.[150] These include (a) managing the programme, (b) learning to collaborate, (c) building from localities outwards, (d) avoiding the colonizing effect of the school, (e) avoiding the dominance of the medical model, (f) financing and (g) evaluating outcomes.[151]

In Canada, the Toronto District School Board has made a commitment to support *all* schools to become FSSs. It defines FSSs as 'the coordinated delivery of health, education, prevention, and social services designed to improve the quality of life for students, families and communities. The programs and services are located inside an operational school'.[152]

In England and Wales, the 2006 Green Paper, *Every Child Matters*, promoted 'full-service extended schools' (FSES), defined as: 'offering the community and their pupils a range of services (such as childcare, adult learning, health and community facilities) that go beyond their core educational function' (Section 2.20). The original aim was to support the development in every local authority of one or more schools to provide a comprehensive range of services, including access to health services, adult learning and community activities, as well as study support and 8am to 6pm childcare. Most FSESs served areas of disadvantage. By the end of the initiative, 138 schools were involved, together with a further 10 funded through the London Challenge.[153]

UK studies have reported positive results for FSSs. A report presented by Colleen Cummings and her colleagues gave the findings from the final year of a three-year evaluation of a national full service extended schools (FSES) initiative.[154] Here are the main points:

- Schools broadly welcomed the FSES initiative. Issues of sustainability and the difficulties of partnership working, which had figured prominently in earlier stages of the evaluation, remained as potentially problematic in the third year. However, enough FSESs had found ways round these difficulties to suggest that they were far from insuperable.
- The FSES approach was impacting positively on students' attainments particularly in the case of those facing difficulties where there was improved engagement with learning.
- FSESs were generating positive outcomes for families and local people particularly where they were facing difficulties.

- The cost-benefit analysis suggested that both the costs and benefits of FSES approaches were high. However, since benefits balanced or outweighed costs, and since they accrued particularly to children and families facing the greatest difficulties, FSES approaches were considered to represent a good investment.
- The FSES approach was commonly associated with schools having better relations with local communities and enjoying enhanced standing in their communities.
- The development of FSES approaches tended to rely heavily on the dynamism of head-teachers and other school leaders.

These findings were supported by a later Ofsted survey of 20 FSES settings, which found that the major benefits to children and parents included enhanced self-confidence, improved relationships, raised aspirations and better attitudes towards learning.[155] A more recent study examined the extent to which FSESs offered five core elements: (1) a varied menu of activities; (2) childcare 8am–6pm 48 weeks per year for primary schools; (3) parenting support including family learning; (4) swift and easy access to targeted and specialist support services; and (5) community access to school facilities. It was found that two-thirds of schools were offering all five elements and the remaining one-third were all offering at least some elements, with secondary schools being more likely than primary and special schools to be offering the full set of core activities. Two-thirds of schools offered extended services as part of a cluster or group of schools and there was evidence that working in clusters helped to develop links with community organizations and avoid duplication of effort. Seven in ten schools were targeting specific groups of pupils or families for support with extended services, most commonly economically disadvantaged families and pupils with disabilities or special educational needs.[156]

According to a Scottish report on the new community schools,[157] there was evidence of the following benefits to students: improved attendance rates, better attainment in examinations, improved employment prospects, less drug abuse and fewer teenage pregnancies. As well, these schools brought benefits to the wider community through a reduction in crime and violence, overall improved health within families, better access to services and resources which might not otherwise be readily available, more productive partnerships between schools, parents and the wider community and reduced parental mistrust of schools and teachers.

3.25 Develop partnerships among relevant agencies

Implicit in the previous section is the notion that ensuring equality of educational opportunity for students from low-SES families necessitates looking 'beyond the school gates'. Thus, in the United Kingdom, a paper prepared for Ofsted noted that 'Systemic solutions will require more than excellence in the application of basic good practice by individual schools; it will require the aligned effort of a range of services and institutions'. It goes on to explain that 'Evidence … points directly to the mutual and accumulative benefits which services can bring to one another when improved health, housing, parenting, home learning and schooling operate in a virtuous circle'.[158]

Since many low-SES families have significant contact with multiple social and other agencies, it is important that there be strong working relationships among them.[159] Increasingly, since the 1990s or so, there has been a distinct trend towards 'wraparound' approaches in providing human services (see section 1.10). This is a system-level approach that quite liter-ally aims to 'wrap' existing services around children and young people and their families to address their problems in an ecologically comprehensive and coordinated way. It calls for radical, transforming systems change manifested in a move from fragmentation to coordi-nated or integrated intervention and from narrowly focused and specialist-oriented, 'silo' services to comprehensive, general approaches.[160]

Wraparound was originally developed in the United States in the 1980s as a means for maintaining youth with serious emotional and behavioural disorders in their homes and com-munities. Recently, it was estimated that the wraparound process is available via nearly 1,000 initiatives in nearly every one of the states in the United States, with the number of them taking implementation state-wide increasing every year.[161]

3.26 Develop early prevention and intervention programmes

Early intervention has two meanings: (a) pre-school provisions and (b) the early identification and remediation of children's lack of progress and behaviour difficulties at school.

First, let's look at the provision of high-quality pre-school education, targeting children from low-SES backgrounds as advocated by writers such as Berliner[162] and Hart and Risley.[163] The main driver of such programmes is research that demonstrates the critical importance of early experiences in establishing the brain architecture that shapes future cognitive, lan-guage, social and emotional development.[164]

According to a UK review, there is abundant evidence of the effectiveness of practices around early intervention and prevention.[165] For example, in England, the Effective Pre-school and Primary Education 3-11 Project studied the developmental trajectories of approximately 2,800 children from age 3 to 11 years.[166] It found that the benefits of pre-school education largely persisted through to the end of Key Stage 2 (age 11). Attendance at pre-school was beneficial for both academic and social/behavioural outcomes, as well as pupils' self-percep-tions. Importantly the quality of the pre-school predicted pupils' developmental outcomes, net of all other influences. For all social outcomes, the benefits of pre-school were greater for boys, for pupils with special educational needs, and (importantly for this review) for pupils from disadvantaged backgrounds. However, for some of the outcomes, notably English, Math-ematics and 'Hyperactivity', only pre-schools of medium or high quality had lasting effects. The higher the academic effectiveness of the pre-school attended, the better the longer term outcomes for children. While attending any pre-school had lasting benefits for 'pro-social' behaviour and academic outcomes, the effects were largely present in medium- to high-quality pre-schools. Children who did not attend pre-school and those who attended low quality pre-school showed a range of poorer outcomes at age 11.

US evidence is similarly supportive of early intervention at the pre-school level, although there are some mixed results. For example, in a randomized control trial, the Abecedarian Project employed a comprehensive education, healthcare and family support programme to focus on low-income, multi-risk families.[167] The programme resulted in reduced incidence of delayed cognitive development, with the most vulnerable children benefiting the most. The long-standing Head Start programme has also reported positive results for its participants, compared with peers in the same SES group in reading and maths scores, although they still lagged behind children from high SES homes.[168] However, these results need to be analyzed in more depth, for there is evidence that some of the gains fade over time and some writers argue that we need to know much more about how early childhood education actually works, in particular, the connections between programme components and particular child outcomes.[169] This is very important when it comes to policy decisions on how programmes should be scaled up in a cost-effective manner.[170]

Second, let me shift the focus to the early identification and remediation of behaviour problems. One example of a study will suffice. In a review, James Buckley from the US Department of Education's Institute of Education Science, concluded that 'a substantial body of research has shown that the early onset of behavioral and mental health problems during elementary school is associated with an increased risk for subsequent severe behavior and academic problems'.[171] He went on to note research that shows that 'in the absence of effective intervention, many students who exhibit serious behavior problems in the early elementary grades … develop more significant antisocial and disruptive behavior patterns by the upper elementary or middle school grades' (p. 195). In a similar vein, one of John Church's major conclusions in a New Zealand review was that 'In order to prevent antisocial children growing up to become antisocial adults, it is desirable that such children be identified as early as possible and as soon as the first signs of antisocial development begin to appear'.[172] He noted that 'improvements in our ability to detect antisocial development probably means that we could identify, by about age 5 if not sooner, a majority of those children who, without suitable intervention, are likely to be at high risk of life-course persistent antisocial behaviour problems'.[173]

3.27 Consider reducing class size – if it is accompanied by other, evidence-based, measures

The OECD describes class size as a controversial topic. Teachers and parents typically consider that smaller classes are beneficial because they allow teachers to focus more on the needs of individual students and allow for a wider range of teaching practices. However, these benefits are not automatic. As noted by Andreas Schleicher, the OECD director of the PISA tests, 'PISA results show no relationship between class size and learning outcomes, neither within nor across countries'.[174] Further, as John Hattie pointed out, teachers in smaller classes tend to adopt the same teaching methods as they were using in larger classes and do not take advantage of the opportunities presented by having fewer students. Not surprisingly, then, in his synthesis of 14 meta-analyses and major studies of reducing class size from 25 to 15 students, Hattie found a low effect size of 0.21.[175] Further, a review of European education systems shows that in most countries, on average, there seems to be no effect of class size on the cognitive skills acquired by students.[176] However, smaller classes may be beneficial for disadvantaged and minority students, especially in the early years.[177]

3.28 Decide on the optimal school size

According to Hattie, school size has a moderate effect on student achievement (effect size = 0.43); he concluded that there was a message about an optimal size, with too small or too large reducing effectiveness. Another study found that increased school size favoured middle- and upper-class students (with an effect equivalent to an extra 0.25 years of school) while it negatively affected low SES students (with an effect equivalent to a loss of 0.67 years of school).[178] Two Canadian researchers examined 57 post-1990 empirical studies of school size effects on a variety of student and organizational outcomes. They concluded that the weight of evidence clearly favoured smaller schools. Students who traditionally struggle at school and students from disadvantaged social and economic backgrounds were found to be the major benefactors of smaller schools. They recommended that elementary schools with large proportions of such students should be limited in size to not more than about 300 students; those serving economically and socially heterogeneous or relatively advantaged students should be limited in size to about 500 students. Secondary schools serving exclusively or largely diverse and/or disadvantaged students should be limited in size to about 600 students or fewer, while those serving economically and socially heterogeneous or relatively advantaged students should be limited in size to about 1,000 students.[179] Similar findings were presented in a recent OECD paper, which concluded that the higher the proportion of minority students, the smaller the optimal school size.[180]

Arguments advanced in favour of smaller schools include the greater likelihood of them fostering student engagement and a sense of belonging than is the case in larger schools.[181] Another possible argument in favour of smaller schools is the reduced likelihood that they will use streaming.[182] There is evidence, too, that in small schools it is easier for the personnel to identify and assist students at risk of dropping out.[183]

3.29 *Manage school choice to avoid segregation and increased inequities*

As I noted in section 3.15, there is considerable evidence that low-SES students' achievement is typically lower in schools where most of the students come from similar low-SES backgrounds, compared with the same students' achievement if they were to receive their education in more mixed SES school environments. Furthermore, there is clear evidence that reducing school segregation by SES does not reduce the performances of high achieving students. Therefore, educational policies that work against the segregation of students and schools based on SES should be an important policy goal.[184]

According to the OECD, providing full parental school choice can result in segregating students by ability, SES background and generate greater inequities across education systems.[185] It is therefore important that choice programmes be designed and managed to achieve a balance between choice and equity. The OECD argued that there are different options possible, including controlled choice schemes that can combine parental choice and ensuring a more diverse distribution of students. In addition, to ensure balance, incentives to make disadvantaged students attractive to high-quality schools, school selection mechanisms and vouchers or tax credits can be alternative options. Policies are also required to improve disadvantaged families' access to information about schools and to support them in making informed choices. For example, there is some evidence that giving parents a choice over schools actually increases the social divide. This was demonstrated in an English study which found that the majoriy of poor parents picked schools that were close to their home, while nearly half of middle-class parents opted for schools for their academic records.[186] At the very least, according to the OECD, school choice requires some balance to 'ensure that all parents and families are able to exercise it and benefit from it, especially disadvantaged parents, who are the ones who exercise it the least'.[187]

Nijmegen, in the Netherlands, provides an example of controlled choice.[188] Here, a central subscription system is used to assign students to primary schools, with the aim of reaching 30% of disadvantaged students in each school. All the primary schools have agreed on a central subscription system based on the distribution of students in different categories. In the event of oversubscription, priority is given to siblings and children who live nearby. Subsequent priority is given to either advantaged or disadvantaged students, in order to reach the required balance, by lottery system. This policy was introduced in April 2009 and has not been evaluated at the time of writing.

3.30 Eliminate grade repetition[189]

According to the OECD, grade repetition is a costly and ineffective way to raising educational outcomes. Alternative strategies to reduce this practice include: preventing repetition by addressing learning gaps during the school year; automatic promotion or limiting repetition to subject or modules failed, with targeted support. Decreasing grade retention rates also requires raising awareness across schools and society about the costs and negative impact on students.

John Hattie is very critical of grade repetition.[190] Indeed, he pointed out that it is difficult to find any study showing a positive effect on student achievement. Rather, the trend is towards negative effects (d = –0.16) for grade repetition. Further, he noted that research indicates that the threat of non-promotion does not motivate students to try harder; on the contrary, it is a de-motivating force, which increases the likelihood of students dropping out of school.

Furthermore, recent research has found an increase in negative behaviour across all students who have higher levels of retained and old-for-grade peers.[191] Increased opportunities to interact with such peers can influence the behaviour of youth who do not share the same risk factors. Conversely, policies that help students stay on track academically have the potential not only to benefit students who are at risk for academic failure, but also to enhance the positive behaviour of other students in the grade.

3.31 Avoid early tracking (streaming) and defer student selection until upper secondary[192]

Eric Hanushek and Ludger W §mann identified tracking effects by comparing differences in outcome between primary and secondary school across tracked and non-tracked systems.[193] Six international student assessments provided eight pairs of achievement contrasts for between 18 and 26 cross-country comparisons. The results suggested that early tracking increases educational inequality and reduces mean performance. The OECD noted that early student selection has a negative impact on students assigned to lower tracks and exacerbates inequities, without raising average performance. It argued that student selection should be deferred to upper secondary education while reinforcing comprehensive schooling prior to that stage.

A recent review carried out by Lynn Mulkey and her colleagues summarized five sets of outcomes associated with tracking.[194] These were: (1) students in higher tracks enjoy a faster pace of instruction; (2) Students in higher tracks often have more effective teachers; (3) students in lower tracks are often in classes where there are more disruptions; (4) teachers of lower tracks have lower expectations of their students; and (5) placement in higher tracks often heightens students' self-esteem, leading to higher achievement.

Due to the disadvantages of streaming (or tracking) outlined above, many schools in the United States are implementing what is referred to as 'detracking', which involves students being deliberately positioned into classes of mixed ability.[195]

3.32 Design equivalent upper secondary education pathways[196]

While upper secondary education is a strategic level of education for individuals and societies, according to the OECD between 10 and 30% of young people starting do not complete this level. Policies to improve the quality and design of upper secondary education can make it more relevant for students and ensure completion. To this end, there are different policy options: making academic and vocational tracks equivalent by improving the quality of vocational education and training, allowing transitions from academic to vocational studies and removing dead-ends; reinforcing guidance and counselling for students; and designing targeted measures to prevent dropout – such as additional pathways to obtain an upper secondary qualification or incentives to stay in school until completion.

Providing young people with pathways into the world of work and/or further education is at the heart of these recommendations. UNESCO and ILO have put forward a comprehensive set of recommendations regarding technical and vocational education and training.[197] These organizations state that 'premature and narrow specialization should be avoided: (a) in principle, the age of 15 should be considered the lower limit for beginning specialization; (b) a period of common studies providing basic knowledge and generic skills should be required for each broad occupational sector before a special branch is chosen'.[198]

A recent US report advocated bringing that country's upper secondary school system more into line with European approaches to vocational education and training (VET).[199] Its key features were as follows:

(a) Throughout northern and central Europe, VET is a mainstream system, this pathway helping most young people make the transition from adolescence to productive adulthood.

(b) In Austria, Denmark, Finland, Germany, the Netherlands, Norway and Switzerland, after grades 9 or 10, between 40 and 70% of young people opt for an educational programme that typically combines classroom and workplace learning over the subsequent three years. This culminates in a diploma or certificate, with real currency in the labour market. In virtually all of these countries, VET also provides a pathway into tertiary education for those who choose to take it.

(c) There are two basic models. The first, usually referred to as an 'apprenticeship' or 'dual system', has students spending three or four days in paid company-organized training at the workplace, with the other day or two in related academic work in the classroom. Germany has the oldest and best-known apprenticeship system, which offers programmes leading to recognized qualifications in about 350 different occupations. A second group of countries has opted for a model in which vocational education is mostly provided in school-based programmes, although they all incorporate at least some work-based learning. These countries typically introduce students to a broad cluster of occupations before narrowing the focus of training in the third year.[200]

(d) From a US perspective, the report noted, perhaps the most important distinction among these countries is the age at which students are separated into different tracks. Germany and Switzerland have separate middle or lower secondary schools based largely on the school's assessment of a student's academic potential. Finland and Denmark, on the other hand, keep all students in a common, untracked comprehensive school up through grade 9 or 10, at which point students and their families, not the school, decide which kind of upper secondary education they will pursue. The report's authors favoured the latter model.

(e) In all of these apprenticeship systems, employer organizations play a major role. They take the lead in defining occupational qualifications, providing paid apprenticeships or other work-based learning opportunities and (in collaboration with educators and trade union partners) assessing student performance and awarding certificates. In Germany, for example, they pay about half of the expenses associated with the system, contributing roughly as much as the government. Approximately one-quarter of German and Swiss employers participate in the dual system.

II School-level strategies

It is important to recognize that schools' roles in addressing the needs of low-SES learners are two-fold. First, all schools should be charged with the responsibility of utilizing their resources to deliver an equitable education to all of its students. Second, some schools may be disadvantaged in that they have a high proportion of low-SES students and need support in managing their responsibilities toward such students. Thus, our attention must focus on the school as an organization.

3.33 Ensure effective school leadership

The literature suggests that good leaders in schools contribute towards improved outcomes and narrowing of the gap between high- and low-SES students. According to a UK review, characteristics of effective school leaders include: a strong vision for their schools; appropriate skills; ability to create the right ethos; ability to engender good relationships with staff, pupils and parents; and getting the right degree of involvement from other relevant agencies. In addition, outcomes for disadvantaged students are influenced by school leaders who have strong behaviour management policies that stress positive ways to teach children to behave well and respect others and who use achievement data as a basis for action with students.[201]

An Ofsted analysis of a sample of UK inspection reports for outstanding schools in areas of economic deprivation also identified school leadership as an important factor.[202] In particular, it highlighted a model in which responsibilities were shared among a strong team of senior staff, so that the success of the school did not depend wholly upon the leadership of the headteacher, as important as that was. A recent report by the Social Mobility and Child Poverty Commission highlighted the role of school leadership, recommending the adoption of a zero tolerance approach to schools which are in terminal failure.[203] Those schools failing to perform for five consecutive years should face wholesale changes in their leadership and be required to become part of a high-performing academy chain. The Commission further recommended the setting up of a new fellowship of Change Leaders, comprising Heads who have previous experience of successfully turning around schools, 'to lead efforts to put failing schools back on the path to success'.

A recent OECD report also identified school leadership as one of five priority recommendations in supporting improvements in low performing disdvantaged schools. Specifically, it advocated:

- developing school leadership preparation programmes to both strengthen school leaders' general expertise to improve learning and teaching;
- reinforcing coaching and mentoring programmes for school leaders, to support them in the search for solutions, and creating networks of schools to achieve durable change in practices and sustainable improvement;
- developing strategies to attract and retain competent leaders in low performing disadvantaged schools, by providing good working conditions, systemic support and incentives to encourage the appointment of high quality school leaders in these schools; and
- providing systemic support for restructuring and re-culturing schools whenever necessary, which may require extra support and external intervention and/or additional resources.

Evidence suggests that the total (direct and indirect) effects of school leadership on student achievement account for about one-quarter of total school effects, and probably more in disadvantaged schools.[204] School leaders influence student achievement through two important pathways: supporting and developing effective teachers and implementing effective organizational processes in their schools. The latter includes the important activities of setting directions through challenging, but achievable, goals, redesigning the school by strengthening its culture, and building collaborative processes within the school and with other schools.[205]

Where schools lack highly competent leaders, ways should be found to recruit them on a continuing basis or to appoint them to assist such schools on a temporary basis. In either case, the new headteachers should be charged with the responsibility of strengthening succession planning and supporting the development of a long-term strategy to improve standards. In a recent speech, David Laws, the UK Schools Minister, noted the presence of school leaders who take on wider responsibilities in more than one school and the appointment of over 850 'national leaders of education'. This programme enables outstanding principals and their schools to provide support to 'improve the teaching and leadership in schools in challenging circumstances'.[206] A similar system is being introduced in New Zealand where a programme, *Investing in Educational Success*, introduced new roles for some of the most skilled teachers and principals to share their expertise with colleagues, with the aim of helping to raise achievement for children and young people throughout the country, not just those from low-SES backgrounds. It is envisaged that the new roles will operate in Communities of Schools, in which schools work together to meet shared challenges. Each Community will include a leadership role in which one principal will support all principals and teachers in the Community to raise achievement and meet shared goals. As well, there will be Across-Community teacher roles – about four or five teachers working closely with other teachers across the Community.[207]

A recent UK paper proposed three approaches to school leadership that have the potential to enhance social justice in schools and to challenge the 'hegemonic trap' of a neoliberal discourse: (1) critical reflection, (2) the cultivation of a common vision of equity, and (3) transforming dialogue.[208] Regarding critical reflection, they cited the work of Kathleen Brown who defined it as 'the examination of personal and professional belief systems, as well as the deliberate consideration of the ethical implications and effect of practices'.[209] In their advocacy of a common vision of equity, they endorsed the work of Australian researchers Richard Niesche and Amanda Keddie, who set up weekly meetings of an Equity and Action Group in a secondary school.[210] Transforming dialogue reflects a democratic approach to leadership that reflects a valuing of student voice and professional participation which aims to enhance understanding.

3.34 Engage families in education[211]

I prefer the concept of 'family engagement' over the more usual 'parent involvement'. The broader concept of family embraces the extended group of family members who may play a major role in child rearing, while, as one writer explains, involvement sometimes has the connotation of 'doing to' while engagement refers to 'doing with'.[212]

The OECD lists giving priority to linking schools with parents and communities as one of its top five recommendations for addressing the needs of low-SES students.[213] It points out that disadvantaged parents tend to be less involved in their children's schooling, for multiple economic and social reasons. Engaged parents encourage more positive attitudes towards school; improve homework habits; reduce absenteeism, disengagement and dropout; and enhance academic achievement. Policies need to be put in place to improve and diversify communication strategies, align school and parental efforts, and identify and encourage individuals from the same communities to mentor students from disadvantaged schools and support their learning.

Ofsted, in the United Kingdom, similarly asserted that educational success depends in large measure upon engaging families. This means developing creative and flexible strategies to make them feel valued, enable them to give greater support to their child's education, and help them make informed decisions about their child's future.[214]

While parent/caregiver engagement has a certain 'common sense' appeal, I do recognize that more evidence is required regarding the impact of this on their children's education, and more longitudinal data are required to understand the true impact on children and young people of such engagement.[215] Nevertheless, John Hattie's meta-analysis of studies of the impact of home variables on children's educational achievement does point the way. His analysis showed that parental aspirations and expectations had a strong relationship with their children's achievement (effect size 0.80), while showing interest in their children's school work, assisting with homework and discussing school progress had a moderate effect size (0.38).[216]

A recent meta-analysis of 51 studies investigated the efficacy of different types of parental involvement on the academic achievement of urban pre-kindergarten to 12th grade children. Results indicated a significant relationship (0.3 of a standard deviation) between parental involvement programmes overall and achievement for children across the age-span involved. It was noted that 'parental involvement initiatives that involve parents and their children reading together (i.e., engaging in "shared reading"), parents checking their children's homework, parents and teachers communicating with one another, and partnering with one another have a noteworthy relationship with academic outcomes'.[217] Other studies have provided similar support for shared reading. First, one study analyzed the relationship between parent involvement in the early years of their children's education and their subsequent performance on the Programme for International Student Assessment (PISA) reading scores at age 15. This study showed that students whose parents reported that they had read a book with their child 'every day or almost every day' during the first year of primary school had markedly higher scores in the PISA 2009 survey than students whose parents rarely read to them. On average, across the 14 countries for which these data were available, the difference was 25 points, the equivalent of well over half a school year. A similar finding was reported even when comparing students of the same socio-economic backgrounds.[218] Second, in 2011 the UK Department for Education published a review of best practices in parental engagement. It stated that 'the evidence of the impact of family literacy, language and numeracy programmes on children's academic and learning related outcomes is extensive and robust ... [These programmes] can have a positive impact on the most disadvantaged families, including the academic outcomes of the children'.[219] Specifically, the review noted that programmes in which parents were trained to listen to their children read produced an effect size of 0.51 (about 4 months of progress), with the largest impacts produced when parents themselves taught specific reading skills to their children, with an effect size of 1.15 (over a year's progress, and over six times more effective than simply encouraging parents to read to their children).[220]

3.35 Focus on literacy and numeracy

In the United Kingdom, an Ofsted analysis of a sample of inspection reports for outstanding schools in areas of economic deprivation identified as one of the factors the provision of a broad and rich curriculum, with a clear focus on raising attainment in the basic skills of literacy and numeracy.[221] The OECD reports that, as shown on PISA results, almost one out of five students across OECD countries lack basic literacy skills, and in some countries this proportion even exceed 25%. It is very likely that those lacking basic skills at this age (15 years) will either drop out from the education system and not finish secondary school, entering the workforce with low skills, or will continue studying but struggling more than their peers and needing additional (and more expensive) support. Similar arguments can be advanced regarding numeracy.

3.36 Take account of the interaction of SES with ethnicity and gender

As I pointed out in Chapter 2, quoting Steve Strand, 'there is something about the particular combination of ethnicity, SES and gender that is uniquely related to attainment'. Suffice to say that schools should closely examine how the SES of their students interacts with the gender and ethnic composition of their students and adjust their programmes accordingly.

3.37 Carefully monitor students' performances

Schools should develop and maintain rigorous monitoring systems that track individual pupils' performance against expectations for their achievement; and tailor flexible intervention programmes with frequent reviews of performances against targets.[222] As noted by the OECD, schools and teachers should ensure that their students are acquiring good understanding and knowledge. Examples of data relevant for the classroom context include information on individual student achievement (formative assessment data, test and report card data), instructional time, disciplinary referrals and absenteeism. In the Netherlands, for example, 85% of schools use a 'learning monitoring system', which contains test results, and which is used to monitor students' progress and development.[223]

3.38 Develop a supportive school culture

Elsewhere, I reviewed the literature on school culture (synonymous with school climate), particularly as it applies to learners with special educational needs.[224] I noted that, increasingly, since around the early 2000s, attention has been paid to how the school as an organization impacts on the behaviour and achievement of its students. I pointed out that a school's culture both determines and reflects how its members behave towards each other: educators with educators, educators with learners, learners with learners, parents with educators, parents with learners … It affects how changes can be introduced into a school. As one writer put it, 'The bottom line for school change is that in order for any change to be effected, it must correspond to the culture of the school.'[225] Alternatively, change agents will have to work on changing the culture of a school if they are to be successful in introducing new ideas. In the United Kingdom, Ofsted, the school inspection arm of the government, identified steps taken to encourage any anti-school subculture to be 'left at the gates' as one of the good practices observed in schools.[226]

A recent US study sought to determine what makes successful schools different from other schools.[227] The definition of success was based on whether or not a school was performing *better than predicted* given the characteristics of the students it serves. Using data from over 1,700 California public middle and high schools, 40 schools were identified that consistently performed better than predicted on standardized tests of maths and English language arts. These schools were labelled 'beating-the-odds' (BTO) schools. School climate was measured by the California Healthy Kids Survey, which included such dimensions of the school environment as safety, academic supports, social relationships and school connectedness. The results of this study show that BTO schools had substantially more positive levels of school climate elements than other schools serving the same types of students and with the same types of staff.

In a similar vein, New Zealand's Education Review Office reported on examples of good practice in student engagement and achievement in seven New Zealand secondary schools rated decile 5 or below with rolls of 200 students or more.[228] These schools were considered to have better outcomes for students than other similar schools. Among the findings was the schools' 'relentless commitment to improvement – improvement focused on success for each and every student'. Among the factors that brought this about was the school culture, in particular the following: (a) the schools focused on students' well-being and on building deeply caring relationships; (b) a 'can do' attitude pervaded the schools – schools believed that all students can succeed and that teachers can find ways to help that happen; and (c) families, parents and community were involved in their teenagers' learning.

The OECD has listed 'a supportive school climate and environment for learning' as one of its top five recommendations for improving the achievement of low-SES students.[229] It argued for the creation of orderly and cooperative school environments in which priority is given to:

- creating positive teacher–student and peer relationships and avoiding an emphasis on discipline alone;
- encouraging students to engage with learning;
- reducing the occurrence of disruptive behaviour;
- promoting the use of data information systems as a school diagnosis tool to identify struggling students and intervening early;
- ensuring that disadvantaged schools provide their students with adequate and timely support such as counselling and mentoring; and
- considering alternative ways of organising instruction time over the day, week or year.

3.39 *Provide additional support for at-risk students*

In a 2014 report, New Zealand's Education Review Office (ERO) presented its findings of an interim evaluation of the Ministry of Education's secondary school initiative, *Achievement 2013-2017*.[230] The focus of this study was on Year 12 students identified as being unlikely to gain National Certificate in Educational Achievement (NCEA) Level 2 without additional support. A total of 2,701 students from 129 schools were identified and given additional support by leaders and teachers. The results were very encouraging: NCEA Level 2 was achieved by 60% of the students and school leaders also reported that attendance had improved and the students were more engaged as a result of the support. The improvements were attributed to the following factors:

- each student was carefully matched with a caring, supportive adult who had regular conversations with them regarding their learning;
- students' progress and achievement were monitored in a timely manner; and
- learning opportunities for students were maximized, with extra targeted teaching provided both during and outside regular school hours.

ERO concluded that these practices encouraged students to take more responsibility for their own learning through helping them gain a better understanding of what they needed to do to achieve success.

In an earlier, 2013, report, ERO presented the findings of its evaluation of the extent to which *primary* schools were using effective strategies to improve outcomes for priority groups of learners.[231] These included Māori, Pacific, special needs and students from low-SES families, who were not achieving at or above National Standards. Of concern was the fact that only 23% of the schools' actions demonstrated the use of highly effective practices students needed to catch up with their peers, with 51% doing so to some extent. Teachers' highly effective practices included the following:

- the good use of assessment data to identify those students for whom they needed to accelerate progress;
- the development of flexible, responsive learning plans for individuals and groups of students;
- the use of an inquiry cycle of teaching and learning by using assessment data to review the impact of their teaching, and changing their strategies as necessary; and
- the use of a range of appropriate teaching strategies, in both individual and group teaching.

3.40 Implement ICT access policies

As far as possible, schools and their governing authorities should aim for one-to-one computer access, particularly for those from low-SES homes. One-to-one access refers to situations where there is one device available for each student in the learning environment. Studies finding positive impacts on student learning typically describe opportunities to learn where there is at least one device per student, and they are readily available for multiple uses by the student throughout the school day.[232]

As well, schools should put in place computer safety programmes and communicate these to parents/caregivers.

III Classroom-level strategies

Nothing is more important for the well-being of students from low-SES backgrounds than what occurs in their day-to-day, minute-by-minute experiences in classrooms. Here, we must consider the appropriateness of the curriculum and associated assessment practices, the quality of the teaching and the nature of the relationships within those environments.

3.41 Employ a universally designed curriculum

A school curriculum should conform to the principles of 'universal design'; in other words, it (a) provides flexibility in the ways information is presented, in the ways students respond or demonstrate knowledge and skills, and in the ways students are engaged; and (b) reduces barriers in instruction, provides appropriate accommodations, supports and challenges, and maintains high achievement expectations for all students.[233] This means designing curricula so that they are accessible to *all* learners. It does not mean developing specific curricula for particular groups of learners, such as those from low-SES backgrounds.

3.42 Ensure equal access to the curriculum

It is important to ensure that all students have equal opportunities to learn. This means that all students should have equivalent access to the full curriculum, not a 'watered-down' version (see section 3.17).

3.43 Set high, but realistic, expectations

In the United Kingdom, an Ofsted analysis of a sample of inspection reports for outstanding schools in areas of economic deprivation identified staff being ambitious in their expectations of students' achievement.[234] Having high, but realistic expectations for low-SES learners is particularly important if they have been exposed to prolonged failure. Teachers should help learners accept that achievement results from effort, as much as from ability[235] and show them that they are personally responsible for their success, by emphasizing the development of an internal locus of control.[236]

3.44 Employ evidence-based teaching strategies

See section 1.22 of Chapter 1.

E Conclusions

Eight broad conclusions may be drawn from the information presented in this chapter:

First, SES refers to an individual's or family's economic and social position in relation to others, based on income, education and occupation. The chapter considers poverty since it forms a subset of SES and is usually, but not always, highly correlated with SES.

Second, a consistent finding of educational research studies is the negative effect of students' low-SES backgrounds on their cognitive development, social behaviours and educational achievement, particularly when SES is considered alongside ethnicity and gender.

Third, SES differences arise from a complex interaction among societal, family and school factors, which overlap with each other. All of these factors, and their interactions with each other, should be taken into account in determining policies and practices.

Fourth, children who come from low-SES backgrounds may lack language and communication skills; they may have limited access to books, Internet and good quality diet; and their parents may have low aspirations for their achievement, provide inadequate role models for their children, have low involvement in school activities, and lack knowledge of how to make their way around the educational system. The result is often that low-SES children have cultural capital and social capital that differs from the prevailing norms and expectations of schools.

Fifth, failure to improve the performance of students from low-income families has an economic and social cost. These concerns are achieving increasing prominence in the current era of globalization, in which governments are seeking to maximize the productivity of all its citizenry and to reduce welfare dependency, while at the same time fulfilling their obligations under human rights treaties and pursuing their particular notions of distributive justice.

Sixth, policies and practices should be evidence-based and their effects carefully evaluated.

Seventh, in determining the educational implications of research into low-SES students, it is important to note that some of them are resilient and achieve 'against the odds'; that schools serving low-SES are similarly heterogeneous, some also succeeding

Table 3.3 Summary of actions to mitigate the effects of low SES

Society (government)	Education system	Schools	Classrooms
• Take steps to increase SES by reducing poverty, increasing employment and improving the education levels of the populace. • Consider adjustments to minimum wages, taxation rates, welfare benefits, housing subsidies, parental leave, child support, and costs of childcare and healthcare to redress disadvantage. • Provide adequate targeted funds to the education system to facilitate its work with low-SES students and their families. • Introduce free and/or subsidized meals for low-SES students. • Develop Full-Service Schools. • Give priority to quality early childhood education. • Give serious consideration to establishing 'children's zones'. • Develop wraparound approaches among various social and other agencies.	• Ensure recruitment and retention of high quality teachers. • Develop weighted funding formulae that conform to the criteria of transparency, adequacy, efficiency, equity (both horizontal and vertical equity), robustness and freedom from unintended consequences. • Reduce class size only if it is accompanied by other, evidence-based, measures. • Prefer smaller schools for low-SES students. • Manage school choice to avoid de facto segregation along SES lines. • Avoid grade repetition. • Avoid early tracking of students and defer selection until upper secondary school. • Ensure that initial teacher education and professional development for teachers includes significant reference to SES.	• Exercise effective leadership. • Link schools with parents and communities. • Facilitate parent-training programmes. • Eliminate biases and prejudices regarding low-SES students. • Avoid streaming and ability grouping. • Consider interactions among SES, ethnicity and gender. • Develop a supportive school culture. • Identify and remediate early signs of anti-social behaviour in children. • Focus on improving literacy and numeracy. • Develop rigorous monitoring systems. • Provide additional support for at-risk students. • Implement School-wide Positive Behaviour Support programmes. • Implement ICT access policies which aim for one-to-one computer access.	• Develop universally designed curriculum. • Ensure that all students have equivalent access to the curriculum. • Set high, but realistic expectations. • Implement evidence-based teaching strategies. • Understand that many children from low-SES may have different cultural capital and worldviews from teachers.

against the odds; and that most educational programmes that are beneficial for students from low-SES backgrounds are appropriate for all students.

Eighth, a range of actions to mitigate the effects of low-SES emerges from the evidence presented in this chapter. These are presented in Table 3.3. The overriding consideration is to develop and implement policies that contribute towards comprehensive inclusiveness at all levels: societal, education system, schools and classrooms.

Notes

1 OECD (2012). *Equity and quality in education: Supporting disadvantaged students and schools.* Paris: Author, p. 15.
2 Rubin, M., Denson, N., Kilpatrick, S., Matthews, K. E., Stehlik, T. & Zyngier, D. (2014). '"I am working-class": Subjective self-definition as a missing measure of social class and socioeconomic status in higher education research.' *Educational Researcher*, 43(4), 196–200.
3 American Psychological Association. URL: http://www.apa.org/topics/socioeconomic-status/ (accessed 20 December 2014). For a detailed explanation, see American Psychological Association Task Force on Socioeconomic Status (2007). *Report of the APA Task Force on Socioeconomic Status.* Washington, DC: American Psychological Association.
4 Schulz, W. (2005). 'Measuring the socio-economic background of students and its effect on achievement in PISA 2000 and PISA 2003.' Paper prepared for the Annual Meetings of the American Educational Research Association in San Francisco, 7–11 April 2005.
5 Cole, M. (2012). 'Social class, Marxism and twenty-first-century capitalism.' In M. Cole (ed.), *Education equality and human rights* (pp. 217–238, p. 217). London: Routledge.
6 Ischinger, B. (2012). 'Foreword.' In OECD (2012), op. cit.
7 Ibid.
8 McKinsey and Company (2009). *The economic impact of the achievement gap in America's schools*, p. 6.
9 Boston Consulting Group (2010). *The mobility manifesto.* London: Sutton Trust.
10 Gladwell, M. (2000). *The tipping point: How little things can make a big difference.* New York, NY: Back Bay Books, p. 12.
11 OECD (2014). *PISA 2012 in focus: What 15-year-olds know and what they can do with what they know.* Paris: Author.
12 Perry, E. & Francis, B. (2010). *The social class gap for educational achievement: A review of the literature.* London: RSA.
13 Teese, R. (2011). *From opportunity to outcomes. The changing role of public schooling in Australia and national funding arrangements.* Melbourne: Centre for Research on Education Systems, University of Melbourne.
14 OECD (2012). op. cit.
15 Schulz op. cit. For example, in the 2003 reading results for PISA, the highest SES weightings occurred in Belgium (23%), Germany (22%), Hungary (22%), Austria (21%), France (20%), UK (19%), Switzerland (18%), Mexico (18%), US (18%) and New Zealand (17%). The lowest weightings were in Iceland (4%), Hong Kong (5%), Indonesia (7%), Brazil (8%), Latvia (8%), Thailand (10%), Finland (10%), Canada (10%), Russia (11%) and Korea (11%).
16 Kupiainen, S., Hautamaki, J. & Karjarlainen, T. (2009). *The Finnish education system and PISA.* Helsinki: Ministry of Education Publications.
17 OECD (2001). *Knowledge and skills for life: First results from the PISA 2000.* Paris: Author.
18 Hattie, J. (2009). *Visible learning: A synthesis of over 800 meta-analyses relating to achievement.* London: Routledge.
19 Sirin, S.R. (2005). 'Socioeconomic status and academic achievement: A meta-analysis.' *Review of Educational Research*, 25(7), 417–453.
20 Reardon, S. 'The widening academic achievement gap between the rich and the poor: New evidence and possible explanations. In G.J. Duncan & R. J. Murnane (eds), *Whither opportunity: Rising inequality, schools, and children's life chances* (pp. 47–69) New York: Russell Sage.

21 Duncan, G. J. & Magnuson, K.A. (2011). 'The nature and impact of early achievement skills, attention skills, and behavior problems.' In G.J. Duncan & R.J. Murnane (eds), *Whither opportunity: Rising inequality, schools, and children's life chances* (pp. 47–69) New York: Russell Sage.

22 Schools Analysis and Research Division (2009). *Deprivation and education: The evidence on pupils in England: Foundation Stage to Key Stage 5.* London: Department for Schools and Families.

23 Miller, G., Chen, E. & Brody, G.H. (2014). 'Can upward mobility cost you your health?' *New York Times*, 16 January 2014.

24 Strand, S. (2014). 'Ethnicity, gender, social class and achievement gaps at age 16: Intersectionality and "getting it" for the white working class.' *Research Papers in Education*, 29(2), 131–171.

25 Brooks-Gunn, J. & Duncan, G.J. (1997). 'The effects of poverty on children.' *Future Child*, 7, 55–71.

26 Yoshikawa, H., Aber, J.L. & Beardslee, W.R. (2012). 'The effects of poverty on the mental, emotional, and behavioral health of children and youth: implications for prevention.' *American Psychologist*, 67, 272–284.

27 Luby, J., Belden, A., Botteron, K., Marrus, N., Harms, M.P., Babb, C., Nishino, T. & Barch, D. (2013). 'The effects of poverty on childhood brain development: The mediating effect of caregiving and stressful life events.' *Journal of the American Medical Association Pediatrics*, 167(12), 1135–1142.

28 Noble, K.G., Houston, S.M., Kan, E. & Sowell, E.R. (2012). 'Neural correlates of socioeconomic status in the developing human brain.' *Developmental Science*, 15, 516–527.

29 Jednor g K., Altarelli I., Monzalvo K., Fluss, J., Dubois, J. Billard, C. & Dehaene-Lambertz, G. (2012). 'The influence of socioeconomic status on children's brain structure.' *PLoS ONE*, 7(8): e42486. doi:10.1371/journal.pone.0042486. For further reviews of the impact of poverty on brain development, see Lipina, S.J. & Colombo, J.A. (2009). *Poverty and brain development during childhood: An approach from cognitive psychology and neuroscience.* Washington, DC: American Psychological Association.

30 Dyson, A., Kerr, K. & Wellings, C. 2013). *Developing children's zones for England: What's the evidence?* London: Save the Children's Fund.

31 See URL: http://hcz.org/ (accessed 14 November 2015).

32 Berliner, D. (2013). 'Effects of inequality and poverty vs. teachers and schooling on America's youth.' *Teachers College Record*, 115(12), 1–15.

33 Wilkinson, R.G. & Pickett, K. (2009). *The spirit level: Why more equal societies almost always do better.* London: Allen Lane.

34 See Closing the Gap website, URL: http://www.closingthegap.org.nz/site-map/the-spirit-level/ (accessed 20 June 2014).

35 Berliner, D. (2004). 'If the underlying premise for no child left behind is false, how can that act solve our problems?' In K. Goodman, P. Shannon & Y. Goodman (eds), *Saving our schools: The case for public education in America* (pp. 167–184). Oakland, CA: RDR Books.

36 Ainscow, M., Dyson, A., Goldrick, S. & West, M. (2012). *Developing equitable education systems.* London: Routledge.

37 Piketty, T. (2014). *Capital in the twenty-first century.* Cambridge, MA: Belknap Press.

38 National Equality Panel (2010). *An anatomy of national inequality in the UK.* London: Government Equalities Office.

39 Child Poverty Action Group (2009). *Ending child poverty.* London: Author.

40 Social Mobility and Child Poverty Commission (2015). *State of the nation: Social mobility and child poverty on Great Britain.* Presented to Parliament pursuant to section 8B(6) of the Child Poverty Act 2010.

41 Several commentators have questioned Piketty's insistence that the rate of return will remain constant, and have suggested instead that it is likely to decline, leading to stagnation and recession: Judis, J.B. (2014). 'Thomas Piketty is pulling your leg: He clearly read Karl Marx. But don't call him a Marxist.' *New Republic*, 6 May 2014.

42 Solow, R.M. (2014). 'Thomas Piketty is right.' *New Republic*. URL: http://www.newrepublic.com/article/117429/capital-twenty-first-century-thomas-piketty-reviewed (accessed 20 July 2014).

43 Summers, L.H. & Balls, E. (co-chairs) (2015). *Report of the Commission on Inclusive Prosperity.* Washington, DC: Center for American Progress, p. 1. URL: https://cdn.americanprogress.org/wp-content/uploads/2015/01/IPC-PDF-full.pdf (accessed 15 November 2015).

44 Central Intelligence Agency (2014). *The world factbook.* URL: https://www.cia.gov/library/publications/the-world-factbook/rankorder/2172rank.html (accessed 30 June 2014).

45 World Bank (2014). *Poverty and equity.* Washington, DC: Author. URL: http://povertydata.worldbank.org/poverty/region/SAS (accessed 1 July 2014).

46 The EFA Global Monitoring Report Team (2014). *Teaching and learning: Achieving quality for all.* Paris: UNESCO.

47 Ibid., p. 14.

48 Dixon, R. (2014). 'The road from beggar to militant.' *Los Angeles Times*, 17 August 2014.

49 Bourdieu, P. & Passeron, J.C. (1977). *Reproduction in education, society and culture.* London: Sage.

50 Reay, D. (2001). 'Finding or losing yourself? Working class relationships to education.' *Journal of Educational Policy*, 16(4), 333-346.

51 Hampden-Thompson, G., Guzman, L. & Lippman, L. (2008). 'Cultural capital: What does it offer students? A cross-national analysis.' In J. Zajda, K. Biraimah & W. Gaudelli (eds), *Education and social inequality in the global culture* (pp. 155-180). New York, NY: Springer, p. 158.

52 Hart, S., Dixon, A., Drummond, M.J. & McIntyre, D. (2004). *Learning without limits.* Maidenhead: Open University Press.

53 Putnam, R.D. (2015). *Our kids: The American dream in crisis.* New York: Simon and Schuster.

54 National Equality Panel, op. cit.

55 Social Mobility and Child Poverty Commission, op. cit.

56 Cassen, R. & Kingdon, G. (2007). *Tackling low educational achievement.* York: Joseph Rowntree Foundation.

57 Hart, B. & Risley, T.R. (2003). 'The early catastrophe: The 30 million word gap by age 3.' *American Educator*, Spring, 4-9. URL: http://www.aft.org//sites/default/files/periodicals/TheEarlyCatastrophe.pdf (accessed 24 February 2016).

58 Department for Children, Families and Schools (2009). *Deprivation and education.* London: Author.

59 Department for Children, Families and Schools (2009). *The extra mile: How schools succeed in raising aspirations in deprived communities.* London: Author.

60 Cabinet Office (2008). *Aspiration and attainment amongst young people in deprived communities.* London: Author.

61 Hampden-Thompson, et al., op. cit.

62 Hatcher, R. (2012). 'Social class and schooling.' In M. Cole (ed.), *Education equality and human rights* (pp. 239-267). London: Routledge.

63 Mitchell, D. R. (1970). 'Education and the disadvantaged child.' In R.J. Bates (ed.), *Prospects in New Zealand education* (pp. 181-198). Auckland: Hodder and Stoughton.

64 Bernstein, B. (1965). 'A socio-linguistic approach to social learning'. In J. Gould (ed.), *Penguin survey of social sciences* (pp. 165-180). London: Penguin Books.

65 *The Economist* (2015). 'An hereditary meritocracy.' *The Economist*, 414(8922), 19-24.

66 Darmon, N. & Drewnowski, A. (2008). 'Does social class predict diet quality?' *American Journal of Clinical Nutrition*, 87(5), 1107-1117.

67 Ministry of Health (2009). *A focus on the health of Māori and Pacific children: Key findings of the 2006/07 New Zealand Health Survey.* Wellington: Author.

68 Cox, A. & Black, R. (2012). *Window on Waikato poverty: Food and Waikato school communities.* Hamilton: Anglican Action.

69 Robertson, A., Lobstein, T. & Knai, C. (2007). *Obesity and socio-economic groups in Europe: Evidence review and implications for action.* Brussels: European Commission.

70 Singh, G.K., Kogan, M.D. & van Dyck, P.C. (2008). 'A multilevel analysis of state and regional disparities in childhood and adolescence obesity in the United States.' *Journal of Community Health*, 33(2), 90-102.

71 Skelton, J.A., Cook, S.R., Auinger, P., Klein, J.D. & Barlow, S.E. (2009). 'Prevalence and trends of severe obesity among US children and adolescents.' *Academic Pediatrics*, 9(5), 322-329.

72 OECD (2012), op. cit.

73 Mullis, I., Martin, M. & Foy, P. (2008). *TIMSS 2007 International mathematics report: Findings from IEA's trends in International Mathematics and Science Study at the fourth and eighth grades.* Chestnut Hill: TIMSS and PIRLS International Study Center, Boston College.

74 Perry, L.B. & McConney, A. (2010). 'Does the SES of the school matter? An examination of socioeconomic status and student achievement using PISA 2003.' *Teachers College Record*, 112(4), 1137-1162.

75 Willms, J.D. (2010). 'School composition and contextual effects on student outcomes.' *Teachers College Record*, 122(4), 1008-1037.

76 OECD (2012), op. cit., p. 107.

77 Harris, D.N. (2010). 'How do school peers influence student educational outcomes? Theory and evidence from economics and other social sciences.' *Teachers College Record*, 112(4), 1163-1197.

78 Campaign Ontario 2000 (2013). *Strengthening families for Ontario's future: 2012 report card on child and family poverty in Ontario*. Toronto: Toronto Family Service. URL: http://www.campaign2000.ca/Ontario/reportcards/2013ReportCardOnChildPovertyOntario.pdf (accessed 29 December 2014).

79 Benn, C. & Chitty, C. (1996). *Thirty years on: Is comprehensive education alive and well or struggling to survive?* London: David Fulton Publishers.

80 Rubin, B. (2008). 'Detracking in context: How local constructions of ability complicate equity-geared reform.' *Teachers College Record*, 110(3), 647–700.

81 OECD (2012), op. cit.

82 Duckworth, K., Akerman, R., Gutman, L.M. & Vorhaus, J. (2009). *Influences and leverages on low levels of attainment: A review of literature and policy initiatives. Research Report 31*. London: Centre for Research on the Wider Benefits of Learning, Institute of Education, University of London, p. 30.

83 Lipsey, M.W. & Wilson, D.B. (1993). 'The efficacy of psychological, educational, and behavioral treatment: Confirmation from meta-analysis.' *American Psychologist*, 48(12), 1181–1209.

84 Hattie, op. cit.

85 Houtveen, T. & Van de Grift, W. (2001). 'Inclusion and adaptive instruction in elementary education.' *Journal of Education for Students Placed at Risk*, 6(4), 389–409.

86 Fogelman, K., Essen, J. & Tibbenhaum, A. (1978). 'Ability grouping in secondary schools and attainment.' *Educational Studies*, 4(3), 201–212.

87 Duckworth et al., op. cit.

88 MacIver, D.J., Reuman, D.A. & Main, S.R. (1995). 'Social structuring of the school: Studying what is, illuminating what could be.' *Annual Review of Psychology*, 46, 375–400.

89 Schmidt, W.H., Burroughs, N.A., Zoido, P. & Houang, R.T. (2015). 'The role of schooling in perpetuating educational inequality: An international perspective.' *Educational Researcher*, 20(10), 1–16.

90 Reeves reported an almost identical finding: Reeves, E. (2012). 'The effects of opportunity to learn, family socioeconomic status, and friends on the rural math achievement gap in high school.' *American Behavioral Scientist*, 56(7), 887–907.

91 Schmidt et al., op. cit., p. 11.

92 UNESCO (2013). *Global media and information literacy assessment framework: Country readiness and competencies*. Paris: Author; and UNESCO (2013). *Media and Information Literacy policy and strategy guidelines*. Paris: Author.

93 Madden, M., Lenhart, A., Duggan M., Cortesi, S. & Gasser, U. (2013). *Teens and technology*. Washington, DC: Pew Research Center. URL: http://www. atlantycalab.com/untangiblelibrary/wp-content/untangible/130315%20-%20PIP_TeensandTechnology2013.pdf (accessed 31 December 2014).

94 Livingstone, S. & Haddon, L. (2009). *EU kids online: Final report*. London: London School of Economics. URL: www.eukidsonline.net (accessed 31 December 2014).

95 OECD (2014). op. cit.

96 For a New Zealand analysis of child poverty, see Boston, J. (2013). *Improving educational performance: Why tackling child poverty must be part of the solution*. Paper prepared for a Symposium on 'Poverty Impacts on Learning' organized by Accent Learning, Karori Campus, Victoria University of Wellington, 24 May 2013. URL: http://igps.victoria.ac.nz/staff/team/Education%20and%20child%20poverty%20V4.pdf (accessed 3 January 2015).

97 Social Mobility and Child Poverty Commission, op. cit.

98 OECD (2014), op. cit.

99 Nettle, D. (2009). 'Social class through the evolutionary lens.' *The Psychologist*, 22(11), 934–937.

100 Berliner, op. cit.

101 OECD (2012), op. cit.

102 Social Mobility and Child Poverty Commission, op. cit.

103 While the focus of this section is on the school sector, I do recognize that, as advocated by the OECD, sufficient resources should be provided to improve the quality of early childhood education and care and to promote access, in particular for disadvantaged families.

104 OECD (2012), op. cit.

105 For a good account of school food programmes, see Harper, C., Wood, L. & Mitchell, C. (2008). *The provision of school food in 18 countries*. Sheffield, UK: School Food Trust.

106 European Commission/EACEA/Eurydice (2014). *Financing schools in Europe: Mechanisms, methods and criteria in public funding*. Eurydice Report. Luxembourg: Publications Office of the European Union. URL: http://eacea.ec.europa.eu/education/eurydice/documents/thematic_reports/170EN.pdf (accessed 18 December 2014).

107   Gonski, D. (Chair) (2011). *Review of funding for schooling: Final report*. Canberra, ACT: Department of Education, Employment and Workplace Relations.

108   See Select Committee on School and Funding, The Senate (2014). *Equity and excellence in Australian schools*. Canberra: Senate Printing Unit, Parliament House, URL: http://www.aph.gov.au/Parliamentary_Business/Committees/Senate/School_Funding/School_Funding/Report/a03 (accessed 15 November 2015).

109   OECD (2012), op. cit., p. 118.

110   Ministry for Economic Affairs and the Interior (2014). *Municipalities and regions: Tasks and financing*. Copenhagen: Author.

111   Personal communication from Professor Hannu Savolainen, University of Jyv skyl , Finland, 18 December 2014.

112   Mourshed, M., Chijoke, C. & Barber. M. (2010). *How the world's most improved school systems keep getting better*. London: McKinsey and Company.

113   See Mitchell, D. (2014). *What really works in special and inclusive education: Using evidence-based teaching strategies*. Second edition. London: Routledge, Chapter 28.

114   De Vijlder, F.J. (nd). *Dutch Education: A closed or an open system?* URL: https://www.academia.edu/1368385/Dutch_Education_a_closed_or_an_open_system (accessed 20 November 2014).

115   Recent research by Jeremy Clark and Sumita Das suggests that attention *should* be paid to the relative weightings of these components. In an evaluation of the relationship between the various factors taken into account in determining decile rankings and school achievement, they found that the marginal effectiveness in targeting low skill occupation was comparatively high, whereas targeting receiving welfare was comparatively low: Clark, J. & Das, S.R. (2015). *Evaluating returns to funding different measures of student disadvantage: Evidence from New Zealand*. Christchurch, New Zealand: Department of Economics and Finance, University of Canterbury.

116   Borge, L.-E. (2006). *Centralized or decentralized financing of local governments? Consequences for efficiency and inequality of service provision*. Working Paper No. 14/2006. Trondheim: Department of Economics, Norwegian University of Science and Technology. URL: http://www.svt.ntnu.no/iso/WP/2006/14efftap_wp.pdf (accessed 20 December 2014).

117   Norway Directorate for Education and Training (2014). 'Facts and analysis of kindergarten, primary and secondary education in Norway.' *Education Mirror*, Oslo: Author. URL: http://utdanningsspeilet.udir.no/en/ (accessed 20 December 2014).

118   Moloi, M. & Chetty, M. (2011). *The quality of primary school inputs in South Africa*. Southern and Eastern Africa Consortium for Monitoring Educational Quality. URL: http://www.sacmeq.org/sites/default/files/sacmeq/reports/sacmeq-iii/policy-brief/sou_school_inputs_15oct2011_final.pdf (accessed 20 December 2014).

119   Nicaise, I., Esping-Andersen, G., Pont, B. & Tunstall, P. (2005). *Equity in education: Thematic review. Sweden country note*. Paris: OECD.

120   Ibid.

121   House of Commons (2014). *Underachievement in education by white working class children – Education Committee*. URL: http://www.publications.parliament.uk/pa/cm201415/cmselect/cmeduc/142/14207.htm (accessed 20 November 2014).

122   The Free School Meal scheme is based on a family being in receipt of any means-tested benefits, such as Income Support, Income-based Jobseeker's Allowance, Income-related Employment and Support Allowance, and support under the Immigration and Asylum Act 1999. In passing, it should be noted that several writers have challenged the validity of employing Free School Meals as a proxy for SES. See Hobbs, G. & Vignoles, A. (2007). *Is free school meal status a valid proxy for socio-economic status (in schools research)?* London: Centre for Economics of Education, London School of Economics; and Shuttleworth, I. (1995). 'The relationship between social deprivation, as measured by individual free school meal eligibility, and educational attainment at GCSE in Northern Ireland: a preliminary investigation.' *British Educational Research Journal*, 21(4), 487–504.

123   The Income Deprivation Affecting Children Index measures in a local area the proportion of children under the age of 16 that live in low-income households.

124   Carpenter, H., Papps, I., Bragg, J., Dyson, A., Harris, D., Kerr, K., Todd, L. & Laing, K. (2013). *Evaluation of pupil premium: Research report*. Reference: DFE-RR282. London: Department for Education.

125   Under a new Ofsted inspection framework, inspectors now look for evidence of what the Pupil Premium has been spent on and how this has impacted on student attainment (ibid.).

126   Biddle, B.J. & Berliner, D.C. (2002). 'A research synthesis: Unequal school funding in the United States.' *Educational Leadership*, 59(8), 48-59.

127   Federal Register / Vol. 79, No. 173 / Monday, September 8, 2014 / Proposed Rules. URL: http://www.gpo.gov/fdsys/pkg/FR-2014-09-08/pdf/2014-21185.pdf (accessed 1 December 2014)

128   What Works Clearinghouse. URL: http://ies.ed.gov/ncee/wwc/documentsum.aspx?sid=19 (accessed 1 December 2014).

129   US Department of Education. (2002). *Comprehensive School Reform (CSR) Program Guidance.* URL: http://www2.ed.gov/programs/compreform/guidance/index.html (accessed 20 December 2014).

130   Borman, G. D. Hewes, G.M., Overman, L.T. & Brown, S. (2003). 'Comprehensive school reform and achievement: A meta-analysis.' *Review of Educational Research*, 73(2), 125-230.

131   Ross, K. & Levačić, R. (eds) (1999). *Needs based resource allocation in education via formula funding of schools.* Paris: International Institute of Educational Planning; Levačić, R. (2006). 'Funding schools by formula.' Paper prepared for International Conference on Educational Systems and the Challenge of Improving Results, 15-16 September 2006, University of Lausanne, Switzerland.

132   Jenkins, A., Levačić, R. & Vignoles, A. (2006). 'Estimating the relationship between school resources and pupil attainment at GCSE.' *DfES Research Report 727*, 85; and Faubert, B. (2012). *In-school policies and practices for overcoming school failure: A literature review.* OECD Education Working Paper. Paris: OECD.

133   Hanushek, E.A. (1997). 'Assessing the effects of school resources on student performance: An update.' *Education Evaluation and Policy Analysis*, 19(2), 141-164.

134   Fazekas, M. (2102). *School funding formulas: Review of main characteristics and impacts.* OECD Education Working Paper 74. Paris: OECD, p. 22.

135   Grubb, W.N., Huerta, L.A. & Goe, L. (2006). 'Straw into gold, revenues into results: Spinning out the implications of the improved school finance.' *Journal of Education Finance*, 31(4), 334-359.

136   For a cost-benefit analysis methodology, see New Zealand Treasury (2011). *Cost benefit analysis primer.* Wellington: The Treasury. URL: http://www.treasury.govt.nz/publications/guidance/planning/costbenefitanalysis/primer (accessed 28 December 2014).

137   Borge, op. cit.

138   Levačić, R. (2008). 'Financing schools: Evolving patterns of autonomy and control.' *Educational Management Administration & Leadership*, 36(2), 221-234.

139   Wikipedia (accessed 20 December 2014).

140   Wylie, C. (2012). *Vital connections: Why we need more than self-managing schools.* Wellington: NZCER.

141   Harper et al., op. cit.

142   Children's Commissioner (2013). *A framework for food in schools programmes in New Zealand.* Wellington: Author. URL: http://www.occ.org.nz/assets/Uploads/Reports/Poverty/A-framework-for-food-in-schools.pdf (accessed 29 December 2014).

143   Pollit, E. & Matthews, R. (1998). 'Breakfast and cognition: An integrative summary.' *American Journal of Clinical Nutrition*, 67(4), 804S-813S.

144   Weinreb, L., Wehler, C., Perloff, J., Scott, R., Hosmer, D., Sagor, L. & Gunderson, C. (2002). 'Hunger: Its impact on children's health and mental health.' *Pediatrics*, 110(4), e41.

145   Kristjansson, E.A., Robinson, V., Petticrew, M., MacDonald, B., Krasevec, J., Janzen, L., Greenhalgh, T., Wells, G., MacGowan, J., Farmer, A., Shea, B.J., Mayhew, A. & Tugwell, P. (2006). 'School feeding for improving the physical and psychosocial health of disadvantaged students.' *Campbell Systematic Reviews*, 2006:14 DOI: 10.4073/csr.2006.14.

146   Benton, D. & Parker, P.Y. (1998). 'Breakfast, blood glucose, and cognition.' *American Journal of Clinical Nutrition*, 67(4), 772S-778S.

147   Other descriptors of essentially the same phenomenon as FSSs include *school-linked services*: Volpe, R., Batra, A., Bomio, S. & Costin, D. (1999). *Third generation school-linked services for at-risk children.* Toronto: Dr R.G.N. Laidlaw Research Centre, Institute of Child Study, OISE, University of Toronto; *collaborative school-linked services*: Wang, M.C., Haertel, G.D. & Walberg, H.J. (1995). *Effective features of collaborative school-linked services for children in elementary school: What do we know from research and practice?* Publication Series #95-16. Philadelphia, PA: National Center on Education in the Inner Cities. ERIC Document Reproduction Service No. ED 399 309; and *full-service community schools*, or simply *community schools*: Sailor, W. & Skrtic, T.M. (1996). 'School-community partnerships and educational reform'. *Remedial and Special Education*, 17(5), 267-270, p. 283; Campbell-Allen, R.,

Shah, M.P.A., Salender, R. & Zazave, R. (2009). 'Full-service schools: Policy review and recommenda-tions.' In Harvard Graduate School of Education, *Wiki Project, GSE A100. Introduction to educational policy.* Cambridge, MA: Harvard Graduate School of Education.

148   Dryfoos, J. (1994). *Full-service schools: A revolution in health and social services for children, youth and families.* San Francisco: Jossey-Bass, p. 142.

149   Scottish Office (1999). *New community schools. The prospectus.* Edinburgh: Author.

150   Adelman, H.S. & Taylor, L. (1997). 'Ideas for a comprehensive, integrated, school-wide approach: System reform to address barriers to learning: beyond school-linked services and full-service schools.' *American Journal of Orthopsychiatry,* 67(3), 408–421; Adelman, H. & Taylor L. (2002). *School-community partnerships: A guide.* Los Angeles: UCLA Center for Mental Health in Schools; and Smith, M.K. (2000, 2004). Full service schooling. *Encyclopedia of Informal Education,* URL: http://www.Infed.org/schooling/f-serv.htm (accessed 20 December 2012).

151   See Mitchell, D. (2012). *Joined-up: A comprehensive ecological model for working with children with complex needs and their families. A review of the literature carried out for the New Zealand Ministry of Education.* Wellington, New Zealand: Ministry of Education. Available on NZ Ministry of Education website: http://www.minedu.govt.nz/~/media/MinEdu/Files/TheMinistry/Consultation/JoinedUp.pdf (accessed 23 May 2016).

152   Toronto District School Board (2010). *Full service schools.* Toronto: Toronto District School Board.

153   Cummings, C., Dyson, A., Muijs, D., Papps I., Pearson D., Raffo, C., Tiplady, L, Todd, L. & Crowther, D. (2007). *Evaluation of the Full Service Extended Schools Initiative: Final report.* Research Report RR852. London: Department for Education and Skills. For a more recent summary of FSES in the UK, see Smith, M.K. (2014). 'Extended schools and services: Theory, practice and issues', *The Ency-clopedia of Informal Education.* URL: http://infed.org/mobi/extended-schools-and-service-theory-practice-and-issues/ (accessed 1 December 2014).

154   Cummings et al., op. cit., pp. 2–3.

155   Ofsted (2006). *Extended services in schools and children's centres.* London: Author. URL: http://www.ofsted.gov.uk/resources/extended-services-schools-and-childrens-centres (accessed 1 December 2014).

156   Carpenter, H., Peters, M. Oseman, D., Papps, I., Dyson, A., Jones, L., Cummings, C., Laing, K. & Todd, L. (2010). *Extended Services evaluation: End of year one report.* London: Department for Education. URL: https://www.gov.uk/government/uploads/system/uploads/attachment_data/file/198000/DFE-RB016.pdf (accessed 1 December 2014).

157   Scottish Office, op. cit.

158   Mongon, D. (2013). 'Educational attainment: White British students from low income backgrounds. Research paper for Ofsted's *Access and achievement in education 2013 review.*' London: Ofsted (June 2013), pp. 4, 37.

159   Ofsted (2008). *White boys from low-income backgrounds: Good practice in schools.* London: Author.

160   Bruns, E.J. & Walker, J.S. (2011). 'Research on the wraparound process: Intervention components and implementation supports.' *Journal of Child and Family Studies,* 20, 709–712.

161   Bruns, E.J., Sather, A., Pullmann, M.D. & Stambaugh, L.F. (2011). 'National trends in implementing wrap-around: Results from the state wraparound survey.' *Journal of Child and Family Studies,* 20, 726–735.

162   Berliner, op. cit.

163   Hart & Risley, op. cit.

164   Duncan, G.J. & Magnuson, K. (2013). 'Investing in preschool programs.' *Journal of Economic Per-spectives,* 27(2), 109–132.

165   For a review, see Springate, I., Atkinson, M., Straw, S., Lamont, E. & Grayson, H. (2008). *Narrowing the gap in outcomes: Early years (0–5).* Slough: NFER.

166   Sylva, K., Melhuish, E.C., Sammons, P., Siraj-Blatchford, I. & Taggart, B. (2004). *The Effective Provi-sion of Pre-School Education (EPPE) Project: Final report.* London: DfES/ Institute of Education, University of London.

167   Feldman, M.A. (ed.) (2004). *Early intervention: The essential readings.* Oxford: Blackwell Publishing.

168   Piggott, T.D. & Israel, M.S. (2005). 'Head Start children's transition to kindergarten: Evidence from the early childhood longitudinal study.' *Journal of Early Childhood Research,* 3(1), 77–104.

169   Duncan & Magnuson, op. cit.

170   Ibid.

171   Buckley, J.A. (2009). 'Introduction to this special issue: Implementing evidence-based interven-tions in elementary schools for students at risk for severe behavior disorders.' *Journal of Emo-tional and Behavioral Disorders,* 17(4), 195–196, p. 195.

172   Church J. (2003). *The definition, diagnosis and treatment of children and youth with severe behaviour difficulties: A review of research*. Wellington: Ministry of Education, p. 50.

173   Ibid., p. 66.

174   Schleicher, A. (2015). 'Seven big myths about top-performing school systems.' *BBC News*, 4 February 2015.

175   Hattie, op. cit.

176   Wossmann, L. & Sch tz, G. (2006). *Efficiency and equity in European education and training systems*. Analytical Report for the European Commission prepared by the European Expert Network on Economics of Education.

177   Krueger, A. (2002). 'Understanding the magnitude and effect of class size on student achievement.' In L. Mishel & R. Rothstein (eds), *The class size debate* (pp. 7–36). Washington, DC: Economic Policy Institute.

178   Howley, C.B. & Howley, A. A. (2004). 'School size and the influence of socioeconomic status on student achievement: Confronting the threat of size bias in national data sets.' *Education Policy Analysis Archives*, 12(52), 1–35.

179   Leithwood, K. & Jantzi, D. (2009). 'A review of empirical evidence about school size effects: A policy perspective.' *Review of Educational Research*, 79(1), 464–490.

180   Abalde, M.A. (2014). *School size policies: A literature review*. Paris: OECD.

181   Crosnoe R., Kirkpatrick, M. & Elder, G. (2004). 'School size and the interpersonal side of education: An examination of race/ethnicity and organizational development.' *Social Science Quarterly*, 85(5), 1259–1274.

182   Walberg, H.J. & Walberg, H.J. III (1994). 'Losing local control.' *Educational Researcher*, 23(5), 19–26.

183   Duncombe, W.D. & Yinger, J.M. (2010). 'School district consolidation: The benefits and costs.' *School Administrator*, 67(5), 10–17.

184   Perry & McConney, op. cit.; OECD (2005). *School factors related to quality and equity: Results from PISA 2000*. Paris: Author.

185   OECD (2012), op. cit.

186   Burgess, S., Greaves, E., Vignoles, A. & Wilson, D. (2015). 'What parents want: School preferences and school choice.' *Economic Journal*, 125(587), 1262–1289.

187   Muset, P. (2012). *School choice and equity: Current policies in OECD countries and a literature review*. Paris: OECD, p. 43.

188   Ladd H., E. Fiske & N. Ruijs (2009). 'Parental choice in the Netherlands: Growing concerns about segregation.' Prepared for School Choice and School Improvement: Research in State, District and Community Contexts, Vanderbilt University, October 2009. URL: http://www.vanderbilt.edu/schoolchoice/conference/papers/Ladd_COMPLETE.pdf (accessed 20 December 2014).

189   OECD (2012), op. cit.

190   Hattie, op. cit.

191   Muschkin, C.G., Glennie, E. & Beck, A.N. (2014). 'Peer contexts: Do old for grade and retained peers influence student behavior in middle school?' *Teachers College Record*, 116(4).

192   OECD (2012), op. cit.

193   Hanushek, E. & W §mann, L. (2006). 'Does educational tracking affect performance and inequality? Differences-in-differences evidence across countries.' *Economic Journal*, 116(510), C63–C76.

194   Mulkey, L.M., Catsambis, S., Steelman, L.C., & Hanes-Ramos, M. (2009). 'Keeping track of getting offtrack: Issues in the tracking of students.' In L.J. Saha & A.G. Dworkin (eds), *International handbook of research on teachers and teaching* (pp. 1081–1100). New York, NY: Springer.

195   Rubin, op. cit.

196   OECD (2012), op. cit.

197   UNESCO/ILO (2002). *Technical and vocational education and training for the twenty-first century: UNESCO and ILO recommendations*. Paris/Geneva: UNESCO/ILO.

198   Ibid., p. 22.

199   Symonds, W.C., Schwartz, R.B. & Ferguson, R. (2011). *Pathways to prosperity: Meeting the challenge of preparing young Americans for the 21st century*. Report issued by the Pathways to Prosperity Project. Cambridge, MA: Harvard Graduate School of Education.

200   See OECD (2010). *Learning for jobs*. Paris: Author. URL: www.oecd.org/edu/learningforjobs (accessed 3 January 2015).

201   Kendall, S., Straw, S., Jones, M., Springate, I. & Grayson, H. (2008). *A review of the research evidence (narrowing the gap in outcomes for vulnerable groups)*. Slough: NFER.

202   Ofsted (2007). *The Annual Report of Her Majesty's Chief Inspector of Education, Children's Services and Skills 2006/07*. London: Author.

203   Social Mobility and Child Poverty Commission, op. cit.

204   Leithwood, K., Louis, K.S., Anderson, S. & Wahlstrom, K. (2004). *Review of research: How leadership influences student learning*. New York, NY: Wallace Foundation.

205   Ibid.

206   David Laws (UK Schools Minister) (2014). Speech to the North of England Education Conference. URL: https://www.gov.uk/government/speeches/david-laws-speech-to-the-north-of-england-education-conference (accessed 1 December 2014).

207   Ministry of Education (2014). Information sheets from the Investing in Educational Success initiative. URL: http://www.education.govt.nz/ministry-of-education/specific-initiatives/investing-in-educational-success (accessed 19 May 2016).

208   Ward, S.C., Bagley, C., Lumby, J., Woods, P., Hamilton, T. & Roberts, A. (2015). 'School leadership for equity: Lessons from the literature.' *International Journal of Inclusive Education*, 19(4), 333–346.

209   Brown, K.M. (2004). 'Leadership for social justice and equity: Weaving a transformative framework and pedagogy.' *Educational Administration Quarterly*, 40(1), 77–108, p. 89.

210   Niesche, R. & Keddie, A. (2011). 'Foregrounding issues of equity and diversity in educational leadership.' *School Leadership and Management*, 31(1), 65–77.

211   See also section 6.20 for more details on parent training programmes

212   Ferlazzo, L. (2011). 'Involvement or engagement.' *Schools, Families, Communities*, 68(8), 10–14.

213   OECD (2012), op. cit.

214   Ofsted (2008), op. cit.

215   Kendall et al., op. cit.

216   Hattie, op. cit., Chapter 5.

217   Jeynes, W. (2012). 'A meta-analysis of the efficacy of different types of parental involvement programs for urban students.' *Urban Education*, 47(4), 706–742.

218   *PISA 2009 results: Overcoming social background: Equity in learning opportunities and outcomes,*Volume II. Reported in Borgonovi, F. (2011). *PISA in Focus 2011/10*. Paris: OECD.

219   Department for Education (2011). *Review of best practice in parental engagement* (September 2011), DFE-RR156, pp. 7–8.

220   Ibid., p. 67.

221   Ofsted (2007). *The Annual Report of Her Majesty's Chief Inspector of Education, Children's Services and Skills 2006/07*. London: Author.

222   Ofsted (2008), op. cit.

223   Akkerman, Y. (2011). *Overcoming school failure: Policies that work, background report for the Netherlands*. Den Haag: Ministry of Education, Culture and Science. URL: http://www.oecd.org/edu/school/49528317.pdf (accessed 3 January 2015).

224   Mitchell (2014), op. cit.

225   Hinde, E.R. (2004). 'School culture and change: An examination of the effects of school culture on the process of change.' *Essays in Education*, 12, Winter.

226   Ofsted (2008), op. cit. In this study, Ofsted undertook a survey in 20 schools across England where white British boys from low-income backgrounds performed better in public tests and examinations than their counterparts in other schools.

227   Voight, A., Austin, G. & Hanson, T. (2013). *A climate for academic success: How school climate distinguishes schools that are beating the achievement odds (Full Report)*. San Francisco: WestEd. URL: http://www.wested.org/online_pubs/hd-13-10.pdf (accessed 10 May 2013).

228   Education Review Office (2014). *Towards equitable outcomes in secondary schools: Good practice*. Wellington: Author. URL: http://ero.govt.nz/National-Reports/Towards-equitable-outcomes-in-secondary-schools-Good-practice-May-2014/National-Report-Summary-Towards-equitable-outcomes-in-secondary-schools-Good-practice (accessed 14 December 2014).

229   OECD (2012), op. cit.

230   Education Review Office (2014) *Achievement 2013-2017: Success for students in 2013*. Wellington: Author. URL: http://ero.govt.nz/National-Reports/Achievement-2013-2017-Success-for-students-in-2013-November-2014 (accessed 15 December 2014).

231   Education Review Office (2013). *Accelerating the progress of priority learners in primary schools (May 2013)*. Wellington: Author.

232 Darling-Hammond, L. Zielezinski, M.B. & Goldman, S. (2014). *Using technology to support at-risk students' learning.* Alliance For Excellent Education and Stanford Center for Opportunity Policy in Education (Scope).

233 Higher Education Opportunity Act of 2008 (PL 110–315) ∔103(a)(24).

234 Ofsted (2007). *The Annual Report of Her Majesty's Chief Inspector of Education, Children's Services and Skills 2006/07.* London: Author.

235 Ames, R. & Ames, C. (1991). 'Motivation and effective teaching'. In L. Idol & B.F. Jones (eds), *Educational values and cognitive instruction: Implications for education* (pp. 247-271). Hillsdale, NJ: Lawrence Erlbaum Associates.

236 Downey, J.A. (2008). 'Recommendations for fostering educational resilience in the classroom.' *Preventing School Failure*, 51(1), 56-64.

4 Race/ethnicity/culture differences

Unity without diversity results in cultural repression and hegemony, [while] diversity without unity leads to Balkanization and the fracturing of the nation-state.
(James Banks[1])

I first became aware that the world was inhabited by people of different races at around the age of five years when I attended a dance with my parents. I recall a dark-skinned man with a cheerful mien singing the Fijian farewell song, 'Isa Lei'. His name was Charlie Baker, I think, and he was a Māori – a member of the race that was the first to settle in New Zealand. During my primary school years some of my fellow students were Māori – mostly of mixed Māori and European heritage – but their racial backgrounds meant little, if anything, to me. We played and learned together, seemingly without any of us being aware of our different ethnicities. (My own background is a mixture of Scottish, English and German, the latter giving rise to some embarrassment during and shortly after World War II.) At high school, too, I had my first contact with a peer who was a 'full' Māori, living at the Arahura pa, a predominantly Māori village just north of Hokitika, where I attended high school. However, I was more interested in Andy's rugby prowess than his ethnicity. It was not until I moved to the North Island to train and work as a school psychologist that I became aware of racial differences in behaviour and achievement. Indeed, my first appointment as a psychologist was to the East Coast region of the North Island, where there was a strong Māori presence. Then, as now, Māori occupied the lower rungs of the achievement ladder and were disproportionately represented in prisons and mental health facilities. At about that time in my career, I began to ask whether this state of affairs reflected racial or socio-economic differences, or some combination of both. In this connection, I was attracted to the writing of Basil Bernstein, the English sociologist, who referred to what he called 'restricted linguistic environments' experienced by 'culturally deprived' children. In later life, my awareness of ethnicity as a factor in the development of children has been heightened by my own family's circumstances. My daughter is married to a man of mixed European and Māori heritage, while my son is married to a Japanese woman. In the latter case, all four of their children are bilingual and bicultural.

In 1900, the black American scholar, W.E.B. Du Bois, stated that 'the problem of the color line' was 'the problem of the twentieth century', in which the question as to how far differences of race – which show themselves chiefly in the color of the skin and the texture of the hair – will hereafter be made the basis of denying over half the world the right of sharing to their utmost ability the opportunities and privileges of modern civilization.[2]

Without doubt, the 'problem of the colour line' has extended into the twenty-first century, at least in America, as witnessed by recent episodes of young black men being killed by police, giving rise to protests and riots in many cities, with the catch cry, 'black lives matter'. Equally without doubt, most countries are becoming more diverse in terms of Du Bois's 'color line'.

Of all the diversities considered in this book, those arising from race, ethnicity and culture are the most complex to unravel. They draw our attention to indigenous peoples and minority nations, migrants (legal and illegal, voluntary and involuntary, refugees (conflict-driven and economic) and temporary or permanent 'guest workers'. They also draw our attention to the relationships that these groups have with their 'host' or 'majority' cultures, both in the past and in the present. Here, a distinction may be made between those whose minority status is 'unchosen' (i.e., indigenous peoples, national minorities and those descended from slaves) and those whose choices led to their being in a minority (e.g., voluntary immigrants).[3] Many refugees occupy the mid ground between these two categories.

Education stands at the fulcrum of the relationships between majority and minority cultures. Determining what model of multicultural education should prevail in increasingly multicultural societies lies at the heart of this relationship.

In this chapter, I will attempt to answer four key questions:

A   What do we mean by race, ethnicity and culture?
B   How do races, ethnicities and cultures differ?
C   What causes racial, ethnic and cultural differences to impact on educational achievement?
D   How should education respond to racial, ethnic and cultural differences?

My overriding aim is to explore how education can contribute towards striking a balance between unity and diversity for different ethnic groups.

A What do we mean by race, ethnicity and culture?

DNA comparisons show that all human populations living today are one species that originated in Africa about 60,000 years ago. Since then, environments, beneficial mutations and natural selection have given rise to considerable variations in such features as skin and eye colour, facial characteristics, resistance to malaria and so on – but not to intelligence.[4]

4.1 Race, ethnicity and culture vary in their meanings

Although the terms race, ethnicity and culture are often used as if they were synonyms, they vary quite markedly in their meanings.

The term *race* is usually based on the premise that human beings vary according to biological and physical differences. According to Phillip Robb, 'the concept of "race" included any [essentializing] of groups of people which held them to display inherent, heritable, persistent or predictive characteristics, and which thus had a biological or quasi-biological basis'.[5] In the nineteenth and early twentieth centuries, this conceptualization of diversity led some to consider the world to be populated by different phenotypes determined by physical attributes such as skin colour, cranial size and shape, and hair type. And, further, people came to believe that different racial groups shared not only physical attributes but they also inherited certain moral and psychological characteristics.[6] We now know that classifying people in this way is fraught with at least four difficulties. First, racial classifications assume that pure phenotypes exist, a notion that is increasingly challenged by the biological intermixing of people of apparently different phenotypes. Second, any claim that racial differences are based on biological differences ignores the fact that people with identical physical attributes are often classified differently and hold different social positions in the same society.[7] Third, there are more within-group differences than between-group differences in the characteristics of the three so-called races (Caucasoid, Negroid and Mongoloid).[8] Fourth, studies of genetic systems have found that differences between individuals within the same tribe or nation account for more variance (84%) than do racial groupings (10%), with skin colour being an exception; thus indicating that racial groups are more alike than they are different, even in physical and genetic characteristics.[9] Stuart Hall, the English sociologist, rejected the biological theory of racial differences, arguing instead that it is the *meaning* of these differences that is the central issue. He proposed that race should be seen as working like a language. He did not deny the reality of the physical differences that exist between people, but stressed that the meanings given to these physical differences is what matters. One writer described the key to Hall's position is that meanings are not fixed in any essential way, but are what Hall calls 'floating signifiers'.[10] However, meanings do become temporarily 'fixed' by ideological processes, and when this occurs these will become the dominant meanings circulating in a particular society. To sum up, 'the idea that race is not ... a set of discrete biological types, but instead is socially constructed, is one of the most important ideas of our time'.[11]

In 1950, UNESCO rejected the idea of a 'racial science', which had been most infamously promulgated by the Nazis, in these words:

> national, religious, geographic, linguistic and cultural groups do not necessarily coincide with racial groups: and the cultural traits of such groups have no demonstrated genetic connections with racial traits ... The scientific material available to us at present does not justify the conclusion that inherited genetic differences are a major factor in producing the differences between the cultures and cultural achievements of different peoples or groups.[12]

This statement leads on to the notion of *ethnicity*, which is is a culturally derived term and is increasingly considered to be more central to human identity than race. Francis Deng defined it as an 'embodiment of values, institutions, and patterns of behavior, a composite whole representing a people's historical experience, aspirations, and worldview'.[13] The concept of ethnicity is also associated with culture and is often used interchangeably with it. Usually, however, ethnicity is used to refer to a group with a common nationality, culture or language. Although cultural background can be a determinant of ethnic identity or affiliation, being part of an ethnic group can also determine culture. As members of an ethnic group interact with each other, ethnicity becomes a means by which culture is transmitted.[14] Because ethnicity incorporates language, religion, demarcations of territory and other cultural traits, changes in people's affinity with any of these factors can occur over time.

UNESCO has defined *culture* as 'the set of distinctive spiritual, material, intellectual and emotional features of a society or social group ... [encompassing] in addition to art and literature, lifestyles, ways of living together, value systems, traditions and beliefs'.[15] In its most general sense, *culture* is 'simply a way of talking about collective identities'.[16] As noted by Frances Raday, these identities may take two forms: *social culture*, which pertains to forms of social organization – how people interact and organize themselves in groups – and *ideological culture*, which refers to what people think, value, believe and hold as ideals.[17] Further, as Raday pointed out, the borders of cultures may not exactly match a country's borders. Thus, within a country there may be a dominant culture and minority subcultures or there may be a mosaic of subcultures. Further, beyond country borders there is a developing global culture, including an international human rights culture (which is of particular relevance to the theme of this book). Raday made one more distinction regarding cultures: the difference between relatively static and homogeneous systems and those that are adaptive and in a state of constant change.

Before leaving this section, it is relevant to mention yet another cultural distinction. Based on the World Values Survey data,[18] political scientists Ronald Inglehart and Christian Welzel have created a 'Cultural Map'.[19] According to this Map, much of the variation in human values between societies can be measured in two broad dimensions: a first dimension of 'traditional vs. secular-rational values' and a second dimension of 'survival vs. self-expression values'. In the first dimension, the United States has higher scores than Europe in the 'traditional' values which emphasize the importance of religion, family ties and deference to authority. Conversely, Europeans score higher on secular-rational values. The United States and European countries have similar values on the second dimension, which reflects economic security and levels of trust and tolerance.

All in all, it can be seen that there are major definitional problems surrounding the notions of race, ethnicity and culture. At best, they represent broad-brush attempts to classify human beings, even if they ignore or downplay considerable diversity within the categories that are created. These categories become even more complex in the situation of 'bi-ethnic' individuals (i.e., one parent with an ethnic majority background and other with an ethnic minority background) and when other intersecting features such as religion, socio-economic status and gender are added to the mix.

For the purposes of this chapter, I will largely be focusing on ethnic differences, except where the sources I cite refer to race or culture.

4.2 Countries differ in their ethnic composition

In an analysis of the ethnic makeup of 160 countries in the early 1990s, Stanford University researcher James Fearon found that about 70% of the countries in the world had an ethnic group that formed an absolute majority of the population.[20] The average size of the second largest group, i.e., the largest ethnic minority, was surprisingly large, at 17%. This figure was close to the average size of the largest minority in every region except the west, where the largest minorities tended to be smaller (and the majority ethnic groups larger). The most ethnically divided region was sub-Saharan Africa. While the rest of the world's regions averaged between 3.2 and 4.7 groups per country, the African countries' average was greater than

Table 4.1 Ethnic fractionalization and cultural fractionalization scores, by western countries

Rank of ethnic frac.	Country	Ethnic frac.	Cultural frac.	Rank of cultural frac.
1	Canada	0.596	0.499	1
2	Switzerland	0.575	0.418	3
3	Belgium	0.567	0.462	2
4	Spain	0.502	0.263	6
5	USA	0.491	0.271	5
6	New Zealand	0.363	0.363	4
7	UK	0.324	0.184	9
8	France	0.272	0.251	7
9	Sweden	0.189	0.189	8
10	Ireland	0.171	0.157	10
11	Australia	0.149	0.147	11
12	Finland	0.132	0.132	12
13	Denmark	0.128	0.128	13
14	Austria	0.126	0.1	14
15	Norway	0.098	0.098	15
16	Germany	0.095	0.09	16
17	Netherlands	0.077	0.077	17
18	Greece	0.059	0.05	18
19	Portugal	0.04	0.04	19.5
20	Italy	0.04	0.04	19.5
21	Japan	0.012	0.012	21

Source: Fearon[20]

eight. The average population share of the largest ethnic group in these countries was 42%, less than a majority, in sharp contrast to all other regions.

As well as ranking countries according to their degree of ethnic fractionalization, Fearon also ranked them according to their 'cultural fractionalization'. The latter ranking was based on the structural distance between languages in a country (i.e., the extent to which languages differ from each other, which is an indicator of the ease or difficulty in learning another language). Table 4.1 shows the results for 21 western countries. From this table, it can be seen that Canada ranked as having the highest scores for both measures, while Japan had the least ethnic and cultural diversity. It can also be seen that there is a close, but not perfect, relationship between the two measures.

4.3 Many countries are multilingual[21]

In the light of the ethnic diversity in many countries, it is not surprising that many have multiple languages. The record for the most languages spoken is probably held by Papua New Guinea where 839 languages have been recorded. It is closely followed by Indonesia with 707 languages, Nigeria with 526 and India with 454. In terms of 'official languages', several countries stand out. These include Luxembourg where most people speak Luxemburgish, and French and German are co-official languages, while English is compulsory for students to learn at school. Singapore has four official languages: English, Mandarin Chinese, Malay and Tamil; however, hardly any people actually speak all four and English is the main lingua franca, it being a required subject in school. A similar situation pertains in Malaysia where everyone can speak the official tongue, Malay, and most people are fluent in English, which is a compulsory subject in school and is widely spoken, often in a creolized form known as 'Manglish'. In addition, Malaysians whose ancestors came from India can speak their familial language in addition to Malay and English, while Chinese Malaysians learn Mandarin in school, but most also speak other dialects. In India, Hindi and English are the official languages and a majority of educated Indians and urban dwellers have knowledge of both. As well, each state has its own official language(s) most of which differ from Hindi. Switzerland has four official languages: German is spoken by about 65%, French by 23%, Italian by about 8% and Romansh is spoken by less than 1% of the total population. In 2004, the Conference of Cantonal Education Directors decided that all Swiss children had to learn a second official language and English by the fifth year of primary school. The former language was to be taught from the third primary year and English from the fifth year. The individual cantons were to decide which languages to introduce first.[22]

4.4 Most countries are becoming more diverse ethnically

Most countries are becoming more diverse in terms of Du Bois's 'color line'. For example, UK census data show that the minority ethnic population[23] grew by 48% between 1991 and 2001, from 3.1 million to 4.6 million, comprising 7.9% of the total population in 2001. Taking data for children aged 5-16 in the United Kingdom, there has been rapid growth in the number of ethnic minorities in recent years; they comprised 26.6% of the population in 2013, compared with 16.8% in 2003.[24] The largest increases were for Other White[25] from 2.1% to 4.3% and Black African from 1.7% to 3.3%.

Similarly, demographic shifts are taking place in the United States and are predicted to continue. Diversity statistics and projections by the US Census Bureau in 2012 showed that by 2060, both Hispanic and Asian populations will more than double; the black population will increase from 13.1% in 2012 to 14.7% in 2060; American Indian, Alaskan Native, Native Hawaiian and other Pacific Island populations will double; and the number of people who identify as being two or more races will more than triple over the same period.[26]

In New Zealand, projections show that it will have greater ethnic diversity in the future.[27] In 2013, 15.6% of the population self-identified with Māori ethnicity – this was projected to increase to 19.5% in 2038. The Pacific share was projected to increase from 7.8 to 10.9%, and the Asian share from 12.2 to 20.9%. In contrast, the European share of the population was projected to decrease from 74.6% in 2013 to 65.6% in 2038. The decline in the European share is largely due to its lower fertility rate.[28] (Note: the percentages do not sum to 100% because people can and do identify with multiple ethnicities.)

In Australia, self-identified ancestries in 2011 were as follows: English 25.9%, Australian 25.4%, Irish 7.5%, Scottish 6.4%, Italian 3.3%, German 3.2%, Chinese 3.1%, Indian 1.4%, Greek 1.4%, Dutch 1.2%, Australian aboriginal 0.5%), other 15.3% and unspecified 5.4%. (Note: over a third of respondents reported two ancestries.)[29]

Canada is another country with a high level of ethnic diversity, as can be seen in the Census figures for 2001: North American (non-Aboriginal) 40.21%; British Isles 33.64%; French 15.89%; Eastern European 8.50%; Southern European 7.87%; East and South East Asian 6.03%; Northern European 3.22%; Caribbean 1.70%; Other European 1.28%; Arab 1.17%; African 0.99%.

As noted by the Council of Europe, in recent decades cultural diversification in Europe has gained momentum as migrants and asylum seekers search for a better life. According to a 2008 White Paper, this reflects several trends: (a) globalization compressing space and time on a scale that is unprecedented; (b) revolutions in telecommunications and the media rendering national cultural systems increasingly porous; and (c) the development of transport and tourism bringing more people than ever into face-to-face contact, engendering more and more opportunities for intercultural dialogue.[30]

B How do races, ethnicities and cultures differ?

Most, but not all, ethnic minorities in most countries fare poorly on a wide range of educational, economic, social and health indicators. Moreover, these indicators interact with each other to produce a compounding effect.

4.5 Most, but not all, ethnic minority groups have lower school achievement than the majority ethnic groups

For some time, most western countries have been concerned at the comparatively poor educational achievement of many ethnic minority groups. As we shall see, while some of this differential performance can be attributed to factors related to low SES, some of it requires consideration of cultural factors related to ethnicity. To illustrate these ethnic differences in educational achievement, I will draw upon data from three countries: the United Kingdom, the United States and New Zealand.[31]

United Kingdom

A comprehensive 2003 UK study reported on the educational attainment of minority ethnic groups.[32] (It is interesting to note that the requirements of the Race Relations Amendment Act (2000) in the United Kingdom specify that monitoring and evaluating the attainment and progress of minority ethnic groups is an essential component of achieving race equality in education.)

- Black Caribbean and Black African children and children for whom English was an additional language made relatively greater progress during pre-school than White children or those for whom English is a first language. These results remained significant even when account was taken of the influence of other important factors, such as mother's education level and socio-economic group.
- Indian and Chinese pupils were more likely to achieve the expected level compared with other ethnic groups at all Key Stages.
- On average, Black, Bangladeshi and Pakistani pupils performed less well than White pupils throughout compulsory schooling.
- Overall, the disparity in achievement between ethnic groups increased significantly over the course of schooling. There was more inequality in attainment between ethnic groups after their time in compulsory education than there was at entry to school.

- While socio-economic factors explained a large part of inequality of attainment, there were still differences in attainment between ethnic groups amongst those pupils who were eligible for free school meals.
- Black Caribbean pupils were around three times more likely than white pupils to be permanently excluded from school.
- Schools that successfully helped minority ethnic children had strong leadership and strong systems, a culture of achievement with high expectations, intensive support for pupils and close links with parents.

In a similar vein, Christian Dustmann and his colleagues found that, with the exception of Black Caribbean students, ethnic minorities (British or foreign born) in England outperformed White British-born students in terms of educational achievements.[33] They noted that these results contrasted to what occurred just before the start of school when, at the ages of 3 and 5, ethnic minority children (except Chinese children) significantly under-performed in early cognitive tests compared with the White British-born pupils. What could account for this turnaround? Dustmann and his colleagues put forward two explanations. First, they believed that language contributes to explaining why ethnic minority pupils improve relative to White British students. In the early years, many minority groups lack language skills, but this changes during their time at school, especially for girls. They presented data showing that, with the exception of Black Caribbean pupils, language alone can explain between 37% (Chinese) and 64% (Pakistani) of the greater progress of ethnic minority pupils relative to White British pupils. Language also helps to explain why Black Caribbean pupils, for most of whom English is the mother tongue, improved less than any other ethnic group. Second, Dustmann and his colleagues put forward the intriguing hypothesis that publication of the league tables employed in the United Kingdom may have provided incentives for teachers to focus their attention on pupils who are most likely to just pass or just fail targets. In the United Kingdom, a similar explanation found empirical support with respect to teacher incentives to meet standards required by the No Child Left Behind Act.[34]

These results highlight the exceptional performances of British Chinese and British Indian students, sometimes leading to them being held up as 'model minority' students. A recent paper by Billy Wong reported that this status comes with a cost for these students.[35] He found that inflated expectations for their school performances can generate a continuous sense of insecurity as they contemplate the fear of failure and the potential damage that failure could inflict on the reputation of their families. Writing from a US perspective, Alejandro Covarrubias and Daniel Liou have challenged the model minority stereotype, arguing that it neglects the history of institutional racism committed against Asian Americans (witness the Chinese Exclusion Act of 1882 and the internment of Japanese during World War II).[36] It also ignores the fact that Asian Americans are vastly diverse populations that cut across ethnicity, culture, gender, socio-economic status, political affiliation, citizenship status and immigrant versus refugee status. When these intersectionalities are taken into account, there is considerable divergence of educational attainment among Asian American students.[37]

According to Dustmann and his colleagues, a possible third explanation, poverty, cannot explain why ethnic minority pupils make greater progress than White British pupils. They did, however, conclude that schools and teacher behaviour do matter when explaining ethnic differences in pupil achievement. Future research is needed to investigate the precise mechanisms by which this occurs.

United States[38]

The National Assessment of Educational Progress (NAEP) comprises the largest nationally representative and continuing assessment of US students at ages 9, 13 and 17. Although test-score gaps have decreased over time, they remained (in 2008) quite large and significant. For example, while the Hispanic-white reading test-score gaps among 9-year-olds and 17-year-olds had narrowed from 1975, they were still large, and the gap for 13-year-olds had not changed much during that period. The same pattern applied to the black–white test score gap. For example, in reading, black 17-year-olds scored about the same as white 13-year-olds in 2008 – an improvement over 1975 when white 13-year-olds scored *better* than black 17-year-olds.

New Zealand

According to 2005 data, approximately 50% of Māori students left school without any qualifications, compared with 21% of their non-Māori counterparts, their retention rate to age 17 was 60% of non-Māori, their rate of suspension from school was three to five times higher depending on gender (girls and boys respectively). As well, Māori students are over-represented in special education programmes for those with behavioural issues, enrol in lower rates in pre-schools, and tend to be over-represented in low stream classes.[39]

4.6   Ethnicity interacts with socio-economic status and gender

As I noted in section 3.7 in Chapter 3, ethnicity interacts with socio-economic status (SES) and gender to influence achievement. This point about intersectionality is emphasized by UK author, Steve Strand, who analyzed the achievement levels of over 15,000 students aged 11, 14 and 16.[40] For example, among low SES boys, White British and Black Caribbean boys were jointly the lowest scoring groups. For low SES girls, Black Caribbean girls joined other minority groups in scoring significantly higher than White British girls. As Strand said, 'there is something about the particular combination of ethnicity, SES and gender that is uniquely related to attainment'.

Intersectional discrimination can occur when a person's multiple characteristics combine to create a distinct identity that is then subject to a unique form of discrimination.[41] This happens when particular stereotypes or prejudices concentrate upon a person based on more than one prohibited ground: for example, Asian females. If disadvantageous treatment is by reason of a person's status as an Asian girl, it cannot be properly analyzed solely under the rubric of either gender or racial discrimination, but requires consideration of both. An example of this intersectionality was outlined in section 2.8, which referred to inequalities suffered by girls and women living in poverty in some developing countries.

4.7   Students with an immigrant background tend to perform worse in school

Results from the OECD Programme for International Student Assessment (PISA) indicate that students with an immigrant background tend to perform worse in school than students without an immigrant background.[42] According to the OECD, several factors are associated with this disparity, including the concentration of disadvantage in the schools that immigrant students attend, language barriers and certain school policies like grade repetition[43] and tracking.[44] Taking the latter point, as Samuel Lucas and Adam Gamoran have noted, 'race matters for tracking, and tracking matters for racial differences in measured achievement'.[45]

4.8   Ethnic gaps in educational achievement are decreasing

Notwithstanding the foregoing, recent UK research carried out by Steve Strand showed that ethnic gaps in educational achievement at age 16 had decreased substantially since the early 1990s.[46] Pupils from most ethnic minority groups were, on average, achieving GCSE results that were as good or better than their White British peers. More specifically, it showed that Indian and Chinese pupils were pulling well ahead of their White British classmates, with Bangladeshi and Black African students improving their GCSE grades significantly and starting to do better, on average, than White British pupils. This is despite the fact that Bangladeshi and black African students are often from very socio-economically disadvantaged backgrounds. The two lowest achieving groups were Black Caribbean and Mixed White and Black Caribbean students. The study also showed that the ethnic gap had reduced in relative terms. While in 2004 the black Caribbean-White British gap was twice as large as the gender gap, by 2013 it was actually smaller (7.2% points compared with a gender gap of 10.1% points). However, both gaps are substantially smaller than the socio-economic gap (as I noted in Chapter 3). Strand commented:

> Huge strides have been made in schools in England in closing the ethnic gap in educational attainment. These results show what can be achieved with targeted funding, particularly the Ethnic Minority Achievement Grant that ran until 2012/2013, and the strong focus through policies, including Excellence in Cities, and programmes through the National Strategies.[47]

4.9   Ethnic identity is stronger among students of colour than White students

Ethnic identity refers to the degree to which individuals identify with their ethnic group. A US study of college students' ethnic identity arrived at two major conclusions.[48] First, 'Students of Color' reported higher levels of ethnic identity than 'White' students, a finding that had been consistently reported in other research. Second, Students of Color reported greater integration between their ethnic and academic identities than White students, a difference that was partially explained by the first finding. The researchers concluded that in order to attract and retain under-represented Students of Color into college programmes, it is important to understand their unique interests and identity-related needs, and how these may impact on their educational decision-making and academic performance.

4.10   Students for whom English is an additional language improve during their school careers

A 2003 UK study found that students for whom English was an additional language (EAL) performed, on average, less well than pupils whose first language was English.[49] Performances of EAL pupils varied by ethnic group, with Bangladeshi and Pakistani pupils doing less well than other groups, regardless of EAL status.

Steve Strand and his colleagues recently reported on the achievement of children with EAL, compared with those whose first language was English (FLE).[50] They found that at the end of their first year of education, only 44% of EAL children achieved 'a good level of development', compared with 54% of FLE children. Later in their school careers, however, the EAL students made more progress than the FLE students and, indeed they had caught up by age 16.

C What causes racial, ethnic and cultural differences to impact on educational achievement?

The ethnic differences which impact on educational achievement can be seen to arise from a complex set of factors. They include the histories of different ethnic groups, multicultural policies which have exacerbated problems, and ethnically separated neighbourhoods and schools.

4.11 Ethnic minorities' histories play a role in determining educational outcomes

Ethnic minorities have diverse histories. Some have been exposed to discrimination and persecution (e.g., Jews in Europe); some have suffered from slavery (e.g., blacks in the United States); many have experienced colonialism (e.g., Māori in New Zealand); some have been victims of civil wars (e.g., Syrian asylum-seekers in Europe), some have suffered economic privations (e.g., African and Asian migrants in the United Kingdom), and still others have histories that combine several of these experiences. For some, these histories are proximal; for others, they are distal, but for all they have significant repercussions for their sense of identity and their educational aspirations.

In many countries, racial and ethnic pluralism has frequently been accompanied by a privileging of some groups over others. In turn, this has led to prejudice, discrimination and even conflict in many countries, historically and contemporaneously. In an analysis of these occurrences, Heewon Chang and Timothy Dodd pointed out that such conflicts were not a result of an inherent incompatibility of groups from differing races or ethnicities, but rather they reflected contexts, ideologies, imbalances of power, marginalizing actions, group perceptions of race and ethnicity and failed negotiations.[51] Chief among these contexts is the legacy of slavery in many parts of the world, especially the United States, and colonialism in many other countries, such as in the African continent and South America, Australia, and my own country, New Zealand. Thus, in seeking explanations of the disparities in educational achievement among Māori students (outlined in section 4.5), several writers have pointed to educational policies and practices that 'were developed and continue to be developed within a framework of neo-colonialism and as a result continue to serve the interests of a mono-cultural elite'.[52] This has led to a growing movement in New Zealand to look within the Māori culture for alternative ways forward. For example, Russell Bishop and his colleagues have argued for investigating the 'sense-making and knowledge-generating processes' of the Māori culture.[53]

4.12 Multiculturalism may be part of the problem, rather than part of the solution

Is multiculturalism the way to go in redressing ethnic inequalities? This concept first appeared in the 1960s and 1970s and came to be associated with the state's approaches to dealing with different races, ethnicities, cultures, social classes and religions in order to provide equal opportunity, individual freedom and group recognition.[54] For the purposes of this chapter, I will confine its scope to ethnic or cultural and linguistic diversity; other chapters address religious and socio-economic diversity.

A recent Council of Europe White Paper pointed to the growing belief in that what had until recently been a preferred policy approach, namely multiculturalism, had been found inadequate, just as there did not seem to be a desire to return to an older emphasis on assimilation. It had this to say about multiculturalism:

> Whilst driven by benign intentions, multiculturalism is now seen by many as having fostered communal segregation and mutual incomprehension, as well as having contributed to the undermining of the rights of individuals – and, in particular, women – within minority communities, perceived as if these were single collective actors.[55]

Other criticisms to have been levelled at multiculturalism include the following:[56]

1   According to Sarah Song, writing in the *Stanford Encyclopedia of Philosophy*, culture is an overly broad concept, which involves religion, language, ethnicity, nationality and race – each with their distinct claims for 'group-differentiated rights'.

2   These 'group-differentiated rights' may restrict the freedom of individual members to pursue their individual rights and liberties.[57] I alluded to this conflict in Chapter 1 when I noted that the twentieth-century articulation of human rights represented a replacement of communitarianism by individualism. Amartya Sen made a related point when he noted that being born into a particular culture is not in itself an exercise of cultural freedom, since it is not an act of choice made after considering other alternatives.[58] Similarly, Canadian Neil Bissoondath argued that official multiculturalism in Canada limited the freedom of minority members by confining them to cultural and geographic ethnic enclaves.[59]

3   Multiculturalism's emphasis on culture and identity may risk diverting attention from the struggle for economic justice, which should involve multi-ethnic class solidarity.[60]

4   Extending protections to minority cultural groups may come at the price of reinforcing the oppression of vulnerable members of those groups (i.e., 'minorities within minorities').[61] These include religious dissenters, sexual minorities, women and children. (Note: I took up this issue in Chapter 2 when I discussed the possible conflict between females' rights and conservative cultural practices.)

5   There is increasing talk of a political retreat from multiculturalism – at least when it involves immigrant groups – as an ideal in western countries. Partly, this is based on fear and anxiety about foreign 'others' and partly it is calling into question the notion of integration into common citizenships. This latter point was made in 2010 by German chancellor, Angela Merkel, who judged that attempts to build a multicultural society in Germany have 'failed, utterly failed'.[62] Similarly, in February 2011, UK Prime Minister, David Cameron, stated that 'the doctrine of state multiculturalism' had failed and would no longer be state policy.[63] Rather, he asserted that the United Kingdom needed a stronger national identity and there should be a tougher stance on groups promoting Islamist extremism.

6   Sen challenged the primacy accorded to culture in determining individuals' identities. He asked: 'Should human beings be categorized in terms of inherited traditions of the community

in which they happen to have been born, taking that unchosen identity to have automatic priority over other affiliations involving politics, profession, class, gender, language, literature, social involvement and many other connections? Or should they be understood as persons with many affiliations and associations, whose relative priorities they themselves choose?'[64]

7   In a related point, Sen pointed out that cultural contacts across the world are leading to such a hybridization of behaviours that it is difficult to identify any local culture as being genuinely indigenous.

8   A distinction can be drawn between multiculturalism and what Sen called 'plural mono-culturalism' – which arises from 'the myth that society is made up of a series of distinct, homogeneous cultures that dance around each other' and 'never the twain meeting'. A related point is Sen's rejection of a 'federational' view in which a multi-ethnic country such as Britain is seen as a collection of ethnic communities. Similarly, Geoffrey Blainey worried that multiculturalism in Australia threatened to transform that country into a 'cluster of tribes'.[65] More recently, Samuel Huntington, in his landmark book *Clash of civilizations*, criticized multiculturalism as 'attacking the identification of the United States with Western civilization at the expense of promoting racial, ethnic and other subnational cultural identities and groupings'.[66]

9   Rather than reducing the risks of racial tension, Kenan Malik believes there is some evidence that setting up ethnic communities within a country creates 'fragmented societies, alienated minorities, and resentful citizenries'.[67] He cited the example of Birmingham, England, when, in 1985, after riots by blacks, Asians and whites, the Birmingham Council set up a series of Umbrella Groups based on ethnicity and faith with substantial funding allocated to each one. Some twenty years later, there were more riots, this time between blacks and Asians. These were at least in part attributed to the tensions created by competition for power and resources and the ignoring of internal conflicts within the various groups. In other words, some versions of multiculturalism may create centrifugal forces in society, as I outlined in section 1.12 in Chapter 1.

10   Multiculturalism cannot override the right of a person to participate in aspects of society that do not conform to the dictates of their traditional culture. Malik, for example, criticized multiculturalism as seeking to 'institutionalize diversity by putting people into ethnic and cultural boxes ... and defining their needs and rights accordingly'.[68] Indeed, a person may well decide that other elements of their identity are more important to them than their ethnic or cultural identity. Thus, Sen argued that a nation should not be perceived as 'a collection of sequestered segments, with citizens being assigned places in predetermined segments'. Moreover, I would argue that while it is true that individuals are usually culture *bearers*, they are not necessarily culture *bound*. Humans have the capacity for change and for creating new cultural identities for themselves through reason and dialogue, and even conflict. In short, personal identities 'constantly mutate'.[69]

4.13   Ethnic minorities tend to live in segregated, high poverty neighbourhoods

In a hard-hitting analysis, Richard Rothstein argued that, in the United States, schools that the most disadvantaged black children attend are typically located in segregated, high-poverty neighbourhoods, far distant from truly middle-class neighborhoods.[70] His central thesis is that education policy is constrained by housing policy: it is not possible to desegregate schools without de-segregating both low-income and affluent neighbourhoods. He pointed out that it has become conventional for policymakers to assert that the residential isolation of low-income black children is now 'de facto', that is, an accident of economic circumstance, demographic trends, personal preferences and private discrimination. But, he argued, the historical record demonstrates that residential segregation is 'de jure', and actually results from racially motivated and explicit public policy in the past whose effects endure to the present.

Rothstein built his case on two intersecting sets of data. First, he drew attention to statistics showing how isolated black children were and that this is increasing. Nation-wide, the share of black students attending schools that had more than 90% from minority backgrounds grew from 34 to 39% from 1991 to 2011.[71] In 1991, black students typically attended schools where 35% of their fellow students were white; by 2011, this had fallen to 28%. Rothstein also noted that in cities with the most struggling students, this isolation was even more extreme. For example, in Detroit, the typical black student attended a school where only 3% of students were white and 84 % were low income. Rothstein argued that 'It is inconceivable that significant gains can be made in the achievement of black children who are so severely isolated.'[72] Other statistics confirm these accelerating trends. For example, Rothstein cited analyses carried out by Paul Jargowsky, which showed that in 2011, 7% of poor whites lived in high-poverty neighbourhoods, up from 4% in 2000; 15% of poor Hispanics lived in such high-poverty neighbourhoods in 2011, up from 14% in 2000; and a 'breath-taking' 23% of poor blacks lived in high-poverty neighbourhoods in 2011, up from 19% in 2000.[73]

Rothstein's second argument revolved around his historical analysis of how, in the United States, residential segregation has actually resulted from racially motivated and explicit public policy in the past. He began this part of his analysis by criticizing a 2007 Supreme Court judgment which prohibited the Louisville and Seattle school districts from making racial balance a factor in assigning students to schools. Desegregation was impermissible if students were racially isolated, not as a result of government policy, but because of societal discrimination, economic factors, or 'any number of innocent private decisions, including *voluntary housing choices*' (my emphasis). This constitutes what Rothstein referred to as a 'de facto' argument. In truth, he argued, the reasons for housing segregation in the United States have their roots in public policy - his 'de jure' argument. Briefly, he outlined a succession of laws and regulations which had the explicit intent of segregating residential areas. These included the racial segregation of federally funded public housing from the inception of this policy during Franklin Roosevelt's New Deal, which was continued during and after World War II. Further, there were episodes of police standing by while mobs torched and stoned houses purchased by blacks in white neighbourhoods.[74] Rothstein concluded by asserting that voluntary choice, magnet schools or 'fiddling' with school attendance zones are insufficient to enable low-income black children in the United States to attend middle-class schools. Instead, he stated,

> narrowing the achievement gap will also require housing desegregation, which history also shows is not a voluntary matter but a constitutional necessity - involving policies

like voiding exclusionary zoning, placing scattered low and moderate income housing in predominantly white suburbs, prohibiting landlord discrimination against housing voucher holders, and ending federal subsidies for communities that fail to reverse policies that led to racial exclusion.[75]

Why should we be concerned about housing segregation? Surely there are some perceived advantages for people – especially migrants – living in close proximity to fellow migrants who share their culture and language and who may provide employment opportunities? There may well be some truth to this claim, but it comes with some costs as well. For example, a German study found that 'co-ethnic concentration' affected immigrants' (and refugees') cultural integration and their participation in the labour market.[76] Residential ethnic clustering strengthened immigrants' retention of an affiliation with their respective country of origin and weakened identification with the host society and, hence, social cohesion. In short, such clustering may have centrifugal, rather than centripetal effects, as I described in Chapter 1, section 1.12. This is not to say that the aim should be assimilation, but rather to strike a balance between unity and diversity.

Similar findings to the German research were reported in the United Kingdom, where a study showed that living in an ethnic enclave was associated with very low levels of British identification and a rather strong affiliation with the respective ethnic groups.[77] The extent of the problem becomes apparent when it is noted that most people from the white ethnic group live in wards with very small populations from ethnic minority groups, while people from ethnic minority groups tend to be found where the share of minorities in the resident population is relatively high.[78] Thus, John Stillwell and Oliver Duke-Williams reported that the 2001 Census showed that although ethnic minority populations had a presence throughout Britain, they remained heavily concentrated in certain London boroughs and metropolitan districts in England.[79] The black population was the most segregated and the Chinese were the least segregated when compared with the rest of the population. They pointed out that there seems to be little doubt that immigration was reinforcing ethnic minority concentration, most conspicuously for the black group.

Singapore stands in contrast to the above. Its population comprises three main ethnic groups: in 2012, Chinese constituted 74.2%, Malays 13.3% and Indians 9.2%. The vast majority (80%) of Singaporeans live in public housing (government-built, but self-owned apartments) and the ethnic groups are deliberately mixed in each housing block. In addition, each of the ethnic communities has a self-help community group, the Malay Mendaki, Indian Sinda and Chinese CDAC. These organizations are funded by members of each community and support children in need.

4.14 Migrant populations are unequally distributed

As I noted in section 1.28, in Chapter 1, currently more than half (54%) of the world's population lives in towns and cities, but it is predicted that by 2050 about 64% of the developing world and 86% of the developed world will be urbanized.[80] Migration is driving much of this increase, making cities increasingly more diverse places in which to live.[81] Urban settlements are characterized by the presence of a great number of very different people in a very limited space – most of them strangers to each other, making it possible to build up a vast array of subcultures close to each other, exposed to each other's influence. However, cities are also home to high concentrations of poverty.[82] According to a recent report from the International Organization for Migration (IOM), cities offer potential access to a variety of resources that are essential for people's well-being and resilience.[83] However, when inadequately managed, migration can actually result in conditions of exclusion and vulnerability for the individuals who are moving:

> Migrants are often faced with legal, cultural and social barriers and obstacles to accessing formal housing, employment, education, health and other social services. These barriers may force them to live in conditions of exclusion, segregation and vulnerability.[84]

Further, IOM noted that although European cities are in general less segregated than American cities, population groups are spatially unequally divided within many European cities. Some neighbourhoods contain an overwhelming majority of a particular group, usually low-income households or specific minority ethnic groups. While moving to neighbourhoods with a high concentration of their own ethnic group may be attractive to migrants when they first arrive in a country (and may, indeed, offer benefits), residential segregation is problematic when it becomes permanent and leads to intergenerational inequalities. According to IOM, reasons for segregation may include discrimination in the housing market or self-segregation, as well as the departure of members of the ethnic majority from the neighbourhood, often termed 'white flight'.

IOM also noted that many cities try to combat residential segregation either by implementing policies that directly tackle segregation or by more indirect integration policies. In addition to anti-discrimination legislation specifically aimed at the housing market, direct policies include the distribution of public housing across a wide range of neighbourhoods; providing rental subsidies and vouchers, and introducing quotas to prevent ethnic minorities from settling in neighbourhoods where they are already overrepresented. Indirect policies address the underlying causes of segregation, such as access to full citizenship, labour market integration and intergroup relations.

4.15   Many students from ethnic minorities attend schools where they constitute a majority

As a consequence of the trends outlined above, ethnic minorities disproportionately populate the schools they attend.[85] This pattern will be illustrated with reference to England and the United States.

In England, in 2013, over 50% of ethnic minority students were in schools where ethnic minorities were in the majority (although not necessarily their own minority). This compared to over 90% of White British pupils who were in majority White British schools. However, there is evidence that this pattern is changing: in 2008 only 49% of ethnic majority pupils in Year 13 were in schools where ethnic minorities predominated, while by 2013 the share had risen to 54%.[86] Apart from the White British majority, the ethnic minority groups who were most likely to be in schools where their own ethnic group was in the majority were Bangladeshis and Pakistanis. Analyses of these data showed that more than half of ethnic minority children would have to move schools in order for there to be an equal spread of ethnic groups relative to the White British across the school system.

Such concentrations of ethnic minority students can have deleterious consequences for students' achievement. This was illustrated in a study of how US teachers and schools contribute to racial differences in the realization of academic potential. In this research, Tina Wildhagen measured whether students earn higher or lower grades than the grades predicted by earlier tests of academic skills.[87] She found that both African American and White students fell short of their academic potential at schools that were composed of 75-100% minority students, with African American students falling short of their academic potential to a greater extent than Whites in these schools. Wildhagen concluded that redoubling efforts to fight the resegregation of America's schools is important for making sure that African American students realize their academic potential. Desegregating predominantly minority schools, in particular, is an important goal, but integration efforts should target predominantly White schools as well.

Wildhagen also noted that schools that are racially integrated must actively work to ensure that African American students are not disadvantaged within them, either through the internal resegregation of students or by fostering school climates that are particularly nonconducive to African American students. She cited several studies that drew attention to the pernicious effects of segregated course-taking regimes within integrated schools, while her own study also revealed that a school's approach to student discipline may be just as harmful as overtly racialized inequality.

4.16   *Racial segregation in education still exists through special education placements*

Partly as a result of the above residential segregation, but also for other reasons, schools in many countries are segregated by race. While most countries have eliminated overt racial segregation in education, vestiges of it remain in the form of racial disproportionality in special education. In the following, I will present evidence of this in the United States and England, with a contrasting pattern in New Zealand.

United States

Racial segregation in education is not a new phenomenon in the United States. As pointed out by Shelley Zion and Wanda Blanchett, there is a history of slaves being forbidden to learn to read, Native American children being removed from their homes and placed in boarding schools, and the outlawing of languages other than English.[88] In more modern times, segregation was embedded in law in 1896, with the Supreme Court ruling in *Plessy v. Ferguson* that state laws requiring racial segregation in public facilities were constitutionally acceptable under the doctrine of 'separate but equal'. This principle remained standard doctrine in US law until its repudiation in the 1954 Supreme Court decision in *Brown v. Board of Education*, which eliminated segregation on the grounds of race because it was deemed to be in violation of the Equal Protection Clause of the Fourteenth Amendment to the Constitution.

However, while racial segregation is unlawful in the United States, elements of it remain in the form of special education placements. Lloyd Dunn was one of the first to recognize racial disproportionality in special education placements in the United States.[89] In his classic 1968 paper, he noted that African American students were over-represented in programmes for students identified as having mild mental retardation. He called attention to the fact that African American children were labeled as mildly mentally retarded and where their white peers were not labelled at all, even when the latter evidenced more significant levels of mental retardation than the former.

It would seem that in the decades since Dunn's paper, the situation has not improved in the United States. For example, 2009 data cited by Wanda Blanchett showed that African American and other students of colour were disproportionately placed in special education, received the most segregated special education placements and were more often referred for discipline reasons.[90] Further, they were identified with Learning Disabled labels more frequently than white students and, once identified, had a risk ratio of up to 3.62 times higher than white children of being placed in segregated classroom settings. In a provocative paper, Beth Ferri and David Connor went so far as to interpret these practices as a legacy of racist practices thought to have been dismantled by *Brown v. Board of Education*. They claimed that the use of 'ableism' was tantamount to 'permitting forms of racism under the guise of disability'.[91] This has taken place because 'Disability has become a more socially accepted, even normalized, category of marginalization for students of color.'[92]

As well as this linkage between racism and disability, disproportionality is a serious matter for other reasons. As noted by the Elementary and Middle Schools Technical Assistance Center:

> For ethnic minority students, misclassification or inappropriate placement in special education programs can have devastating consequences. The problem is exacerbated when it results in a child's removal from the regular education setting, the core curriculum, or both. Students faced with such exclusionary practices are more likely to encounter a limited curriculum and lower teacher expectations. As a result, these students often have more negative post-school outcomes as evidenced by their lack of participation in post-secondary education and limited employment opportunities. In some districts, the disproportionate representation of ethnic minority students in special education classes also results in significant racial separation.[93]

In a similar vein, British researchers Steve Strand and Geoff Lindsay had this to say:

> Both over-and under-representation are problematic if they are associated with reduced access to the most appropriate forms of education, whether by inappropriate placement in special education programs for students who do not need such support and who may then miss out on a mainstream curriculum, or by a lack of support for students who would benefit from special education provision. In either case, inappropriate matches may reduce students' educational opportunities.[94]

Similar potentially negative outcomes have been noted by researchers from the United States (e.g., Alfredo Artiles and his colleagues[95]) and from Canada (e.g., Gillian Parekh and her colleagues[96]).

The 22nd Annual Report to Congress in 2000 presented the race/ethnicity breakdown of special education enrolments for the United States.[97] This information is summarized in Table 4.2

Table 4.2 Special educational enrolments in the United States, by ethnicity, 1997-1998

Ethnicity	Students by ethnicity (%)	
	Students in general population (%)	Students in special education population (%)
Asian/Pacific Islander	3.8	1.7
Black (non-Hispanic)	14.8	20.2
Hispanic	14.2	13.2
American Indian	1.0	1.3
Caucasian (non-Hispanic)	66.2	63.6

from where it can be seen that compared with their presence in the general population, Black (non-Hispanic) students were considerably over-represented in special education. In 10 of the 13 disability categories, the percentage of the special education population composed of Black students equalled or exceeded the resident population percentage. At the most extreme, Black students' representation in the mental retardation and developmental delay categories was more than twice their national population estimates. (In passing, it is worth noting that an opposite situation pertained in South Africa where, under apartheid, Whites were over-represented in special education.[98])

Conversely, in the United States, there is clear evidence that students of colour are under-represented in gifted programmes relative to White students. Even among students with high standardized test scores, Black students are less likely to be assigned to gifted services in both maths and reading, a pattern that persists when controlling for other background factors, such as health and socio-economic status, and characteristics of classrooms and schools.[99] Data from the US Department of Education revealed that as of 2009, African American students constituted 16.7% of the student population but just 9.8% of students in gifted programmes. Similarly, Hispanic students constituted 22.3% of students but only 15.4% of students receiving gifted services.[100]

In the United States, Alfredo Artiles explored the issue of ethnic minority over-representation in some detail.[101] He noted that African Americans and Native Americans were disproportionately represented in special education, especially in the high incidence categories of learning disabilities, mental retardation and emotionally disturbed.

England

According to 2007 data for England, the ethnic groups with the highest percentages of students classified as having special educational needs were Travellers of Irish heritage (2.6% with statements and an incredible 55.5% without statements), closely followed by Gypsy/ Roma students (2.5% and 49.2%, respectively). At the other end of the continuum were Chinese students (1.2% and 11.1%, respectively) and Indian students (1.2% and 14.2%). By comparison, the figures for the majority group, White British, were 1.8% and 20.0%, respectively. In a 2009 study, Steve Strand and Geoff Lindsay found that poverty and gender had stronger associations than ethnicity with the overall prevalence of students with special educational needs (SWSEN).[102] However, after controlling for these effects, significant over- and under-representation of some minority ethnic groups relative to White British students remained.

Another UK study,[103] which focused on the intersection of ethnicity and disabilities, reported similar patterns:

- Black Caribbean and Mixed White and Black Caribbean pupils were around 1.5 times more likely to be identified as having Behavioural, Emotional and Social Difficulties than White British pupils;
- Bangladeshi pupils were nearly twice as likely to be identified as having Hearing Impairments than White British pupils;
- Pakistani pupils were between 2 and 2.5 times more likely to be identified as having Profound and Multiple Learning Difficulties, Visual Impairments, Hearing Impairments or Multi-sensory Impairments than White British pupils;
- Asian and Chinese pupils were less likely than White British pupils to be identified as having Moderate Learning Difficulties, Specific Learning Difficulties and Autistic Spectrum Disorders; and
- Travellers of Irish Heritage and Gypsy/Roma pupils were over-represented among many categories of special educational needs, including Moderate, and Severe Learning Difficulties and Behavioural, Emotional and Social Difficulties.

New Zealand

Against the trends in the United States and England, the ethnic distribution of the 1.1% of the total schooling population who were classified as having high or very high needs, matched that of the general schooling population.[104] Thus, Māori students made up 21.7% of such students, compared with them making up 23.3% of the school population. The comparable figures for European students were 53.2% for both special needs funding and the school population.

Before exploring possible explanations for ethnic disproportionality, it is necessary to consider quite serious caveats regarding its evidential basis – at least of that coming out of the United States. Thus, Donald MacMillan and Daniel Rechsly argued that the over-representation of ethnic minorities in special education is not a straightforward matter.[105] In their critique of the US literature, they argued that data suffer from four major problems. First, quite different results are obtained when percentages of groups in categories or programmes are used, compared with the more commonly cited data on percentage of categories or programmes by groups. Second, they urged caution in relying on aggregated data on race/ethnicity from sources that use different approaches to recording these features (in a related point, they noted that most data collection fails to account for biracial students). Third, in noting the considerable variability in rates of disability across states, particularly in categories requiring subjective judgments, they questioned the validity of these designations. Fourth, they found that social class, rather than race/ethnicity, may be the more significant variable to focus on when considering over-representation.

However, if we accept that since ethnic disproportionality seems to be widespread, it is appropriate to turn our attention to possible explanations. These are many and varied and include such factors as the lack of congruence between minority cultures and school cultures, the legacy of deficit thinking about racial minorities, bias towards racial minorities, the history of school segregation (at least in the United States), resource inequalities, asynchronous power relationships between school authorities and minority parents, culturally inappropriate or insensitive assessment practices, and inadequate professional development opportunities for teachers.[106]

4.17 The ethnic composition of schools makes a difference to the achievement of ethnic minority students

A UK study reported on the situation of 34,000 ethnic minority pupils in mainly White schools.[107] The results indicated that children from Black Caribbean, Indian and Pakistani backgrounds in mainly White schools outperformed similar pupils in urban multi-ethnic schools at GCSE level but not at the end of Key Stage 2. The results were interpreted as showing secondary school aged children from minority ethnic backgrounds shared in whatever educational advantages were available in these mainly White schools to the same degree as children from a White background.

D How should education respond to racial, ethnic and cultural differences?

4.18 Introduction

In this section I will present strategies that have been shown to be effective in improving the educational outcomes of students from ethnic minority backgrounds. I will be drawing upon empirical research, as well as best practices identified by such bodies as UNESCO and the Council of Europe. In presenting this material I am conscious of the need to 'accommodate both universalism and cultural pluralism',[108] as Rob Reich put it, 'to navigate successfully between protecting the *pluribus* while also promoting an *unum*'.[109] I am also conscious of the importance of applying the principles of distributive justice that I outlined in section 1.9 of Chapter 1. In particular, I believe that John Rawls's 'difference principle' applies: namely that divergence from strict equality (as in sameness of treatment) is justifiable so long as any unequal treatments would make the least advantaged in society better off than they would otherwise be.

Some important caveats
Before addressing educational approaches to addressing equity challenges posed by students from ethnic minorities, it is necessary to take into account four caveats:

- Students from different, and even similar, ethnic backgrounds are heterogeneous.
- Schools serving ethnic minorities are heterogeneous.
- Most educational programmes that are beneficial for students from ethnic minorities are beneficial for all students.
- Ethnicity interacts with socio-economic status and gender as determinants of educational achievement.

As with other chapters in this book, the educational implications of the ethnic differences outlined involve complex interactions among, family, school and societal factors. These were outlined in section 1.10 in Chapter 1 and are portrayed in Figure 4.1. They will be addressed in turn.

The strategies are broadly grouped into three overlapping levels:

1   society and system-level accommodations;
2   school-level accommodations; and
3   classroom-level accommodations.

I Society and system-level accommodations

This level of analysis includes the societal component of my ecological model, described in Section 1.10 of Chapter 1. In particular, it considers the role of government in setting macro-level priorities, as well as in developing policies relating to students from diverse ethnic backgrounds. Depending on the jurisdiction, system-level accommodations targeting such students may be at the national, regional or district levels or some mix of all three.

4.19   Understand the histories and contemporary situations of ethnic minorities

Education systems should ensure that the school curriculum includes consideration of the diverse groups within their societies and in a range of other countries. This should involve an historical perspective on oppression and inequality and learning to be critical thinkers able to analyze historical and contemporary issues centring on ethnic diversity.

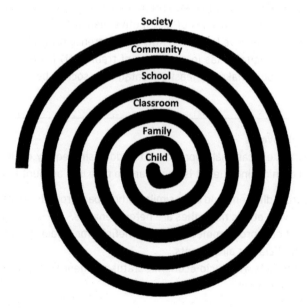

Figure 4.1 A comprehensive ecological model

4.20   *Recognize that individuals have a qualified right to have their cultural identities protected through education*

Many international instruments spell out the rights of individuals to have their cultural identities protected through education. One example is article 26.2 of the Universal Declaration of Human Rights of 1948, which states that:

> Education shall be directed to the full development of human personality and to the strengthening of respect for human rights and fundamental freedoms. It shall promote understanding, tolerance and friendship among all nations, racial and religious groups, and shall further the activities of the United Nations for the maintenance of peace.

Further, in the Preamble to UNESCO's 1945 Constitution, the founding member states declared as indispensable 'the wide diffusion of culture and the education of humanity for justice and liberty and peace'. Thus, they committed to the development of 'the means of communication between their peoples and to employ these means for the purposes of mutual understanding and a truer and more perfect knowledge of each other's lives'.

According to UNESCO, these basic principles are elaborated in many other international standard-setting instruments.[110] These include: the International Convention on the Elimination of All Forms of Racial Discrimination (1965), the International Covenant on Economic, Social and Cultural Rights (1966), the Convention on the Rights of the Child (1989), the Declaration on the Elimination of All Forms of Intolerance and of Discrimination Based on Religion or Belief (1981) and the International Convention on the Protection of the Rights of All Migrant Workers and Members of Their Families (1990).

Specifically, the cultural responsibilities of education are addressed in Article 29 of the Convention on the Rights of the Child (1989), which states that:

> the education of the child shall be directed to ... the development of respect for the child's parents, his or her own cultural identity, language and values, for the national values of the country in which the child is living, the country from which he or she may originate, and for civilizations different from his or her own.

These responsibilities were also addressed in the UNESCO Universal Declaration on Cultural Diversity (2001), which affirmed that (a) 'all persons are entitled to quality education and training that fully respect their cultural identity' (Article 5). The Declaration also made a series of recommendations, which included: 'promoting through education an awareness of the positive value of cultural diversity and improving to this end both curriculum design and teacher education' (Annex II), and 'incorporating, where appropriate, traditional pedagogies into the education process with a view to preserving and making full use of culturally appropriate methods of communication and transmission of knowledge' (Annex II).

In Europe, Article 6 of the 1995 *Framework Convention for the Protection of National Minorities*, obliges the contracting parties to

> encourage a spirit of tolerance and intercultural dialogue and take effective measures to promote mutual respect and understanding and co-operation among all persons living on their territory, irrespective of those persons' ethnic, cultural, linguistic or religious identity, in particular in the fields of education, culture and the media.[111]

4.21   Recognize the rights of students to have their cultural identities respected and to choose their own identities

In the UN Convention on the Rights of the Child (1989), it is specified that students have the right to respect for their own cultural identities, languages and values, for the national values of the countries in which they are living, and for the countries from which they may have originated. These rights coexist with students' freedom to pursue their own individual rights and liberties, including the freedom to choose their own cultural identities.

4.22   Avoid disproportionality in special education placements through legislation, regulation and careful monitoring

In section 4.16 of this chapter, I addressed ethnic disproportionality in special education enrolments. We turn now to considering how this problem could be dealt with through legislation and regulation. In section 4.34 I will propose actions at the school level.

In the United States, the reauthorization of Individuals with Disabilities Education Act 2004 made several statutory provisions to address the problem of disproportionality. First, it required states and local education agencies to develop policies and procedures to prevent the over-identification of students with racial, cultural, ethnic and linguistic diversity (RCELD). Second, it required school districts to gather and analyze data and identify disproportionality across disability categories, in special education placements, and in disciplinary actions. Third, local education agencies with high rates of students with RCELD in special education were required to implement early identification services and to reserve a maximum amount of federal funds (15%) for early intervention services. Finally, the Office of Special Education Programs in the Department of Education was required to monitor state compliance with the IDEA regulations by reviewing state data on performance indicators, including two directly related to disproportionality. As well, the Department of Education's Office of Civil Rights (OCR) was required to undertake pro-active compliance reviews of disproportionate representation.

4.23   Adopt and implement inclusivist policies

One of the over-riding themes of this book is that education systems should adopt and implement inclusivist policies. It is time that the concept of inclusion be broadened to incorporate other areas of marginality than disability. This means taking steps to reduce, if not eliminate, the segregation of children on the basis of their race/ethnicity. As I pointed out in Chapter 1, section 1.8, Gordon Allport's Intergroup Contact Theory suggests that contact between members of different groups can work to reduce prejudice and intergroup conflict. [112] He claimed that prejudice is a direct result of generalizations and oversimplifications made about an entire group of people based on incomplete or mistaken information. Such prejudice may be reduced if there is greater contact, enabling one to learn more about a category of people different from oneself. Ideally, according to Allport, such contact situations should be characterized by four key conditions: equal status, intergroup cooperation, common goals and support by social and institutional authorities.

Allport's theory found confirmation in a 2006 meta-analysis carried out by Thomas Pettigrew and Linda Tropp.[113] In their synthesis of the results from 515 studies, they found clear evidence that greater intergroup contact was generally associated with lower levels of prejudice (mean r = −0.215). Their results also showed that intergroup contact effects typically generalized beyond participants in the immediate contact situation. Not only did attitudes toward the immediate participants usually become more favourable, but so too did attitudes toward the entire outgroup, outgroup members in other situations, and even outgroups not involved in the contact. Moreover, the relationships between contact and prejudice held up across samples involving different age groups, geographical areas and contact settings. Finally, Pettigrew and Tropp found that Allport's optimal conditions for contact were best conceptualized as functioning together to facilitate positive intergroup outcomes rather than as entirely separate factors.

Miles Hewstone has been a strong advocate of contact theory and the practice of intergroup contact in the promotion of intergroup harmony. He has argued that it is the lack of or biased knowledge about the outgroup that promotes prejudice. Further, intergroup contact is both a cognitive process, and an affective one.[114]

Adoption of inclusivist policies means taking steps to desegregate schools where there are disproportionate numbers of any one ethnic group. Following *Brown v. Board of Education* (see 4.16), which required the integration of US educational facilities 'with all deliberate speed', various attempts have been made to do this. More recently, there have been encouraging developments in making schools more diverse. For example, in 2015 the New York City Council passed the School Diversity Accountability Act. This legislation required the city Department of Education to provide detailed demographic data on schools and to identify the steps it planned to take to improve diversity within schools. It also required the Department to adopt a policy that considers diversity in its school assignment process for students. As well, advocates are trying to introduce a system of 'controlled choice', where parents can still assert their preferences, but the district administration ensures that each school's enrolment reflects the community's diversity.[115] These steps are not before time as a recent report found the New York State's schools to be some of the most segregated in the country.[116]

Other desegregation methods have been employed, with mixed success. Perhaps the best-known approach was the bussing of children in the United States. This was often subverted by 'white flight' to majority white schools or to private schools and is rarely used now. Furthermore, in 2007, the US Supreme Court in *Parents Involved in Community Schools v. Seattle School District No. 1* determined that school assignment plans that used individual students' race or ethnicity as the sole factor in school assignment was unconstitutional. The challenge would appear to be one of finding a desegregation plan that would be beneficial to both ethnic minority and white students. 'Magnet schools' may be that solution, according to Christine Rossell in her book, *The carrot or the stick*.[117] These schools gave whites an incentive to transfer to other schools because they were able to offer specialized programmes and curriculum that their own neighbourhood school did not offer. Therefore, it was in the self-interest of the parents to send their children to a school in a minority neighborhood because of the better opportunities. This is a further example of the principle of interest convergence that I discuss in section 4.24 and below. What's more, courts have approved magnet schools as a means to achieve desegregation. Other approaches that are being tried include (a) school twinning, (b) school sharing, (c) joint teaching, (d) school mergers[118] and (e) communities of schools.[119]

4.24   Find interest convergence in improving the lives of ethnic minorities

You may recall Derek Bell's claim that I cited in section 1.13 in Chapter 1 in which he stated that 'the interests of Blacks in achieving racial equality will be accommodated only when it converges with the interests of whites'.[120] The lives of people in majority cultures would be improved if the negative indicators associated with many (but not all) ethnic minorities could be reversed. In many countries, this could see ethnic minorities achieve higher levels of education, which would prepare them for fuller participation in an increasingly technological workplace; it could see their rates of imprisonment and psychiatric disorders reducing; and it could see a lessening of their disaffection with society and radicalization. Quite apart from discharging human rights obligations, improving these and other such indicators are surely ones which majority cultures would find in convergence with their own interests and should spur them to take action to redress inequalities.

In Chapter 1, I pointed out another example of interest convergence, this time involving immigrants. This referred to Germany's decision to accept up to 800,000 asylum seekers in 2015. As I noted, in part at least this was driven by economic considerations in a country experiencing labour shortages and low fertility levels. Thus, the interests of refugees and German society converged.

Interest convergence can only happen if those in the majority culture are prepared to relinquish some of their power and privilege in the interests of the wider picture. This is a challenging situation for societies and for teachers, principals and parents. But, as I argued in Chapter 3 (section 3.5) with reference to SES, I believe that in many countries we have also reached a 'tipping point' in our approach to ethnic minorities. I hope that the ideas I traverse in this chapter go some way towards redressing existing inequalities.

One example of a way forward was recently articulated by an OECD Labour and Employment Ministerial Meeting, which acknowledged that refugees and their children need relevant support. This would include helping them to develop and fully utilize their skills in order to integrate in the labour market and society and contribute to the host country.[121]

4.25   Adopt Mother Tongue-Based Multilingual Education

> *Language is one of the most universal and diverse forms of expression of human culture, and perhaps even the most essential one. It is at the heart of issues of identity, memory and transmission of knowledge.*[122]

Mother Tongue-Based Multilingual Education (MT-BMLE) requires the use of the mother tongue as the language of instruction in the classroom. This policy is based on the assumption that by starting in the language they know best, children will be able to build a strong foundation at school, which then enables them to make an effective transition into other national or international languages in due course. Although UNESCO has encouraged mother tongue instruction in early childhood and primary education since 1953,[123] monolingualism in official or dominant languages is still the norm around the world.[124] In a 2007 report, UNESCO pointed out the advantages of multilingual education in the early years.[125] For example, when children are offered opportunities to learn in their mother tongue, they are more likely to enrol and succeed in school and their parents are more likely to communicate with teachers and participate in their children's learning. Mother tongue-based education especially benefits disadvantaged groups, including children from rural communities and girls, who tend to have less exposure to an official language. According to a review carried out by Jessica Ball, research confirms that children learn best in their mother tongue as a prelude to and complement of bilingual and multilingual education.[126] Whether children successfully retain their mother tongue while acquiring additional languages depends on several interacting factors. Studies show that six to eight years of education in a language are necessary to develop the level of literacy and verbal proficiency required for academic achievement in secondary school. In addition, according to Ball, research increasingly shows that children's ability to learn a second or additional languages does not suffer when their mother tongue is the primary language of instruction throughout primary school. It would seem that fluency and literacy in the mother tongue lays a cognitive and linguistic foundation for learning additional languages. If, however, children are forced to switch abruptly or transition too soon from learning in their mother tongue to schooling in a second language, their first language acquisition may be attenuated or even lost. Even more importantly, their self-confidence as learners and their interest in what they are learning may decline, leading to lack of motivation, school failure, and early school leaving.

4.26 Provide additive bilingual programmes that promote the maintenance of students' first language while learning a second

A 2015 paper noted that the number of dual language programmes is on the increase across the United States.[127] This is a positive trend for, as I noted in section 4.10, research favours additive bilingual programmes that promote maintenance of the first language while learning a second.[128] However, paradoxically, there is also a possibility that dual immersion programmes might actually benefit the dominant English-speaking population more than language minority students.[129] This was confirmed in an Illinois study of the distribution of such programmes, where it was found that they appeared mostly in white, middle-class communities rather than in predominantly Latino ones.[130] The authors argued that this inequity was driven by ideological and cultural capital differences among communities.

4.27 Provide targeted teaching for students for whom the host nation's language is an additional language

Earlier, in section 4.10, I noted the improved standing of students with English as an additional language as they progressed through the UK education system. Steve Strand and his colleagues pointed to a growing proficiency in the English language as an explanation for the closing of the gap between EAL and FLE students' achievement

In another recent study, Victoria Murphy and Adam Unthiah of Oxford University carried out a systematic review of intervention studies on children whose home language was not English (EAL) and who were taught through the medium of English.[131] Whereas non-EAL children develop in homes whose linguistic environment mirrors that of their educational context, this is not the case for children with EAL. Research has shown that many of them are likely to have less vocabulary knowledge than their non-EAL peers, which in turn can have negative consequences on their English language and literacy development and they may struggle in listening and reading comprehension.

Murphy and Unthiah's review included 29 studies, all bar two of which were carried out in the United States, with most focusing on primary school pupils. Not surprisingly, most of the interventions were aimed at some aspect of language and were focused on developing vocabulary knowledge. Within these interventions, the target was either academic vocabulary, phonological and/or morphological awareness. While EAL children in these studies did not have a problem with single word reading, decoding and alphabetic knowledge, they were significantly behind their non-EAL peers in comprehension. This was probably because their general vocabulary knowledge was less well elaborated relative to non-EAL peers. If children with EAL typically have good decoding skills, as has been demonstrated in numerous studies, yet nonetheless lag behind non-EAL peers in reading comprehension, then vocabulary is a good candidate for intervention, as are comprehension strategies and training to enhance students' abilities to analyze words through their morphological structure.

4.28 In multilingual countries, consider teaching two and possibly three languages

According to the Council of Europe (2007), 'plurilingualism' should be understood in a dual sense as it constitutes (1) a conception of the speaker as fundamentally plural, and (2) a value in that it is the basis of linguistic tolerance, an essential element of intercultural education.[132]

According to Ulrike Jessner, there are three types of third language learners:

- Children growing up with three languages from birth.
- Bilingual children learning a third language – in many cases English – at school at an early age, as is the case in the Basque Country in Spain. Also as I noted in section 4.3, Switzerland requires children to learn two of the country's four official languages and English by the fifth year of primary school, making a total of three languages.
- Bilingual migrant children moving to a new linguistic environment such as Kurdish/Turkish children learning German in Austria.[133]

So what does the research tell us about teaching and learning three languages? In what follows, I will draw upon a recent review of 43 studies carried out by Camilla Dyssegaard and her colleagues.[134] Here are their main findings: First, as Jessner has pointed out, the learning process of acquiring a second language (L2) differs greatly from that of third language learning. The main difference is that third language (L3) learners can use two languages as base languages in third language acquisition while second language (L2) learners can only use their first language as the base language. When learning an L2, one can either learn L1 and L2 simultaneously or learn the two languages sequentially, and third language acquisition presents more temporal diversity than second language acquisition. Second, studies regarding immersion programmes indicate that these programmes often have a positive impact. It also appears that students in immersion programmes who are learning an L2 and an L3 at an early age develop age appropriate skills in their L1 and L2 at the same time. This seems to indicate that immersion programmes do not constitute a source of overload. Third, findings indicate that both social factors and educational factors are important when it comes to understanding bilingual and trilingual development in contexts of two languages, a majority language and a minority language, e.g., Spanish and Basque. Fourth, findings also show that when one of the languages that a bilingual learner knows is a minority language, then he or she obtains better results in L3 when his or her minority language is valued and used at home. Fifth, exposure outside school may play an important role in a student's third language acquisition. Sixth, studies appear to indicate positive effects of well-educated teachers and direct feedback to students. Seventh, late starters in most cases seem to out-perform early starters in regards to third language proficiency when the amount of instruction time is held constant. This may be explained by older students' greater cognitive ability or by the amount of instruction received by early starters being more spread out than that received by older learners. Eighth, not surprisingly, high levels of proficiency in L1 and L2 have a positive impact on L3 acquisition. As an explanation for these findings, several studies point to the fact that bilinguals could have an advantage in terms of a higher level of metalinguistic awareness and the ability to use two other linguistic systems when learning a third language. Finally, some studies suggest that the typological relation between the students' previously acquired languages and the L3 they are acquiring may facilitate the acquisition of certain L3 skills.

4.29 Implement intercultural education

Two major concepts relating to cultural diversity in education have been identified: 'multicultural education' and 'intercultural education'.[135] Both stand in contrast to an assimilationist approach which would have schools give priority to teaching students to become effective citizens of a 'melting pot' state. According to James Banks, Director of the Center for Multicultural Education at the University of Washington in the United States, 'the assimilationist views the modernized state as universalistic rather than characterized by strong ethnic allegiances and attachments'[136] and believes in 'the full socialization of all individuals and groups into the shared national civic culture'.[137]

Multicultural education

Multicultural education has been used to describe education that is intended to take account of the culturally diverse nature of human society. For it to be implemented successfully, Banks argued that institutional changes must be made, including: changes to the curriculum; the teaching materials; teaching and learning styles; the attitudes, perceptions and behaviours of teachers and administrators; and in the goals, norms, and culture of the school.[138] He further advocated that five dimensions of multicultural education be taken into account: content integration, the knowledge construction process, prejudice reduction, an equity pedagogy, and an empowering school culture and social structure.[139]

Let me be clear: multicultural education should be so designed as to avoid the criticisms of multiculturalism that I outlined in Section 4.12. This means, for example, that it should not equate to an education system that comprises an aggregation of diverse monocultural schools; nor should it equate to schools that comprise a series of separate monocultural classes, and nor should it comprise classes with students grouped largely on the basis of their ethnicity. I believe Banks's approach bypasses these criticisms. However, to avoid any possible ambiguity of meaning, I prefer to use the term *intercultural education*, which is favoured by UNESCO and is widely used in Europe. I believe it constitutes the way forward.

Intercultural education

Intercultural education is a dynamic concept that refers to the relations between cultural groups. UNESCO defined it as 'the existence and equitable interaction of diverse cultures and the possibility of generating shared cultural expressions through dialogue and mutual respect'.[140]

According to a landmark set of guidelines on intercultural education published by UNESCO, in order to strengthen democracy, education systems need to take into account the multicultural character of society, and aim at actively contributing to peaceful coexistence and positive interaction between different cultural groups.[141] To achieve this goal, UNESCO has advocated intercultural education.[142] This aims to go beyond passive coexistence, to achieve a developing and sustainable way of living together in multicultural societies through the understanding of, respect for and dialogue between the different cultural groups. The aims of intercultural education are summarized under the 'four pillars of education', as identified by the Delors Commission.[143] These comprise:

- *learning to know*: bringing students into contact with other languages and areas of knowledge;
- *learning to do*: the acquisition of necessary competencies that enable the individual to find a place in society;
- *learning to live together*: carrying out joint projects and learning to manage conflicts in a spirit of respect for the values of pluralism, mutual understanding and peace; and
- *learning to be*: taking account of students' potential including their cultural potential and their right to difference.

According to UNESCO, three principles stand out in intercultural education:

Principle I: it respects the cultural identity of learners through the provision of culturally appropriate and responsive quality education for all. This principle can be achieved in three ways. First, it requires the use of appropriate curricula and teaching and learning materials. Second, it implies the development of culturally appropriate teaching methods. Third, it should involve interactions between the school and its community and the involvement of the learners and/or their communities in the educational processes.

Principle II: intercultural education should provide every learner with the cultural knowledge, attitudes and skills necessary to achieve active and full participation in society. This principle can be achieved in three ways. First, it requires the guaranteeing of equitable opportunities in education. Second, curricula and teaching and learning materials should be culturally appropriate. Third, teaching methods should be attended to.

Principle III: intercultural education should provide all learners with cultural knowledge, attitudes and skills that enable them to contribute to respect, understanding and solidarity among individuals, ethnic, social, cultural and religious groups and nations. As with the previous principles, this one can be achieved in three ways. First, the curricula should contribute to such perspectives as the discovery of cultural diversity, awareness of the positive value of cultural diversity and respect for cultural heritage. Second, teaching and learning methods should (a) treat the heritages, experience and contributions of different ethnic groups with comparable dignity, integrity and significance; and (b) correspond to the values taught. Third, learners should be assisted to acquire skills to communicate and cooperate beyond cultural barriers and to share and co-operate with others.

Like UNESCO, the Council of Europe has also advocated intercultural education. Thus, in 2003, the European ministers of education developed what became known as the 'Athens Declaration' on intercultural education.[144] They premised their recommendations on four factors: (a) the diversity of European societies in terms of ethnicity, culture, languages and religions; (b) the social conflicts and disagreements that may result from the coexistence of different value systems; (c) a wish to preserve the multicultural nature of European society; and (d) an awareness of the disturbing persistence in European societies of xenophobic and racist practices, violence and intolerance.

The Athens Declaration on intercultural education was subsequently strengthened in a Council of Europe White Paper on intercultural dialogue.[145] As I noted in Chapter 1, this document argued for 'a vibrant and open society without discrimination, benefiting us all, marked by the inclusion of all residents in full respect of their human rights'.[146] It saw an intercultural approach as offering a forward-looking model for managing cultural diversity and preventing ethnic, religious, linguistic and cultural divides on the basis of shared universal values and sustaining social cohesion.

The White Paper stated that achieving inclusive societies needed a new approach, and that 'intercultural dialogue was the route to follow'.[147] This was understood to comprise 'an open and respectful exchange of views between individuals, groups with different ethnic, cultural, religious and linguistic backgrounds and heritage on the basis of mutual understanding and respect'.[148] Such an approach provides the best chance to bring about social cohesion, understood by the Council of Europe to denote the capacity of a society to ensure the welfare of all its members, minimizing disparities and avoiding polarization.

For the purpose of the White Paper, intercultural dialogue was defined 'as a process that comprises an open and respectful exchange of views between individuals and groups with different ethnic, cultural, religious and linguistic backgrounds and heritage, on the basis of mutual understanding and respect. It requires the freedom and ability to express oneself, as well as the willingness and capacity to listen to the views of others'.[149] Further, freedom to choose one's own culture is fundamental to intercultural dialogue – a critical point when it comes to education of children. In the words of the White Paper:

> Simultaneously or at various stages in their lives, everyone may adopt different cultural affiliations. Whilst every individual, to a certain extent, is a product of his or her heritage and social background, in contemporary modern democracies everyone can enrich his or her own identity by integrating different cultural affiliations. No one should be confined against their will within a particular group, community, thought-system or worldview, but should be free to renounce past choices and make new ones – as long as they are consistent with the universal values of human rights, democracy and the rule of law.[150]

The White Paper provided detail on the learning and teaching of intercultural competences, which it deemed to be essential for democratic culture and social cohesion. Its recommendations will be incorporated in the following sections.

4.30 Ensure that teacher education programmes prepare educators to work with ethnically diverse students

Teachers and school leaders are at the heart of ensuring that students from all ethnic backgrounds receive a sound, appropriate education. This means that close attention should be paid to the content of teacher education programmes and the cultural sensitivity of those responsible for delivering it. Specifically, this means

- introducing intercultural learning and practice in the initial teacher education and professional development of teachers;[151]
- ensuring that educators are equipped with cultural self-awareness, attitudes/ expectations, beliefs, knowledge, and skills, as well as the socio-political contexts of education in culturally and linguistically diverse communities.[152]

Dialogical professional development is a useful approach to working with teachers and principals. Known in New Zealand by its Māori name as *Te Whakapakari*, it involves groups of teachers or school leaders engaging in critical reflection, underpinned by social justice positioning and high trust of teachers.[153] The participants work in small 'learning circles' within their own school or with colleagues in nearby or similar schools. Facilitators access readings and experiences and encourage crucial dialogue on this material, with discussion of the relevance of the writers' ideas for the participants' classrooms and communities. The leadership of the circles can rotate among the participants.

II School-level strategies

Schools' roles in addressing the needs of students from diverse ethnic backgrounds are twofold. First, all schools have the responsibility of utilizing their resources to deliver an equitable education to all of their students. Second, some schools may be disadvantaged in that they have a high proportion of students from ethnic minorities and need support in managing their responsibilities toward such students. School-level strategies that have been found to work include the following.

4.31 Develop a school-wide strategy for targeting success for ethnic minorities

In New Zealand, the Education Review Office (ERO) is responsible for reviewing the performances of schools every three years and more often if a school is causing concern. In 2014, it suggested that improvements in Māori students' achievement resulted when schools:

- integrated elements of students' identity language and culture into teaching and learning;
- used their student achievement data to target resources for optimal effect;
- provided early intensive support for those students at risk of falling behind;

- created productive partnerships with parents, whānau [family], hapu [community], iwi [tribe], communities and business focused on educational success;
- retained high expectations of students to succeed in education as Māori.[154]

In elaborating on the relationship with parents and whānau, ERO noted that teachers and leaders who understood this intent:

- listened to what whānau knew about their child's interest and what worked for them;
- involved parents in setting goals and agreeing on next learning steps;
- developed a shared language about learning and achievement with students and their parents and whānau; and
- valued students' well-being and were genuinely interested in them and their whānau.

4.32   Ensure that the school does not discriminate on the grounds of ethnicity

Discrimination can take many forms, ranging from the deliberate to the unconscious, from the widespread to the occasional. School leaders should conduct regular audits of their school to eliminate any such practices by, for example, examining grouping and labeling practices, sports participation, disproportionality in achievement, and interactions of staff and students across ethnicities to ensure no biases.[155]

4.33   Encourage interactions between the school and its community

Increasingly, in many countries the 'borders' between schools and the communities they serve are becoming blurred. As I pointed out in section 3.24 in Chapter 3, this is reflected in the development of Full-Service Schools in which various community agencies share the same campus. Other approaches that have been recommended include the following:[156]

- use the school as a centre for social and cultural activities, both for educational purposes and for the community;
- encourage the participation of traditional artisans and performers as instructors;
- decentralize the development of contents and methods to take into account cultural differences from one region to another;
- support the participation of students, parents and other community members from different cultural backgrounds in school governance, decision-making, planning and the implementation of education programmes.

4.34   Avoid disproportionality in special education placements through actions at the school level

Research has shown that reducing disproportionality requires a comprehensive approach that encompasses teacher education, culturally appropriate assessment and instruction, cultural sensitivity and effective home and school collaboration.

Before presenting these, I would like to observe that, for the most part, the principles described are relevant to all students, not just those from ethnic minorities. The truism that 'good teaching is good teaching' surely applies: the principles of learning and pedagogy apply similarly to all students. Certainly, they need culturally appropriate teaching, but they also share the same needs as other students for sound, evidence- based teaching, such as outlined by John Hattie[157] and in my own writing.[158]

Writing on behalf of the National Center for Culturally Responsive Educational Systems, Shernaz Garcia and Alba Ortiz presented a comprehensive overview of how disproportionate representation can be prevented 'through culturally and linguistically responsive pre-referral interventions'.[159] By 'pre-referral', they meant taking steps to avoid referring students for special education by 'differentiating students with disabilities from those whose academic or behavioral difficulties reflect other factors, including inappropriate or inadequate instruction'.[160] In making their case, Garcia and Ortiz argued

> it is critical that the pre-referral intervention process is culturally and linguistically responsive; that is, educators must ensure that students' socio-cultural, linguistic, racial/ ethnic, and other relevant background characteristics are addressed at all stages, including reviewing student performance, considering reasons for student difficulty or failure, designing alternative interventions and interpreting assessment results.[161]

Garcia and Ortiz went on to specify key elements of culturally – and linguistically – responsive pre-referral intervention for culturally and linguistically diverse students. These included the following:

- schools should recognize the fact that all students have cultures composed of social, familial, linguistic and ethnically related practices that shape the ways in which they see the world and interact with it;
- all educators should share responsibility for educating all students, through culturally responsive curricula and instruction and by creating learning environments in which their culturally and linguistically diverse students can be successful;
- educators should recognize that culturally and linguistically diverse learners are best served by curricula and instruction that build on their prior socio-cultural and linguistic knowledge and experiences;
- schools should offer an array of programmes and services that accommodate the unique learning characteristics of specific groups of students, including community-based programmes and support services;
- educators should create collaborative relationships with students and their families, by recognizing parents/family members as valuable partners in promoting academic progress and by working with them from a posture of cultural reciprocity;
- schools should implement early intervention strategies as soon as learning problems are noted.

III Classroom-level strategies

As I have emphasized throughout this book, nothing is more important for the well-being of students whatever their backgrounds than what occurs in their day-to-day, minute-by-minute experiences in classrooms. Here, we must consider the appropriateness of the curriculum and associated assessment practices, the quality of the teaching and the nature of the relationships within those environments.

4.35   *Recognize the histories of students from different ethnic minorities*

Students from different ethnic groups come to school with a wide range of experiences associated with their ethnicities. Some have suffered from trauma associated with conflict in their country of origin, some will have been raped, some will have been forcibly enlisted as child soldiers, some will have been exposed to religious persecution, some will have been malnourished, and some will not speak the language of their new country. For some, these experiences will be fresh in their minds, for others they will have been conveyed to them by their parents or their grandparents. All will need to be understood and accommodated to by their teachers and school principals.

A related point is that many such students have had diverse educational histories. As pointed out by Jim Anderson and his colleagues for the Council of Europe, they may have moved from one country to another in the course of their educational careers and as a result have had to shift their learning from one language to another.[162] As well, they may have experienced different approaches to curricula and pedagogy.

4.36   *Emphasize positive relationships with students*

A New Zealand research project entitled *Te Kotahitanga* (unity) investigated Māori secondary school students' perceptions of what was involved in improving their educational achievement.[163] The most important influence to emerge centred on the quality of the in-class face-to-face relationships and interactions between students and their teachers. These findings led to the development of an Effective Teaching Profile, which then formed the basis of a professional development intervention. When implemented with a group of 11 teachers in four schools, this was associated with improved learning, behaviour and attendance outcomes for Māori students. The authors noted that deficit theorizing by teachers was the major impediment to Māori students' educational achievement for it results in teachers having low expectations, which creates a self-fulfilling prophecy of school failure. In a follow-up study, it was found that schools in their fourth through to seventh year of the project's implementation were maintaining the changes made in teaching practices with the associated gains in Māori students' achievement made earlier.[164] I believe this project's themes have wide applicability, both inside and outside New Zealand.

4.37   *Support students' linguistic acquisition and development*[165]

Many students from ethnic minorities will have one or more languages that differ from the school's language of instruction. Thus, teachers should support their students both in the language of schooling and in the other languages they use outside the school – as well as any other languages they are learning at school. Teachers should also be aware of the linguistic demands of the curriculum and have the skills to make it accessible to students from a variety of language backgrounds and at different stages of competence in the language of schooling. In this sense, every teacher is a language teacher.

A related point is that in some countries there are complementary schools, in the evenings or at weekends, set up to develop competence in students' home languages and to study topics of cultural significance to their communities. As pointed out by Jim Anderson and his colleagues, in Europe, these schools are administered in a range of ways.[166] Some are supported by foreign governments (e.g., the Italian government has sponsored classes and schools across Europe for children of Italian origin); some may be sponsored by the national or local government of the country in which the children live (e.g., in Scandinavia where 'mother tongue' classes after school are often provided by the municipality for immigrant children); and some may be set up independently by cultural groups (for example, there are Chinese schools in several European countries designed to ensure that children of Chinese descent have the opportunity to become literate in Chinese and to participate in cultural activities). Teachers should make themselves familiar with any such complementary programmes and, if possible, coordinate with them.

4.38 Engage with families of all students, including those from ethnic minorities

There can be no doubt that parents and caregivers play a major role in the development and education of their children. According to John Hattie, the effect size for the impact of parent involvement on children's academic achievement has been calculated from meta-analyses to be 0.51.[167] The challenge for educators is to create collaborative relationships by recognizing parents/family members as valuable partners in promoting academic progress and by working with them from a posture of cultural reciprocity,[168] mutual respect, open communication, shared responsibility and collaboration.[169]

4.39 Ensure that curricula content reflects consideration of cultural diversity

The content of what is taught in schools should be carefully selected and presented to take account of the cultural diversity not only of the students, but also of society and the wider world. One of the aims should be to eliminate prejudices about culturally distinct groups. This principle can be achieved by following guidelines such as:

- use examples and content from a variety of cultures to illustrate key concepts in subjects;[170]
- include consideration of racial attitudes and how they can be modified;[171]
- impart knowledge about the history, traditions, languages and cultures of minorities to majority groups;[172]
- impart knowledge about society as a whole to minorities;[173]
- develop an awareness of the positive value of cultural diversity;[174]
- develop a critical awareness of the struggles against racism and discrimination;[175]
- acquire knowledge about cultural heritage;[176]
- develop an awareness of the increasing global interdependence between peoples and nations;[177]
- develop an awareness not only of rights, but also of duties incumbent upon individuals, social groups and nations toward each other;[178]
- make learning about democracy and intercultural education key components of educational reform;[179]
- disseminate examples of good practice which emphasize intercultural and pluralist approaches in school textbooks;[180]
- encourage students to reflect critically on their own responses and attitudes to experiences of other cultures;[181]

- focus the teaching of history, not only on the history of one's own country, but include learning the history of other countries and cultures, as well as how others have looked at the students' own society (i.e., multiperspectivity);[182]
- ensure that history teaching is not an instrument of ideological manipulation, of propaganda or is used for the promotion of intolerant and ultra-nationalistic, xenophobic, racist or anti-Semitic ideas.[183]

By following these guidelines the principles of universal design for learning that I described in section 1.26 in Chapter 1 would be assured.

4.40 Ensure that pedagogy is evidence-based and culturally responsive

As I have argued elsewhere, children have similar needs for sound, evidence-based pedagogy.[184] Only to a limited extent can we say that there are teaching strategies that are specific to different cultural groups. What constitutes effective teaching for such students is invariably effective for all learners. With these caveats, here are some strategies that should be taken into account:

- modify teaching strategies to facilitate the achievement of students from diverse ethnic and cultural groups;[185]
- integrate non-formal and traditional forms of teaching such as story-telling, drama, poetry and song;[186]
- include activities resulting from collaboration with cultural institutions;[187]
- promote learners' active participation in the education process.[188]

A recent US study provides some helpful, research-based, leads into culturally responsive pedagogy. It employed a Culturally Responsive Instruction Observation Protocol (CRIOP) as a framework for providing 52 hours of professional development for 27 teachers. [189] CRIOP comprised seven elements: Classroom Relationships, Family Collaboration, Assessment, Curriculum/ Planned Experiences, Instruction/Pedagogy, Discourse/Instructional Conversation and Sociopolitical Consciousness/Diverse Perspectives. Of the 456 students in the study, 87.3% received free or reduced lunches, and 28% were classified as English Language Learners. The results showed that students of high implementers of the CRIOP had significantly higher achievement scores in reading and mathematics than students of low implementers.

4.41 Take account of different worldviews of students and their families

A truism of teaching is that one should start from what the student already knows and build out from that. This is no less true for starting with an understanding of students' worldviews – their 'sense-making and knowledge-generating processes' that I briefly mentioned in section 4.11. This can be done by adopting strategies such as:

- recognizing that all students have cultures composed of social, familial, linguistic and ethnically related practices that shape the ways in which they see the world and interact with it;[190]
- helping students to understand, investigate and determine how implicit cultural assumptions, frames of references and biases within a discipline influence the ways in which knowledge is constructed;[191]

- sensitizing students to the idea that humans have developed a range of different ways of life, customs and worldviews, and that this breadth of human life enriches all of us;[192]
- incorporating an appreciation of different expressions of creativity, including artefacts, symbols, texts, objects, dress and food into learning about one another.[193]

4.42   Take account of any possible mismatches of cultural and social capital

As I emphasized in section 1.21 in Chapter 1, in their everyday interactions with their students and their parents, teachers have to take into account possible differences in values, beliefs and worldviews. This also means taking account of students' popular culture, including their navigation of social media and their participation in video games.[194] To do otherwise would be to deny their identities and their rights to hold on to their cultures. This principle is not an absolute one, however, for teachers also have obligations to develop critical thinking and media literacy in their students and to present them with other ways of looking at their place in the world – as outlined in the above section on intercultural education.

4.43   Educate students to be citizens of diverse societies in a globalized world

As we have seen in this chapter, migration within and across nation-states is leading to an increasing amount of racial, ethnic, cultural, linguistic and religious diversity in nation-states. This phenomenon is posing challenges to our concepts of citizenship and, by extension, citizenship education.[195] Strictly speaking, according to UNESCO, citizenship education can be defined as

> educating children, from early childhood, to become clear-thinking and enlightened citizens who participate in decisions concerning society. 'Society' is here understood in the special sense of a nation with a circumscribed territory which is recognized as a state.[196]

However, in addressing this issue, I will be taking a broader brush. In keeping with my overriding concern for inclusivism, I believe that citizenship education should contribute to inclusivism at all levels: schools, communities, societies and globally. Indeed, despite its somewhat narrow definition, UNESCO also adopted this perspective when it stated that citizenship education had three main objectives:

- educating people in citizenship and human rights through an understanding of the principles and institutions which govern a state or nation;
- learning to exercise one's judgment and critical faculty; and
- acquiring a sense of individual and community responsibilities.

Earlier, at a meeting of world Ministers of Education, the importance of citizenship education was emphasized in the following statement:

> We, the Ministers of Education (of the world) strive resolutely to pay special attention to improving curricula, the content of textbooks, and other education materials including new technologies with a view to educating caring and responsible citizens committed to peace, human rights, democracy and sustainable development, open to other cultures, able to appreciate the value of freedom, respectful of human dignity and differences, and able to prevent conflicts or resolve them by non-violent means.[197]

In turn, according to UNESCO, these objectives suggested four major themes for citizenship education:

- The relations between individuals and society: individual and collective freedoms, and rejection of any kind of discrimination.
- The relations between citizens and the government: what is involved in democracy and the organization of the state.
- The relations between the citizen and democratic life.
- The responsibility of the individual and the citizen in the international community.

James Banks has written extensively on citizenship education. In a 2011 article, he rejected assimilationist conceptions of citizenship education and argued instead that it should enable students to acquire the knowledge, skills and commitments needed to become effective civic participants in their communities, nation-state and the world.[198] He noted that many people have multiple national commitments, live in more than one nation, and practise 'flexible citizenship'. Such an approach is necessary, according to Banks, since approximately 200 million migrants (in 2008) were living outside the nation in which they were born, representing about 3% of the world's population. Banks also referred to 'multicultural citizenship' in which immigrant and minority groups retain important aspects of their languages and cultures, as well as having full citizenship rights. This requires striking a delicate balance of diversity and unity. As Banks put it,

> Schools must nurture, support, and affirm the identities of students' diverse groups if we expect them to endorse national values, become cosmopolitans, internalize human rights values, and work to make their local communities, nation, region, and the world more just and humane.[199]

In response to terrorist attacks in Europe, the European Ministers of Education in 2015 issued a *Declaration on promoting citizenship and the common values of freedom, tolerance and non-discrimination through education*.[200] They stated that they remained united in their efforts to promote freedom of thought and expression, social inclusion and respect for others, as well as to prevent and tackle discrimination in all its forms. Accordingly, they resolved to combine their efforts 'to prevent and tackle marginalisation, intolerance, racism and radicalisation and to preserve a framework of equal opportunities for all'.

E Conclusions

Eight broad conclusions may be drawn from this chapter:

First, consideration of race, ethnicity and culture draws our attention to indigenous peoples, minority nations, migrants (legal and illegal, voluntary and involuntary), refugees (conflict-driven and economic) and temporary or permanent 'guest workers'. It also draws our attention to the relationships that these groups have with their 'host' or 'majority' cultures, both in the past and in the present. This chapter focuses on *ethnicity*, defined as an 'embodiment of values, institutions, and patterns of behavior, a composite whole representing a people's historical experience, aspirations, and worldview'.[201]

Second, most countries are becoming more diverse ethnically. This reflects such factors as: (a) globalization compressing space and time on a scale that is unprecedented;

Table 4.3 Summary of actions to accommodate to ethnic diversity

Society (government)	Education system	Schools	Classrooms
• Recognize that individuals have a right to have their cultural identities protected through education. • Recognize the rights of people to have their cultural identities respected and to choose their own identities. • Adopt and implement inclusivist policies in housing and social services. • Find interest convergence in improving the lives of ethnic minorities. • In multilingual countries, consider teaching two and possibly three languages.	• Ensure that the curriculum considers diverse groups within their societies and in a range of other countries. • Ensure that the curriculum contains an historical perspective on oppression and inequality and how to critically analyze historical and contemporary issues centring on ethnic diversity. • Adopt and implement inclusivist policies in education. • Avoid disproportionality in special education placements through legislation, regulation and monitoring. • Adopt Mother Tongue-Based Multilingual Education. • Promote maintenance of students' first language while learning a second. • Implement intercultural education. • Ensure that teacher education prepares educators to work with ethnically diverse students.	• Develop a school-wide strategy for targeting success for ethnic minorities. • Ensure that the school does not discriminate on the grounds of ethnicity. • Encourage interactions between the school and its community. • Avoid disproportionality in special education placements through actions at the school level. • Provide professional development for all staff on strategies for educating students from diverse ethnic backgrounds.	• Recognize the histories of students from different ethnic minorities. • Emphasize positive relationships with students. • Support students' linguistic acquisition and development. • Engage with families of all students, including those from ethnic minorities. • Ensure that curricula content reflects consideration of cultural diversity. • Ensure that pedagogy is culturally sensitive. • Take account of different worldviews of students and their families. • Take account of any possible mismatch of cultural and social capital. • Educate students to be citizens of diverse societies in a globalized world.

(b) revolutions in telecommunications and the media rendering national cultural systems increasingly porous; and (c) the development of transport and tourism.

Third, most, but not all, ethnic minorities in most countries fare poorly on a wide range of educational, economic, social and health indicators. Moreover, these indicators interact with each other to produce a compounding effect. Similarly, ethnicity interacts with socio-economic status and gender to influence educational achievement.

Fourth, ethnic minorities' histories play a role in determining educational outcomes. This draws our attention to proximal or distal experiences of discrimination, persecution, slavery, colonialism, civil wars, economic privations and combinations of several of these experiences.

Fifth, many criticisms have been levelled at multiculturalism. These include (a) group-differentiated rights restricting the freedom of individual members to pursue their individual rights and liberties, (b) the risk to societal integration, and (c) the propriety of children being categorized in terms of the inherited traditions of the community in which they happen to have been born. Therefore, intercultural education, rather than multicultural education, is the preferred approach to educating ethnic minorities.

Sixth, since ethnic minorities tend to live in segregated, high poverty neighbourhoods, they attend similarly segregated schools that are disproportionately populated by other ethnic minorities. While most countries have eliminated overt racial segregation in education, vestiges of it remain in the form of racial disproportionately in special education. Inclusivist policies should be pursued to counteract these trends. This may mean finding policies that maximize interest convergence.

Seventh, countries should develop language policies that include (a) promoting the maintenance of students' first language while learning the host language, and (b) considering teaching three languages in multilingual countries, and (c) supporting students' linguistic acquisition and development.

Eighth, educational strategies for targeting success for ethnic minorities should include (a) developing interactions between schools and their communities, (b) engaging with families, (c) emphasizing positive relationships with students, (d) designing curricula content to reflect consideration of cultural diversity while at the same time preparing students to be citizens of a globalized world, and (e) employing a pedagogy which is culturally sensitive and takes account of any different worldviews of students and their families. Initial teacher education and professional development programmes for existing teachers should prepare educators to acquire these skills to work with ethnically diverse students. Table 4.3 summarizes the range of actions to mitigate the effects of ethnic minority status presented in this chapter.

Notes

1 Banks, J.A. (2011). 'Educating citizens in diverse societies.' *Intercultural Education*, 22(4), 243–1251, p. 248.
2 Du Bois, W.E.B. (1900). 'Address to the nations of the world.' In P. Foner (ed.) (1970). *W.E.B. Du Bois speaks: Speeches and addresses 1890–1919* (pp. 124–27). New York, NY: Pathfinder Press.
3 Kymlicka, W. (2001). *Politics in the vernacular: Nationalism, multiculturalism, and citizenship.* Oxford, UK: Oxford University Press.
4 Nisbett, R.E., Aronson, J., Blair, C., Dickens, W., Flynn, J., Halpern, D. & Turkheimer, E. (2012). 'Intelligence: New findings and theoretical developments.' *American Psychologist*, 67, 130–159.

5   Robb, P. (ed.) (1995). *The concept of race in South Asia.* Oxford: Oxford University Press, p. 1.

6   For recent, controversial, arguments that that races differ innately in such features as intelligence, personality, sexual behaviour, and criminal behaviour, see Rushton, J.P. (2000). *Race, evolution and behavior.* Second edition. Port Huron, MI: Charles Darwin Research Institute; and Wade, N. (2014). *A troublesome inheritance: Genes, race, and human history.* New York, NY: Penguin.

7   Chang, H. & Dodd, T. (2001). 'International perspectives on race and ethnicity: An annotated bibliography.' *Electronic Magazine of Multicultural Education.* Spring, 2001.

8   Betancourt, H. & Lopez, S.R. (1993). 'The study of culture, ethnicity and race in American psychology.' *American Psychologist*, 48(6), 629–637.

9   Zuckerman, M. (1990). 'Some dubious premises in research and theory on racial differences: Scientific, social, and ethical issues.' *American Psychologist*, 45, 1297–1303; and McChesney, K.Y. (2015). 'The science you need to know to explain why race is not biological.' *Sage Open*, 5(4), DOI: 10.1177/2158244015611712.

10 Hall, S. (1997). *Race, the floating signifier.* Media Education Foundation, cited by Hiles, D. (2007). 'Human diversity and the meaning of difference.' Paper presented at 10th European Congress of Psychology, Prague, 3–6 July 2007.

11 McChesney, op. cit.

12 UNESCO (1950). *The race question.* Paris: Author.

13 Deng, F. (2015). *Ethnicity: An African predicament.* Washington, DC: Brookings Institution Press. URL: http://www.brookings.edu/research/articles/1997/06/summer-africa-deng (accessed 15 December 2015).

14 Betancourt & Lopez, op. cit.

15 UNESCO (2001). *Universal declaration on cultural diversity.* Paris: Author, p. 1.

16 Kuper, A. (1999). *The anthropologists' account.* Cambridge, MA: Harvard University Press, p. 3.

17 Raday, F. (2003). 'Culture, religion, and gender.' *International Journal of Constitutional Law*, 1(4), 663–715, p. 666.

18 The World Value Survey, headquartered in Stockholm, Sweden, consists of nationally representative surveys of people's values and beliefs conducted in almost 100 countries, using a common questionnaire. See www.worldvaluessurvey.org (accessed 23 May 2016).

19 Welzel, C. (2013). *Freedom rising: Human empowerment and the quest for emancipation.* Cambridge: Cambridge University Press.

20 Fearon, J.D. (2003). 'Ethnic and cultural diversity by country.' *Journal of Economic Growth*, 8(2), 195–222.

21 Atlas and Boots (2016). *The world's most multilingual countries.* URL: http://www.atlasandboots.com/worlds-most-multilingual-countries-ranked/ (accessed 14 January 2014).

22 Dyssegaard, C.B., Egeberg, J.dH, Sommersel, H.B., Steenberg, K. & Vestergaard, S. (2015). *A systematic review of the impact of multiple language teaching, prior language experience and acquisition order on students' language proficiency in primary and secondary school.* Copenhagen, Denmark: Danish Clearinghouse for Educational Research, Department of Education, Aarhus University.

23 In 2001, Indians were the largest minority group (1.8% of the population), followed by Pakistanis (1.3%), Mixed ethnic backgrounds (1.2%), Black Caribbeans (1.0%), Black Africans (0.8%), Bangladeshi (0.5%) and Chinese (0.4%).

24 Strand, S., Malmberg, L. & Hall, J. (2015). *English as an Additional Language (EAL) and educational achievement in England: An analysis of the National Pupil Database.* Educational Endowment Foundation and the Bell Foundation. URL: https://educationendowmentfoundation.org.uk/uploads/pdf/EAL_and_educational_achievement2.pdf (accessed 2 January 2016).

25 'Other White' comprises persons who are neither British nor Irish and are dominated by European-born individuals.

26 US Census Bureau (2012). *U.S. Census Bureau projections show a slower growing, older, more diverse nation a half century from now.* Release CB12-243. URL: https://www.census.gov/newsroom/releases/archives/population/cb12-243.html (accessed 4 January 2016).

27 Note: In interpreting the following statistics, it should be recognized that people can and do belong to more than one ethnic group. For example, in New Zealand's 2001 Census of Population and Dwellings, 526,281 people identified with the Māori ethnicity. Of these people, 212,889 (or 40%) also identified with a European ethnicity. Similarly, of the 231,798 people who identified with a Pacific ethnicity, 31,548 (or 14%) also identified with the Māori ethnicity.

28 Statistics New Zealand (2015). *National Ethnic Population Projections: 2013(base)-2038.* URL: http://www.stats.govt.nz/browse_for_stats/population/estimates_and_projections/NationalEthnic PopulationProjections_HOTP2013-38.aspx (accessed 9 January 2016).

29 CIA (2016). *The world factbook.* URL: https://www.cia.gov/library/publications/the-world-factbook/geos/as.html (accessed 9 January 2016).

30 Council of Europe (2008). *Living together as equals in dignity. White Paper on intercultural dialogue.* Strasbourg: Author.

31 For a range of other countries, see P.A.J. Stevens & A.G. Dworkin (eds), *The Palgrave handbook of race and ethnic inequalities in education.* New York: Palgrave Macmillan.

32 Bhattacharyya, G., Ison, L. & Blair, M. (2003). *Minority ethnic attainment and participation in education and training: The evidence.* Annesley, Nottingham: Department for Education and Skills.

33 Dustmann, C., Machin, S. & Schonberg, U. (2010). 'Ethnicity and educational achievement in compulsory schooling.' *Economic Journal,* 120(546), 272-297.

34 Neal, D.A. & Whitmore-Schanzenbach, D. (2010). 'Left behind by design: Proficiency counts and test-based accountability.' *Review of Economics and Statistics,* 92(2), 263-83.

35 Wong, B. (2015). 'A blessing with a curse: Model minority students and the construction of educational success.' *Oxford Review of Education,* 41(6), 730-746.

36 Covarrubias, A. & Liou, D.D. (2014). 'Asian American education and income attainment in the era of post-racial America.' *Teachers College Record,* 116(6), 1-38.

37 Lee, S.J. & Kumashiro, K.K. (2005). *A report on the status of Asian Americans and Pacific Islanders in education: Beyond the 'model minority' stereotype.* Washington, DC: National Education Association.

38 This material is sourced from Dworkin, A.G. & Lopez Turley, R.N. (2014). 'United States of America.' In Stevens & Dworkin, op. cit., pp. 559-607.

39 Bishop, R., Berryman, M., Cavanagh, T. & Teddy, L. (2009). 'Te Kotahitanga: Addressing educational disparities facing Māori students in New Zealand.' *Teaching and Teacher Education,* 25(5), 734-742.

40 Strand, S. (2014). 'Ethnicity, gender, social class and achievement gaps at age 16: intersectionality and "getting it" for the white working class.' *Research Papers in Education,* 29(2), 131-171.

41 Butler, A. & Butler, P. (2015). *The New Zealand Bill of Rights Act: A commentary.* Second edition. Wellington, NZ: LexisNexis, p. 880.

42 OECD (2015). *Immigrant students at school: Easing the journey towards integration.* Paris: Author.

43 See section 3.30 in Chapter 3 for a discussion of grade repetition.

44 See section 3.17 in Chapter 3 for a discussion of tracking.

45 Lucas, S.R. & Gamoran, A. (2002). 'Tracking and the achievement gap.' In J.E. Chubb & T. Loveless (eds), *Bridging the achievement gap* (pp. 171-198). Washington, DC: Brookings Institution Press.

46 Strand, S. (2015). *Ethnicity, deprivation and educational achievement at age 16 in England: Trends over time.* Research Report DFE-RR439B. Manchester, UK: Department for Education.

47 Ibid., abstract.

48 Lovey, W. & Moin, S. (2013). 'Integrating identities: Ethnic and academic identities among diverse college students.' *Teachers College Record,* 115(8), 1-24.

49 Bhattacharyya et al., op. cit.

50 Strand et al., (2015), op. cit.

51 Chang & Dodd, op. cit.

52 Bishop et al., op. cit., p. 735; and Bishop, R. (2011). *Freeing ourselves.* Rotterdam: Sense Publishers.

53 Ibid.

54 Catarci, M. & Fiorucci, M. (2015). 'Preface.' In M. Catarci & M. Fiorucci (eds), *Intercultural education in the European context: Theories, experiences, challenges.* Burlington, VT: Ashgate Publishing.

55 Ibid., p. 19.

56 Song, S. (2014) 'Multiculturalism'. *The Stanford Encyclopedia of Philosophy,* Spring 2014 edn, Edward N. Zalta (ed.), URL: http://plato.stanford.edu/archives/spr2014/entries/multiculturalism/ (accessed 26 December 2015).

57 Ibid.

58 Sen, A. (2006). 'The uses and abuses of multiculturalism.' *New Republic,* 27 February 2006.

59 Bissoondath, N. (1994). *Selling illusions: The cult of multiculturalism in Canada.* Toronto: Penguin Books.

60 Song, op. cit.

61 Ibid.

62 Weaver, A. (2010). 'Angela Merkel: German multiculturalism has "utterly failed".' *The Guardian*, 17 October, 2010. URL: http://www.theguardian.com/world/2010/oct/17/angela-merkel-german-multiculturalism-failed (accessed 27 December 2015).

63 Kuenssberg, L. (2011). 'State multiculturalism has failed, says David Cameron.' *BBC News*, 5 February 2011. URL: http://www.bbc.com/news/uk-politics-12371994 (accessed 27 December 2015).

64 Sen, op. cit.

65 Blainey, G. (1984). *All for Australia*. North Ryde, NSW: Methuen Haynes.

66 Huntington, S.P. (1996). *The clash of civilizations and the remaking of world order*. New York: Simon & Schuster, p. 305.

67 Malik, K. (2015). 'The failure of multiculturalism: Community versus society in Europe.' *Foreign Affairs*, 94(2), 21-32, p. 21.

68 Ibid., pp. 21-22.

69 Ibid., p. 28.

70 Rothstein, R. (2015). 'The racial achievement gap, segregated schools, and segregated neighborhoods: A Constitutional insult.' *Race and Social Problems*, 7(1), 21-30.

71 Orfield, G., Frankenberg, E., Ee, J. & Kuscera, J. (2014). *Brown at 60: Great progress, a long retreat and an uncertain future*. Los Angeles, CA: The Civil Rights Project/Proyecto Derechos Civiles. URL: http://civilrightsproject.ucla.edu/research/k-12-education/integration-and-diversity/brown-at-60-great-progress-a-long-retreat-and-an-uncertain-future/Brown-at-60-051814.pdf (accessed 3 January 2016).

72 Rothstein, op. cit., p. 22.

73 Jargowsky, P.A. (2013). *Concentration of poverty in the new millennium: Changes in the prevalence, composition, and location of high-poverty neighborhoods*. The Century Foundation and Rutgers Center for Urban Research and Education. URL: http://www.tcf.org/assets/downloads/Concentration_of_Poverty_in_the_New_Millennium.pdf (accessed 3 January 2016).

74 Rubinowitz, L.S. & Perry, I. (2002). 'Crimes without punishment: White neighbors' resistance to black entry.' *Journal of Criminal Law and Criminology*, 92(2), 335-428.

75 Rothstein, op. cit., p. 28.

76 Constant, A.F., Schüller, S. & Zimmermann, K.F. (2013). *Ethnic spatial dispersion and immigrant identity*. Discussion paper 7868. Bonn, Germany: IZA.

77 Battu, H. & Zenou, Y. (2010). 'Oppositional identities and employment for ethnic minorities: Evidence from England.' *Economic Journal*, 120(542), 52-71.
    Bell, B. & Machin, S. (2012). 'Immigrant enclaves and crime.' *Journal of Regional Science*, 53(1), 118-141.

78 Owen, D. (1994). 'Spatial variations in ethnic minority group populations in Great Britain.' *Population Trends*, 78, 23-33.

79 Stillwell, J. & Duke-Williams, O. (2005). 'Ethnic population distribution, immigration and internal migration in Britain: What evidence of linkage at the district scale?' Paper prepared for the British Society for Population Studies Annual Conference at the University of Kent at Canterbury, 12-14 September 2005.

80 'Urban life: Open-air computers'. *The Economist*, 27 October 2012.

81 International Organization for Migration (2015). *World migration report 2015 - Migrants and cities: New partnerships to manage mobility*. Geneva: Author.

82 United Nations Population Fund (2015). *Urbanization*. New York: Author. URL: http://www.unfpa.org/urbanization (accessed 23 October 2015).

83 Organization for Migration, op. cit.

84 Ibid., p. 81. It must be noted that there is considerable variation among countries with regard to the employment of migrants. For example, data for 2015 showed that 64.7% of foreign-born migrants were employed in OECD countries, compared with 67.7% for natives. The four countries with highest levels of employment of migrants comprised Iceland (84.2%), Switzerland (77.0%), Chile (74.2%) and New Zealand (73.0%). The lowest levels were in Turkey (44.9%), Belgium (50.8%), Greece (53.4%) and Mexico (53.8%). OECD (2016). *Employment and unemployment in figures*. Paris: Author. URL: http://www.oecd.org/employment/ministerial/employment-in-figures.htm (accessed 19 January 2016).

85 Demos (2015). *Education: Integration hub*. URL: http://www.integrationhub.net/module/education/ (accessed 15 December 2015).

86 Ibid.

87   Wildhagen, T. (2012). 'How teachers and schools contribute to racial differences in the realization of academic potential.' *Teachers College Record*, 114(7), 1–27.

88   Zion, S. & Blanchett, W. (2011). '[Re]conceptualizing inclusion: Can critical race theory and interest convergence be utilized to achieve inclusion and equity for African American students?' *Teachers College Record*, 113(10), 2186–2205.

89   Dunn, L.M. (1968). 'Special education for the mildly retarded: Is much of it justifiable?' *Exceptional Children*, 35, 5–22.

90   Blanchett, W.J. (2010). 'Telling it like it is: The role of race, class, and culture in the perpetuation of learning disability as a privileged category for the white middle class.' *Disability Studies Quarterly*, 30(2).

91   Ferri, B. & Connor, D. (2005). 'Tools of exclusion: Race, disability, and (re)segregated education.' *Teachers College Record*, 107(3), 453–474, p. 454.

92   Ibid.

93   Elementary and Middle Schools Technical Assistance Center (2010). *The disproportionate representation of racial and ethnic minorities in special education*. URL: http://www.emstac.org/registered/topics/disproportionality/intro.htm (accessed 7 January 2016).

94   Strand, S. & Lindsay, G. (2009). 'Evidence of ethnic disproportionality in special education in an English population.' *Journal of Special Education*, 43(3), 174–190, p. 175.

95   Artiles, A.J., Kozleski, E.B., Trent, S.C., Osher, D. & Ortiz, A. (2010). 'Justifying and explaining disproportionality, 1968–2008: A critique of underlying views of culture.' *Exceptional Children*, 76, 279–299.

96   Parekh, G., Killoran, I. & Crawford, C. (2011). 'The Toronto connection: Poverty, perceived ability, and access to education equity.' *Canadian Journal of Education*, 34, 249–279.

97   US Department of Education (2000). *Twenty-Second Annual Report to Congress on the Implementation of the Individuals with Disabilities Education Act*. Washington: Author.

98   Department of Education (2001). *Education White Paper 6. Special needs education: Building an inclusive education and training system*. Pretoria: Republic of South Africa Department of Education.

99   Grisson, J.A. & Redding, C. (2016). 'Explaining the underrepresentation of high-achieving students of color in gifted programs.' *AERA Open*, URL: http://ero.sagepub.com/content/2/1/2332858415622175 (accessed 25 January 2016).

100 US Department of Education. (2010). *Civil rights data collection, 2009–2010: National and state estimations*. URL: http://ocrdata.ed.gov/StateNationalEstimations/Projections_2009_10 (accessed 25 January 2016).

101 Artiles, A.J. (2003). 'Special education's changing identity: Paradoxes and dilemmas in views of culture and space.' *Harvard Educational Review*, 73(2), 164–202.

102 Strand & Lindsay, op. cit.

103 Read, J., Spencer, N. & Blackburn, C. (2007). *Can we count them? Disabled children and their households*. Full project report to the ESCR. URL: http://www2.warwick.ac.uk/fac/cross_fac/healthatwarwick/research/currentfundedres/disabledchildren/res-000-22-1725-5k.pdf (accessed 19 May 2016).

104 Personal communication with Education Counts official, New Zealand Ministry of Education, August 2015.

105 MacMillan, D.L. & Rechsley, D.J. (1998). 'Overrepresentation of minority students: the case for greater specificity or reconsideration of the variables examined.' *Journal of Special Education*, 32(1), 15–24.

106 Elementary and Middle Schools Technical Assistance Center, op. cit; Fiedler, C.R., Chiang, B., Haren, B.V., Jorgensen, J., Halberg, S. & Boreson, L. (2008). 'Culturally responsive practices in schools: A checklist to address disproportionality in special education.' *Teaching Exceptional Children*, 40(5), 50–59; Gabel, S.L., Curcic, S., Powell, J.J.W., Khader, K., & Albee, L. (2009). 'Migration and ethnic group disproportion in special education: an exploratory study.' *Disability in Society*, 24(5), 625–639; Losen, D. J. & Orfield, G. (2002). *Racial inequality in special education*. Cambridge, MA: Harvard Education Press; and Skiba, R.J., Poloni-Staudinger, L., Simmons, A.B., Feggins-Azziz, R. & Chung, C.-G. (2005). 'Unproven links: can poverty explain ethnic disproportionality in special education?' *Journal of Special Education*, 39(3), 130–144.

107 Cline, T., de Abreu, G., Fihosy, C., Gray, H., Lambert H. & Neale, J. (2002). *Minority ethnic pupils in mainly white schools*, Research Report RR365, Department for Education and Skills.

108   UNESCO. *UNESCO guidelines on intercultural education*. Paris: Author. URL: http://unesdoc.unesco.org/images/0014/001478/147878e.pdf, p. 11 (accessed 20 December 2015).

109   Reich, R. (2002). *Bridging liberalism and multiculturalism in American education*. Chicago, IL: University of Chicago Press, p. 116. Note: e pluribus unum, is Latin for *out of many, one*, and is on the Seal of the United States.

110   UNESCO (2006), op. cit.

111   Council of Europe (1995). *Framework Convention for the Protection of National Minorities: An explanatory report*. Strasbourg: Author, p. 4. It is interesting to note that the Convention contained no definition of the notion of 'national minority' since it was 'impossible to arrive at a definition capable of mustering general support of all Council of Europe member States' (p. 12).

112   Allport, G.W. (1954). *The nature of prejudice*. Cambridge/Reading, MA: Addison Wesley.

113   Pettigrew, T.F. & Tropp, L.R. (2006). 'A meta-analytic test of intergroup contact theory.' *Journal of Personality and Social Psychology*, 90(5), 751-783.

114   Hewstone, M, Paolini, S. Cairns, E., Voci, A. & Harwood, J. (2006) 'Intergroup contact and the promotion of intergroup harmony.' In R.J. Brown & D. Capozza, D. (eds), *Social identities: Motivational, emotional, cultural influences*. Hove, UK: Psychology Press.

115   Collette, M. (2015). 'Why New York City is experimenting with new ways to desegregate public schools.' *Slate*, 20 July 2015.

116   Kucsera, J (2014). *New York State's extreme school segregation: Inequality, inaction and a damaged future*. Los Angeles: The Civil Rights Project. URL: http://civilrightsproject.ucla.edu/research/k-12-education/integration-and-diversity/ny-norflet-report-placeholder (accessed 9 January 2016).

117   Rossell, C. H. (1990). *The carrot or the stick*. Philadelphia, PA: Temple University Press.

118   Cantle, T. (2013). 'Segregation of schools: The impact on young people and their families and communities.' Paper to the Accord Coalition and All-Party Parliamentary Groups, London, February 2013.

119   New Zealand Ministry of Education (2016). *Communities of schools: The engine room of Investing in Educational Success*. URL: http://www.education.govt.nz/ministry-of-education/specific-initiatives/investing-in-educational-success/communities-of-schools-making-a-difference/ (accessed 10 January 2016).

120   Bell, D. (1980). '*Brown v. Board of Education* and the interest convergence dilemma.' *Harvard Law Review*, 93(3), 518-533, p. 523

121   OECD (2016). *Ministerial statement: Building more resilient and inclusive labour markets*. OECD Labour and Employment Ministerial Meeting, Paris, 15 January 2016. URL: http://www.oecd.org/employment/ministerial/labour-ministerial-statement-2016.pdf (accessed 17 January 2016).

122   UNESCO (2006), op. cit., p. 13.

123   UNESCO (1953). *The use of the vernacular languages in education*. Monographs on Foundations of Education, No. 8. Paris: Author.

124   Ball, J. (2009). *Enhancing learning of children from diverse language backgrounds: Mother tongue-based bilingual or multilingual education in early childhoodand early primary school years*. Prepared for UNESCO. URL: http://eyeonkids.ca/docs/files/unesco_mother-tongue_based_ey_2010.pdf (accessed 15 December 2015).

125   UNESCO (2007). *Strong foundations: Early childhood care and education*. Paris: Author. URL: http://unesdoc.unesco.org/images/0014/001477/147794e.pdf (accessed 19 May 2016).

126   Ball, op. cit.

127   Morales, P.Z. & Rao, A.B. (2015). 'How ideology and cultural capital shape the distribution of Illinois' bilingual education programs.' *Teachers College Record*, Date published: September 28, 2015. URL: http://www.tcrecord.org (accessed 15 December 2015).

128   Garc a, O. (2009). *Bilingual education in the 21st century*. Oxford, UK: Wiley-Blackwell; Genesee, F., Lindholm-Leary, K., Saunders, W.M. & Christian, D. (eds) (2006). *Educating English language learners: A synthesis of research evidence*. New York, NY: Cambridge University Press; and Goldenberg, C. (2008). 'Teaching English language learners: What the research does – and does not – say.' *American Educator*, 32(2), 8-44.

129   Vald s, G. (1997). 'Dual-language immersion programs: A cautionary note concerning the education of language-minority students.' *Harvard Educational Review*, 67(3), 391-394.

130   Morales & Rao, op. cit.

131 Murphy, V.A. & Unthiah, A. (2015). *A systematic review of intervention research examining English language and literacy development in children with English as an Additional Language (EAL)*. Education Endowment Foundation and the Bell Foundation.

132 Council of Europe (2007). *From linguistic diversity to plurilingual education: Guide for the development of language education policies in Europe*. Strasbourg: Author.

133 Jessner, U. (2008). 'Teaching third languages: Findings, trends and challenges.' *Language Teaching*, 41(1), 15–56.

134 Dyssegaard et al., op. cit.

135 Although James Banks points out that 'intercultural education' is rarely used outside Europe, as I note below, it has also been adopted by UNESCO, suggesting its global acceptance.

136 Banks, J.A. (2006). *Cultural diversity and education: Foundations, curriculum, and teaching*. Boston: Pearson, p. 115.

137 Ibid.

138 Banks (2006), op. cit., p. 3.

139 Ibid., p. 5.

140 UNESCO (2005). *Convention on the Protection and Promotion of the Diversity of Cultural Expressions*. Article 8. Paris: Author.

141 Ibid.

142 UNESCO (2006), op. cit.

143 Delors, J. (chairman) (1996). *Learning: The treasure within: Report to UNESCO of the International Commission on Education for the Twenty-first Century*. Paris: Author.

144 Council of Europe (2003). *Intercultural education: Managing diversity, strengthening democracy. Declaration by the European ministers of education on intercultural education in the new European context*. Athens, Greece: Author.

145 Council of Europe (2008), op. cit.

146 Ibid., item 1.

147 Ibid, p. 9.

148 Ibid., p. 10.

149 Ibid., p. 17.

150 Ibid., p. 18.

151 Ibid.

152 Garcia, S.B. & Ortiz, A.A. (2006). *Preventing disproportionate representation: Culturally and linguistically responsive pre-referral interventions*. National Center for Culturally Responsive Educational Systems.

153 Carpenter, V.M. (2014). 'Pedagogies of hope: Dialogical professional development.' In V.M. Carpenter & S. Osborne (eds), *Twelve thousand hours: Education and poverty in Aotearoa New Zealand* (pp. 123–144). Auckland, NZ: Dunmore Publishing.

154 Education Review Office (2015). *Accelerating student achievement: A resource for schools*. Wellington, New Zealand: Author.

155 Banks (2006), op. cit.

156 UNESCO, op. cit.

157 Hattie, J. (2009). *Visible learning: A synthesis of over 800 meta-analyses relating to achievement*. London: Routledge.

158 Mitchell, D. (2014). *What really works in special and inclusive education: Using evidence-based teaching strategies*. Second edition. London: Routledge.

159 Garcia & Ortiz, op. cit., p. 1.

160 Ibid., p. 4.

161 Ibid.

162 Anderson, et al., op. cit.

163 Bishop et al., op. cit.

164 Bishop, R., Berryman, M., Wearmouth, J., Peter, M. & Clapham, S. (2012). 'Professional development, changes in teacher practice and improvements in indigenous students' educational performance: A case study from New Zealand.' *Teaching and Teacher Education*, 28, 694–705.

165 Anderson, J., H lot, C., McPake, J. & Obied, V. (2010). *Professional development for staff working in multilingual schools*. Strasbourg: Council of Europe.

166 Ibid.

167   Hattie, op. cit.
168   Garcia & Ortiz, op. cit.
169   Zhang, C. & Bennett, T. (2003). 'Facilitating the meaningful participation of culturally and linguistically diverse families in the IFSP and IEP process.' *Focus on Autism and Other Developmental Disabilities*, 18(1), 51-59.
170   Banks (2006), op. cit., p. 5.
171   Ibid.
172   UNESCO (2006), op. cit.
173   Ibid.
174   Ibid.
175   Ibid.
176   Ibid.
177   Ibid.
178   Ibid.
179   Council of Europe (2003). op. cit.
180   Ibid.
181   Council of Europe (2008). op. cit.
182   Ibid.
183   Ibid.
184   Mitchell (2014), op. cit.
185   Banks (2006), op. cit.
186   UNESCO (2006), op. cit.
187   Ibid.
188   Ibid.
189   Powell, R., Cantrell, S.C., Malo-Juvera, V. & Correll, P. (2016). 'Operationalizing culturally responsive instruction: Preliminary findings of CRIOP research.' *Teachers College Record*, 118(1), 1-46.
190   Garcia & Ortiz, op. cit.
191   Banks (2006), op. cit.
192   National Council for Curriculum and Assessment (2005). *Intercultural education in the primary school*. Dublin: Author.
193   Council of Europe (2008), op. cit.
194   A national survey by the Kaiser Family Foundation in the US found that with technology allowing nearly 24-hour media access as children and teens go about their daily lives, the amount of time young people spend with entertainment media has risen dramatically, especially among minority youth. Survey results showed that 8-18 year-olds devoted an average of 7 hours and 38 minutes to using entertainment media across a typical day (more than 53 hours a week). Kaiser Family Foundation (2010). *Generation M2: Media in the lives of 8- to 18-year-olds*. URL: http://kff.org/other/event/generation-m2-media-in-the-lives-of/ (accessed 22 January 2016).
195   Banks (2011), op. cit.
196   UNESCO (1998). *Citizenship education for the 21st century*. Paris: Author.
197   UNESCO (1995). *Declaration and integrated framework of action on education for peace, human rights and democracy*. Paris: Author.
198   Banks (2011), op. cit.
199   Ibid., p. 248.
200   European Education Ministers (2015). *Declaration on promoting citizenship and the common values of freedom, tolerance and non-discrimination through education*. Paris: Author.
201   Deng, op. cit.

5 Religions/beliefs differences

Religious differences entered my consciousness when I was about ten years old and living in Ross, a small town on the west coast of New Zealand, where there was a 'state' school and a convent school for Roman Catholics. Before then, I was vaguely aware that I was a Protestant - a Presbyterian. This was brought home to me when an uncle and an aunt both 'turned' to marry Catholics, behaviour that upset some of my wider family. Although we state school pupils looked down on those attending the convent school, just as they probably looked down on us, it never stopped the boys from both schools playing together. Whether this co-mingling was because of some degree of religious tolerance or out of necessity occasioned by the small number of peers, I cannot be sure.

I once attended a Catholic mass and was bewildered by the Latin liturgy. I think I was also brought up to hold the Catholics' adherence to the Roman Pope in some sort of doubt. I must say, however, that my attendance at the Presbyterian Church with my mother (but not my father) was only slightly more satisfying, albeit for social rather than religious reasons. It was about this time, at the age of 12 or 13, that I began to doubt my religious beliefs. I certainly appreciated being schooled in a secular education system, even if there were occasional half-hour religious instruction lessons.

In this chapter, I will examine the nature and place of religion in societies and the relationship between religion and education. Each issue requires attending to several questions:

A What is the nature of religion and its place in society?
B What rights do people have to pursue their religions or beliefs?
C What form should religion in education take?

A What is the nature of religion and its place in society?

Religions are ubiquitous: people in every society subscribe to some form of religion or belief system. Questions that arise here include: What is the definition of religion? What is the range of religions across the world and within countries? How does religion intersect with other diversities? How stable are religious beliefs? and What are the functions of religion?

5.1 There is no universally recognized definition of religion

What exactly constitutes religion is a matter of considerable debate. Although there is no universally accepted definition, most definitions include some transcendental belief in or service to a divine, while some broaden the concept to include nontheistic and even atheistic beliefs.[1]

Jared Diamond, Professor of Geography at the University of California, has identified five common elements in definitions that have been advanced: 'belief in the supernatural, shared membership in a social movement, costly and visible proofs of commitment, practical rules for one's behavior (i.e., "morality"), and a belief that supernatural beings and forces can be induced (e.g., by prayer) to intervene in worldly life'.[2] Diamond argued that while these attributes vary in strength among world religions, all of them are necessary and one of them alone is insufficient in determining the presence of a religion. Further, he recognized that some of these attributes are present in non-religious movements such as political philosophies and even among sports fans. Also, there are grey borderline movements such as Buddhism, Confucianism and Shintoism about which there is uncertainty as to whether they constitute religions or philosophies of life.

According to Diamond, virtually all religions hold some supernatural beliefs specific to that religion and that appear implausible to people other than the adherents of that particular religion. He offered several examples, including the Christian belief that a woman who had not been fertilized by a man became pregnant and gave birth to a baby boy, whose body after death was carried up to a place called heaven, and the Islamic belief that men who sacrifice their lives in a battle for their religion will be carried to a paradise populated by beautiful virgin women. Diamond noted that recent religious scholarship interprets such beliefs as serving to display one's depth of commitment to one's religion: it takes true commitment to 'espouse some irrational belief that contradicts the evidence of our senses, and that people outside of religion would never believe'.[3]

Yet another perspective on religion was put forward earlier by Ninian Smart, a professor of religious studies, who began his book with the comment that 'throughout history and beyond in the dark recesses of men's earliest cultures, religion has been a vital and pervasive feature of human life'.[4]

He identified six dimensions of religion:

1   The ritual dimension: shown through worship, prayers, offerings and the like, involving both an inner and an outer aspect.
2   The mythological dimension, which is quite neutral as to the truth or falsity of the story enshrined in the myth. These stories may be about God or gods, but also about the historical events of religious significance in a tradition.
3   The doctrinal dimension, which represents an attempt to give system, clarity and intellectual power to the faith.
4   The ethical dimension: throughout history religions usually incorporate a code of ethics intended to govern the behaviour of individuals and the community.
5   The social dimension: religions are not just systems of belief: they are also organizations or parts of organizations, which have social significance.
6   The experiential dimension: for example, a Christian believes that 'God does speak to men in an intimate way and that the individual can and does have an inner experience of God.'[5]

What distinguishes religious from other forms of belief? Brian Leiter, Professor of Jurisprudence at the University of Chicago Law School, identified three features of religious belief systems.[6] First, they make 'categorical demands' on adherents that they must satisfy regardless of costs; second, they are insulated from ordinary standards of evidence and reasoning as used in common sense and science; third, they offer existential consolation in response to human suffering and death. Leiter went on to claim that the first two features mean that religious beliefs should have no special protection; indeed, they have a special potential to cause harm and should make us alert to the limits of religious toleration. He also pointed out that nonreligious sources are just as capable of offering existential consolation as religion (e.g., therapy and meditation). How these views play out in determining the role of religion in education will be explored in subsequent sections of this chapter.

5.2 The world has diverse religions

According to 2012 data from the Pew Research Centre,[7] the global population comprised the following major religious groups by percentage:

Christian	31.5
Muslim	23.2
Unaffiliated	16.3
Hindu	15.0
Buddhist	7.1
Folk religions	5.9
Other religions	0.8
Jewish	0.2

The educational significance of these statistics is obvious: given the variety of religions (and sects within most of them), and assuming that their followers usually believe theirs to be the one true religion (or sect), it is not reasonable to design a universal approach to defining the role of religion in education.

5.3 Countries vary in their degree of religious diversity

How ought the different degrees of religious diversity that occur in different societies affect education? In addressing this question, it is important to take account of the different degrees of religious diversity in different countries. Clearly, what might be considered appropriate in countries with high degrees of religious homogeneity may not be acceptable for more religiously diverse countries, particularly when some of them contain large minorities of people professing no religious affiliation, including atheists.

This variation is well illustrated in the Pew Research Center's 2010 analysis using a *Religious Diversity Index*. Using this scale, 12 out of the 232 countries and territories were rated as having a very high degree of religious diversity. These comprised Singapore, Taiwan, Vietnam, South Korea, China, Hong Kong, Guinea-Bissau, Togo, Ivory Coast, Benin and Mozambique and Suriname. Singapore had the highest score, with 34% Buddhist, 18% Christian, 16% religiously unaffiliated, 14% Muslim, 5% Hindu and < 1% Jewish, with the remainder of the population belonging to folk or traditional religions (2%) or to other religions (10%).

Other countries with high levels of religious diversity included (in order) New Zealand, Netherlands, Malaysia, France, Belgium, Latvia, Australia, Sweden, Canada and Germany. For example, in New Zealand those professing to be Christians accounted for 45.6%, Hindu 2.1%, Buddhist 1.4%, Islam 1.1%, other 1.4% and no religion 38.5% (the total exceeds 100% as people could identify with more than one of the categories). Furthermore, within the Christian group, there was considerable diversity with Catholics accounting for 11.6%, Anglicans for 10.8%, Presbyterians and Congregationalists for 7.8%, Methodists for 2.4%, Pentecostalists for 1.8%, Maori Christians for 1.3% and other sects for 9.9%.[8]

Those with moderate levels of religious diversity included the United Kingdom, Luxembourg, Russia, Israel, the United States, Austria, Finland, Italy, Denmark and Norway. For example, the United States ranked 68th among the 232 countries and territories, with Christians constituting a sizeable majority (78%) and of the seven other major religious groups, only the religiously unaffiliated claimed a substantial share (16%). All other religious groups combined accounted for about 5%.

Countries with low levels of religious diversity included Argentina, Indonesia, Lithuania, Ireland, Serbia, Mexico, Samoa, Turkey, Iran and Morocco.

5.4 Religions vary in their racial diversity

Religion clearly intersects with with race. This relationship is clearly shown in US survey data where, in general, African Americans are more likely than whites and Hispanics to hold Christian beliefs. More specifically, here are some representative findings: 70% of black Americans read the Bible outside of formal worship, compared with just 44% of white Americans; nearly half of blacks pray several times a day, compared with just 27% of whites; and 51% of blacks, compared with 37% of whites, strongly agree that they have a personally meaningful relationship with God.[9] A similar racial divide in religiosity has also been reported in the United Kingdom, where South Asian and Black groups are more religious than White natives, with Pakistanis and Bangladeshis standing out as being the most religious.[10]

In the United States, religions vary in their racial composition. According to a 2014 Pew Center survey,[11] the most racially diverse religion in the United States is the Seventh-Day Adventists with 37% being white, while 32% are black, 15% are Hispanic, 8% are Asian and another 8% are another race or mixed race. Although Jews (90% white) and Hindus (91% Asian) are not very diverse, the five least diverse groups are all Protestant denominations (the Evangelical Lutheran Church in America, the Lutheran Church-Missouri Synod, and the United Methodist Church, which are all more than 90% white). Meanwhile, two of the largest historically black Protestant denominations, the National Baptist Convention and the African Methodist Episcopal Church, have almost exclusively black members.

5.5 Women are more religious than men – in western societies

Just as religion clearly intersects with race, so too it intersects with gender. As noted by Marta Trzebiatowska and Steve Bruce, there is clear evidence from western countries that women are more religious than men, and not by small margins.[12] For example, US Harris Poll data from 2003 showed that women are more likely than men to hold either Christian or non-Christian religious beliefs. Thus, of the 90% of adults who believed in God, 93% were women and 86% were men and the 84% who believed in the survival of the soul after death included 89% of women but only 78% of men.[13] In a similar vein, the Pew Research Center found significant gender differences on various markers of religion: affiliation with a religion (86% women, 79% men), an absolutely certain belief in God or a universal spririt (77% vs 65%), and saying that religion is very important in their lives (63% vs 49%).[14]

Two other countries will suffice to support the consensus that women are more religious than men. First, in New Zealand 2006 Census data showed that females exceeded males in three religions: Christianity, Buddhism, and Spiritualism and New Age Religions; although in the remaining religions (e.g., Hinduism and Islam), males exceeded females. However, although women tended to claim religious affiliation more than men, the increasing trend of 'No Religion' applied almost equally to both: 32% of men and 29% of women. Second, 2014 data for the United Kingdom showed a clear sex difference in the proportion of people who reported they were Anglican: 34.3% for women and 27.7% for men. In contrast to New Zealand, 48.6% of men were more likely to declare that they did not belong to a religion, compared with 40.0% of women.[15]

5.6 *Religion plays a variable role in people's lives*

According to a 2002 international survey of 44 countries by the Pew Research Center, there is considerable variation in the importance people place on religion in their lives.[16] Religion was much more important to Americans than to people living in other developed nations. Nearly six-in-ten (59%) people in the United States said religion played a very important role in their lives. This was considerably higher than the percentages of self-avowed religious people in such developed countries as Poland (36%), United Kingdom (33%), Canada (30%), Italy (27%), Germany (21%), Japan (12%), France (11%) and Czech Republic (11%). Indeed, Americans' views were closer to people in many developing nations than to the publics of developed nations. In Africa, for example, in the ten countries sampled, no fewer than eight-in-ten people in any country saw religion as being very important personally. Similarly, majorities in every Latin American country also subscribed to that view, with the exception of Argentina (39%). In the predominantly Muslim nations of Indonesia, Pakistan, Mali and Senegal, too, more than nine-in-ten respondents rated religion as personally very important. In Turkey (65%) and Uzbekistan (35%), however, people were more divided over religion's importance.

In another study, Australians were asked in the 2009 Survey of Social Attitudes 'How important is religious faith or spirituality in shaping your life's decisions, such as career, relationships and lifestyle?' Religion was rated as very important by 13%, important by 25%, of little importance by 23%, and not important by 38%.[17]

American scholars Pippa Norris and Ronald Inglehart have put forward an interesting explanation for the patterns of religiosity and secularization around the world.[18] Basing their work on detailed analyses of the World Values Surveys conducted between 1981 and 2007 in almost 90 countries, they observed that the people of virtually all advanced industrial societies have been moving towards more secular orientations since the 1960s, even as religiosity persists in poorer nations and failed states. To account for these trends, Norris and Inglehart developed a theory of 'existential security'. They argued that religion persists where people bear high levels of risk due to inequality, poverty and inadequate social provisions by the state. Conversely, more equal, less impoverished societies with comprehensive welfare provisions have become increasingly secular; thus, they enjoy higher levels of existential security and have less need to turn to religion. This finding is supported in a recent comprehensive study of religious beliefs in 583 societies, which found that belief in 'moralizing high gods' is more prevalent among societies that inhabit poorer environments and are more prone to ecological distress.[19] It is supported, too, in Denmark and Sweden, both of which are among the least religious nations in the world today *and* are also among the most secure nations, with the gap between rich and poor being smaller than in other industrialized democracies.[20] This existential security explanation is not new, with Karl Marx's arguing in the nineteenth century that when life is hard, people turn to religion for comfort.

So how does the United States, with its high incomes and high levels of religiosity, fit within this theory? Norris and Inglehart believe this can be explained by the fact that, among advanced countries, the United States is the most unequal, underinsured and poverty-ridden, with low levels of social spending as a percentage of GDP. This inequality heightens a sense of insecurity and leads to greater religiosity. The theory of existential security being related to religiosity is yet another example of intersectionality that I have alluded to in other chapters of this book.

But there are other possible explanations of irreligiousity. For example, in examining why Swedes and Danes have remarkably low levels of traditional religious belief and church attendance (as noted above), Phil Zuckerman advanced four explanations in addition to existential security. First, citing the work of Roger Stark and his associates,[21] he argued that the effects of a long-standing Lutheran monopolies in both countries has been to reduce competition, and hence marketing of different religions, with consequential lowered interest and involvement in religion. Second, Zuckerman suggested that the high proportion of women in the paid workplace has influenced their religious commitment. Third, he pointed to the high levels of education, citing US research that showed, for example, that while 86% of Americans with no college education believe in the resurrection of Jesus, only 64% of those with postgraduate degrees did.[22] Fourth, he suggested that successive Social Democrat governments in both countries have been relatively anti-religious and have sought at times to dilute religion's influence in society. For example, they changed the school curriculum to ensure that Christianity is not taught in in an evangelical manner, but is taught in a more 'social sciences' manner as being one among several religious traditions.

5.7 The times, they are a-changin'

In recent years, the populations of many western societies have become increasingly diverse, with increasing numbers of people reporting no religion. For example, the 2011 Census in England and Wales found that between 2001 and 2011, there was a decrease in people who identify as Christian from 71.7% to 59.3%, with a corresponding increase in those reporting no religion from 14.8% to 25.1%. (As well, Muslims increased from 3.0% to 4.8% during this period.)

Another example of increasing religious diversity is afforded by New Zealand. Between 1966 and 2006, three major shifts took place.[23] First, there was a decline in those professing Christian affiliations. For example, in 1966, 89.14% of the population identified with some form of Christianity, whereas in 2006 this had declined to 54.21%. Second, there was an increasing pluralization of religious affiliations. This was reflected in immigration resulting in an explosion of those professing to be Hindus, Buddhists, Muslims, Jews and Sikhs. Collectively, their numbers grew from 0.31% of the population in 1986 to 4.12% in 2006. The third shift was the dramatic increase in those professing 'no religion'. These figures grew from 1.22% in 1986 to 32.99% in 2006.[24]

5.8 Religion serves a variety of functions

Organized religion has its roots at least in Neolithic times, around 11,000 years ago. Why did it develop and how is it sustained in almost every society? The word 'religion' derives from the Latin *religare*, which means 'to bind', interpreted by some to refer to the state of being tied to God and bound to Him. So, how does religion serve to bind its adherents? To answer this question, scholars of religion typically ask: what functions do religions perform? Arguing from the perspective of an evolutionary biologist, Jared Diamond put forward a persuasive approach. By way of background, he postulated that biological evolution proceeds in two stages. First, variations that occur between individuals are generated by mutations and re-combinations of genes. Second, because of natural selection and sexual selection, there are resulting differences among individuals in how they survive, reproduce and pass on their genes to the next generation. As Diamond expressed it, 'Thus, gene mutations and re-combinations provide the origins of biological diversity, while natural selection and sexual selection sieve that starting material by the criterion of function.'[25] With reference to the development of religions, Diamond identified several functions that they may have served in the past and, in some contexts, they continue to serve in the present:

1 The search for causal explanations

One of the distinguishing features of the human species is our sophisticated ability to deduce cause, agency and intent, attributes that help us to survive across hugely diverse environments. We are 'hardwired' into seeking ways of interpreting the world, to find meaning and even purpose. According to Diamond, we keep trying out causal explanations, even when our search for them leads to supernatural beliefs such as attributing agency to inanimate things such as plants, the wind, volcanoes and the stars.

Explanation was an early function of religion. Sometimes these explanations were natural and eventually became established through science; at other times, they were supernatural and religious. However, in modern Western society, religion's explanatory power has increasingly become usurped by science with the origins of the universe being attributed to the Big Bang and the subsequent operation of the laws of physics, astronomy, meteorology and evolutionary biology. Nevertheless, as Diamond pointed out, creationists still invoke God as a 'First Cause' who created the universe and every plant and animal species, including humans.

2 Defusing anxiety

Diamond argues that a second early function of religion was its role in defusing our anxiety over problems and dangers beyond our control. By resorting to prayers, rituals, ceremonies, consulting shamans and oracles, we convince ourselves that at least we are doing something, aren't helpless and feel in charge to some degree. Ambiguity and uncertainty due to complexity is thus reduced. As with the previous function, this role for religion decreased as science and knowledge assumed greater significance in dealing with our problems and as state governments became more capable of protecting the interests of its citizenry, even if it is still present in many traditional societies.

3 Providing comfort

Diamond believes that religion's role in providing comfort, hope and meaning when life is hard has probably expanded in recent times (i.e., the last 10,000 years). He pointed out that 'most religions provide comfort by in effect denying death's reality, and by postulating some sort of afterlife for a soul postulated as associated with the body'.[26] Many religions go further, asserting that something even better awaits us after death: eternal life, reunion with one's loved ones, and freedom from cares, to the point where some even reject life in the present world. Diamond argued that this comforting function of religion is greater in more populous and recent societies for three reasons: social stratification and inequality is greater in large complex societies, compared with more egalitarian small-scale societies; life became harder as hunter-gatherers became farmers and assembled in larger societies; and complex populous societies have more formalized moral codes. In support of this hypothesis, he further pointed out that poorer social strata, regions and countries tend to be more religious than richer ones: they need more comforting. He cited research showing that among the world's nations, the percentage of citizens who say that religion is an important part of their daily lives is 80-99% for most nations with a per capita GDP under $US10, 000, but only 17-43% for most nations with a per capita GDP over $US30, 000. Within the United States, the highest religious commitment and the most radical Christians are found among the most marginalized, underprivileged social groups. As I discussed in section 5.6, this probably reflects Norris and Inglehart's theory that religion offers existential security to such people.

4 Developing social cohesion and preaching political obedience

Sociologists Emile Durkheim[27] and Talcott Parsons[28] argued that religion is one of the most important agents of socialization and social control, providing social cohesion and social solidarity. Durkheim, for example, referred to the role of shared values and common symbols associated with religion in maintaining the internal stability of societies and enabling them to survive over time. Similarly, anthropologist Bronislaw Malinowski observed that religion established attitudes that were foundational to the collective existence and survival of societies through reverence for tradition and courage in the struggle with difficulties and at the prospect of death.[29]

According to Diamond, as societies became more complex, the power of the state and religion became integrated. The chief or king became portrayed as being related to the gods or even as being a god (e.g., the Japanese emperor at the time of World War II). At the very least, they had the capacity of being able to intercede with the gods on behalf of the peasants, e.g., to ensure a good harvest. In more recent times within the Judaeo-Christian world, this symbiotic relationship between religion and state has been significantly weakened, but not so in some Muslim countries with theocratic governments (e.g., present-day Iran).

A related explanation is Marx's claim that religion served to disguise the realities of the underlying capitalist economic system and to counter the suffering of the labouring classes. As famously he stated,

> Religious suffering is, at one and the same time, the expression of real suffering and a protest against real suffering. Religion is the sign of the oppressed creature, the heart of a heartless world, and the soul of soulless conditions. It is the opium of the people.[30]

5 Regulating behaviour towards strangers

Diamond considers that all major religions teach what is right, what is wrong, and how one should behave towards strangers. As societies grew in size, it became necessary to formulate rules of peaceful behaviour to apply among all members of the society, including those who may be strangers. In many cases, these rules were claimed to have their origins in the gods or in God himself. Diamond cites the power of the Ten Commandments in Jewish and Christian societies as a prime example.

6 Justifying wars

Religion has been and continues to be used as a justification for wars. In religious terms, according to Diamond, it does this by arguing that the preceding principles apply only to one's behaviour towards fellow citizens within the chiefdom or state, unless those citizens happen to belong to another religion. This latter point follows from most religions claiming to have a monopoly on the truth, and that all other religions are wrong. This principle is sometimes accompanied by adherents of a religion believing that they are not merely permitted, but actually obliged, to kill and steal from believers in wrong religions (e.g., between Christians and Muslims at the time of the Crusades and, more recently, in Bosnia and Serbia), or sects within a religion (e.g., as we see with the common occurrence of conflicts between Shiites and Sunnis in the present day and between Catholics and Protestants in England and Europe in the past and, more recently, in Northern Ireland).

B What rights do people have to pursue their religions or beliefs?

International and most national human rights instruments are unanimous in asserting individuals' rights to pursue their own religions, generally provided that these rights do not harm other people. However, as we shall see, these rights can sometimes come into conflict with other rights, such as those held by children and women. Also, both in the past and contemporaneously, the rights of people to pursue their own religion have been and are compromised in various countries.

5.9 Individuals have a qualified right to pursue their religions or beliefs

Many international and national instruments spell out the rights of individuals to pursue their own religions or beliefs. Here is a selection of them:

The Universal Declaration of Human Rights

As I outlined in Chapter 1, the linchpin to human rights becoming enshrined is undoubtedly the Universal Declaration of Human Rights. It covers a range of rights, but Articles 18 and 26 are of particular relevance to religions and beliefs:

> Article 18: Everyone has the right to freedom of thought, conscience and religion; this right includes freedom to change his religion or belief, and freedom, either alone or in community with others and in public or private, to manifest his religion or belief in teaching, practice, worship and observance.
>
> Article 26(2): Education shall be directed to the full development of the human personality and to the strengthening of respect for human rights and fundamental freedoms. It shall promote understanding, tolerance and friendship among all nations, racial or religious groups.

International Covenant on Civil and Political Rights

Freedom of religion and belief is also recognized in this document, which was adopted by the United Nations in 1966. Article 18 of the Covenant states:

1 Everyone shall have the right to freedom of thought, conscience and religion. This right shall include freedom to have or to adopt a religion or belief of his choice, and freedom, either individually or in community with others and in public or private, to manifest his religion or belief in worship, observance, practice and teaching.
2 No one shall be subject to coercion which would impair his freedom to have or to adopt a religion or belief of his choice.
3 Freedom to manifest one's religion or beliefs may be subject only to such limitations as are prescribed by law and are necessary to protect public safety, order, health or morals or the fundamental rights and freedoms of others.
4 The States Parties to the present Covenant undertake to have respect for the liberty of parents and, when applicable, legal guardians to ensure the religious and moral education of their children in conformity with their own convictions.

International Covenant on Economic Social and Cultural Rights

This Covenant recognizes that children have a right to education, as set out in Article 13(1):

> The States Parties to the present Covenant recognize the right of everyone to education. They agree that education shall be directed to the full development of the human personality and the sense of its dignity, and shall strengthen the respect for human rights and fundamental freedoms. They further agree that education shall enable all persons to participate effectively in a free society, promote understanding, tolerance and friendship among all nations and all racial, ethnic or religious groups, and further the activities of the United Nations for the maintenance of peace.

Convention on the Rights of the Child

Article 14(1) of this Convention, which came into force in 1990, includes the following:

> States Parties shall respect the right of the child to freedom of thought, conscience and religion.
>
> States Parties shall respect the rights and duties of the parents and, when applicable, legal guardians, to provide direction to the child in the exercise of his or her right in a manner consistent with the evolving capacities of the child.

In a similar vein, Article 29(1) specifies that the education of a child should take account of

> (c) The development of respect for the child's parents, his or her own cultural identity, language and values, for the national values of the country in which the child is living, the country from which he or she may originate, and for civilizations different from his or her own;
>
> (d) The preparation of the child for responsible life in a free society, in the spirit of understanding, peace, tolerance, equality of sexes, and friendship among all peoples, ethnic, national and religious groups and persons of indigenous origin;

These two Articles should be read in conjunction with Article 3, which requires that in all actions concerning children, 'the best interests of the child shall be a primary consideration', and Article 12, which states that 'the views of the child [should be] given due weight in accordance with the age and maturity of the child'. Clearly, these Articles are of crucial significance for educators.

United Nations Convention on the Rights of Persons with Disabilities

The Preamble to this Convention includes religion as one of the premises to the specified rights:

> Concerned about the difficult conditions faced by persons with disabilities who are subject to multiple or aggravated forms of discrimination on the basis of race, colour, sex, language, religion, political or other opinion, national, ethnic, indigenous or social origin, property, birth, age or other status.

The European Convention for the Protection of Human Rights and Fundamental Freedoms

This Convention, which came into force in 1950, includes Article 9, which is concerned with freedom of thought, conscience and religion:

> 1. Everyone has the right to freedom of thought, conscience and religion; this right includes freedom to change his religion or belief and freedom, either alone or in community with others and in public or private, to manifest his religion or belief, in worship, teaching, practice and observance.
> 2. Freedom to manifest one's religion or beliefs shall be subject only to such limitations as are prescribed by law and are necessary in a democratic society in the interests

of public safety, for the protection of public order, health or morals, or for the protection of the rights and freedoms of others.

United Kingdom's Human Rights Act

The United Kingdom is a signatory to the European Convention and the policy of successive British governments has been to support religious freedom. The 1998 Human Rights Act is the primary legislation outlining religious rights, guaranteeing freedom of thought, conscience and religion and prohibiting discrimination on the basis of religion. Article 9 of this Act specifies:

- the freedom to change religion or belief;
- the freedom to exercise religion or belief publicly or privately, alone or with others; and
- the freedom to exercise religion or belief in worship, teaching, practice and observance.
- freedom to manifest one's religion or beliefs shall be subject only to such limitations as are prescribed by law and are necessary in a democratic society in the interests of public safety, for the protection of public order, health or morals, or for the protection of the rights and freedoms of others.

United States Bill of Rights

The Bill of Rights is the collective name for the first ten amendments to the United States Constitution. The First Amendment, passed by Congress in 1791 (but which did not become applicable in all states until 1947), includes the provision that reflected Thomas Jefferson's desire to create a 'wall of separation between church and state':

Congress shall make no law respecting an establishment of religion, or prohibiting the free exercise thereof.

However, in 1878, the US Supreme Court found that while laws cannot interfere with religious belief and opinions, laws can be made to regulate some religious practices (e.g., human sacrifices, and the Hindu practice of suttee – the funeral custom where a widow was expected to immolate herself on her husband's pyre or commit suicide). The Court stated that to rule otherwise, 'would be to make the professed doctrines of religious belief superior to the law of the land, and in effect permit every citizen to become a law unto himself'.[31]

It is important to realize that the United States, unlike France, is not a secularist state, but rather a 'disestablishmentarian state' which prohibits the establishment of any one religion, or religion generally.[32]

The American Convention on Human Rights (The Pact of San Jose, Costa Rica)

This *Convention*, which covers the Organization of American States, came into force in 1978. Its preamble includes the recognition that states will recognize specified rights and freedoms 'without any discrimination for reasons of race, color, sex, language, religion, political or other opinion, national or social origin, economic status, birth, or any other social condition'. Article 12 is concerned with freedom of conscience and religion and specifies that:

1   Everyone has the right to freedom of conscience and of religion. This right includes freedom to maintain or to change one's religion or beliefs, and freedom to profess or disseminate one's religion or beliefs, either individually or together with others, in public or in private.
2   No one shall be subject to restrictions that might impair his freedom to maintain or to change his religion or beliefs.
3   Freedom to manifest one's religion and beliefs may be subject only to the limitations prescribed by law that are necessary to protect public safety, order, health, or morals, or the rights or freedoms of others.
4   Parents or guardians, as the case may be, have the right to provide for the religious and moral education of their children or wards that is in accord with their own convictions.

New Zealand Human Rights Act

This *Act*, which came into force in 1993, specifies religious belief as a prohibited ground of discrimination. It also includes ethical belief as a prohibited ground, describing it as 'the lack of a religious belief, whether in respect of a particular religion or religions or all religions'.

Australian Constitution

Chapter V, Section 116 of the *Constitution*, which deals with freedom of religion and belief, states:

> The Commonwealth shall not make any law for establishing any religion, or for imposing any religious observance, or for prohibiting the free exercise of any religion, and no religious test shall be required as a qualification for any office or public trust under the Commonwealth.[33]

However, because the Constitution does not affect the legislative powers of the states and territories, which have more responsibility than does the Commonwealth for social regulation that may affect religious practice, the protection afforded by the Constitution is limited. Views vary on how far and how adequately Section 116 provides individuals with an avenue of legal redress if their rights have been violated.[34]

Canadian Human Rights Act

This *Act* of 1985, includes religion as a prohibited ground of discrimination.

Finnish Constitution

The *Constitution of Finland* states that 'Everyone is equal before the law' (2:3) and that '[d]emocracy entails the right of the individual to participate in and influence the development of society and his or her living conditions' (1:2). Moreover, it says that '[n]o one shall, without an acceptable reason, be treated differently from other persons on the ground of sex, age, origin, language, religion, conviction, opinion, health, disability or other reason that concerns his or her person' (2:6).

Irish Constitution

The *Constitution* guarantees freedom of worship, and forbids the state from creating an established church. Article 44.1, as originally enacted, explicitly recognized a number of Christian denominations, as well as 'Jewish Congregations'; it also recognized the 'special position' of the Roman Catholic Church. Although these provisions were removed in 1973, the Constitution still contains a number of explicit religious references in Article 44.1, including:

> The State acknowledges that the homage of public worship is due to Almighty God. It shall hold His Name in reverence, and shall respect and honour religion.

Norwegian Constitution

The *Constitution of the Kingdom of Norway* contains Article 2, which specifies that:

(1) All inhabitants of the Realm shall have the right to free exercise of their religion.
(2) The Evangelical-Lutheran religion shall remain the official religion of the State. The inhabitants professing it are bound to bring up their children in the same.

China's Constitution

China's *Constitution* provides for freedom of religion, with the caveat that the government protects what it calls 'normal religious activity' defined in practice as activities that take place within government-sanctioned religious organizations and registered places of worship.

5.10 There is potential tension between the rights of parents and their children

From the above outline of rights pertaining to religion and beliefs, it can be seen that there is an apparent tension between the rights of parents to determine the religious education of their children and the state's obligations to see that children receive an education in conformity with the requirements spelled out in human rights instruments. Thus, as Ingvill Plesner has noted, 'this tension becomes particularly acute when parents wish their child's religious instruction to be solely within their own tradition and that tradition is hostile to notions essential to rights such as equality, respect for others and religious freedom for all'.[35]

5.11 There is potential tension between religious freedom and gender equality

As I mentioned in Chapter 2, women's rights can clash with cultural practices and religious norms. Frances Raday has presented a detailed analysis of what she called this 'pervasive problem for constitutional law', describing how it has been addressed in international law and in various courts.[36] She pointed out that gender equality rights clashing with cultural practices or religious norms is widespread and is 'probably the most intractable aspect of the confrontation between cultural and religious claims and human rights doctrine'.[37] How should this issue be resolved? Raday pointed out that UN conventions give precedence to gender equality, arguing that 'where there is a clash between cultural practices or religious norms and the right to gender equality, it is the right to gender equality that must have normative hegemony'.[38] This clash can also be seen as one between individual and group rights, as I discussed in section 4.12 in Chapter 4, or between individualism and communitarianism, as I outlined in section 1.7 of Chapter 1.

5.12 Various religions have suffered, and are suffering, from varying degrees of intolerance

Historically and contemporaneously, adherents to certain religions have suffered persecution and even death for their beliefs.

History is replete with wars fought on the basis of religion, sometimes on that ground alone, sometimes in conjunction with economic and ethnic differences. Thus occurred the Muslim conquests of the seventh and eighth centuries, including the wars against Christians in the Iberian Peninsula; the Christian Crusades against Muslims in Jerusalem during the eleventh to thirteenth centuries; and the Wars of Religion, involving Protestants and Catholics, in the sixteenth and seventeenth centuries in Europe. More recent times have seen religious conflicts between Pakistani Muslims and Indian Hindus; between Catholics and Buddhists in Vietnam; between Christians and Muslims in Nigeria; between Jews and Muslims in the Middle East; between Buddhists and Muslims in Myanmar; among Sunni Muslims, Christians and Shiite Muslims in Lebanon ... the list could go on, and no doubt will continue into the future.

Despite the various human rights instruments, even in the twenty-first century, religious freedom is very limited in some countries, as can be seen in the reports of two agencies charged with monitoring countries' adherence to their citizens' religious rights.

The first of these is the United Nations Special Rapporteur on Freedom of Religion or Belief. Set up in 1948, this office has a brief 'to promote the adoption of measures at the national, regional and international levels to ensure the promotion and protection of the right to freedom of religion or belief'. In his 2014 report,[39] the then Rapporteur, Heiner Bielefeldt, noted that 'violence committed "in the name of religion", that is, on the basis of or arrogated to religious tenets of the perpetrator, can lead to massive violations of human rights, including freedom of religion or belief'. He recommended, inter alia, 'concerted actions by all relevant stakeholders, including States, religious communities, interreligious dialogue initiatives, civil society organizations and media representatives, in order to contain and eventually eliminate the scourge of violence committed in the name of religion' (p. 1). With specific reference to education, the Rapporteur advised that:

> Textbooks used for school education should not contain negative stereotypes and prejudices, which may stoke discrimination or hostile sentiments against any groups, including the followers of certain religions or beliefs.
>
> States should use all available means, including education and community outreach, in order to promote a culture of respect, non-discrimination and appreciation of diversity within the larger society.

(p. 21)

The second monitoring agency is the United States Commission on International Religious Freedom (USCIRF).[40] In its 2015 report, USCIRF noted that nine countries had earlier been classified as being of particular concern: Burma, China, Eritrea, Iran, North Korea, Saudi Arabia, Sudan, Turkmenistan and Uzbekistan. To that list, it added another eight countries: Central African Republic, Egypt, Iraq, Nigeria, Pakistan, Syria, Tajikistan and Vietnam. As well, it placed the following ten countries on Tier 2: Afghanistan, Azerbaijan, Cuba, India, Indonesia, Kazakhstan, Laos, Malaysia, Russia and Turkey.

In recent times, the most egregious example of religious persecution is undoubtedly provided by the Islamic State of Iraq and the Levant (ISIL). As described by USCIRF, ISIL's rise, spread and its June 2014 declaration of a so-called 'Islamic State' which cuts across Iraq and Syria, is particularly threatening for the future of human rights and religious freedom in Iraq, Syria and the region. According to USCIRF,

> ISIL espouses an extreme, violent religious ideology that allows for no religious diversity. While ISIL targets all Iraqis who oppose it, religious minority communities have suffered especially egregious, devastating and large-scale abuses, including forced expulsion from their historic homelands, forced conversion, rape and enslavement of women and children, torture, beheadings and massacres.[41]

Although not as extreme as ISIL, Pakistan is one of the countries that either perpetrates or tolerates some of the worse abuses of religious freedom. USCIRF noted that it had received reports of preferential treatment for Muslim students, who can receive extra credit for memorizing the Koran, making it easier for them to obtain government jobs or university placement. Also, in a 2011 study, USCIRF found that an alarming number of Pakistan's public schools and privately run madrassas devalued religious minorities in both textbooks and classroom instruction. The madrassa education system generally relied on very old religious texts and for the most part did not educate children about the value of religious tolerance and diversity.

Turkey is cited by USCIRF as an example of a Tier 2 country. There, the constitution makes religious and moral instruction compulsory in public primary and secondary schools, with a curriculum established by the Ministry of National Education. While non-Muslim children can be exempted, there were reports of societal and teacher discrimination against those who opt out. Alevis, who comprise 25% of Turkey's total population and are the country's second largest religious community, have complained that they are not allowed to have their children opt out of Sunni Islamic courses (while Christian and Jewish students may do so). Although the Turkish government and many Alevis view them as heterodox Muslims, many Sunni Muslims do not accept that definition and consider Alevis to be non-Muslims. Indeed, some identify as Shia Muslim, while others reject Islam and view themselves as a unique culture. In September 2014, the European Court of Human Rights ruled that Turkey's compulsory religious education for Muslim students violates the right of Alevi parents to have their children educated consistent with their own convictions. Additionally, after complaints by religious minority communities, the Ministry of Education reported that it has made an effort to revise textbooks to not portray minorities in a derogatory manner.

Religious intolerance must be addressed within those countries where it is present, with schools providing avenues for addressing it through the curriculum and models provided by teachers. In addressing this issue, UNESCO pointed out that laws are necessary but not sufficient for countering intolerance in individual attitudes.[42] According to UNESCO, intolerance is very often rooted in ignorance and fear: fear of the unknown, of the other, other cultures, nations, religions. It is also closely linked to an exaggerated sense of self-worth and pride, whether personal, national or religious. These notions are taught and learned at an early age. Greater emphasis therefore needs to be placed on teaching children about tolerance and human rights, about other ways of life. Children should be encouraged at home and in school to be open-minded and curious.

Intolerance has repercussions that go well beyond the borders of the countries where it is widespread, for it often leads to the displacement of whole communities and the creation of refugees. Educators in countries that host religious refugees are thus faced with the challenge of providing safe havens for traumatized children and ensuring that they are not exposed to further discrimination.

C What form should religion in education take?

Given the diverse nature of religions across the world, the diverse ways in which rights are interpreted and the unique histories of different countries, it is not surprising that there are many contrasting approaches to including religion in education.

5.13 Religion in schools takes many different forms

Given that countries vary in their religious makeup (outlined in section 5.3), the varying attractiveness of religion to different racial groups (section 5.4) and to different genders (section 5.5), as well as the significance of religion in people's lives (section 5.6), it is not surprising that the place of religion in education is dealt with in diverse ways in different countries. Nor is this variation surprising when consideration is given to the level of doctrinal disagreements within religious communities, between religious communities, and between religious and non-religious views.[43]

This variation in approaches to religion in schools includes:

(a) the establishment of faith schools with or without government support;
(b) the presence of religious instruction inside or outside of school hours and which may involve compulsory or voluntary participation, the latter permitting parents and/or children to opt in or opt out; and
(c) religious education, which may range from teaching about different religions, with or without critical appraisal, to embedding religion in a broader consideration of moral education.[44]

These different approaches may be portrayed as a continuum ranging from strict secularism to religious instruction. Carolyn Evans,[45] an Australian academic, has outlined six broad conceptualizations of religious education:

1 *Strict secularism*: there is no discussion of religion at all in the classroom.
2 *Incidental religious education*: religion is taught about only to the extent that it is necessary to understand other subjects (for example, the role of religion in particular wars or religious imagery in certain poems).
3 *Plural religious education*: students learn about the basic practices, beliefs, rituals etc. of a variety of religions. They are presented with information about these religious

traditions but are not taught that any of them are (un)true. The instruction may also extend to philosophies and beliefs of a non-religious nature.

4   *Sectarian religious instruction*: students are broken up into groups (normally sectarian-based) and given instruction in their religion. An alternative class (perhaps in philosophy or secular beliefs) is given to students who do not wish to have religious instruction.

5   *Unitary religious education*: there are classes about the dominant religion of the state. The classes present information about the religion, but teachers do not claim that the religion is true. However, the classes deal either exclusively or predominantly with a single religion.

6   *Religious or ideological instruction*: there is only one class in religion available and that is religious instruction in the dominant religion. The religion is taught as true and children may be prepared for participation in religious rituals.

So how should we decide what is the most acceptable approach? What criteria should we use in coming to a decision? Like Charles Clarke and Linda Woodhead, in their recent analysis of religion and beliefs in English schools,[46] I believe that religious instruction has no place in schools if it involves instructing students in a particular faith (a) without critical questioning, (b) without consideration of alternative options, and (c) distorting other forms of religion and granting them no legitimacy. Reluctantly, however, I would have to accept that, in a free society, if such activities exist, they should take place in families, Sunday Schools and madrassas, that is, outside of schools. I say 'reluctantly' because I believe that *religious instruction*, as I have perceived it, is almost certainly indoctrination and is even, according to Christopher Hitchens and Richard Dawkins, almost tantamount to child abuse.[47] On the other hand, as I will discuss later, *religious education* is a necessary component of a child's education.

I have other objections to both faith schools and religious instruction:

First, there is evidence that selection by religion in England is associated with selection by socio-economic status. This was shown by *The Guardian's* analysis of 2010 English school enrolments, which showed that state faith schools were not taking a fair share of the poorest pupils in their area.[48]

Second, since religious identities often overlap with ethnic identities, it follows that some faith schools effectively exclude some ethnic groups. For example, children from families claiming no faith are excluded from faith schools, unless there are insufficient applicants from their faith. Given the stance I take on faith schools, perhaps this is a good thing!

Third, as pointed out by David Bell, head of England's Ofsted, there is a risk that many students educated in faith schools have little understanding of other faiths and little appreciation of their wider obligations to society. He criticized Islamic schools in particular, calling them 'a threat to national identity'.[49]

Fourth, as I have traversed throughout this book, I oppose any form of selection and segregation, whether it is on the grounds of gender, socio-economic status, ability, ethnicity – and religion. Schools should be comprehensive institutions catering for all children. I discussed this issue in Chapter 1, but let me summarize my arguments here: (a) inclusion supports social cohesion (i.e., it is a centripetal force); (b) inclusion enables all children to learn about and understand human diversity, including religious diversity; (c) inclusion promotes social mobility; (d) inclusion facilitates access to a wide range of schools (e.g., in England people of no faith are effectively excluded from one-quarter of schools);[50] (e) inclusion helps to change stereotypes, discriminatory attitudes and prejudice through intergroup contact;[51] and (f) inclusion helps people to think more globally and adapt to an intercultural world.

Fifth, I believe that it is inappropriate for teachers to be permitted, even encouraged, to proselytize on behalf of particular religions, which is inevitable in faith schools and in religious instruction. In this connection, I question whether teachers who personally adhere to an 'exclusivist' position regarding a particular religion or denomination can be expected to deal with students from different religions or denominations. How should teachers respond to students' questions regarding religion, including questions regarding their own religious beliefs? Increasingly, in these days of widespread access to the Internet and to social media, students will have access to a range of views on religion. In these circumstances, is it reasonable to expect teachers to take a neutral position?

Sixth, should teachers prevent their students from freely expressing their religious beliefs? How can a teacher avoid their students proselytizing, especially when this may be a fundamental, core belief of their religion? A related point is the potential for a mismatch between children's and teachers' cultural capital, which I described in section 1.21 in Chapter 1. This could well arise when either the teacher or a student has strongly held religious beliefs and associated worldviews which are at variance with the other person's. This requires teachers to become familiar with those beliefs and worldviews and to take them into consideration when it is appropriate, for example in the teaching of science and social studies.

Seventh, I question how teacher-led religious studies can be reconciled with the increasing educational trend towards blended learning, with its emphasis on personalized learning, online learning and student-led inquiry.[52]

Last, how can (should) religious instruction be integrated with other subjects in the school curriculum? This issue is particularly important in the case of science, as has been noted in the United Kingdom when, in 2014, in answer to a parliamentary question on teaching or supporting creationism in faith schools, the UK Secretary of State for Education replied as follows:

> State-funded schools, including free schools and academies, should not teach creationism as an evidence-based scientific theory. Outside of science lessons, it is permissible for schools to cover creationism as part of religious education lessons, providing that this does not undermine the teaching of established scientific theory. Academies and free schools are required to teach a broad and balanced curriculum and the model funding agreement now prohibits the teaching of creationism as an evidence-based theory.[53]

The complexity of steering an acceptable path through these choices is well illustrated by a set of guidelines drawn up in 2007 by a widely representative European committee.[54] Known as the Toledo Guidelines, these provided guidance as to how religion might be taught in public schools, including how to prepare curricula, develop appropriate teacher education and ensure respect for internationally protected rights. While the committee advocated teaching *about* religions and beliefs, it recognized that this approach might be perceived as indoctrination into relativism or secularism by some religious believers, or as indoctrination into religion by some humanists. It is to this theme of indoctrination I now turn.

5.14 Indoctrination has no place in education

> *Give me a child of seven, and I will show you the man.*
> (attributed to the Jesuits)

The concept of indoctrination lies at the heart of deciding what role, if any, religion should play in education. Whichever approach is taken towards religious education, indoctrination has no place in education systems.

Indoctrination is not a new concept. For example, the German philosopher, Arthur Schopenhauer, an atheist, had this to say in the nineteenth century:

> But religions admittedly appeal, not to conviction as the result of argument, but to belief as demanded by revelation. And as the capacity for believing is strongest in childhood, special care is taken to make sure of this tender age. This has much more to do with the doctrines of belief taking root than threats and reports of miracles. If, in early childhood, certain fundamental views and doctrines are paraded with unusual solemnity, and an air of the greatest earnestness never before visible in anything else; if, at the same time, the possibility of a doubt about them be completely passed over, or touched upon only to indicate that doubt is the first step to eternal perdition, the resulting impression will be so deep that, as a rule, that is, in almost every case, doubt about them will be almost as impossible as doubt about one's own existence. Hardly one in ten thousand will have the strength of mind to ask himself seriously and earnestly – is that true?[55]

More recently, American philosopher, Philip Smith, defined indoctrination in these terms:

> To indoctrinate has come to mean, especially in educationist circles, to teach a set of beliefs or a point of view in such a manner as to create the impression openly or subtly that what is taught is so true and important to the individual or social well-being that, by contrast, all possible alternatives are false and dangerous.[56]

Indoctrination is a complex issue, which I shall try to unravel in what follows. In doing so, I shall draw heavily upon the writings of my compatriot, Ivan Snook.[57]

- According to William Kilpatrick,[58] one of America's leading Progressivists during the first half of the twentieth century, a distinction should be drawn between *intentional* and *nonintentional* indoctrination. While some indoctrination might be inevitable with young children, even in these situations, the ultimate intent should be to the contrary. In Kilpatrick's view, parents can avoid accusations of indoctrination if they intend to give reasons when it becomes possible and use no methods which would inhibit free inquiry later. Thus, intentions cannot be divorced from the methods used.
- Indoctrination requires consideration of the *content* of what is taught. It clearly takes place when (a) teaching an ideology (or doctrine) as if it were the only possible one with any claim to rationality; (b) teaching, as if they are certain, propositions the teacher/parent knows are uncertain and are substantially disputed by other competent authorities; and (c) teaching propositions which are false and known by the teacher/parent to be false. As Snook put it: 'A person indoctrinates P (a proposition or set of propositions) if he teaches with the intention that the pupil or pupils believe P regardless of the evidence.'[59]

He went on to say that 'a person is indoctrinating if (i) in his [sic] teaching he is actively desiring that the pupils believe what he is teaching regardless of the evidence, or (ii) he foresees that as a result of his teaching such an outcome is likely or inevitable'.[60]

- Indoctrination usually involves some or all of the following *methods*: (a) the teacher is authoritarian, allowing little discussion or questioning; (b) the content is 'drummed in' in some way; and (c) there are threats of some sort that are held over the child. These methods amount to a 'non-rational approach'. However, method by itself is not a sufficient condition for deeming an activity indoctrination; it has to be considered in relation to the content outlined above.

- A counterpart to indoctrination is brainwashing. Both involve the manipulation of what people believe. Kathleen Taylor, from the University of Oxford, has identified five core techniques in brainwashing: (i) isolation (including physical isolation or separation from other belief systems), (ii) control (restricting the information and range of views to which people have access), (iii) uncertainty (reminding people of the chaos of what lies outside a given belief system), (iv) repetition (e.g., regular communal chanting or singing) and (v) emotional manipulation (e.g., associating positive feelings and images with the belief system and fear and uncertainty with the alternatives).[61] Elaborating on these, Stephen Law noted that the extent to which they apply varies from cult to cult and that they also apply to non-religious cults and regimes such as the present regime in North Korea. He also asserted that 'religious schools of the sort that tended to predominate in the United Kingdom up until the 1960s very clearly ticked all five boxes'.[62] Somewhat provocatively, Law went on to ask whether those who favour faith-based schools would accept the establishment of party political schools in which children are educated to uncritically accept particular political creeds.

So how can religious education avoid or, at least, temper any suspicion that it is indoctrination (or brainwashing)? Snook suggested four possible 'escape routes' to avoid indoctrination: (i) cease teaching religion altogether (unless it involves teaching *about* religion), (ii) delay all teaching of religion until the child is old enough to investigate it, (iii) make religion 'a stance towards the world' or (iv) change the method and/or content so radically that it cannot be said that the teacher intends the pupils to hold beliefs regardless of the evidence. Like Snook, I favour (iii) and (iv), but am prepared to accept (i). Above all, I agree with Snook on the importance of rationality, of children learning the importance of distinguishing between what is true and what is false.

This stance, which I have developed in the preceding analysis, is reflected in two recent approaches to religious education.

The first of these has been put forward by Michael Hand, a philosopher of education at the University of Birmingham in England. He has argued that the only adequate justification for compulsory religious education in schools is what he and his colleagues call the 'possibility-of-truth case'.[63] He contrasted this position with the 'religious choice case' presented by writers such as the American philosopher Harry Brighouse.[64]

First, let us examine the *possibility of truth case*. According to Hand, the foremost task of religious education is to 'ensure that pupils understand the meaning of religious propositions and can evaluate the evidence and argument bearing on the question of their truth'.[65] Thus, they would be in a position to examine arguments for and against the existence of God, the immortality of the soul and life after death, miracles and different forms of textual authority. They would be encouraged to question their own religious beliefs and come to judge for themselves which religious or irreligious worldview is the most plausible. This position echoes that advocated by Nobel-prize-winning economist, Amartya Sen, who pointed out that

> education is not just about getting children, even very young ones, immersed in an old, inherited ethos. It is also about helping children to develop the ability to reason about new decisions any grown-up person will have to take.[66]

Like Hand, Sen went on to suggest that we should be offering children an education that 'would best enhance [their] ... capability ... to live "examined lives" as they grow up'.[67]

Second, there is the contrasting *religious choice case*. As Brighouse argued, since personal autonomy should be the basic aim of education, children therefore have a right to make and act on well-informed judgments about how to live their own lives. This includes the right to make a choice as to which, if any, religion to follow. As Brighouse put it 'Not only do we need knowledge of the alternatives, we also need self knowledge, habits of mind, and strength of character to make the appropriate alternative choices'.[68]

Hand presented two objections to the religious choice case. First, he noted that some critics dismiss it because it reduces religion to a matter of taste, just like selecting food from a supermarket. Second, he felt that 'there is something awry with the notion of choosing beliefs'.[69] He disputed the claim that we can exercise direct control over what we believe (referred to as 'direct doxastic voluntarism' by philosophers). He argued that 'in religion, as in other areas of life, changes of belief are rarely under our direct control'.[70] Hand's emphasis here is on the word 'direct' as he allows for the possibility that we can, and should, exercise *indirect* control over our religious beliefs. We do this by considering relevant evidence and argument bearing on the truth of certain beliefs – a notion that lies at the heart of Hand's favouring of the possibility of truth case. As he put it, 'We cannot choose our religious beliefs, but we can choose how hard to think about them, how critically to examine their grounds, how open-mindedly to consider contrary views and alternative perspectives'.[71] Thus, schools should equip children to 'conduct such examinations as competently and carefully as possible', 'with an open mind', letting their beliefs 'be determined by the evidence'.[72] The task of religious education is ultimately to enable children to answer not 'Which, if any, of these ways of life is right for me?' but 'Which, if any, of these claims about the world is true?'.[73]

This leads me to support the teaching of philosophy in schools or, as it is sometimes referred to, 'Philosophy for Children' (P4C). This approach began with the work of Matthew Lipman, who founded the Institute for the Advancement of Philosophy for Children at Montclair State University in the United States in 1974. As of 2006, P4C was practised in 45 countries, usually as a supplementary or extra-curricular activity.[74] It typically involves a teacher presenting a thought-provoking stimulus, such as a text image or video clip, around which the students then frame philosophical questions, with the teacher engaging in a Socratic dialogue with them. At its heart is conceptual analysis and thinking critically and independently about moral issues, including religious questions.

5.15 How can interest convergence be achieved?

As I have indicated in the preceding chapters, shifts in policies and behaviours when there are two or more groups with different interests are more likely to occur when all groups can perceive a benefit accruing to them. So, how might this principle apply if there is a proposed shift from faith-based religious instruction to religious education, as I have portrayed it in this chapter? My argument is that all parties would benefit from such an approach if it leads to the inclusivism I am advocating throughout this book (see previous section). I do recognize, however, that certain religious groups would find this anathema and would be reluctant to relinquish schools in which their children are fully immersed in their faith. Ultimately, governments have to arrive at settlements that do justice to competing interests.

5.16 Countries deal with religion in education in different ways

As I noted in section 5.13, religious education takes many different forms. Likewise, as we shall see in this section, countries have reached a wide range of settlements regarding their approaches to religious education. These reflect a range of factors, including the increasing religious and cultural diversity of many societies, increasing secularization, the emergence of new ways of believing and belonging, concerns about social cohesion, the challenge of integrating immigrants with diverse values and beliefs into their new societies, states' different interpretations of their obligations to meet national and supranational human rights covenants and their own constitutions, changing pedagogical philosophies and practices, parent choice, increases in school accountability, political transformations and historical settlements reached in various countries.[75] These and other factors have resulted in a range of country-specific provisions for religion in education, including financial arrangements, the aims of religious schools and the type and degree of public scrutiny they are exposed to, responsibility for designing the curriculum, pedagogy, the recruitment of teachers, the gender composition of schools, school choice and the selection of students, the protections afforded to students from different or no religious backgrounds and so on. Invariably, the settlements reached in various countries reflect accommodations reached among competing interests, sometimes after periods of intense confrontations. It is not surprising, therefore, that these settlements continue to be the subject of political pressures, debate, contestation and even litigation as various parties seek to have their views accepted.

Space permits only a limited review of various jurisdictions' approaches. In this section, I will outline how 11 countries deal with religion in their education systems.[76] These are arranged alphabetically.

But before describing the various countries' approaches, it is useful to consider the situation in Europe. In her introduction to the 2015 publication, *The Future of Religious Education in Europe*, Kristina Stoeckl claimed that European societies are now secularized societies.[77] This means three things: (1) there is a differentiation of politics, economics, science and culture from religion; (2) religion is pushed out of the public into the private sphere; and (3) the decline of religious belief in modern societies.

Stoeckl went on to describe three approaches to the teaching of religion in European schools. First, there is the *confessional religious education approach*, which holds that children benefit from single-faith-teaching as it enables them to formulate an authentic personal religious (or non-religious) stance as a precondition to religious tolerance. Second, there is the *study-of-religions approach*, which places religion in the school curriculum just as any other subject with the aim of informing children about the range of religious beliefs and worldviews in the world. Third, there is an *inclusive approach*, which occupies a middle-ground between the previous two. It starts from the study of various religious and non-religious worldviews but also incorporates representatives of various faiths speaking about their religions. Stoekl observed that while these three models compete with each other, confessional religious education is a reality in many European countries and is likely to remain so. The validity of this latter view will become apparent in the settlements relating to religious education arrived at in the various countries described below.

Belgium (Flemish Community)

Flanders shapes its own education laws within the Belgian federal structure. One of the features of the Belgian Constitution is educational freedom (Article 24) and its consequential requirement to provide generous subsidies to private schools (including religious schools). Schools receiving subsidies belong to the Free Subsidised Education Network, which receives public funds equivalent to those granted to public schools, while at the same time retaining the right to determine their own curriculum, assessment methods and pedagogy. Since 2013, however, these schools are required to participate in centralized examinations and be subject to inspections. In other words, the Flemish Community adopted a conditional-funding model. These requirements have led to challenges from the Haredi (the ultra-Orthodox Jewish) community who wished to retain the right to provide an exclusively religious education for boys. To do so, they would have had to forego their membership of the Free Subsidised Education Network and become independent schools. [78]

Denmark

The free school movement emerged in the nineteenth century as a protest against the dominance of the state in education and the role Danish People's Church played in the curriculum. Thus, in 1855, parents were granted the right to assume responsibility for the education of their own children and to create 'free schools'. This benefited both those wanting to found non-religious schools, as well as those seeking to establish religious schools. [79]

In a recent paper, Tore Olsen explored how the right to fund non-governmental 'free schools', including religious ones, functioned as one of the strongest expressions of Danish 'free-mindedness' or tolerance. [80] It allowed parents to choose a school for their children according to their own ideological, religious, cultural and pedagogical convictions. However, as Olsen noted, the existence and freedoms of these schools are now under debate. New clauses in the law on free primary schools demand that they 'shall prepare the students to live in a society like Denmark, with freedom and democracy'. Monitoring mechanisms have been reinforced to ensure that private schools live up to academic standards and teach 'freedom and democracy' to a sufficient degree.

England

Here, religion figures in education in three ways: faith schools, religious instruction and religious education.

First, *faith schools*[81] are schools that follow the national curriculum but which have a particular religious character and/or formal links with a religious organization. They are free to teach religious studies in accordance with their own religion and are permitted to take applicants' religion into account when appointing teaching staff. The term is most commonly applied to state-funded faith schools, although many independent schools and academies also have religious characteristics. Faith schools may give priority to students who are of the religion they cater for. However, state-funded faith schools must admit other applicants if they cannot fill all of their places. The term 'faith school' was introduced in Britain in 1990 following calls from Muslims for institutions comparable to the existing Christian church schools. Faith schools have to follow the national curriculum except for religious studies, where they are free to have acts of worship 'in accordance with the beliefs of the religion or denomination specified for the school'.

In England in 2014, 37% of primary school students and 19% of secondary school students attended state-funded faith schools. The proportion of such schools has increased gradually since 2000 when the figures were 35% and 16% respectively.[82] These 2014 statistics comprised 7,735 schools, of which 6,824 were state-maintained and 911 were independent (i.e., fee-paying private schools); 4,865 were Church of England, 2,101 were Catholic, 153 were Muslim and 92 were Jewish. Only 6% of both Church of England and Catholic faith schools were independent compared with 53% of Jewish[83] and 91% of Muslim schools.[84] By retaining an independent status, these schools retained their autonomy not to follow the statutory national curriculum.

In 2014, 24% of students in faith schools in England belonged to ethnic minorities, slightly less than the average for non-faith schools. Christian faith schools are the most ethnically mixed, with White British (and Irish) and Black Africans and Black Caribbeans well represented in the same school.[85]

At secondary level, students attending state-funded faith schools tend to do better than those attending non-faith state schools, but not by much. In 2013, for example, 64% of pupils in faith schools achieved 5 or more A* to C grades, including English and Maths at GCSE, compared with 60% in non-faith schools. However, when it is considered that students in faith schools were less likely to be eligible for free schools meals (14%) compared with schools with no religious character (18%), and consequently more likely to have a strong academic record prior to secondary school, these results are not surprising.[86] Put another way, faith schools do not seem to provide a pathway for children from low-SES homes.

Second, *religious instruction* is compulsory in England for all students in local authority maintained schools aged 5 to 16 years, unless they are withdrawn from these lessons by their parents. In faith schools it must be provided in accordance with the beliefs of the religion or denomination specified in the order that designates the school as having a religious character.

The UK Education Act of 1944 introduced the requirement for daily prayers in all state-funded schools, but later acts changed this requirement to a daily 'collective act of worship'. Such acts of worship are required to be 'wholly or mainly of a broadly Christian character'. More broadly, religious instruction generally allows for instructing students in a particular faith, (a) without critical questioning, (b) without consideration of alternative religions or non-religious options, and even (c) distorting other forms of religion and granting them no legitimacy.[87]

Third, the legal requirements governing *religious education* (RE) were set out in the Education Reform Act of 1988 and confirmed by the Education Acts of 1996 and 1998. Although RE is a statutory subject, it is not part of the National Curriculum. Its content in maintained schools[88] is determined at the local authority level but an agreed syllabus should 'reflect the fact that the religious traditions in Great Britain are in the main Christian while taking account of the teachings and practices of the other principal religions represented in Great Britain'.[89] According to English writers Charles Clarke and Linda Woodhead, RE is concerned with encouraging students 'to learn "about" and "from" religious and non-religious worldviews ... It develops knowledge about a range of beliefs and values, an ability to articulate and develop one's own values and commitments, and the capacity to debate and engage with others'.[90] It appears that their definition of RE is more aspirational than reflective of the real situation in England. Thus, according to the schools watchdog, Ofsted, more than half of England's schools are failing students on religious education. In a recent report, it highlighted low standards, weak teaching, problems in developing a curriculum, weak leadership and management, weak examination provisions, confusion about the purposes of RE and gaps in the training of teachers.[91]

Further, Clarke and Woodward questioned the requirement that RE 'should reflect the fact that the religious tradition in Great Britain is in the main Christian'. As I noted above, this assertion is becoming less and less valid, with adherents to Christianity constituting only just over half of the population. Clarke and Woodhead also pointed out that RE syllabuses are to be determined by the 152 local authorities, although a 2004 national framework for RE was agreed to by all traditional religions in the United Kingdom, as well as humanists. However, this framework does not have statutory force. Accordingly, Clarke and Woodhead recommended that a national RE curriculum be established on the advice of an advisory council on RE. They also noted the importance of assuring the supply of properly qualified teachers and improved professional development opportunities. Given the neutrality of the RE they envisaged, Clarke and Woodhead also recommended that parents' right to withdraw their children from this part of the curriculum should no longer exist. They went on to assert that a nationally agreed RE syllabus should be extended to 'all students in schools of every type in England', including 'faith schools'.[92] Notwithstanding this recommendation, they also recommended that faith schools should clearly advertise and explain the kind of religious (or non-religious) 'ethos and formation' which they offer.[93]

A second influential report relevant to a consideration of the nature and role of RE was also published in 2015.[94] Authored by an inter-faith panel convened by the Woolf Institute of Cambridge, the report included a significant section on education. Among its recommendations were the following:

• The basic approach should be informed by human rights values and standards.
• Religious practices should not be required in publicly funded schools, but also they should not be prohibited.

- A national entitlement of content and outcomes (i.e., syllabus) should be flexibly applied at the level of the individual school.
- Education about religion and belief is essential because it is in schools and colleges that there is the best and earliest chance of breaking down ignorance and developing individuals who will be receptive of the other, and ask difficult questions without fear of offending. This is vital for the fruition of our vision for a fairer, more cohesive society.
- A key element of any effective work designed to improve learning about religion and belief must be encounter. At the basic level this means that participants in the teaching and learning process must at the very least be able to meet people different from themselves in terms of background, heritage and worldview. Quality encounter, however, must go beyond just knowing about different religions and beliefs, and engage participants in an interactive process of building relationships based on awareness, honesty, dialogue and trust.
- Governments across the United Kingdom should repeal requirements for schools to hold acts of collective worship or religious observance and issue new guidelines building on current best practice for inclusive assemblies and times for reflection that draw upon a range of sources, that are appropriate for pupils and staff of all religions and beliefs, and that will contribute to their spiritual, moral, social and cultural development.
- UK governments should recognize the negative practical consequences of selection by religion in schools, and that most religious schools can further their aims without selecting on grounds of religion in their admissions and employment practices.
- UK governments should expect publicly funded schools to be open for the provision of religion- or belief-specific teaching and worship on the school premises outside of the timetable for those who request it and wish to participate.
- UK governments should require state inspectorates to be concerned with every aspect of the life of faith schools, including religious elements currently inspected by denominational authorities.
- UK governments should ensure that in all teacher education attention is given to religion and belief that is of a similar level to that which is given to reading and maths, so that every primary class teacher is confident and competent in this curriculum area.
- UK governments should clarify and emphasize that in all phases and sectors of the education system respectful and thoughtful discussion of contrasting opinions and worldviews is essential, and that all staff have skills in the educative handling of sensitive and controversial issues.

Finland[95]

Fewer than 2% of Finnish children attend private schools, including religious schools, even though they are state-funded. Religious Education (RE) is a compulsory subject both in comprehensive schools and upper secondary schools in Finland because it is considered to support the development of the child's own identity and worldview, and also establishes a foundation for intercultural dialogue. Since the 1923 Primary School Act, every pupil has been eligible to receive RE according to his or her own religion, if the denomination is registered, if there is a minimum of three pupils who belong to that specific religion in a municipality and if such is available. This provision was intended to guarantee the rights of minorities and to ensure that children receive an education in accordance with their family's convictions. Since the 1980s, as an alternative to RE, non-religious children have studied a subject called 'Life Perspective Studies' (sometimes referred to as 'Ethics and Philosophy of Life', or simply 'Ethics'), which includes ethics, worldview studies and comparative religion. Pupils can also apply for exemption from RE in schools, and instead take part in education given by their own religious community outside of school. Pupils using this opportunity most often belong to the Jehovah's Witnesses or the Mormons. Religious education outside the school curriculum is not, however, recognized by the municipalities, and therefore these pupils do not receive a grade for RE in their school report. While the Christian faith – specifically Lutheranism and to a lesser extent the Orthodox and Catholic faiths – is still the norm in Finland, the various choices of RE have led some scholars to describe it as 'separative', rather than 'integrative', to use the terminology of Norwegian scholar, Wanda Alberts.[96] Even though it seems that this model has a fairly wide support, some people are concerned at the implications of the growing religious plurality of Finnish society and argue for some sort of integrated RE, using the Swedish model with a general knowledge of religion as an example.

Curricula for different religions are created jointly by religious communities and educational authorities, a process that is becoming more and more complex and expensive, according to some writers. The general principle in the national core curriculum is that the goal of any religious or ethical education should be to support the student in building his or her own, individual identity and worldview. It is intended that the curriculum for a religion be clearly in line with the general aims of the school, rather than those of a particular religious community. In more detail, the objectives of RE aim at familiarizing the pupil with his or her own religion and with the Finnish spiritual tradition (not described, but seemingly from the Lutheran point of view), introducing the pupil to other religions, helping the pupil to understand the cultural and human meaning of religions, and educating the pupil in ethical living while helping him or her to understand the ethical dimension of religion.[97]

The main content of Lutheran RE in the first five grades focuses on the Bible, ethical issues and Lutheran church life, as well as introducing 'common and divergent features of Judaism, Christianity and Islam'. Orthodox RE, at this level, contains instruction in the church year and saints, in what it means to be a church member, in the Bible, in liturgical life and dogma and in ethical values. In similar fashion to Lutheran RE, it also deals with Judaism, Christianity and Islam. From the sixth to the ninth grade, both curricula aim at deepening pupils' understanding of their own religion and the religion of others, as well as supporting 'the formation of the pupil's own worldview and ethical points of view'. In addition, pupils should be familiarized with world religions.[98]

The goal of Ethics is 'to give the pupils the material to grow into independent, tolerant, responsible, and judicious members of society', and to support their 'growth into full, democratic citizenship' in a globalizing and swiftly changing society. It should be 'guided by the sense of the pupil's opportunities to grow into a free, equal, and critical creator of a good life'. The first five grades of Ethics contain instruction in human relations and moral growth, self-knowledge and cultural identity, human rights and issues concerning the environment and nature. From the sixth to the ninth grade, the aim of Ethics is to 'deepen the pupil's understanding of their own philosophies of life and conceptions of the world', and to provide fundamental information about a variety of worldviews and religions. The contents of Ethics at this stage focus on citizenship and a good society, different philosophies, culture, ethics and good life, and on the future for individuals, society and nature.[99]

In order to qualify as an RE teacher, a teacher needs a certain number of credits in the relevant religion, either included in a Master's Degree or taken as additional studies. Four universities provide training for Lutheran RE teachers and one can also study to be a teacher of Islam and Buddhism. Teachers are not required to be members of the religious community whose religion they teach.

It is estimated that of the pupils taking part in basic education, 93% participate in Lutheran RE, 1.3% in Orthodox RE, 2.9% in Life Perspective Studies and 1.2% in Muslim education. In recent years, schools in larger population centres have seen the advent of Islam study groups catering to children from immigrant and refugee backgrounds. Like many European countries, Finland is becoming increasingly culturally plural, with Muslims often being seen as the most challenging for the social and political order.[100]

France

In secular, highly centralized France, although religious schools are classified as private schools, they can enter into a 'contract with the state', which creates substantial opportunities for public funding, and obliges schools to comply with the national curriculum.[101] Relative to most European countries, religious schools in France have a relatively small 'market share' of students.

Germany

According to Joachim Willems, religious education (RE) in Germany takes the form of 'Protestant RE', 'Catholic RE' and, in some states, 'Islamic RE', 'Jewish RE', etc.[102] RE is state-funded, with state authorities and cooperating religious organizations both required to approve the curricula and teaching materials. The state and religious organizations cooperate in the selection and training of teachers, but RE teachers require a certification issued by their religious organization. Willems reasons that with different RE programmes existing side-by-side in one school, students learn that there are different religious worldviews. According to Germany's Basic Law, parents have the right to decide whether their children shall receive religious instruction.

In 2006, a group of experts convened by the Evangelical Church in Germany defined 12 'religious competences' to be taught in Protestant RE lessons.[103] These included (1) students learning to reflect on and communicate about their religious or worldview convictions; (2) knowledge about the history of Christian theology; (3) discerning and interpreting fundamental forms of religious language; (4) the ability to make statements about other religious convictions; (5) the ability to communicate with adherents of other religions; (6) the ability to articulate religious doubts, criticism and indifference towards religion; (7) the ability to apply criteria for the evaluation of different forms of religion; and (8) the ability to perceive religious elements and motives in culture (literature, art, music, films, sport) and reflect on the societal relevance of religious ideas.

Iran

In 2006, the population of Iran was 98% Muslim, of which 89% were Shia and 9% Sunni. The Iranian Constitution establishes Shia Islam as the state religion and permits limited tolerance for some religious groups (e.g., Christians and Jews), but not for Baha'is and Kurds who are regarded as apostates from Islam and their civil rights are severely circumscribed.[104] As noted by Hossein Godazgar,[105] after the 1978-79 revolution, school textbooks were rewritten so as to deemphasize pre-Islamic Iranian history and to glorify Islam instead. The teaching of religion in schools was also changed. Before the revolution it had been called 'religious education' and concentrated on moral issues, but after the revolution it was renamed 'Islamic education' and expanded to include the Islamic worldview and ideology, the Koran, and a detailed study of the principles of Shiism. To implement these values, a deliberate attempt was made to employ teachers who had graduated from teacher training colleges where a commitment to the values of the revolution was inculcated. Furthermore, teachers had to take courses to further their education, with a heavy emphasis on theology and the Koran.

Ireland

In Ireland, all primary and the vast majority of secondary schools are non-governmental, albeit that they are incorporated into the system of state schools. Furthermore, most of the primary schools are faith schools (mostly Catholic). Thus, religious schools are fully funded by the state.[106] However, according to a recent paper by Nathalie Rougier and Iseult Honohan, there is a shift towards a more varied pluralism, or greater 'diversity of schools', in which multi- or non-denominational schools feature more prominently, rather than towards either a secular system or a privileged recognition of religious schools.[107] These developments entail a change in the historical balance of religious equality and freedoms; from leaning more towards collective religious freedom and equality among religions, to tilting more towards individual religious freedom and non-discrimination. Rougier and Honohan see these developments as entailing a change in the historical balance of religious equality and freedoms: 'from leaning more towards collective religious freedom and equality among religions, to tilting more towards individual religious freedom and non-discrimination'.[108]

Netherlands

Historically, schools in the Netherlands were seen as nation-forming institutions based on liberal, non-sectarian, Christianity. Thus, religious and state schools came to enjoy statutory equality. Recent legislative changes have been introduced to enforce non-discrimination laws upon religious schools with regard to hiring teachers, selecting students and respecting sexual diversity.[109]

New Zealand[110]

New Zealand's first schools were private, set up by missionaries to teach Māori children and the children of missionaries in the 1820s. When provincial governments became responsible for education from the 1850s, they often simply subsidized existing private schools. In 1876, provincial governments were abolished and in the following year the Education Act 1877 was passed. This established a 'free, compulsory and secular' national system of primary educa-tion to be provided by the state. In response, the Catholic Church began to set up its own net-work of schools. Protestant churches tried to get prayer and Bible study included in the state system, but were unsuccessful, so, in the early twentieth century, Anglican, Presbyterian and Methodist churches formalized their links with existing private schools.

Two significant developments took place in the second half of the twentieth century. First came the Education Act of 1964, Section 77 of which reiterated that teaching in state schools should be 'entirely of a secular nature'. However, Section 78 provided that school boards, in consultation with their principals, could effectively close their schools for up to 60 minutes a week, and for no more than 20 hours a year, so that religious instruction could take place in those time slots.

The second development resulted from a crisis in the Catholic education system: the cost of running their schools was overwhelming many parishes. Faced with a possible influx of Catholic school students into a state education system that was already full, the government, in 1975, introduced the Private Schools Conditional Integration Act. In return for using the New Zealand Curriculum, this Act allowed private schools to gain substantial government funding, and permitted them to maintain their special character, charge fees and restrict entry. As of July 2013, there were 331 state-integrated schools, of which 238 identified as being Catholic. Many of the remaining state-integrated schools were Christian, but there were also Rudolf Steiner, Montessori and Jewish schools. In total, state-integrated schools educated approximately 11.5% of New Zealand's student population in 2013.

In a similar classification to those I outlined in Section 5.10, New Zealand's Human Rights Commission has identified three ways in which religion can be located in schools: religious observance, religious instruction and religious education.

- Religious observance involves reciting prayers, singing hymns or participating in other aspects of religious practice. This is not neutral, as it either assumes or encourages adherence to a particular belief. An example is if prayers are said in a school assembly.
- Religious instruction means teaching aspects of a faith in its own right and carries with it an implicit or explicit endorsement of a particular faith and/or encourages students to engage with and make decisions about accepting it on a personal level.
- Religious education, or religious studies, refers to teaching about religion(s) as part of a broader context. An example is the role religion has played in politics, culture, art, history or literature. Religious education does not require students to engage with the religions being studied at a personal level or make choices about accepting those beliefs. Religious education can take place as part of the usual school curriculum.

Different rules regarding religion in schools apply to primary and secondary schools and there are further differences to schools with a designated religious character.

As I noted above, primary schools can provide religious instruction and religious obser-vance, but only if three main conditions are met. First, schools may 'close' for instruction for up to one hour a week with a maximum total of 20 hours a year. Second, this must be done in a way that allows students to opt out freely if they (or their parents) want to and receive appropriate supervision and instruction when they do opt out. Third, the New Zealand Bill of

Rights Act 1990 permits religious instruction and observance in schools as long as it is done in a way that does not discriminate against anyone who doesn't share that belief. Whether or not primary schools include religion in their day-to-day life is up to their Boards of Trustees (the bodies responsible for governing schools).

Religious instruction is usually provided through the Churches Education Commission, which organizes Christian Religion Education volunteers. Teachers or principals may lead prayers or other religious observances in their schools, but the Human Rights Commission points out the difficulties in practice for students to separate 'Mrs Jones the teacher' from 'Mrs Jones the person' and suggests it is best avoided. Schools must also ensure that teaching is secular during the hours they are open for instruction. They are free, however, to teach about different religions and the role that religion has played in politics, culture, art, history and literature. Indeed, knowing about, and understanding, the beliefs of others is an important part of the New Zealand Curriculum. Teaching creationism as science, however, would be a breach of the need to be secular.

The situation is slightly different for secondary schools, where teaching does not have to be explicitly secular. Under the Education Act 1989 (Section 72), Boards of Trustees are accorded considerable discretion about what they choose to do by way of providing religious instruction. However, secondary schools are also required to comply with the Bill of Rights, so if they do provide religious instruction or observance then it must be in a non-discriminatory way and students must be able to opt out if they wish.

Private schools (sometimes called independent schools, and to be distinguished from state-integrated schools) receive some government funding, but most of their support is provided by school fees and endowments. They do not have to follow the national curriculum. Like state-integrated schools, most private schools are Christian, the older ones being linked to the Anglican and Presbyterian denominations. In addition, there are also many smaller, more recently established, private schools with a strong Bible-based perspective, and a very few secular private schools.

Private and state-integrated schools are not obliged to provide a wholly secular education. If a state-integrated school has a special character provision in their charter that is religious in nature, then it can offer religious instruction and observance appropriate to that religious character without closing the school. However, parents can still choose to withdraw students from particular observances, on the grounds, for example, that the student is of a different faith (who are permitted, nevertheless, to enrol in such schools).

These arrangements are increasingly coming under criticism. For example, in 2015, the Secular Education Network[iii] wrote an open letter to the Secretary of Education claiming that Section 78 of the Education Act 1964 'erode(d) the secular nature of our schools through fictitious "closure" whilst classes in religious instruction are held'. It further asserted that religious instruction 'presents a narrow Christian perspective and requires parents to declare their personal religious views in relation to it'. Further, 'parents then have to make the unenviable choice between setting their children apart from their peers or allowing volunteers to proselytise to their children'.

The Network also expressed concern that, because schools were technically closed for the duration of religious instruction, the Ministry of Education and the Education Review Office did not have jurisdiction over what was taught and by whom. Finally, the Network was at pains to emphasize that 'secularism is not the same as promoting atheism – it takes no position on the existence of deities – and only secularism can provide a religiously neutral environment in schools, allowing families to practice their chosen religion at home, in church, Sunday School, synagogue, temple etc'.

United States

The place of religion in education in the United States contrasts sharply with what applies in England. As of 2014-2015, just under two million students were enrolled in US Catholic schools, 17% of whom were non-Catholics. Enrolments in Catholic schools reached a peak in the 1960s when there were more than five million students. The decline in enrolments appears to be accelerating. Between 2005 and 2014/15 elementary school enrolments in Catholic schools declined by 30% in the 12 urban dioceses and 20% in the rest of the United States.[112] This decline is attributable, at least in part, to schools having to charge higher tuition fees as the number of religious clergy fell away and were replaced by better paid lay teachers.[113] Tuition fees paid by families in 2014-2015 constituted 68% of the actual per student expenses. The difference between the per student cost and the tuition charged is obtained primarily through direct subsidy from parish, diocesan or religious congregation resources and from fund-raising activities. Based on the public schools costs, it is estimated that Catholic schools provide almost $22 billion dollars a year savings for the nation.[114] As well as Catholic schools, there are schools run by other denominations, Orthodox Jews, and various Fundamentalist schools, the latter especially in the South. Most parochial school principals report that their schools' most important educational goal is religious development.[115]

The constitutional context for these arrangements needs to be understood. As I mentioned in section 5.9, the United States Bill of Rights should not be interpreted as promoting a secularist state, but rather a 'disestablishmentarian state' which prohibits the establishment of any one religion, or religion generally. However, the situation is by no means clear-cut, as noted in a recent paper by Janice Russell and James Richardson.[116] They claimed that 'the original supposition of separation of church and state seemed to be more an ideal than a reality when it comes to the inclusion of religion in education'. As will be seen in what follows, decisions in this field involve balancing the competing principles contained in the First Amendment to the Constitution, namely (a) free speech, (b) the prohibition of laws respecting the establishment of religion (referred to as the 'Establishment Clause') and (c) the prohibition of laws preventing the free exercise of religion (referred to as the 'Free Exercise Clause'). The interpretation of these First Amendment clauses has exercised, and continues to exercise, US courts at the state and federal levels. The Russell and Richardson paper provides a comprehensive outline of the ebb and flow of decisions regarding the place of religion in education in the United States. Here are some of the main ones:

- In 1971, the US Supreme Court established what became known as the 'Lemon test', which stated three criteria that should be met if a statute were to meet the Establishment Clause. First, a statute must have a secular purpose; second, the goal of the statute must not advance or inhibit any religion; third, the statute must not lead to excessive entanglement between church and state.

- The Supreme Court has ruled that the practice of prayer during the school day is 'wholly inconsistent' with the Establishment Clause. At that time, the Court made it clear that they supported the study of religion, but not the practice of religion in public schools. The rationale for this and other similar decisions was expressed by Justice Anthony Kennedy who argued for the Supreme Court that: 'One timeless lesson is that if citizens are subjected to state-sponsored religious exercises, the State disavows its own duty to guard and respect that sphere of inviolable conscience and belief which is the mark of a free people.'[117]

- The Supreme Court has ruled that student-led prayer during school football games also violates the Establishment Clause. Subsequently, however, courts in California and Florida ruled that genuinely student-led religious speech in school assemblies, athletic competitions and graduation ceremonies was not in violation of the Establishment Clause, but was permitted under students' First Amendment rights to free speech. The Supreme Court declined to hear appeals of these decisions, but later it ruled that religious meetings in universities or colleges were more permissible than in schools because students are assumed to be more mature and not as susceptible to religious teachings and coercion.

- In 1999, the state of Louisiana introduced 'a brief time in prayer or meditation', to be observed in all public schools. The Supreme Court ruled that this was in direct violation of the Establishment Clause.

- The Free Exercise Clause has resulted in several challenges to the widespread requirement in American public schools that students should recite the Pledge of Allegiance and salute the flag at the beginning of each school day. For example, in 1940, Jehovah's Witnesses objected to this practice on the grounds that it constitutes an act of idolatry as the Bible calls on individuals to worship only God. The Supreme Court rejected this argument, finding in favour of schools requiring students to show their loyalty through a salute or recitation of the pledge.

- According to Russell and Richardson, the extent to which the state should financially support parochial schools 'has seen profound change over the course of American history', with the Supreme Court developing 'a convoluted and meandering course concerning the ability of states to support, in various ways, the system of mainly Catholic schools.'[118] They pointed out that many states have experimented with ways to support parochial schools while meeting the Constitutional requirements to separate church and state. These have included the loan of textbooks, transportation to and from parochial schools and special needs funding. The Supreme Court ruled that these provisions constituted a 'child benefit', rather than support for parochial schools – a decision that led to proposals to furnish other types of aid. For example, in 2002, the Supreme Court permitted the use of vouchers that enabled children to attend schools of their parents' choice, including parochial schools. Again, the Court argued that vouchers did not violate the Establishment Clause because they were provided to individuals and not to schools.[119] However, the Supreme Court has also ruled that the principle of child benefit did not apply to states providing salaries for teachers in parochial schools, even when these were limited to those who taught secular subjects. This was considered to be a step too far, violating the Establishment Clause. Thus, as I indicated above, Catholic schools (and also Jewish schools) are largely self-funded and receive only limited state assistance.

To make matters even more complicated, charter schools have to be thrown into the mix. These are schools which, like traditional public schools, are directly subsidized by a combination of state and local taxes, but receive autonomy from various federal and state rules and regulations that govern public schools. By 2012, there were approximately 6,000 charter schools educating some two million children (coincidentally, about the same number as were enrolled in Catholic schools). There would appear to be nothing stopping charter schools from developing religious content, thus evading the First Amendment strictures and, according to some writers, 'having it both ways'.[120] However, in 2015, the Washington state Supreme Court and the Colorado state Supreme Court both ruled that charter schools were unconstitutional, the former ruling that they cannot be classified as 'common schools', and therefore could not have 'access to restricted common school funding'. At the time of writing (2016), the US Supreme Court had not addressed this issue.

It is also worth noting that the US Supreme Court has taken a position on the teaching of evolution in schools. In 1968, the Court considered the constitutionality of a 1928 Arkansas law forbidding the teaching of evolution in public schools. It found that this law was unconstitutional because it violated the separation of church and state. It further argued that this decision did not constitute a breach of the state's obligations to be neutral, not favouring one religious or anti-religious view over another.[121]

Another significant ruling was the decision that religious believers do not have the right of exemption from 'neutral, generally applicable laws'. Thus, an earlier decision to exempt Amish parents from Wisconsin's compulsory schooling law was reversed in 1990. Brian Leiter, whose work I cited earlier in section 5.1, further illustrates this notion of neutral, generally applicable laws. He argues for a principle of toleration that prohibits the state from suppressing religious claims of conscience unless they harm others. Thus, he distinguishes between prohibiting Sikh boys from wearing a *kirpan*, or ceremonial knife, to school, and the French ban on headscarves, yarmulkes, large crosses and other religious symbols in public schools. The former is justified; the latter is not. The distinction rests on the presumed potential for harm.

It cannot be said that these and other decisions of the Supreme Court are the last word on defining the role of religion in American schools. As the United States, like many other countries, becomes increasingly diverse with respect to religious and non-religious beliefs, debate and litigation is bound to continue. There will continue to be arguments regarding what constitutes 'secular' and 'religious' actions. Harvard law professor, Noah Feldman, for example, has disputed the assumption that these two categories are binary.[122] He notes that while some things are inherently religious (e.g., prayer), many things that are not religious are not inevitably secular, and vice versa. For example, while a gymnasium has a secular use, it can also be consecrated for the purposes of religious worship. Thus, Feldman introduced the notion of 'dual use' in which something can be at once secular to one person and religious to another. He cited the example of the way in which Sunday is recognized as being both a secular holiday in many countries when most workers don't work as well as being the Sabbath for many religions.

D Conclusions

Although there is no universally accepted definition of religion, most include some transcendental belief in or service to a divine. As well, religions make demands on their adherents that must be satisfied regardless of costs and they are insulated from ordinary standards of evidence and reasoning. In return, religion offers to their followers several benefits, including a way of finding meaning in how the world works, defusing anxiety over problems and dangers, providing comfort and hope when life is hard, and developing social cohesion.

The role of religion in education, let alone in society more generally, is a sensitive, contentious and complex issue, with many opposing voices. In determining the way forward, many principles have to be taken into account. The relative weight given to each of them varies among countries and has fluctuated over time; it may well continue to do so as globalization and immigration alter countries' demographic profiles.

Ten interlocking principles stand out:

First, we must recognize that many countries, especially western countries, are religiously diverse and are rapidly becoming even more so. This diversity includes a significant and growing proportion of people who profess to having no religion or to being atheists. In this connection, account must be taken of the variation in importance people place upon religion in their lives.

Second, in defining the role of religion in education not only should we pay due regard to religious diversity, the degree of which varies from country to country, but we must also consider each country's unique history, demographic profile, political system, and how education is arranged. A universal approach is therefore untenable, except for general principles.

Third, cognizance must be taken of the rights of individuals to pursue their own religions or beliefs, as expressed in many international and national instruments, beginning with the 1948 Universal Declaration of Human Rights. This means taking whatever steps are possible to eliminate religious intolerance, discrimination, prejudice and persecution. Schools have a major role in this regard.

At the same time, it must be recognized that tensions arise between competing rights, in particular the potential conflict between the rights of parents to determine the religious education of their children and the state's obligations to see that children receive an education in conformity with the requirements spelled out in human rights instruments. Similarly, when women's rights clash with religious norms, UN conventions give precedence to gender equality.

Fourth, the concept of indoctrination lies at the heart of deciding what role, if any, religion should play in education. In this chapter, I assert that indoctrination, and its bedfellows brainwashing and coercion, have no place in education systems. The essence of indoctrination is that it allows little questioning of whatever belief is being promulgated and it takes place without recourse to evidence. Such an approach is anathema to educators who value the spirit of inquiry in their students.

Fifth, whatever approach to religious education is adopted, it should always take account of children's cognitive maturity. They should not be required to accept beliefs before they are capable of seeking and evaluating evidence for them. Most certainly, they should not be coerced into accepting beliefs. It is important, too, to respect children's development of personal autonomy.

Sixth, it is important to differentiate between religious *instruction*, which involves being taught religious beliefs as truth, and religious *education*, which involves learning about religions. Throughout this chapter, I have taken the position that religious instruction has no place in schools, particularly if it is supported by the state. Not only is it indefensible pedagogically, but it also impinges on the separation of church and state.

I have also taken the position that, with provisos, religious education is acceptable, even desirable. As well as providing opportunities to learn *about* diverse religious and non-religious beliefs and worldviews (including indigenous traditions), religious education should be broadened to include moral[123] and ethical education and assisting students to articulate and develop their own values and commitments. It could well be extended into teaching philosophy in schools. Such a curriculum should prepare children to live in an increasingly complex, pluralistic and globalized world.

It should be developed in consultation with a wide range of stakeholders, including but not limited to relevant religious bodies and representatives of secular belief systems, and be guided by principles such as those I have outlined in this chapter. There need not be any provision for parents to have their children opt out of it, any more than, say, mathematics or writing.[124] Nor should any group have the power to veto such a curriculum at a school or classroom level.

Seventh, arising from the previous points, it is clear that religious education is a morally and pedagogically complex task. It is therefore important that it be taught by trained teachers and not left to volunteers who may consciously or unconsciously fall into proselytization. One is entitled to expect that teachers' professionalism and codes of ethics would prevent them from pursuing their own religious views. This does not necessarily mean excluding representatives of various religions from participating as guest speakers in religious education.

Eighth, I recognize that in free, democratic societies, parents have the right to seek out religious instruction in their own faith for their children. While I have some reservations about this voluntary embracement of what I consider to be indoctrination, I accept that parents or caregivers can make such arrangements, provided they do not occur under the aegis of the state's education system. I would hope that in raising their children in a specific religious tradition, parents take steps to ensure that their child does not develop an exclusivist religious belief and has the right to an open future.[125]

Having said that, I must note (with some degree of scepticism) a somewhat contrary position advanced by the late Terence McLaughlin, a philosopher of education and a committed and practising Catholic. He argued that parents' raising their children within a faith is actually more likely to mean they achieve autonomy on reaching adulthood. He put forward an 'initiation thesis', which centred on the view that those initiated into a religious practice are better enabled to make informed judgments eventually.[126]

Ninth, as I have emphasized throughout this book, I oppose any form of selection and segregation, whether it is on the grounds of gender, socio-economic status, ability, ethnicity – and religion. Schools should be comprehensive institutions catering for all children. Arguments for taking this inclusivist position include, but are not limited to, the following: (a) inclusion supports social cohesion (i.e., it is a centripetal force); (b) inclusion enables all children to learn about and understand human diversity; (c) inclusion helps to change

Table 5.1 Summary of proposed actions regarding religion in education

Society (government)	Education system	Schools	Classrooms
• Accept and promote obligations under Article 18 of the *Universal Declaration of Human Rights* to respect individuals' rights to pursue their religions or beliefs and to freely change their religions or beliefs. • Respect that individuals' freedom to manifest a religion or beliefs is subject to 'limitations prescribed by law and are necessary to protect public safety, order, health or morals or the fundamental rights and freedoms of others' as specified by Article 3 of the *International Covenant on Civil and Political Rights*. • Promote understanding and tolerance among religious groups (*International Covenant on Economic, Social and Cultural Rights*). • Make no laws that promote the establishment of a religion (United States *Bill of Rights*). • Develop and maintain a separation between religion and the state (United States *Bill of Rights*). • Take steps to reduce religious disproportionality in schools.	• Respect the freedom of parents/guardians to ensure the religious and moral education of their children, as specified in Article 4 of the *International Covenant on Civil and Political Rights*. • In exercising this freedom, parents/guardians should give due weight to the views of the child 'in accordance with their age and maturity' (Article 12 of *Convention on the Rights of the Child*). • Respect the country's relevant articles in human rights legislation and constitution. • Formulate and promote policies of inclusive education that embrace all forms of diversity, including religious diversity. • Prohibit indoctrination and proselytization in state-supported schools. • Exclude religious instruction in schools that are funded by or sanctioned by the State. • Develop a religious and moral education curriculum that includes (a) consideration of alternative worldviews, (b) critical questioning, (c) the absence of distortion of any religion or belief, and (d) cognizance of children's levels of cognitive maturity. • Ensure that trained teachers are responsible for delivering the religious and moral education curriculum.	• Ensure that textbooks do not contain negative stereotypes and prejudices that may stoke discrimination or hostile sentiment against any religion. • Ensure that evolution is taught as part of the science curriculum, but that creationism is not. • Ensure that students are taught about their rights and responsibilities under international human rights conventions and their own country's human rights legislation. • Implement a policy that students develop skills of critical thinking so that their beliefs become determined by evidence. • Explore ways of developing contacts between students in faith-based schools and other schools through, for example, school twinning.	• Employ the principles of universal design for learning to accommodate to all students' ways of learning and expressing their knowledge and skills. • Teach critical thinking skills. • Accept that students may well have worldviews at variance with those held by the teacher and respond to this difference with knowledge of students' beliefs and tolerance of them. • Make the development of tolerance and the avoidance of prejudice and discrimination part of the everyday classroom life. • Discuss with parents how their religions should be taken into account in classroom discourse.

stereotypes, discriminatory attitudes and prejudice through intergroup contact; and (d) inclusion helps people to think more globally and to adapt to an intercultural world. A related point is that educators should seek to develop 'reflective pluralism' in their students through engaging with people and groups whose religious practices are fundamentally different from one's own.[127]

Having taken this inclusivist position, I am aware that geography might make its implementation difficult. In Northern Ireland, for example, Protestants and Catholics live quite separately, such distributions on the basis of religion being the case in many other countries. However, referring again to Northern Ireland, there is evidence that intergroup contact in schools is strongly associated with more positive orientations to ethno-religious outgroups.[128]

Tenth, it behoves teachers to understand and accept that students may have different worldviews from their own. Their religious beliefs and those held by their students and their parents may be at variance to their own. This discrepancy may well test a teacher's tolerance. At a minimum, it challenges teachers to familiarize themselves with the range of beliefs held by their students.[129]

The way in which these principles come together in determining a country's approach to religion in education is summarized in Table 5.1. In keeping with the ecological framework I have adopted for this book, this outlines actions that should be taken at multiple levels: societal (i.e., governmental), education system, schools and classrooms.

Notes

1   Raday, F. (2003). 'Culture, religion, and gender.' *International Journal of Constitutional Law*, 1(4), 663–715.
2   Diamond, J. (2012). *The world until yesterday*. London: Allen Lane, p. 329.
3   Ibid., p. 343.
4   Smart, N. (1969). *The religious experience of mankind*. Englewood Cliffs, NJ: Prentice Hall, p. 11.
5   Ibid., p. 22.
6   Leiter, B. (2013). *Why tolerate religion?* Princeton, NJ: Princeton University Press.
7   Pew Research Center (2012). *The global religious landscape*. URL: http://www.pewforum.org/2012/12/18/global-religious-landscape-exec/ (accessed 15 July 2015).
8   Source: CIA, *The world factbook*. URL: https://www.cia.gov/library/publications/the-world-factbook/ (accessed 20 November 2015).
9   Briggs, D. (2015). Are black Americans the most religious of all? *The Huff Post*. URL: http://www.huffingtonpost.com/david-briggs/are-black-americans-the-m_b_6769296.html (accessed 15 November 2015).
10 Manning, A. & Georgiadis, A. (2012). 'Cultural integration in the United Kingdom.' In Y. Algan (ed.), *Cultural integration of immigrants in Europe* (pp. 260–284). Oxford: Oxford University Press.
11 Pew Research Center (2015). *The most and least racially diverse U.S. religious groups*. URL: http://www.pewresearch.org/fact-tank/2015/07/27/the-most-and-least-racially-diverse-u-s-religious-groups/ (accessed 15 November 2015).
12 Trzebiatowska, M. & Bruce, S. (2012). *Why are women more religious than men?* Oxford: Oxford University Press.
13 Taylor, H. (2003). *The religious and other beliefs of Americans 2003*. URL: http://www.theeffect.org/resources/articles/pdfsetc/Religious%20Beliefs%20US%202003.pdf (accessed 10 November 2015).
14 Pew Research Center (2008). *The stronger sex – spiritually speaking*. URL: http://www.pewforum.org/2009/02/26/the-stronger-sex-spiritually-speaking/ (accessed 19 May 2016).

15 Clemens, B. (2014). *The British election study 2015: Religious affiliation*. URL: http://www.brin.ac.uk/news/2014/the-british-election-study-2015-religious-affiliation/ (accessed 15 November 2015).

16 Pew Research Centre for the People and the Press (2002) 'Among wealthy nations ... U.S. stands alone in its embrace of religion,' Pew Global Attitudes Project. Washington, DC: Author. URL: http://www.pewglobal.org/files/pdf/167.pdf (accessed 24 August 2015).

17 Kaldor, P., Hughes, P. & Black, A. (2010). *Spirit matters: How making sense of life affects well-being*. Melbourne: Mosaic.

18 Norris, P. & Inglehart, R. (2011). *Sacred and secular: Religion and politics worldwide*. Second edition. Cambridge: Cambridge University Press.

19 Botero, C.A., Gardner, B., Kirby, K.R., Bulbulia, J., Gavin, M.C. & Gray, R.D (2014). 'The ecology of religious beliefs.' *Proceedings of the National Academy of Sciences*, 111(47), 16784-16789.

20 Zuckerman, P. (2009). 'Why are Danes and Swedes so irreligious?' *Nordic Journal of Religion and Society*, 22(1), 55-69.

21 Stark, R. & Finke, R. (2000). *Acts of faith: Explaining the human side of religion*. Berkeley, CA: University of California Press.

22 Taylor, H. (2003). *The religious and other beliefs of Americans 2003*. URL: http://www.theeffect.org/resources/articles/pdfsetc/Religious%20Beliefs%20US%202003.pdf (accessed 10 November 2015).

23 Hoverd, W.J. (2008). 'No longer a Christian country? Religious demographic change in New Zealand 1966-2006.' *New Zealand Sociology*, 23(1), 41-65.

24 The increase in people with no religious affiliation is accelerating in other countries. For example, in Finland the figure grew from 12.7% in 2000 to 17.7% in 2009.

25 Diamond, op. cit., p. 334.

26 Ibid., p. 351.

27 Durkheim, E. (1952 (1912)). *The elementary forms of the religious life*. New York, NY: Free Press.

28 Parsons, T. (1951). *The social system*. New York, NY: Free Press.

29 Malinowski, B. (1948; 1925). *Magic, science and religion*. Garden City, New York, NY: Doubleday.

30 Marx, K. (1843). *Critique of Hegel's philosophy of right*. Marxist Internet Archive. URL: https://www.marxists.org/archive/marx/works/1843/critique-hpr/intro.htm#05 (accessed 10 July 2015).

31 Reynolds v. United States 98 U.S. 145 (1878). URL: https://supreme.justia.com/cases/federal/us/98/145/case.html (accessed 23 August 2015).

32 Mansueto, A. (2011). 'For sapiential literacy.' In E.B. Coleman and K. White (eds), *Religious tolerance, education and the curriculum* (pp. 121-129). Rotterdam: Sense Publishers.

33 Commonwealth of Australia (1900). *Commonwealth of Australia Constitution Act*. Canberra: Parliament of Australia.

34 Robertson, G. (2009). *The statute of liberty*. Sydney: Vintage Books.

35 Plesner, I.T. (2004).'Promoting tolerance through religious education'. In T. Lindholm, W.C. Durham, B. Tahzib-Lie, E.A. Sewell, and L. Larsen (eds), *Facilitating freedom of religion or belief: A deskbook* (pp. 792-812). Leiden: Martinus Nijhoff Publishers, p. 805.

36 Raday, op. cit., p. 663.

37 Ibid., p. 665.

38 Ibid., p. 710.

39 United Nations (2014). *Report of the Special Rapporteur on Freedom of Religion or Belief, Heiner Bielefeldt*. Geneva: Author. URL: http://www.ohchr.org/EN/Issues/FreedomReligion/Pages/Annual.aspx (accessed 23 August 2015).

40 United States Commission on International Religious Freedom (2015). *Annual Report 2015*. URL: http://www.uscirf.gov/sites/default/files/USCIRF%20Annual%20Report%202015%20%282%29.pdf (accessed 20 August 2015).

41 Ibid, p. 96.

42 UNESCO (2014). *Learning to live together*. URL: http://www.unesco.org/new/en/social-and-human-sciences/themes/fight-against-discrimination/promoting-tolerance/ (accessed 20 August 2015).

43 Bouma, G. Cahill, D., Dellal, H. & Zwartz, A. (2011). *Freedom of religion and belief in 21st century Australia*. A research report prepared for the Australian Human Rights Commission.

44 For an overview of these approaches, see David, D.H and Miroshnikova, E. (eds)(2013). *The Routledge international handbook of religious education*. London/New York: Routledge.

45 Evans, C. (2008). 'Religious education in public schools: An international human rights perspective.' *Human Rights Law Review*, 8(3), 449-473.

46 Clarke, C. & Woodhead, L. (2015). *A new settlement: Religion and belief in schools*. The Westminster Faith Debates, p. 33. URL: http://faithdebates.org.uk/wp-content/uploads/2015/06/A-New-Settlement-for-Religion-and-Belief-in-schools.pdf (accessed 15 July 2015).

47 Dawkins, R. (2006). *The God delusion*. Boston, MA: Houghton Mifflin; and Hitchens, C. (2007). *God is not great: How religion poisons everything*. New York, NY: Twelve.

48 Shepherd, J. & Rogers, S. (2012). 'Church schools shun poorest pupils.' *The Guardian*, 5 March 2012.

49 Halpin, T. (2005). 'Islamic schools are a threat to national identity.' *The Times*, 18 January 2005.

50 Cantle, T. (2013). 'Segregation of schools: The impact on young people and their families and communities.' Paper to the Accord Coalition and All-Party Parliamentary Groups, London February 2013 and Liberal Democrat Conference Fringe meeting, March 2013. URL: http://tedcantle.co.uk/wp-content/uploads/2013/03/075-Segregated-schools-divided-communities-Ted-Cantle-2013a.pdf (accessed 17 July 2015).

51 Paolini, S., Hewstone, M., Cairns, E., Voci, A. & Harwood, J. (2006). 'Intergroup contact and the promotion of intergroup harmony.' In R.J Brown and D. Capozza (eds), *Social identities: Motivational, emotional, cultural influences* (pp. 209-238). Hove, UK: Psychology Press.

52 Powell, A., Watson, J., Staley, P., Patrick, S., Horn, M., Fetzer, L., Hibbard, L. Oglesby, J. & Verma, S. (2015). *Blending learning: The evolution of online and face-to-face education from 2008-2015*. International Association for K-12 Online Learning. URL: http://www.inacol.org/wp-content/uploads/2015/07/iNACOL_Blended-Learning-The-Evolution-of-Online-And-Face-to-Face-Education-from-2008-2015.pdf (accessed 15 July 2015).

53 House of Commons Debates, 30 June 2014. URL: http://www.publications.parliament.uk/pa/cm201415/cmhansrd/cm140630/text/140630w0001.htm#14063048000150 (accessed 20 July 2015).

54 ODIHR Advisory Council of Experts on Freedom of Religion or Belief (2007). *Toledo guiding principles on teaching about religions and beliefs in public schools*. Warsaw: Author.

55 Schopenhauer, A. (translated 1910). *Religion: A dialogue*. URL: http://www.gutenberg.org/files/10833/10833-h/10833-h.htm (accessed 2 September 2015).

56 Smith, P.G. (1964). *Philosophy of education: Introductory studies*. New York: Harper and Row, p. 257.

57 Snook, I (1972). *Concepts of indoctrination: Philosophical essays*. Boston: Routledge and Kegan Paul; and Snook, I.A. (1972). *Indoctrination and education*. London: Routledge and Kegan Paul.

58 Kilpatrick, W.H. (1951). *Philosophy of education*. New York: The Macmillan Co., p. 123.

59 Snook (1972), op. cit., p. 47.

60 Ibid., p. 50.

61 Taylor, K. (2005). 'Thought crime.' *The Guardian*, 8 October 2005.

62 Law, S. (2008). 'Religion and philosophy in schools.' In M. Hand and C. Winstanley (eds), *Philosophy in schools* (pp. 41-57). London and New York: Continuum, p. 51.

63 Hand, M. (2015). 'Religious education and religious choice.' *Journal of Beliefs and Values*, 36(1), 31-39; and Hand, M. & White, J. (2004). 'Is compulsory religious education justified? A dialogue.' *Journal of Education and Christian Belief*, 8(2), 101-112.

64 Brighouse, H. (2009). 'Moral and political aims of education.' In H. Siegel (ed.), *The Oxford handbook of philosophy of education* (pp. 35-51). Oxford: Oxford University Press.

65 Hand, op. cit., p. 31.

66 Sen, A. (2006). *Identity and violence: The illusion of destiny*. London: Penguin, p. 160.

67 Ibid.

68 Brighouse, op. cit., p. 36.

69 Hand, op. cit., p. 36.

70 Ibid.

71 Ibid.

72 Ibid., p. 38.

73 Ibid.

74 Hand, M. & Winstanley, C. (2008). 'Introduction.' In M. Hand and C. Winstanley (eds), *Philosophy in schools* (pp. x-xviii). London/New York: Continuum.

75 See, for example, Mausen, M. & Bader, V. (2015). 'Non-governmental religious schools in Europe: Institutional opportunities, associational freedoms, and contemporary challenges.' *Comparative*

Education, 51(1), 1-21; & Norris, P. & Inglehart, R. (2011). *Sacred and secular: Religion and politics worldwide*. Cambridge: Cambridge University Press.

76 For a more detailed presentation on the range of approaches to religious education around the world, see David, D.H. & Miroshnikova, E. (eds) (2013). *The Routledge international handbook of religious education*. London/New York, Routledge; and Mausen & Bader, op. cit.

77 Stoeckl, K. (2015). 'Knowledge about religion and religious knowledge in secular societies: Introductory remarks to *The future of religious education in Europe*.' In K. Stoeckel (ed.), *The future of religious education in Europe* (pp. 1-6). Florence, Italy: European University Institute.

78 See Perry-Hazan, op. cit.

79 Rangvid, B.S. (2008). 'Private school diversity in Denmark's national voucher system.' *Scandinavian Journal of Educational Research*, 52(4), 331-354.

80 Olsen, T.V. (2015). 'The Danish free school tradition under pressure. *Comparative Education*, 51(1), 22-37.

81 Wikipedia. URL: https://en.wikipedia.org/wiki/Faith_school (accessed 16 July 2015).

82 Long, R. & Bolton, P. (2014). *Faith schools FAQs*. London: Library of House of Commons.

83 For more details of Haredi schools in England, see Perry-Hazan, L. (2015). 'Curricular choices of ultra-orthodox Jewish communities: Translating international human rights law into educational policy.' *Oxford Review of Education*, 41(5). DOI: 10.1080/03054985.2015.1074564.

84 Although not state schools, there are around 700 unregulated madrassas in Britain, attended by approximately 100,000 Muslim children. URL: https://en.wikipedia.org/wiki/Parochial_school (accessed 19 May 2016).

85 Demos Integration Hub (2015). *Education*. URL: http://www.integrationhub.net/module/education/ (accessed 18 July 2015).

86 Ibid.

87 Clarke & Woodhead, op. cit.

88 Maintained schools are state-funded schools which receive their funding from local authorities and are required to follow the National Curriculum.

89 Education Reform Act 1988 section 8 (3).

90 Ibid.

91 Ofsted (2013). *Religious education: Realising the potential*. URL: https://www.gov.uk/government/uploads/system/uploads/attachment_data/file/413157/Religious_education_-_realising_the_potential.pdf (accessed 1 October 2015).

92 Ibid., p. 42.

93 Ibid., p. 49.

94 Butler-Sloss, E. Baroness (chair) (2015). *Living with difference: Community, diversity and the common good. Report of the Commission on Religion and Belief in British Public Life*. Cambridge, UK: Woolf Institute.

95 This section draws mainly on two sources: Halonen, V. (2010). *The role of religion in the Finnish comprehensive school curriculum*. University of Tampere: Finnish Institutions Research Paper. URL: https://www15.uta.fi/FAST/FIN/REL/vh-relig.html (accessed 1 October 2015), and Sakaranaho, T. (2013). 'Religious education in Finland.' *Temenos*, 49(2), 225-254.

96 Alberts, W. (2010). 'The academic study of religions and integrative religious education in Europe.' *British Journal of Religious Education*, 32(3), 275-290.

97 Finnish National Board of Education (2004). *National core curriculum for basic education intended for pupils in compulsory education*. Helsinki: Author, p. 202. URL: http://www.oph.fi/english/sources_of_information/core_curricula_and_qualification_requirements/basic_education (accessed 1 October 2015).

98 Ibid., pp. 202-211.

99 Ibid., pp. 213-218.

100 Turner, B.S. (2011). *Religion and modern society: Citizenship, secularisation and the state*. Cambridge: Cambridge University Press.

101 Pons, X., van Zanten, A. & Da Costa, S. (2015). 'The national management of public and Catholic schools in France: Moving from a loosely coupled towards an integrated system?' *Comparative Education*, 51(1), 57-70.

102 Willems, J. (2015). 'Religious education and the student's fundamental right to freedom of religion: Some lessons and questions from Germany.' In K. Stoeckel (ed.), *The future of religious education in Europe* (pp. 27-38). Florence, Italy: European University Institute.

103 Comenius-Institut (2006). Cited by Willems, ibid.

104 See Abdullahi An-Na'im (1987). 'Religious minorities under Islamic law and the limits of cultural relativism.' *Human Rights Quarterly*, 9(1), 1-18.

105 Godazgar, H. (2008). *The impact of religious factors on educational change in Iran: Islam in policy and Islam in practice.* Lampeter, Wales: The Edwin Mellen Press.

106 O'Mahony, C. (2012). 'Ireland.' In C.L. Glenn and J. de Groof (eds), *Balancing freedom, autonomy and accountability in education*, Volume 2 (pp. 245–259). Nijmegen, Netherlands: Wolf Legal.

107 Rougier, N and Honohan, I. (2015). 'Religion and education in Ireland: growing diversity – or losing faith in the system?' *Comparative Education*, 51(1), 71-86.

108 Ibid., p. 71.

109 Maussen, M. & Vermeulen, F. (2015). 'Liberal equality and toleration for conservative religious minorities: Decreasing opportunities for religious schools in the Netherlands?' *Comparative Education, 51*(1), 87-104.

110 This section draws heavily upon two documents: Human Rights Commission (2009). *Religion in New Zealand schools: Questions and concerns.* Wellington: Author. URL: https://www.hrc.co.nz/files/9414/2387/8011/HRC-Religion-in-NZ-Schools-for-web.pdf (accessed 10 October 2015); and Megan Cook. 'Private education – Private schools in New Zealand', *Te Ara: The Encyclopedia of New Zealand*, updated 7 May 2013. URL: http://www.TeAra.govt.nz/en/private-education/page-1 (accessed 10 October 2015).

111 Secular Education Network. *Religious indoctrination is dividing our children. Open Letter to Acting Secretary For Education: Peter Hughes.* URL: http://religioninschools.co.nz/for-parents-and-caregivers/letter-to-secretary-for-education-chief-executive/ (accessed 19 May 2016).

112 National Catholic Educational Association (2015). *United States Catholic elementary and secondary schools 2014-2015: The annual statistical report on schools, enrollment and staffing.* URL: https://ncea.org/data-information/catholic-school-data (accessed 1 October 2015).

113 As of 2014-2015, lay professional staff in Catholic schools comprised 97.2% of the workforce, ibid.

114 Ibid.

115 National Center for Educational Statistics (1994). *Private schools in the United States: A statistical profile, 1993-94. Catholic parochial schools.* URL: https://nces.ed.gov/pubs/ps/97459ch2.asp (accessed 1 October 2015).

116 Russell, J.R. & Richardson, J.T. (2011). 'Religious values and public education in the United States.' In E.B. Coleman and K. White (eds), *Religious tolerance, education and the curriculum* (pp. 11-26). Rotterdam: Sense Publishers.

117 *Lee v. Weisman*, 120 L.Ed. 2D467, 484,518 (1992), p. 484.

118 Russell and Richardson, op. cit., p. 21.

119 Not all states permit this to occur: see Forman, J. (2007). 'The rise and fall of school vouchers: A story of religion, race and politics.' *UCLA Law Review*, 54, 547-604.

120 Green, P., Baker, B. & J. Oluwole, J. (2013). 'Having it both ways: How charter schools try to obtain funding of public schools and the autonomy of private schools.' *Emory Law Journal*, 63(2), 303-337.

121 *Epperson v. Arkansas*, 393 U.S. 97, 113 (1968).

122 Feldman, N. (2007). 'The way we live now: Universal faith.' *The New York Times*, 26 August 2007.

123 The Scottish education system uses the phrase 'Religious and Moral Education'.

124 I recognize that doing away with the opting out principle may create difficulties for some parents or caregivers – and teachers. Total exemption from religious education as I have envisaged it is inappropriate because of its value in preparing children to live in an increasingly pluralistic world. Partial exemption from those aspects of the curriculum that may cause concern to certain groups of parents is complicated, if not untenable, in a modern classroom where curricula elements are integrated and interwoven and where issues may arise spontaneously. As pointed out by Carolyn Evans (op. cit.), in those circumstances, schools need to find ways of dealing with controversial topics, including religion, in ways that are sensitive to the equality of all students, their right to education and their claims to religious freedom and non-discrimination. Sometimes partial exemptions will be part of such an approach, but it is not the answer to all problematic questions. Part of the way forward lies in teachers following the Toledo guidelines of ensuring that their teaching is 'fair, accurate, and based on sound scholarship' (ODIHR Advisory Council of Experts on Freedom of Religion or Belief, op. cit.).

125 Morgan, J. (2005). 'Religious upbringing, religious diversity and the child's right to an open future.' *Studies in Philosophy and Education*, 24, 367-387.
126 Carr, D., Halstead, M. & Pring, R. (eds) (2008). *Liberalism, education and schooling: Essays by T.M. McLaughlin*. St Andrews: Imprint Academic.
127 Wuthnow, R. (2005). *America and the challenge of religious diversity*. Princeton: Princeton University Press.
128 Hughes, J., Campbell, A., Lolliot, S., Hewstone, M. & Gallagher, T. (2013). 'Inter-group contact at school and social attitudes: Evidence from Northern Ireland.' *Oxford Review of Education*, 39(6), 761-779.
129 For a discussion of this topic, see Abo-Zena, M. (2013). 'Religion and education: Does the separation between church and state require a separation between self and school?' *Teachers College Record*, ID Number: 17195.

6 Different abilities

The only people we can think of as normal are those we don't yet know very well.
(Sigmund Freud)

Physical prowess was a differentiating feature that I became aware of from an early age. As a pre-schooler I used to cheer on my father, who was a champion axeman, taking vicarious pride in his skill. At school, I became aware that my athletic ability was above average, to the degree that I regularly won races and jumps, even holding school records at one stage. I was a good rugby player, mainly because of my speed, although I rather lacked the robustness and courage required to advance to higher levels. As a boy, I constantly measured myself against other boys in tests of strength and speed. I think my first awareness that not all people have physical attributes necessary for managing their lives, let alone for excelling in sport, took place when I was at primary school. At one stage, we lived next door to a veteran of World War I – to me, a somewhat frightening man with one eye, one arm and one leg, who always seemed to be grumpy. My early heroes were wrestlers, whose exploits were regularly broadcast on pre-television radio. They were closely followed by the successes of New Zealand's renowned rugby team, the All Blacks, initially via the radio, then through film and eventually through television. Despite my admiration for physical prowess and my modest successes in such pursuits, I resolved quite early in my life that I did not want to follow my father into occupations that centred on physical work, such as farming. Rather, I came to prefer the more sedentary and cerebral life of academia.

A related point has to do with physical health. I believe I am a member of perhaps the first generation to benefit from advances in medicine, without which people in my parents' generation and earlier suffered early deaths. Thus, there are effective treatments for heart disease, some cancers, diabetes and many others, resulting from such discoveries as penicillin and other antibiotics, surgical procedures and preventive medicine. I am a beneficiary of several of these.

Also when I was quite young, I intuitively became aware of variations in intellectual abilities. Fortunately, I found most learning came fairly easily to me, but as I progressed through school I began to notice that some of my fellow students struggled to learn. For the most part, I attributed this difference to hard work and perseverance, not to innate intelligence. However, at quite an early age, around five or six, I grew friendly with Les, a roustabout at the local hotel in the Fox Glacier township where my family lived. Les seemed to like talking with

us children and we enjoyed his innocent interest in us. But I sensed he was different from the other adults: he was slow of speech and somewhat 'simple' in his manner. Later, when I was about ten years old, and living in Ross, I became aware of Jimmy, a semi-hermit who used to walk into town every week or so for his supplies. He was a short man in his sixties, dressed in baggy pants and a jersey. Like Les, he liked the company of boys and in the summer he always sought us out to play cricket with him in the local domain. Jimmy had a speech impediment and seemed slow on the uptake. To my later embarrassment, we used to tease him, not only for his lack of prowess at cricket, but for his speech, lifestyle and clothing. Then, when I went to high school in Hokitika, I attended occasional rugby matches where groups of patients from the local psychiatric hospital were often present. One patient in particular stood out. He was a middle-aged man who did not seem to be able to relate normally to other people, but who had a remarkable ability to work out dates. For example, he could quickly tell a questioner on what day a particular date fell.

At University, one of the significant experiences I had was to visit a hospital for people with intellectual disabilities ('mental handicap' in those days). There I was shocked to see large numbers of people lying in beds or sitting around in chairs engaging in repetitive movements or making strange sounds. So, from an early age, I became aware that my fellow human beings were diverse in their physical and mental faculties, as well as in their personalities, an awareness that was later to dominate my career. However, my early work as a primary school teacher was with students considered to be 'gifted and talented'. In those days, students in intermediate (i.e. middle) schools were rigidly streamed and because of my university qualifications I was assigned a 'top stream' class and had a year as a seconded teacher working on a post-Sputnik programme for gifted students. In my early career as a school psychologist, I worked with children with special educational needs and their families – who have remained my focus as a university teacher, researcher and writer.

In their 2011 *World Report on Disability*, the World Health Organization and the World Bank hit the headlines with the announcement that there were one billion people with disabilities in the world.[1] They described disability as being part of the human condition, pointing out that almost everyone will be temporarily or permanently impaired at some point in their lives. They further noted that responses to disability have changed since the 1970s, prompted largely by the self-organization of people with disabilities and by the growing tendency to see disability as a human rights issue. As we shall see in this chapter, however, it is instructive to acknowledge that

> despite the magnitude of the issue, both awareness of and scientific information on disability issues are lacking. There is no agreement on definitions and little internationally comparable information on the incidence, distribution and trends of disability.[2]

How best to educate children with different abilities is one of the most dominant and controversial issues confronting educators around the world today. It is a complex and dynamic issue that demands careful and systematic analysis. It requires that we examine such fundamental questions as: What paradigm should drive our approach to educating such children? How should they be classified; indeed, should they be classified at all? How should they be funded? How best to teach them? How should they be assessed? How important is the place in which they are educated? What choices should their parents have? What supports do they require? How can the agencies that are involved with their education, health and welfare be coordinated?

In this chapter, I will consider a range of general issues bearing upon children with different abilities, focusing on those with disabilities. Unfortunately, space limitations preclude me from examining those with exceptional abilities, i.e., gifted and talented. As with the other substantive chapters, this one will be structured around the following broad questions:

A　What do we mean by ability differences?
B　How do students with different abilities differ in their achievement?
C　What causes differences in abilities?
D　How should education accommodate to students with different abilities?

A　What do we mean by ability differences?

6.1　*There are three main types of ability differences*

For the purposes of this chapter, I am focusing on three main categories of differences in ability manifested by children. First, some vary significantly in their health and physical ability, with some excelling in sports and other physical activities and others having disabilities such as cerebral palsy, deafness, visual impairment and health problems. Second, children vary in their cognitive/intellectual development, with some excelling and others experiencing difficulties in constructing thought processes, including remembering, reasoning, problem solving and information processing, and the application of these abilities to achieve major developmental tasks. Children with cognitive difficulties include those with intellectual disabilities, learning disabilities, autistic spectrum disorder, dyslexia and attention deficit hyperactivity disorder. Third, personality plays an important role in children's relationships with peers and adults, influencing classroom behaviour and contributing to academic achievement. Dysfunctional personality characteristics include those that manifest themselves in emotional disturbance, antisocial behaviour and delinquency. Such behaviours pose particular challenges to teachers and families, sometimes creating risks to the children themselves and to their peers.

6.2　*Persons with disabilities are heterogeneous*

According to the *World Report on Disability*, generalizations about 'disability' or 'people with disabilities' can mislead.[3] It emphasized that persons with disabilities have diverse personal factors with differences in gender, age, socio-economic status, sexuality, ethnicity, or cultural heritage. Each has his or her personal preferences and responses to disability. Also, while disability correlates with disadvantage, not all people with disabilities are disadvantaged. Further, as I pointed out in Chapter 1 (section 1.14), diversities intersect with each other. More specifically, abilities/disabilities intersect with gender (Chapter 2, section 2.40) and ethnicity (Chapter 4, section 4.16). As well, we should note the observation of the World Health

Organization and the World Bank that disability has a bidirectional link to poverty: 'disability may increase the risk of poverty, and poverty may increase the risk of disability'.[4]

6.3 The aim should be to respect and enhance the human rights of children with disabilities

In December 2006, the 61st session of the United Nations General Assembly confirmed the *Convention on the Rights of Disabled Persons* (UNCRPD), which came into force on 3 May 2008. Disabled people's organizations were closely involved in its development. As of February 2016, a total of 160 countries had ratified it, notably not Finland, Iceland, Ireland, the Netherlands and the United States[5], among others.[6]

The UNCRPD is based on the social model of disability, which perceives disability to be largely a social construct, as I will describe in the following section. Thus, in its Preamble it is stated that 'disability results from the interaction between persons with impairments and attitudinal and environmental barriers that hinder their full and effective participation in society on an equal basis with others'.

Article 2 defines discrimination as:

> any distinction, exclusion, or restriction on the basis of disability which has the purpose or effect of impairing or nullifying the recognition, enjoyment or exercise on an equal basis with others, of all human rights and fundamental freedoms in the political, economic, social, cultural civil or any other field. It includes all forms of discrimination, including denial of reasonable accommodation.

Article 2 goes on to define 'reasonable accommodation' as 'necessary and appropriate modification and adjustments not imposing a disproportionate or undue burden, where needed in a particular case'.

Article 24 deals specifically with education and is of particular relevance to the theme of this book. It states that:

1. States Parties recognize the right of persons with disabilities to education. With a view to realizing this right without discrimination and on the basis of equal opportunity, States Parties shall ensure an inclusive education system at all levels, and life-long learning, directed to:

    (a) The full development of the human potential and sense of dignity and self worth, and the strengthening of respect for human rights, fundamental freedoms and human diversity;
    (b) The development by persons with disabilities of their personality, talents and creativity, as well as their mental and physical abilities, to their fullest potential;
    (c) Enabling persons with disabilities to participate effectively in a free society.

2. In realizing this right, States Parties shall ensure that:

    (a) Persons with disabilities are not excluded from the general education system on the basis of disability, and that children with disabilities are not excluded from free and compulsory primary education, or from secondary education, on the basis of disability;

(b) Persons with disabilities can access an inclusive, quality, free primary education and secondary education on an equal basis with others in the communities in which they live;

(c) Reasonable accommodation of the individual's requirements is provided;

(d) Persons with disabilities receive the support required, within the general education system, to facilitate their effective education;

(e) Effective individualized support measures are provided in environments that maximize academic and social development, consistent with the goal of full inclusion.

The *Convention* established a committee for monitoring its implementation by those countries who ratified it, a committee that must include the participation of experts with disabilities (article 34). The UN recognizes that countries vary in their readiness to implement the Convention and therefore refers to the need for evidence of 'progressive realization' of its principles and policies.

As we shall see in this chapter, meeting the obligations of the *Convention* requires countries to dedicate extra resources to the education of children with disabilities. As I argued in section 1.9 of Chapter 1, I believe this is justifiable by invoking philosopher John Rawls's 'difference principle'. This posits that divergence from strict equality in resource allocation is permissible so long as it would make the least advantaged in society materially better off.

6.4 Three different paradigms dominate approaches to educating students with disabilities

A paradigm is an ideology or frame of reference – the way one perceives, understands, or interprets a topic or issue. Individuals interpret (often unknowingly) everything they experience through paradigms, frequently without questioning their accuracy. People simply assume that the way they view things is the way things really are or the way they should be. Paradigms are so ingrained in culture that they seem 'natural'. They are a primary source of our attitudes and actions.[7] The originator of the term, Thomas Kuhn, defined a paradigm as 'universal achievements that for a time provide model problems and solutions to a community of practitioners'.[8]

During its history, the broad field of special education has been the site of quite different paradigms, which posit certain relationships between individuals with disabilities and their environments. In this section, I will examine the three most dominant paradigms: the psycho-medical paradigm, the socio-political paradigm and the organizational paradigm.

Until recently, special education has been dominated by *a psycho-medical paradigm*, which focuses on the assumption that deficits are located within individual students.[9] Historically, this paradigm has been the most widespread and has been used in both the diagnosis and educational treatment of children with disabilities. In this model, students receive a medical diagnosis based on their psychological and/or physical impairments across selected domains and both strengths and weakness are identified for education and training.[10] Those with similar diagnoses and functional levels are grouped together for instructional purposes. This paradigm is problematic for several reasons.[11] First, it leads to the attribution of student failure to a defect or inadequacy within the individual, thus masking the role that highly constraining educational systems play in creating failure. Second, it wrongly suggests homogeneity within various diagnostic categories. Third, many students enrolled in special education do not manifest demonstrable pathologies. Fourth, studies show that instruction based on categories is generally not effective.

In contrast to the psycho-medical paradigm, several writers regard disability as a *sociopolitical construct*, which focuses on structural inequalities at the macro-social level being reproduced at the institutional level.[12] For example, schools may not adapt their instruction to differences in children's language backgrounds, leading to them being classified as having a disability. To these two paradigms, a third, *organizational paradigm*, has been added.[13] In this recently emerged paradigm, special education is seen as the consequence of inadequacies in mainstream schools and, consequently, ways should be found to make them more capable of responding to student diversity. Disabilities are perceived as a function of the interaction between individual students and their physical, social and psychological environments. Instructional techniques and learning opportunities should therefore be structured to compensate for environmental deficiencies to ensure that children learn and achieve skills of adaptive living. This can be achieved through such means as schools implementing findings from research into effective teaching, operating as problem-solving organizations, and supporting teachers through the change process.

While most countries have a mix of paradigms underlying their educational provisions for students with disabilities, the preponderant one remains the psycho-medical model, which retains its adherents even when other paradigms that place an emphasis on the environment have gained traction in recent years. It cannot yet be said that that the field has undergone a Kuhnian 'paradigm shift', in which traditional paradigms are discarded in favour of the new. In their *World Disability Review*, however, the World Heath Organization and the World Bank argued that while the medical model and the social model are often presented as dichotomous, disability should be viewed neither as purely medical nor as purely social, but a balanced approach is needed. Instead, they promoted a 'bio-psycho-social model' as representing a workable compromise between the two paradigms. As we shall see in section 6.23, UK scholar, Geoff Lindsay, shares this view, arguing that there is an imbalance of emphasis on the social model compared with the medical model.[14] It is not a matter of one or the other model but of finding the right balance between the two and of understanding how each interacts with the other.

6.5 Countries differ widely in their definitions and categorization of ability differences

Given the diversity of paradigms outlined above, it is not surprising that making international comparisons of provisions for children with disabilities is fraught with difficulties. As we shall see in this section, there is no universal agreement as to how these students should be referred to, how they should be defined and what, if any, categories they should be divided into. It should be noted that this is a very fluid situation as countries change their approaches to ability differences.

This diversity reflects a variety of factors, including different philosophical positions, the history of organizations/systems, local traditions within school districts, legal foundations, and fiscal policies and constraints.[15] It is further compounded by the 2008 UNESCO International Conference on Education resolution that Member States should adopt a broadened concept of inclusive education that addresses the diverse needs of *all learners* not just those with disabilities.[16]

In this section, I will examine various definitions and classifications of disabilities, discuss some problems with classification systems, and outline terminological issues.

In order to discuss policy differences and to gather comparable statistics, various bodies have sought to compare definitions across countries.[17] As suggested above, they have found comparisons difficult, as the definitions vary even within nations, as well as reflecting considerable variation across countries. Thus, for example, the category, *special educational needs*, is limited in some countries to students with disabilities, while in others it extends to social disadvantage, those with minority ethnic backgrounds and, in some cases, gifted children.[18]

In order to deal with this diversity, the OECD obtained agreement across countries to re-allocate their national categories into three types, for the purpose of obtaining data for international comparisons[19]:

Category A: Disabilities: students with disabilities or impairments viewed in medical terms as organic disorders attributable to organic pathologies (e.g., in relation to sensory, motor or neurological defects).

Category B: Difficulties: students with behavioural or emotional disorders, or specific difficulties in learning. The educational need is considered to arise primarily from problems in the interaction between the student and the educational context.

Category C: Disadvantages: students with disadvantages arising primarily from socio-economic, cultural and/or linguistic factors. The educational need is to compensate for the disadvantages attributable to these factors. This category is dealt with in Chapters 3 and 4 in this book.

The OECD noted that most countries found it easiest to contribute data in relation to category A (disabilities), while many found it less easy to contribute data in relation to categories B (difficulties) and C (disadvantages).

In category A, the number of national sub-categories varied from two for England to 19 in Switzerland, with most countries having 12 or 13 sub-categories; nine sub-categories are found in virtually every country. These common categories comprised students with blindness or partial sight, deafness or partial hearing, emotional or behavioural difficulties, physical disabilities, speech and language problems, health needs requiring hospitalization, moderate or severe learning problems, and specific learning difficulties. Certain countries cited IQ scores to define some categories (France, Greece, Italy, the Netherlands, Slovak Republic and Switzerland). Emotional and behavioural problems were not recognized as a separate category in Greece, Hungary, Italy or Turkey. Certain countries had a separate category for autism (Czech Republic, Germany, Poland, Slovak Republic, Turkey and the United States). Only Poland had a category for children who are in 'danger to addiction'.

The range between countries was less for category A (disabilities) (Korea – 0.47% to the United States – 5.16%) than for either category B (difficulties) (Italy – close to or at 0%, to Poland – 22.29%), or category C (disadvantages) (Hungary – close to or at 0% to the United States – approximately 23%). Italy, Japan and Poland identified no categories within category B (difficulties) and Turkey was the only country to recognize 'gifted and talented' students in category B.

According to the OECD, countries differed the most in relation to category C. The most common categories across countries related to students whose first language was not that of their host country and/or who were immigrant, migrant or refugee children. Four countries (Belgium (Flemish Community), Germany, Mexico and Spain) had a category that included 'Travelling children'. Only Belgium (the French Community) and Mexico specified rural areas or areas of small population. Few countries specifically mentioned socio-economic disadvantage (the exceptions included France, Mexico and the Netherlands). Few countries specifically included children who offend.

Some countries have taken a strong stance in relation to categorization. Three warrant further description. Sweden has generally adopted an anti-categorization approach to special educational needs and has opposed the use of medical categories for educational purposes. Given the reluctance to categorize children, psychometric assessment techniques have not been widely used. An exception to the Swedish anti-categorization stance is the recognition of deaf or hearing impaired students as a separate group who may have the option of attending a special school for the deaf. Despite the dislike of categories, it has been noted that there has been a marked increase in Sweden's identification of some types of impairment, in particular ADHD.[20] Denmark and England were two other countries not to take a categorical approach, although the former did make a distinction between more extensive special needs (about 1%) and those with less extensive needs, including those with disadvantages (about 12%).

Given the influential role played by the United States in international developments in special education, it is relevant to consider that country's approach to the classification of SWSEN. The first point to make is that under the Individuals with Disabilities Education Act, the US legislation focuses on no fewer than 13 disability categories. These fall into three major types:

1 *Sensory disabilities*: visual impairments, hearing impairments, deaf-blindness;
2 *Physical and neurological disabilities*: orthopedic impairments, other health impairments, traumatic brain injury, multiple disabilities, autism; and,
3 *Developmental disabilities*: specific learning disabilities, speech and language impairments, emotional disturbance, mild mental retardation and developmental delay.

The 2002 *President's Commission on Excellence in Special Education* was very critical of what it referred to as America's 'proliferation of categories and assessment guidelines that vary in their implementation, often with little relation to intervention'.[21] It pointed out that many of the 13 categories emerged as a result of advocacy groups' efforts to promote recognition for their specific constituencies and that 'the necessity of all 13 categories and their relation to instruction is not firmly established'.[22]

The Commission's conclusion regarding categorization in the United States is worth noting in full as I believe it has wide and current applicability:

The Commission could not identify firm practical or scientific reasons supporting the current classification of disabilities in IDEA. The intent of IDEA is to focus
on the effective and efficient delivery of special education services. The Commission is concerned that federal implementing regulations waste valuable special education resources in determining which category a child fits into rather than providing the
instructional interventions a child requires. The priority should always be to deliver services, with assessment secondary to this aim. When schools are encouraged by federal
and state guidelines to focus on assessment as a priority - and often for gate keeping
functions to control expenditures - the main victims are the students themselves, whose
instructional needs are not addressed in the cumbersome assessment process. Thus,
the overall Commission recommendation for assessment and identification is to simplify
wherever possible and to orient any assessments towards the provision of services.[23]

Special educational classifications based on disabilities are problematic for several
reasons.[24] First, as I pointed out in section 6.4 in the description of the psycho-medical paradigm, they tend to attribute student failure to a defect or inadequacy within the
individual student, thus masking the role that highly constraining educational systems
may play in creating failure. Second, they wrongly suggest homogeneity within various
diagnostic categories. Third, some students with disabilities do not manifest special educational needs. Fourth, studies show that instruction based on disability categories is of
limited utility. Fifth, since all disability categories are continuous in nature (as opposed
to being discrete entities such as gender), they require some judgment to be exercised
about the relevant cut-off points for special educational purposes, which is not always
a straightforward task. Sixth, issues of category boundaries also arise through the
co-occurrence of various disabilities. For example, according to the American Psychiatric
Association around half of clinic-referred children with ADHD also have an oppositional defi-
ant disorder or a conduct disorder.[25] Finally, since disability categories may militate against
seeing the student holistically, care is needed that classification of a disorder or disability
does not come to be seen as a defining the child.

In light of such problems, the validity and reliability of some categories of disability may be
questionable, leading to some 'very wide variations in the supposed prevalence of conditions'
For example, studies reported by the authors of the *Diagnostic and Statistical Manual of Mental Disorders Fourth Edition Text Revision (DSM-IV-TR)* showed a wide range in estimates of
the prevalence of particular disorders.[26] For example, 'oppositional defiance disorder' varied
from 2% to 16%, and 'conduct disorders' ranged from 1% to 10% in the general population.

As well as the diversity of categories outlined above, there are differences in the way the
broad field of educational provisions are described internationally. There are three main divisions: 'special education', 'inclusive education' and hybrids of the two. Australia provides a
good case in point. As summarized in a recent review,[27] many state departments in Australia
now refer to services using some reference to disability, for example: NSW - 'Disability Programs'; Tasmania - 'Students with Disabilities'; South Australia - 'Disability Services'; and
Victoria - 'Students with Disabilities'. In contrast, two states use the term 'Inclusive Education'
to describe their services: Western Australian services are known as 'Inclusive Education' and
Queensland employs a hybrid term, 'Inclusive Education and Learning and Disability Support'.

Tony Shaddock and his colleagues also pointed out that only the two territory governments, Australian Capital Territory (ACT) and Northern Territory, currently use 'Special Education' as a descriptor of services: 'Special Education and Wellbeing' (NT) and 'Special Education' (ACT). They concluded that in Australia, the use of 'special' to describe services for students with a disability was clearly not the preferred option. Other countries reflect this diversity of terminology: for example, the United States prefers 'special education', Japan 'special support education', Scotland 'educational provision for pupils with additional support needs', and Europe in general and South Africa 'special needs education' (the latter administered by the Directorate of Inclusive Education). It should not be assumed that this diversity of terminology is merely semantic, for, in most cases, it represents significant differences in the perceptions of children's disabilities and the scope of provisions designed for them.

An alternative to categorizations such as those outlined above is the Response to Intervention (RtI) model. In brief, this involves: (a) tracking the rate of growth in core subjects for all students in the class; (b) identifying students whose levels and rates of performance are significantly below their peers; and (c) systematically assessing the impact of evidence-based teaching adaptations on their achievement.[28] Above all, RtI is an approach focused on outcomes and on the evaluation of intervention; it thus integrates student assessment and instructional intervention. The RtI framework provides a system for delivering interventions of increasing intensity. Data based decision-making is the essence of good RtI practice.

In the United States, RtI has a statutory and regulatory foundation. Thus, the re-authorization of IDEA in 2004 moved away from the identification of a child with a specific learning difficulty on the basis of a severe discrepancy between achievement and intellectual ability. Instead, it favoured a process in which the child 'responds to scientific, research-based intervention', as specified in P.L. 108-446. Further, subsequent regulations required that prior to being referred for classification as a child with a specific learning disability, he or she should have been provided with 'appropriate high quality, research-based instruction in regular education settings' and that 'data-based documentation of repeated assessments of achievement at reasonable intervals, reflecting formal assessment of student progress during instruction' be provided. Only then, if the child has not made adequate progress after an appropriate period of time, could the child be referred for an evaluation to determine if special education should be provided. It would seem, too, that the development of RtI was provoked, at least in part, by concern that over 50% of IDEA funding was being spent in learning disability programmes, with around 70% of special education activities being related to learning disability cases.[29] However, it must be emphasized that RtI is not limited to students with learning disabilities, but is intended for all those who are at risk for school failure, as well as students with identified disabilities. It is increasingly being seen as an approach to adapting instruction to meet the needs of students who are having problems learning in the general curriculum. Thus,

> the purpose of an RtI system, which combines evidence-based instruction, increasing intensity of academic and behavioural supports, and progress monitoring, is to increase the number of at risk students whose needs are addressed so that they may learn successfully in general education before their problems become so severe that they need special education services.[30]

6.6 *Cultural perspectives on disability differ*

Culture may be defined as 'an historically unique configuration of the residue of the collective problem solving activities of a social group in its efforts to survive and prosper within its environment(s)'.[31] As will be seen below, it is a complex, multi-dimensional construct that goes some way to helping us understand how disability and issues such as inclusive education are interpreted in different societies. I will illustrate these relationships with reference to three disparate cultures: Japanese, the Middle East and the Māori in New Zealand.

Japan

Some years ago, I carried out a study of how Japanese schools accommodated to student diversity, in particular to students with disabilities.[32] In preparing for this project, I recognized that it must be situated in an understanding of the Japanese cultural context. Eight interlocking core values seemed to relate to the concept of student diversity within education:[33]

1   Japanese schools are not much concerned with individual differences. For example, a vice-principal asserted that 'Japanese education, as a whole, is not set up to accommodate individual differences. What we do here is provide education according to collectively established frames of reference'.

2   With rare exceptions, people are born with equal capacities to achieve. Thus, a principal explained that since a basic premise of Japanese education is that students are born with equal abilities, it does not make much sense to talk about 'ability differences' (*noryokusa*). Instead, it would be better to refer to 'difference in mastery levels' (*shujukudo*). The latter term implies that individual differences are created as a result of schoolwork and individual effort, rather than naturally given ability.

3   Individual differences are created through cumulative effort, not innate ability. In general, Japanese believe that eventual success depends not on one's innate capacities, but on one's efforts over a long period to accumulate knowledge (*tsumikasane*). Hence, potential is regarded in Japan as egalitarian – everyone has it, but some work harder than others to develop it. Except for students with clearly recognizable disabilities (who are mainly placed in special schools or special classes), teachers see all students as being capable of succeeding in school. Similarly, the presence of gifted students is not denied, but Japanese generally believe that such people are rare, and that one does not need a special talent to do well in school.

4   Since all students are equal, any special attention is seen as discriminatory. Japanese teachers thus feel ability grouping is discriminatory and impinges on students' rights to equal educational opportunity. Apart from violating the principle of fairness, Japanese teachers believe that ability-based grouping would have potentially detrimental effects on slow learners and would hurt students emotionally so much that they would lose their motivation to study.

5   Self-discipline is important and is moulded through experiencing hardship. Japanese culture values self-discipline, a personality characteristic that is moulded through experiences involving hardship (*kuro*), endurance (*gaman, nintai, shimbo, gambaru*), effort (*doryoku*), and the utmost self-exertion (*isshokemmei*). Japanese believe that hardship

builds character, and that anyone can acquire the habit and virtue of self-discipline. Suffering or hardship is believed to have a beneficial effect on the self, deepening and maturing it, removing self-centredness.

6   Effort and motivation to do well are as important as success. The Japanese give higher regard to people who are motivated than to those with only ability or talent. In short, the motive to do well is considered to be a virtue in its own right. Furthermore, motivation is viewed as a characteristic that teachers can actively cultivate. Japanese teachers and parents often use the expression, 'If you tried your hardest, it wouldn't matter if you succeeded or not.'

7   A supportive family environment that values education and motivates students is critical for their success. Where does motivation to study come from? 'Family environment', the majority of Japanese teachers, parents, and students would answer. Insofar that there are individual differences in ability, these primarily arise as the result of lack of effort (as noted above) which can, in turn, be mainly attributed to differences in upbringing and a lack of family support. Key to this is the mother's responsibility for creating a positive relationship with her children through *amae*, the assurance of security and unconditional love. Further, this begins early in life, as reflected in the proverb, 'The spirit of a two-year-old will last until 100.'

8   Much education is relations-oriented and emphasizes the importance of group life. Japanese culture prizes the relational aspect of self in interaction with others, the surrounding environment, aspects of oneself, and experiences Thus, in Japan, the educational enterprise is not just individual; instead, it is a series of carefully nurtured relationships, beginning with the family, extending to the school, and including identification with successively larger communities. For the Japanese, the most highly valued qualities are those that make a person 'human-like' (*ningen-rashii*) and the most valued quality is an ability to maintain harmony as members of a group or society. This ideal of group living (*shudan seikatsu*) means that while school achievements are important, they should be judged as a demonstration of a capacity to be a good social person. This does not mean, however, that the individual is entirely subordinated. Cooperating with others does not necessarily mean giving up the self, but in fact results from inner self-control and self-discipline and is the appropriate means by which one expresses and enhances oneself.

9   Education should be concerned with the whole person. It follows from the preceding core values that schools would have as their goal the creation of well-rounded human beings. Several writers have observed that this is indeed the case and that Japanese teachers consider students' emotional, social, physical and mental development to be as important as their cognitive development. Knowledge transmission is secondary to a more comprehensive emphasis on developing human beings (*ningen*), and at the core of ningen is *kokoro* (the centre of the physical, cognitive, spiritual, aesthetic and emotional self).

Middle East

In an insightful analysis, Ronald Brown pointed out that while a family's perception of and response to disability in the Middle East varied with exposure to modern western practices and their education level, cultural factors contine to play important roles.[34] He identified four cultural factors as playing a significant part in a family's response to a disability:

1   Image of wholeness: The ideal person fulfils traditional cultural values and norms, the totality of which contributes to a sense of wholeness in the mature person. These values include honour, courage, hospitality, marriage, procreation and active participation in family and community life. As Brown noted, the presence of a disability contradicts the cultural image of wholeness and this can lead to resistance of information that confirms the existence of any imperfection, or, if it is incontrovertible, then the disabled person might be seen as a member of a separate community, different and isolated from the mainstream of life.

2   Shame and family honour: In the Middle East, shame occurs as a result of a loss of honour resulting from some misdeed or condition created by a family member. It accrues not only to the individual, but also to the whole family. And it need not be an intentional act as it is sufficient that a condition that violates cultural norms exists. This factor can lead to a family suffering external judgments of inadequacy which may persist and lead to families taking protective measures such as avoiding any diagnosis of disabiity or any classification of the child as requiring special education. In some cases it may lead to the child kept in the home and in isolation from the extended family and the community.

3   Denial: As already suggested, the need to avoid family shame will often prolong parents' denial of a child's disability or leave it incomplete. This is particularly likely to occur when the child demonstrates few or none of the outward signs of disability such as deafness, blindness or physical disability. Brown pointed out that the outward appearance of normality is often vigorously reinforced by extended family members who encourage the parents to reject any suggestion of a problem. This may lead to parents embarking on a search for more favourable medical opinions and to them rejecting recommendations for any form of special educational assistance.

4   Fatalism: Traditionally, disabilities have been viewed as absolute and inalterable. This emanates from the belief that without some form of divine intervention, nothing can be done to ameliorate the condition, or, in some cases, nothing should be attempted since it is 'God's will'. Fatalism is an obstacle to any form of special education or inclusive education as it promotes apathy and a wait-and-see posture.

Māori in New Zealand

The Māori are the indigenous people of New Zealand and constitute approximately 15% of the population. My compatriots, Angus Macfarlane and Sonja Macfarlane, have stated that there are four key components in developing a culturally responsive pedagogy, the latter with respect to Māori children with special educational needs:[35]

1   Building relationships (*whanaungatanga*): this focuses on establishing relationships that take account of kinship and common locality. It means knowing students' names and how to pronounce them and knowing their backgrounds. It means teachers being accessible, approachable and part of the classroom learning community. It means establishing positive links with families (*whanau*) and the community.

2   Ethic of caring (*maaakitanga*): this is the cornerstone of culturally responsive pedagogy, according to both writers. It centres on respect, kindness, caring and compassion for others. It involves reciprocity, built on the faith, as one writer put it, 'that one day that which one has contributed will be returned'.[36] Translated into classroom practice, it means creating a safe haven, an unconditional caring atmosphere and sound intercultural communication.

3   Self-awareness and self-determination (*rangatiratanga*): this involves educators being aware of the impact their own culture may have on their interactions with their students. It means that they have an understanding of their own worldviews, cultural identities, biases, stereotypes and deficit beliefs they may hold about Māori.

4   Unity and bonding (*kotahitanga*): this core value means developing a sense of unity and inclusiveness within educational communities, which recognizes the personal prestige (*mana*) of every person. It means building up schools as communities, which are culturally safe for students from different cultural groups.[37]

While arguing that these four pillars are core cultural referents for working with Māori students, Angus Macfarlane rightly, in my view, suggested they are also appropriate for signalling to students from other cultures that their culture matters. In other words, they have universal applicability across all diversities.

6.7 Globally, perspectives on disability are changing

Other issues compound the problems of definition and categorization when attempts are made to determine the prevalence of disability. These were described in a report by UNESCO Institute for Statistics and UNICEF.[38] These bodies noted that, until recently, only data on the most visible or severe disabilities were reported, but that the availability and quality of information on children with disabilities has been improved by a shift in focus towards their functioning, as well as consideration of mild and moderate disabilities and impairments. However, these advancements have not yet reached all data collection systems.

Notwithstanding these problems, in 2011, the *World Report on Disability* estimated that more than 1 billion people (or 15% of the global population) live with some form of disability, with estimates for the number of children up to the age of 14 living with disabilities ranging between 93 million and 150 million.[39] Not surprisingly, UNESCO's Institute for Statistics and UNICEF have argued that such global estimates are speculative since they are derived from data whose quality is too varied and methods too inconsistent to provide any reliable evidence. They further note that attempts to generate global figures have been hampered by the lack of a common definition of disability and that, not surprisingly, international and national disability prevalence rates fluctuate wildly, depending on the different surveys used and the different questions asked.

This may change in the future as there is growing consensus that definitions of disability should include social as well as the more traditional medical factors. For example, the preamble to the UN's 2006 *Convention on the Rights of Persons with Disabilities* recognizes that 'disability is an evolving concept and that disability results from the interaction between persons with impairments and attitudinal and environmental barriers that hinders their full and effective participation in society on an equal basis with others'.[40] This emphasis on functional capacity gained prominence in the International Classification of Functioning, Disability and Health (ICF), developed by WHO[41] and subsequently in the International Classification of Functioning, Disability and Health for Children and Youth (ICF-CY).[42] More recently, in 2012, the World Health Organization and other stakeholders agreed to merge ICF and ICF-CY into one classification to arrive at a comprehensive ICF that addresses all aspects of functioning across a person's lifespan. However, this shift towards a social approach to disability is not yet fully embedded in practice and the ways in which disability is measured remain predominantly medical, with a continued focus on specific physical or intellectual impairments.

In light of the above, it is not surprising that the *World Disability Report* noted that estimates of the prevalence of children with disabilities vary substantially depending on the definition and measure of disability.[43] It cited the Global Burden of Disease estimate of the number of children aged 0–14 years experiencing 'moderate or severe disability' at 93 million (5.1%). It also cited another data set in which UNICEF in 2005 estimated the number of children with disabilities under age 18 at 150 million. As an example of the wide variance in prevalence estimates, the *World Disability Report* cited a review of the literature in low- and middle-income countries in which prevalence varied from 0.4% to 12.7% depending on the study and assessment tool. Finally, it mentioned a review in low-income countries that pointed to the problems in identifying and characterizing disability as a result of the lack of cultural and language-specific tools for assessment.

B How do students with different abilities differ in their achievement?

6.8 On the whole, students with disabilities have low levels of academic achievement

Despite low academic achievement being one of the chief factors in identifying children with special educational needs, there is surprisingly little information on their actual achievement. However, at least two countries, the United States and the United Kingdom, have begun to disaggregate their achievement data to enable some conclusions to be drawn. For the most part, these are a cause for concern.

United States

As pointed out by Margaret McLaughlin and her colleagues, until recently, there were few available data pertaining to educational outcomes of students with disabilities in the United States.[44] This changed with the 1997 Individuals with Disabilities Education Act that required that students with disabilities participate in large-scale state assessments.

In their summary of available achievement data, McLaughlin and her colleagues noted that almost two-thirds of the students with disabilities scored at or below the 25th percentile on standardized tests of reading and mathematics. Among the various groups of disabilities, 73% of students with learning disabilities scored below the 25th percentile, as did 85% of the students classified as having mental retardation or multiple disabilities.

In contrast, 25% of students with speech or visual impairments scored above the 50th percentile, while 10% of students with visual impairments scored in the top quartile on the reading assessments and 24% scored in the top quartile of a standardized math assessment. They noted that, in 2003/2004, it was not possible to make comprehensive state-by-state comparisons for only 70% of the states were reporting disaggregated assessment rates for students with disabilities.

United Kingdom

In 2009, the Lamb Inquiry reported that 'educational achievement for children with SEN/D [special educational needs/disability] is too low and the gap with their peers too wide'.[45] It attributed this to the long-term effects of the overall educational system and a society that places insufficient value on achieving good outcomes for disabled children and children with SEN/D and that too many schools focus the best teachers on those children with the highest abilities. As well as low achievement, the Lamb Inquiry drew attention to the disproportionate exclusion of children with SEN/D from schools, noting that they were eight times more likely to be excluded than their peers.

However, there is some encouraging evidence of improvements in the achievements of these students in the United Kingdom. Thus, between 2005/2006 and 2010/2011, the percentage of pupils without SEN at the end of Key Stage 4 achieving 5 or more GCSEs at grades A* to C had increased from 66.3% to 88.9%. The comparable data for students with SEN without a statement had increased from 19.8% to 59.2%, while for students with SEN with a statement it had increased from 8.7% to 24.9%.[46]

6.9 People with disabilities are disadvantaged when it comes to employment

Even in developed countries, employment rates for people with disabilities are very low.[47] In a US study, for example, among all working-age (18-64) people with disabilities, only 21% said they were employed full- or part-time, compared with 59% of working-age people without disabilities. In England, an overview of disability and the transition to adulthood noted that disabled children (a) were at high risk of growing up in poverty, (b) were less likely than non-disabled to achieve adult goals in employment, economic independence, personal autonomy, independent housing, and (c) were less likely than non-disabled to live independently of their parents.[48]

These problems are caused or accentuated by situations in which many children with disabilities do not attend school or they drop out at primary or secondary education level, undoubtedly causing them to sequentially be unemployed or underemployed.[49] Even those who complete their secondary education are at risk for unemployment or under-employment resulting from low expectations and discrimination from employers and the community. This is both a social and an economic loss, which must be actively addressed and redressed.

6.10 Disproportionality is widespread in special education

As I have already noted, special education systems in many countries have disproportionate representations of boys (Chapter 2, sections 2.24, 2.40), children from low socio-economic homes (Chapter 3, section 3.11) and children from ethnic minorities (Chapter 4, sections 4.16, 4.22, 4.23 and 4.34). Disproportionality is generally defined as 'the representation of a particular group of students at a rate different than that found in the general population'.[50] In many countries, this apparent over-representation in special education of certain groups has caused concern to policy-makers who worry about the probability of such students being misidentified, misclassified, and inappropriately placed in special education programmes. It is interesting to observe that placement in special education is seen as a negative outcome by many of those who express concern about the over-representation of certain groups. Indeed, it is ironic to consider over-representation to be a problem if students are purportedly gaining the advantage of special education![51]

Gender

As I pointed out in Chapter 2, there is clear international evidence of a gender imbalance in the incidence of disabilities (section 2.25) and in special education enrolments (section 2.24).

Ethnicity

Disproportionate representation of students from ethnic minority backgrounds in special education has been a persistent concern in the field since the 1980s, particularly in the United States[52] and the United Kingdom.[53] In passing, it is worth noting that an opposite situation pertained in South Africa where, under apartheid, *whites* were over-represented in special education.[54] Two countries have detailed statistics on the ethnicities of students classified as having special educational needs – the United States and England. Some of these data were summarized in section 4.16 in Chapter 4 and won't be repeated here.

If we accept that since ethnic disproportionality is highly likely to be a valid construct, it is therefore appropriate to turn our attention to possible explanations for it. These are many and varied and include such factors as poverty and socio-economic disadvantage (see Chapter 3 and below), the lack of congruence between the cultural capital of families and schools (see Chapter 1), the legacy of deficit thinking and bias relating to racial/ethnic minorities (see Chapter 4), the history of school segregation (at least in the United States), resource inequalities, asynchronous power relationships between school authorities and parents, culturally inappropriate or insensitive assessment practices, and inadequate professional development opportunities for teachers.[55] It is to the first of these explanations – poverty – that I shall briefly turn my attention.

Poverty[56]

The consistent overlap of race and poverty in the United States has led some to suggest that race is simply a 'proxy' for poverty and that 'ethnic disproportionality in special education is in large measure an artefact of the effects of poverty'.[57] Support for a race-poverty connection in explaining disproportionality in special education can be found in a range of sources. For example, a group of American writers have argued that there are at least four assumptions implicit in a logical sequence linking poverty and disproportionality in special education:[58]

1   Minority students are disproportionately poor and hence are more likely to be exposed to a variety of socio-demographic stressors associated with poverty.
2   Factors associated with living in poverty leave children less developmentally ready for schooling and ultimately yield negative academic and behavioural outcomes.
3   Students who are low achieving or at risk for negative behavioural outcomes are more likely to be referred to, and ultimately found eligible for, special education services.
4   Therefore, poverty is an important contributing factor that increases the risk, presumably in a linear fashion, of special education placement for minority students.

C What causes differences in abilities?

6.11 Introduction

Given the great range of differences in human abilities, it is not surprising that many factors account for them. In this section, I will present an overview of classification systems and then focus on two more specific causes: those linked to brain functioning and those associated with disasters and conflicts.

6.12 Disabilities arise from multiple causes

There are broadly two main causes of disabilities in children – endogenous factors originating from within the individual and exogenous factors originating from outside of the individual.[59] Endogenous factors are those that reflect characteristics of the child such as temperament and neurobiological deficits. Exogenous factors are those that represent influences external to the child, such as malnutrition, family stress, constrained social networks and, as we shall see below, disasters and conflicts. Despite the fact that research has continued to focus on single factor explanations of primary causal significance, current conceptualizations are beginning to acknowledge the complex interactions between both factors.[60]

In more detail,[61] endogenous factors include the following:

- Chromosomal disorders such as Down syndrome, fragile X-chromosome syndrome, Prader-Willi syndrome, Rett syndrome, neurofibromatosis and tuberous sclerosis.
- Hereditary disorders such as phenylketonuria, galactosemia and Tay-Sachs disease.

Exogenous factors include:

- Congenital factors, which can be grouped as follows: (1) metabolic: neonatal hypothyroidism; (2) toxic: lead poisoning, foetal alcohol syndrome, prenatal exposure to substances; and (3) infections: rubella, syphillis and toxoplasmosis.
- During the prenatal period, there are possible pregnancy complications, such as toxemia and uncontrolled diabetes, intrauterine malnutrition, vaginal haemorrhages, placenta previa and umbilical cord prolapse.
- During the perinatal period, there are common birth complications, such as prolonged foetal suffering with neonatal anoxia, asphyxia related with suffocation, and inadequate use of high forceps.
- During the postnatal period, complications include encephalopathy from hyperbilirubinemia and infections (encephalitis and meningitis).

- Socio-cultural factors, chief of which is poverty, play an important role, particularly in developing countries. There is clear evidence of links between poverty and poor prenatal, perinatal and postnatal health care, adolescent maternity, family instability, poor natal health care due to multiple and inadequate caregivers and health professionals, low level of stimulation and education, in addition to infant mistreatment.[62]

6.13 It is important to understand the relationship between the functioning of the brain and disabilities

The brain, with its 100 billion nerve cells, is the seat of our mental faculties, regulating our bodily functions, as well as performing such higher functions as language, reasoning and memory. Much has been learned about the relationship between the brain and disabilities as a result of the development of brain imaging techniques such as electroencephalograms (EEG), positron emission tomography (PET), brain electrical activity mapping (BEAM) and Magnetic Resonance Imaging (MRI). Much, too, has been learned from experiments on animals, especially rats, as well as on humans.

Research is increasingly confirming that neurological factors contribute to a range of disabilities, as a result of either significant or minimal central nervous system dysfunction. Some of these will be summarized in this section.

Traumatic brain injury (TBI)

TBI typically impacts on cognitive and neurobehavioural functioning.[63] Individuals with TBI experience a range of cognitive deficits, including varying degrees of impairment in attention, memory, speed of information processing, communication, executive functioning, affective stability and social functioning.

Learning disabilities

A recent review outlined research on dyslexia, which shows evidence of an unusual structure of one region of the brain – the 'planum temporale'.[64] In approximately 70% of normal brains this area is typically asymmetrical, whereas in individuals with dyslexia it is mostly symmetrical. Since the planum temporale is important to language, some writers suggest that this unusual symmetry must be related to the occurrence of dyslexia. However, Pullen et al. urge caution in drawing this conclusion, noting the limitations of technologies to measure brain physiology and electrical activity in individuals with dyslexia.

Attention deficit/hyperactivity disorder (ADHD)

In a review of the literature, Karen Rooney notes that brain imaging research has provided 'suggestive evidence' that the pre-frontal cortex, frontal lobes, basal ganglia cerebellum, corpus callosum and right parietal regions of the brain are involved in the occurrence of ADHD.[65]

Emotional and behavioural disorders

Among the biological and social factors implicated in emotional and behavioural disorders is traumatic brain injury (TBI). As noted by James Kauffman and Timothy Landrum, studies of children who have experienced TBI show evidence of associated emotional and behavioural effects, including failure to comprehend humour or read social cues; becoming easily tired, angered or frustrated; irritability; extreme mood swings; and even depression.[66]

6.14 Disasters and conflicts can cause or exacerbate disabilities

As my colleague, Valerie Karr, and I pointed out in our recent book, *Conflict, Disaster and Disability: Ensuring Equality,*[67] people with disabilities are among the most adversely affected when natural disasters strike or during armed conflicts. They experience higher mortality rates, have fewer available resources, have less access to help, and are often overlooked during emergency evacuation, relief, recovery and rebuilding efforts. This situation is contrary to Article 11 of UN *Convention on the Rights of Persons with Disabilities,* which requires that states must take all necessary measures to ensure the protection and safety of people with disabilities during situations of armed conflict, humanitarian emergencies and natural disasters.

As we noted, the UN obligations are of considerable significance given the sheer numbers of people affected by disasters and conflict around the world. Taking four of the most common natural disasters – earthquakes, tropical cyclones, floods and droughts – a 2004 United Nations report estimated that 75% of the world's population lived in areas affected at least once during the period 1980-2000.[68] The same report noted that, during that period, more than 1.5 million people were killed by natural disasters, at a rate of 184 deaths per day; these fatalities occurred disproportionately in countries classified as low human development. There are two types of armed conflicts. Derived from the Geneva Conventions of 1949, international humanitarian law distinguishes between (a) international armed conflicts, opposing two or more states, and (b) non-international armed conflicts, between governmental forces and non-governmental armed groups, or between such groups only.[69] Taken together, according to the United Nations Development Programme, during the 1990s a total of 53 armed conflicts resulted in 3.9 million deaths.[70]

Disasters and conflicts not only contribute to the incidence of disabilities, but they also increase the vulnerability of those who already have disabilities. They consistently escalate the incidence of disabilities through physical injuries and mental trauma. As well, those with existing disabilities may acquire new impairments. Children with existing or new disabilities are particularly at risk because of their often-limited ability to report abusive experiences. Disasters and conflicts exacerbate the vulnerabilities of people with disabilities, leading them to get stuck in a vicious circle of poverty.

Another compounding factor is refugee/displaced person status. Most such people, particularly those with disabilities, face a daunting array of barriers to their participation and well-being. These include language difficulties, financial pressures, trauma, concern for families in their home countries and difficulties in accessing services. In some receiving countries, refugees with disabilities are often overlooked and neglected, even hidden, leading to increased exclusion and isolation. Furthermore, when services for them are made available, they tend to focus on those with physical impairments, seldom on those with sensory impairments and almost never on those with intellectual impairments.

There is clear evidence that disasters and conflicts have a disproportionate impact on people with disabilities. According to emergency management statistics, when natural disasters strike, those with disabilities die in far higher percentages of the population than other people[71] and have far fewer resources and access to help in refugee camps and in post-disaster environments. For example, in the case of Hurricane Katrina in New Orleans, persons with disabilities were left behind in the evacuation efforts.[72] In addition, environmental barriers – such as destroyed roads and blocked passages – created greater obstacles to those with mobility issues. In the case of the 2004 earthquake and associated tsunami in Japan, the death rate among persons with disabilities was at least twice as high as among the general population. Similarly, over 40% of the fatalities in the 2009 bushfires in Australia were categorized as 'vulnerable' and included people with disabilities. Other situations of conflicts and disasters similarly impact disproportionately on persons with disabilities for such reasons as disruptions to their normal physical, social and economic networks, and the inaccessibility of evacuation facilities. In addition, there can be destruction of institutions that provide services to people with disabilities, the displacement of key staff, the unavailability or inaccessibility of information about risks, support agencies not knowing how to help those with disabilities, disrupted social support networks, assistive devices being lost or damaged and the lack of procedures for tracking people with disabilities in times of crises. Further, for persons with disabilities living in emergency shelters, sanitary latrine arrangements may be inaccessible and where food aid is distributed in refugee camps, those with disabilities are often at the back of the queue and many go hungry.[73] Persons with disabilities are also more exposed to risks, such as physical and sexual violence, discrimination and harassment in times of disasters and conflicts. Of those with disabilities, children are most at risk.

D How should education accommodate to students with different abilities?

6.15 Introduction

In this section, I will present strategies that have been shown to be effective in improving the educational outcomes of learners with disabilities. As with the previous chapters, the strategies are broadly grouped into three overlapping levels:

1   society and system-level accommodations;
2   school-level accommodations; and
3   classroom-level accommodations

I Society and system-level accommodations

6.16 Sign, ratify and abide by the UN Convention on the Rights of People with Disabilities

As I noted in section 6.3, the *Convention on the Rights of Persons with Disabilities* came into force on 3 May 2008. For the benefit of all people with disabilities, the remaining countries should sign and ratify this *Convention*. Even more importantly, all countries should abide by its various articles, particularly Article 24 as far as this chapter is concerned. The *Convention* could well form the basis of legislation, policies and practices regarding children with disabilities.

6.17 Recognize the economic benefits of accommodating to children with disabilities

As with other disadvantaged people, there are distinct economic benefits to providing people with disabilities with economic opportunities. The *World Report on Disability* pointed out that failure to do so carries wide-ranging and substantial indirect costs.[74] Economic costs include (a) the loss of productivity from insufficient investment in educating disabled children, (b) exits from work or reduced work related to the onset of disability, and (c) the loss of taxes related to the loss of productivity. Non-economic costs include social isolation and stress. Losses increase when family members leave employment or reduce the number of hours worked to care for family members with disabilities.

The *World Report on Disability* noted that estimating disability-related loss in productivity and associated taxes is complex and requires statistical information, which is seldom available. However, one such estimate, for Canada using data from the 1998 National Population Health Survey, suggested that the loss of work through short-term and long-term disability was 6.7% of GDP. In a different analysis, Bangladesh data has shown that the cost of disability due to foregone income from a lack of schooling and employment, both of people with disabilities and their caregivers, was estimated at US$ 1.2 billion annually, or 1.7% of GDP.[75]

6.18 Ensure that children with disabilities receive education

According to UNESCO Institute for Statistics and UNICEF, children with disabilities are among the most disadvantaged in terms of missing out on education. As well as the problems in determining the prevalence of disability, which I indicated in Section 6.5, these bodies attribute this situation to several other factors. These include education systems that are not adapted or equipped to meet the basic needs of such children and the lack of everything from accessible school buildings to teachers who have been trained to teach in inclusive settings. As well, they often miss out because continuing stigma around disability excludes them from the wider society. Other 'supply barriers' include (a) children with physical disabilities being confronted by inaccessible school facilities, (b) children with visual or hearing impairments struggling in environments with inadequate light or poor acoustics, (c) problems with transport often preventing children with disabilities from making the journey to school, (d) inflexible curricula and examination systems, and (e) the lack of appropriate training and support for teachers to teach children with disabilities in regular schools. Very often, these barriers are exacerbated by the intersection of disability with poverty, gender, ethnicity and geographic location, which contribute to children with disabilities facing multiple forms of discrimination that lead to their exclusion from society and education.

The cumulative result of these factors is the low participation rate of children with disabilities in education. For example, a 2004 study in Malawi found that a child with a disability was twice as likely to have never attended school than a child without a disability.[76] As well, while India has achieved close to universal enrolment in primary education, a 2009 survey showed that out of 2.9 million children with disabilities, 990,000 (34%) were out of school. The percentages were even higher among children with multiple disabilities (59%), intellectual disabilities (48%) and speech impairments (36%).[77]

Fortunately, many countres are beginning to address this situation, spurred along by their ratification of the UN's 2006 *Convention on the Rights of People with Disabilities*. As noted by UNESCO's Institute for Statistics and UNICEF, there are two main strands to this shift: broad social reforms beyond the education sector and reforms within the sector itself. Broad social reforms are increasingly promoting inclusive education for children with disabilities at all levels (including early childhood education) and supporting the practice and culture of inclusion across education systems by reviewing national policies in all relevant sectors – health and social, as well as education. Sector-wide strategies, programmes and budgets should be reviewed to determine whether they include concrete actions to support children with disabilities and their families. These strategies include making curricula and learning materials, processes and assessments accessible and applicable to every child. As well, teachers should receive practical training and ongoing support for teaching in inclusive settings and have the backing of schools and communities that are committed to inclusive approaches.

6.19 Develop early prevention and intervention programmes

According to the *World Disability Report*, early identification and intervention can reduce the level of educational support children with disabilities may require throughout their schooling and ensure they reach their full potential.[78] Children with disabilities may require early access to specialist health and education professionals such as occupational therapists, physiotherapists, speech therapists and educational psychologists to support their learning. The importance of such services being coordinated was emphasized in a review of early childhood interventions in Europe.[79] For further discussions of early prevention and intervention, see section 1.27 in Chapter 1 and section 3.26 in Chapter 3.

6.20 Engage parents in their children's education

Parents[80] play important, if not critical, roles in educating and supporting their children. They are first and foremost parents, with all the rights and responsibilities of that role, but they are also sources of information, partners in designing and implementing programmes for their children, and 'consumers' of education.[81] As well, some of them may be in need of direct support, in the form of training, counselling or psychiatric care.

Parents have also played and continue to play a critical role in advocating on behalf of their children for better services. For example, one of the earliest advocates of family involvement in rehabilitation and special education, Gunnar Dybwad, recounted how parents of children with mental retardation banded together in many countries during the 1940s and 1950s to demand justice for their children and an end to discriminatory practices.[82]

Further, parents are most probably the only people who are involved with their child's education throughout their entire school years – and beyond. They are thus likely to have great interest in their child's learning overall and be the most affected by the outcomes of any schooling decisions. Parents know their child's development and the factors that may be responsible for their special educational needs better than anyone else. They often have insights into what motivates their child and which teaching and management strategies are most effective. Thus, in the United States, for example, it is mandatory for parents to be involved in the development of Individual Education Plans and they have due process rights to enforce such plans.[83]

Working with parents increases the likelihood of consistency in expectations of behaviour at home and at school. It also increases the opportunities for reinforcing appropriate behaviours and increasing the range of reinforcers that are available to do this. Children will obtain positive messages about the importance of their education if they see their parents and educators working together.

Special consideration must be given to disabled parents' involvement in their children's education. A recent UK study reported on findings from 24 case studies involving parents who had a range of impairments. Common themes included the perceived importance and benefits of involvement, the need for effective communication and access, and the significance of an inclusive school ethos.[84]

In the United Kingdom, there are quite explicit prescribed statutory duties and guidance about various roles and responsibilities concerning all parents' involvement in the education of their children with special educational needs. The former are expressed in the Special Educational Needs and Disability Act 2001 and the Education Act 1996, and the latter in the *Special Educational Needs Code of Practice* of 2001. One of the fundamental principles underpinning the latter was stated as 'parents have a vital role to play in supporting their child's education' (p. 8). Similarly, critical success factors included special education professionals and parents working in partnership and special education professionals taking into account the views of individual parents in respect of their child's particular needs. Key principles in communicating and working in partnership with parents included the following guidance for professionals:

- acknowledge and draw on parental knowledge and expertise in relation to their child;
- focus on the children's strengths as well as areas of additional need;
- recognize the personal and emotional investment of parents and be aware of their feelings;
- ensure that parents understand procedures, are aware of how to access support in preparing their contributions, and are given documents to be discussed well before meetings;
- respect the validity of differing perspectives and seek constructive ways of reconciling different viewpoints;
- respect the differing needs parents themselves may have, such as a disability, or communication and linguistic barriers; and
- recognize the need for flexibility in the timing and structure of meetings.

I turn now to parent training programmes. There is considerable evidence for the efficacy of such programmes, two of which will be summarized here. First, there is *Parent Management*

Training – sometimes referred to as Behavioural Parent Training – in which parents are typically helped to use effective behavioural management strategies in their homes. This strategy is often based on the assumption that children's conduct problems result from maladaptive parent–child interactions, such as paying attention to deviant behaviour, ineffective use of commands and harsh punishments. Thus, parents are trained to define and monitor their child's behaviour, avoid coercive interchanges and positively reinforce acceptable behaviour by implementing developmentally appropriate consequences for their child's defiance. Such parent training includes a mixture of didactic instruction, live or videotaped modelling and role-plays. The emphasis is on teaching behavioural strategies, which focus on transmitting knowledge about antecedents and consequences of behaviour. Parents learn to observe and identify problematic behaviours in their children and to reframe them in ways that may lead to insight into the reasons behind them.[85]

Second, there is the *Incredible Years* programme – a variant of Parent Management Training – but which includes programmes for children and teachers, as well as parents. Aimed at children aged from birth to 12 years and their parents, Incredible Years comprises a series of two-hours per week group discussion (a minimum of 18 sessions for families referred because of abuse and neglect). The programme contains videotaped modelling sessions, which show a selection from 250 vignettes of approximately 2 minutes each in which parents interact with their children in both appropriate and inappropriate ways. After each vignette, the therapist leads a discussion of the relevant interactions and solicits parents' responses. Parents are taught play and reinforcement skills, effective limit-setting and non-violent discipline techniques, problem-solving approaches promoting learning and development, and ways of becoming involved in their children's schooling.[86] As well, *Incredible Years* has an add-on programme to facilitate parents in supporting their child's schoolwork. In addition, there is a classroom programme, with over 60 lesson plans for all age ranges of children[87] and a teacher-training programme in classroom management of children with externalizing and internalizing problems that operates similarly to that of the parent-training programme.[88] *Incredible Years* has been adopted successfully in the United States (where it originated), and countries such as England, Wales, Ireland, Norway, Sweden, Denmark, New Zealand and Russia. According to research by John Reid and his colleagues, the programme was as efficacious for parents of the most disadvantaged children, as for those parents with a higher socio-economic demographic.[89]

6.21 Ensure that students with disabilities and special educational needs have access to the general curriculum

In the United States, the Individuals with Disabilities Education Act of 1997 and the No Child Left Behind Act of 2001 required school districts to provide access to the general education curriculum for students with disabilities. Similar requirements are in place in many other countries, including Scotland, England, Finland, South Africa and New Zealand. Increasingly, the notion of two separate curricula – one for mainstream students and another for students with disabilities – is being seen as inappropriate. The move towards inclusion is accelerating this trend away from two-tier education systems.[90]

In developing an inclusive curriculum, governments should take account of the key characteristics of such a curriculum as identified in international documents, namely: flexibility, relevance and adjustability to the diverse characteristics and needs of lifelong learners.[91] These requirements have given rise to - or reflected in - the idea of *universal design for learning*, in which the aim is to create curricula that are flexible enough to embrace all students, including those with disabilities.[92] It does this by providing students with (a) multiple means of representation (e.g., different modalities of vision, hearing and touch and through means such as audio, video, text, speech, Braille, photographs and computers), and (b) multiple means of action or expression (e.g., through writing, speaking, drawing and video recording).

6.22 Ensure that students with disabilities and special educational needs have access to the national or state assessments

Just as many countries are moving towards providing access to the general education curriculum for students with disabilities, so too they are moving towards expecting such students to participate in national or state assessment regimes.[93] These moves are part of the standards-based reform in education that is dominating much of the educational and political discourse around the world. For example, in the United States, accountability in special education in the past was defined exclusively in terms of students' progress on Individual Education Plans. That changed in the Individuals with Disabilities Act of 1997, which required all students, including those with disabilities, to participate in their states' accountability systems. However, both that Act and the No Child Left Behind Act of 2002 required the provision of alternative assessments for students who could not participate in state or district assessments with or without accommodations. Similar requirements are present in the United Kingdom, New Zealand and many other countries.

6.23 Develop and implement inclusive education policies

In almost every country, inclusive education has emerged as one of the most the dominant issues in the education of SWSEN. Since around the 1970s the field of special needs education has moved from a segregation paradigm through integration to a point where inclusion is central to contemporary discourse. Even so, in many countries the concept of inclusion is not unproblematic, both conceptually and practically.[94]

The almost universal shift towards inclusive education reflects four main factors. First, inclusive education, if it is handled appropriately, will result in students with disabilities gaining academically and socially and will improve their self-esteem. Second, it is now generally accepted that such students have a right to be educated alongside their non-disabled peers, as reflected in Article 24 of the UN *Convention on the Rights of Disabled Persons* (see section 6.3). You may recall that this includes the statement, 'With a view to realizing this right without discrimination and on the basis of equal opportunity, States Parties shall ensure an inclusive education system at all levels.' Third, inclusive education increases the probability of students with disabilities acquiring competitive employment, higher earnings and enrolment in other vocational education opportunities, and becoming taxpayers rather than recipients of welfare. A fourth argument is sometimes advanced that inclusive education is more economically viable than special school placement, given the expense involved in transporting and accommodating students in special schools that might be some distance from their homes.[95] It is also worth noting that research indicates that other students do not suffer from being educated alongside their disabled peers. Indeed, they have been shown to gain academically, as well as obtaining a greater appreciation of the diversity of society and of social justice and equality.[96]

In his review of efficacy studies of inclusion, UK scholar Geoff Lindsay concluded that they do not provide a ringing endorsement of the concept.[97] Among the criticisms he put forward is what he believed to be an imbalance of emphasis on the social (environmental) model compared with the medical (within child) model. While supporting the trend towards the social model, Lindsay felt that a narrow adherence to it has promoted the notion that inclusion is solely a question of rights and that the question of its efficacy in practice is irrelevant. He argued that it is not a matter of one or the other model but of finding the right balance between the two and of understanding how each interacts with the other. Similarly, US writers Kevin Kavale and Mark Mostert have claimed that the evidence is mixed at best and clearly suggests the need for caution.[98] They noted, for example, that analyses of regular classrooms in the United States show that they are places where undifferentiated, large group instruction dominate and teachers make few adaptations, with the result that there is little individualized programming. Other writers have criticized the employment of what they perceive to be rhetoric on behalf of inclusive education, at the expense of empirical evidence. Thus, with a US frame of reference, Douglas and Lynn Fuchs argued that 'the field's rhetoric has become increasingly strident and its perspective increasingly insular and dissociated from general education's concerns'.[99] They felt that radical proponents of full inclusion want nothing less than the elimination of special education and its continuum of placements. In a similar vein, Kavale and Mostert complained that the ideology of full inclusion has influenced policy and practice disproportionately to its claims of efficacy. Further, James Kauffman questioned the validity of some assumptions made by 'full inclusionists', suggesting that they have 'lost their heads about place, about the spaces occupied by people with disabilities' and that physical access does not necessarily imply instructional access.[100]

While I accept the validity of many of these criticisms, my own perspective is that until inclusive education has been implemented in a fully comprehensive way, it is premature to make judgments as to its efficacy. Much of research to date seems to have looked at inclusive education mainly in placement terms, rather than as a full suite of provisions, as I have described in section 1.8.

One of the consequences of adopting inclusivist policies is the re-examination of the role of special schools. For example, a 2003 report from the European Agency for Development in Special Needs Education noted a trend in European countries in which special schools and institutes were being transformed into resource centres, with such functions as (a) training teachers and other professionals, (b) developing and disseminating materials and methods (c) supporting mainstream schools and parents, (d) providing short term or part-time help for individual students, and (e) supporting students to enter the labour market.[101] For example, in

Sweden in 2001, all special schools, except for those providing sign language education, were re-designated as special needs resource centres to support inclusion in mainstream classes. A specialist teacher working as a member of the mainstream school staff mainly supplied this support. Another example is provided by South Africa. When it emerged from the apartheid era, South Africa was determined to create special needs education as a non-racial and integrated component of its education system. Thus, in a 2001 White Paper, a phased conversion of special schools to resource centres was recommended.[102]

6.24 Protect the rights of children with disabilities at times of disasters and conflicts

In section 6.14, I mentioned the book on disasters and conflict that I co-edited with Valerie Karr. I turn now to six of the recommendations we drew from the 25 substantive chapters.

First, underpinning all of the chapters was the explicit or implicit claim that persons with disabilities have the same rights as all others in a society to have their needs taken fully into account in disasters and conflicts. This does not imply that they should be treated exactly the same as all other persons, but rather that they should enjoy equal legal rights, while at the same time receiving additional support that takes account of their particular needs.

Second, account should be taken of the fact that children – particularly those with disabilities – are especially vulnerable at times of disasters and conflicts. As noted by one of our writers, a UNICEF report from 2003 indicated that in the previous decade 2 million children died due to armed conflicts and 6 million were severely injured, many of whom became permanently disabled.[103]

Third, action plans to deal with the impact of disasters and conflicts should be designed and implemented at all levels – globally, nationally, regionally and locally. At every phase of the cycle in dealing with disasters and conflicts, a multi-level approach is called for. The United States has perhaps the most comprehensive, multi-level structure for dealing with hazards, engaging federal, state, local, tribal and territorial governments, the private sector and non-governmental organizations.[104]

Fourth, persons with disabilities should be mainstreamed in the design and implementation of action plans. Such involvement could be at the level of individuals or via disability organizations representing their interests.

Fifth, action plans should be comprehensive and include consideration of the basic needs of people with disabilities. They should ensure that persons with disabilities have appropriate access to basic requirements such as: (a) health services, including medication and physiotherapy; (b) nutrition; (c) water; (d) shelter; (e) sanitation; (f) education, including sex education; (g) security and protection; (h) transport; (i) communication systems available in multiple formats, including ICT; (j) assistive devices; and (k) employment opportunities.

Sixth, it is essential to recognize that social networks at the community level play a critical role helping people with disabilities deal with conflicts and disasters. As Daniel Aldrich has pointed out, scholars are increasingly incorporating a recognition of the role of social networks and social capital in determining outcomes in disasters.[105]

6.25 Develop policies on transition from school to post-school situations for children with disabilities[106]

The importance of taking a life-long and life-wide perspective on the education of people with disabilities is being more recognized. This draws our attention to the importance of preparing students for making an effective transition from school to post-school situations. The International Labour Office defines transition as:

> a process of social orientation that implies status change and role (e.g., from student to trainees, from trainee to worker and from dependence to independence), and is central to integration into society ... Transition requires a change in relationships, routines and self-image. In order to guarantee a smoother transition from school to the workplace, young people with disabilities need to develop goals and identify the role they want to play in society.[107]

The purposes of transition programmes for students with disabilities are many: to provide them with the academic and social skills to enable them to become competitively employed and/or to continue their participation in education, to enhance their economic and social welfare, and to enjoy an enhanced quality of life through becoming as independent as possible. To achieve these goals, transition programmes should be the shared responsibility of many agencies and organizations: education, labour, welfare, health, NGOs and, of course, governments at various levels within country systems.

For many countries, however, effecting a successful transition programme from school to post-school life for students with disabilities is an ongoing challenge. Unfortunately, numerous countries fail to effectively manage the process. Common underlying reasons are society's lack of awareness of people with disabilities, lack of understanding of their situation and lack of knowledge on how to include them, as well as discrimination and over-protection. Even where there is legislative support for the employment of people with disabilities, they continue to face considerable stigmatization. An increasing challenge is to find work in situations where disruptive technology is rapidly displacing jobs that might otherwise have been filled by individuals with major disabilities.

The result is that individuals with disabilities are frequently overlooked as a productive labour force with many of them not working and not looking for work, but relying on their parents or family, or living on social welfare for their economic and physical support. Sometimes they are even considered by their families and communities to be shameful persons who do not need to be educated. Even in developed countries, employment rates for people with disabilities are very low. In a US study, for example, among all working-age (18-64 years) people with disabilities, only 21% said they were employed full- or part-time, compared with 59% of working-age people without disabilities.[108] Also, in England, an overview of disability and the transition to adulthood noted that disabled children were at high risk of growing up in poverty, were less likely than non-disabled to achieve adult goals in employment, economic independence, personal autonomy, independent housing and were less likely than non-disabled to live independently of their parents.[109]

Underlying assumptions

In designing transition systems for students with disabilities, the following assumptions are made:

- Transition to adulthood is a complex process, with many factors affecting students' lives after they finish their schooling: their own and their family's characteristics, economic conditions, community contexts and the availability of services.[110]
- People with disabilities are at a disadvantage on the open labour market, not necessarily because of any inherent incapacity associated with their disability, but because of their low level of access to education and training and their lack of appropriate qualifications.[111]
- People with disabilities are diverse, with varying abilities, interests and needs.
- Quality transition programmes for students with disabilities must be based on the expectation that all such students can achieve successful post-school outcomes, including post-secondary education and training, meaningful employment and a satisfying quality of life as an adult.
- Societies have a responsibility to identify and remove barriers confronting people with disabilities in education and employment.
- There is no single pre-determined pathway for persons with disabilities throughout the transition process. One size does not fit all. Rather, there should be multiple options with flexibility to switch between school education, further education and workplace experience with relative ease.
- Educational and employment opportunities and outcomes are likely to vary considerably from person to person and from society to society.[112]
- Quality transition programmes result from the support and commitment of qualified and knowledgeable personnel who collaborate with each other, with the families of students with disabilities, and with the students themselves.
- Students with disabilities have diverse abilities, interests, needs and aspirations and these can change over time as they mature and gather more experiences. Thus, transition planning should be seen as an ongoing process, rather than a once-and-for-all event.[113]
- The focus of transition planning is on what the person with a disability is capable of performing, whilst at the same time paying due regard to the challenges their disabilities create. In other words, the underlying philosophy driving the education of students with disabilities should be a strengths-based model, rather than a deficit model.[114]
- The student with a disability is central to transition planning.
- The ultimate aim of transition planning is to enhance the individuals' quality of life as citizens and as members of their culture, to maximize their potential for work and education, and to help them achieve a satisfying balance between independence and interdependence.

In the remainder of this section, I will briefly summarize a set of Standards, arranged in six domains, that I developed for the Jakarta office of UNESCO in 2011. They were intended for the use of governments, ministries, agencies and individuals involved in planning and implementing comprehensive transition systems for students with disabilities from school to post-school settings, especially work. The Standards have been developed from international best practices, legislation, policies and research literature, as well as comments from participants in two workshops I conducted in South East Asia. I recognize that most of the Standards have their origins in developed countries and that not all countries are in a position to implement all of them because of limitations in resources. As is the case with the UN *Convention on the Rights of Persons with Disabilities*,[115] 'progressive realization' of most of the Standards, in line with the resources of individual countries, is expected.

Domain I: Raise awareness on the right to education and the right to employment. For example, steps are taken to raise awareness in the community on the unemployment and underemployment of people with disabilities.

Domain II: Strengthen policies: For example, policies are put in place through legislation and regulations to ensure equal opportunities for students with disabilities to access quality school-to-post-school education and/or work transition programmes, including vocational training.

Domain III: Strengthen personnel involved in transition: For example, school principals and school governing bodies receive training to take on leadership roles in conducting school-to-post-school transition programmes for students with disabilities.

Domain IV: Strengthen school educational services for students with disabilities: For example, the specific curricula of school to post-school transition programmes are comprehensive and relevant to the needs of students with disabilities and in designing curricula for students with disabilities, a wide range of potential occupations is considered. Transition-specific curricula include components that are valued by employers and that correlate with essential job duties.

Domain V: Strengthen cooperation: For example, a Joint Committee (perhaps called the 'National Transition Team') consisting of representatives of key ministries is established to collaboratively manage school to post-school transition for students with disabilities. Its functions would include aligning legislation, policies and resources and developing a comprehensive national plan to assist and promote transition.[116]

Domain VI: Strengthen monitoring, evaluation and accountability: For example, indicators and benchmarks to monitor and evaluate the implementation of school-to-post-school transition programmes are put in place. These include procedures for tracking the transition progress of students with disabilities are developed and implemented.

6.26 *Develop equitable funding and resourcing models*

The means of allocating resources to students with disabilities or special educational needs, and the quantum of those resources, has long exercised policy-makers around the world and continues to do so. As we shall see in this section, the issue of funding is impinged on and, in turn, impinges upon almost every issue explored in this chapter. Thus, for example, there is a reciprocal relationship between funding and such issues as paradigms of special educational needs, categorization and inclusive education.

Historically, funding arrangements for special education have often been kept administratively separate from the mechanisms that govern fiscal resources for general education.[117] Reasons for this include the fact that special educational services have traditionally been reserved for students with identified disabilities who were considered to have a clear and justifiable need for extra resources and specialized interventions over and above that provided to other students in the regular classroom. In most jurisdictions, these and other factors have contributed to the creation of separate budgetary arrangements to ensure extra funding to support the educational needs of eligible students. Since the early 2000s or so, however, funding models for special education have been under review in several countries. Several drivers for such reviews have been identified, including rising costs, concerns over efficiency and equity in the use of resources, and concerns about the incentives inherent in funding formulae for contra-indicated practices, such as exclusion from mainstream education and over-referral into special education.[118]

I will now explore the variety of ways in which additional support for students with disabilities (and special educational needs) is provided and the various tensions that arise in different funding models. I will examine four main topics: (a) the relationship between funding and student achievement, (b) levels of funding, (c) various funding models, and (d) general principles of funding.

Relationship between funding and student learning outcomes

As noted by Australian researchers, Tony Shaddock and his colleagues, in their 2009 review of the literature, there is not a strong body of evidence to show that finance in itself has a direct and major effect on student learning outcomes.[119] For example, they cited John Hattie as reporting an effect size on student learning of only 0.14 for 'finances'.[120] Hattie suggested that this lack of association is probably due to factors such as the source of the data (from well-resourced countries only), that most school finances are fixed, and that disbursements within schools involve whole *school* expenditure. Shaddock and his colleagues concluded, however, that the stark reality is that available research does not demonstrate a strong, *direct* causal relationship between finances and educational outcomes; rather, the big effects on student learning are attributable to individual *teacher* differences. They pointed out that 'some minimum level of resourcing is necessary, and after that, the key consideration in regard to finances and educational outcomes is how well the finances are spent'.[121] Thus, research has found that particular *types* of expenditure do have a positive impact on student learning. For example, Hattie found that increased per student expenditure on professional learning for teachers and paying salaries to attract high quality and experienced teachers have only modest effects on student outcomes. Further, there is evidence that the quality of the learning space affects learning. For example, in a recent book, after reviewing more than 30 studies, I concluded, 'Learners who spend time in well-designed, well-maintained classrooms that are comfortable, well-lit, reasonably quiet and properly ventilated with healthy air learn more efficiently and enjoy their educational experiences'.[122]

Levels of funding

In the United States, funding varies considerably according to the category of disability. One study,[123] for example, found that expenditure for students with specific learning disabilities was 1.6 times that for regular education students, while expenditure for those with multiple disabilities was 3.1 times higher. Overall, per student education expenditure for students who received special education services was 1.91 times greater than expenditure for students who received no special education services. Another US review of special education funding found that although the costs of special education in the United States were rising, data suggested that 'rather than rising numbers of high cost special education students or extravagant services per student, the primary source of rising special education costs seems to be the rising numbers of students being referred to, and identified as needing, special education'.[124] This trend was reflected in data indicating that the US special education population had been growing steadily as a percentage of the total student population, from 8.96% in 1987-1988 to 10.74% in 2000-2001, and 11.46% in 2005-2006.

Across all OECD countries, students with disabilities cost two to four times as much to educate as regular students. For those with disabilities, the cost was higher in special schools, compared with mainstream education, by a ratio of about 1.2:1.[125]

Various funding models

Three special education funding models can be identified: (a) demand, (b) supply, and (c) output. Each one has advantages and disadvantages, with the consequence that many countries employ mixed models.

Sometimes referred to as an input model or categorical funding, the demand-driven approach to funding students with special educational needs is based on allocating individual funding to identified students, the amount based on the student's degree and type of disability or need for support. Complete reliance on this model has been criticized as having the following unintended effects:[126]

- it offers perverse incentives to over-identify or 'play the system';
- playing the system results in a reduction in funds for each deserving student;
- the strong focus on disability, difference and deficit is upsetting for parents and has deleterious effects on inclusive culture and practice;
- it leads to the 'medicalization' of diversity in order to attract additional funds; and
- where funds are tied to the formal identification of particular disabilities, resources may be used on expensive diagnosis and/or litigation.

In contrast to a demand-driven model, a supply-driven model permits control over levels and patterns of expenditure. In order to guard against the 'perverse incentive' to over-identify students with special educational needs and/or 'play the system', the supply-driven model usually caps the number of students who can be considered eligible for additional funding. For example, the United States capped the proportion of students with learning disabilities at 12% of the school-age population.

A related model is a census-based approach in which schools receive a set amount of funding based on their total enrolment. In one example the amount per student was set at a level designed to cover the costs of special education for the 15% of students estimated to have mild disabilities, with an additional amount provided to cover the costs associated with the 1% of the school population expected to have severe disabilities. Other writers have concluded that census-based models could be improved by introducing a weighting formula to compensate schools with higher enrolments of students with special educational needs and to allow funding of prevention programmes.[127]

Also, it has been argued that supply-driven approaches would permit students with special educational needs to be served outside special education and would reduce the incentives to over-identify.[128] Further, it has been noted that supply-driven models have the advantage of being quantifiable and can be used to determine the extent to which additional resources are being used efficiently and effectively. They also enable comparisons to be made between and within countries.[129] On the other hand, supply-driven models raise issues of equity in states and districts with higher disability prevalence rates. They can also jeopardize procedural safeguards if students are not identified as having special needs, and may threaten current levels of funding.[130]

In the output model, schools are 'rewarded' for effectiveness and excellence and are retrospectively funded for tasks completed, rather than 'tasks to be done', as is mostly the case at present.[131] It does, however, suffer from 'perverse disincentives' (e.g., a school may be so successful that it no longer qualifies for additional funding). Even so, the approach deserves further attention as *part* of the funding mix, because in focusing on quality outcomes, it aligns special education with the mainstream accountability agenda and it can at least be defined – and presumably measured.[132]

General principles of funding[133]

Research on the impact of different funding models for SWSEN suggests that the following general principles should be taken into account by policy-makers:

- The funding of education and special education is extraordinarily complex.
- In efforts to resolve funding issues, the starting point should not be how to fund special education, but rather how to fund general education.
- There is no single, 'best' funding model. Every model has strengths and weaknesses, incentives and disincentives, and positive and negative outcomes that may affect different students differentially, so a combination of funding models seems inevitable.
- From an economic efficiency viewpoint, it is best to allocate resources where they will do the most good, for example, to early identification and intensive education for students who struggle with learning.
- Resources should be allocated in ways that are coherent with, and promote, system policy, for example, towards greater inclusivity, lifting the performance of all students and particularly those functioning in the lowest quartile and improving equity.
- Undue perverse incentives and disincentives should be avoided.
- Resources should be directed to approaches for which there is evidence of effectiveness in improving students' learning outcomes.

- Arrangements to ensure accountability, including the monitoring of the use of resources and outcomes for children, should be included.
- Funding should be transparent and equitable, with individual schools clear about the resources available to them.
- Funding should be allocated in ways that give schools the flexibility, within appropriate accountability frameworks, to implement practices that work for them and assist teachers to meet the learning needs of students with special educational needs.

6.27 Develop wraparound services

Increasingly, since the 1990s or so, there has been a distinct trend towards 'joined-up thinking' in providing human services. The challenge of educating children with disabilities is essentially a multidisciplinary enterprise, requiring the highest possible levels of collaboration, both at the individual level and at the system level. This means dismantling 'silos' or, at the very least, avoiding 'silo thinking' in which professionals or agencies compete rather than cooperate.

According to Tony Shaddock and his colleagues, a feature of leading practice throughout the world is a move towards 'integrated support', 'service integration' or 'wraparound services', all of which are concerned with the delivery of specialized services in a more coordinated and integrated manner.[134] Such coordination should take place at an institutional level, at an agency level, and at a government level among ministries. Shaddock and his colleagues noted that the literature on service integration highlighted the following factors:

- the active involvement of the child and support for parents as the primarily responsible party;
- conceptualization of schools as the predominant learning environment for children and as a community resource;
- co-location of services where possible;
- alignment of client assessments and case management; and
- clear and realistic objectives of service integration; leadership support; time allocation for joint planning; and clarity around administrative arrangements, funding and resources.

The concept of 'wraparound' was originally developed in the United States in the 1980s as a means of maintaining youth with serious emotional and behavioural disorders in their homes and communities. As described by Timothy Landrum, these students had historically been educated in more restrictive environments than their peers with other disabilities, and this included out-of-community placements for a disproportionate number of them.[135] He went on to note that partly in reaction to this pattern of services, a trend that gained considerable traction in the 1990s was a heightened focus on comprehensive, or wrap-around services designed to keep these students in their home environments. In a nutshell, such an approach comprises system-level interventions that quite literally aim to wrap existing services around children and young people and their families to address their problems in an ecologically comprehensive way. Wraparound has continued to expand in the United States, both in uptake and in its scope. According to Leonard Bickman and his colleagues, in 2003, 88% of US states and territories were using some form of a wraparound approach to provide services to children and adolescents with, or at risk of developing, severe emotional disorders.[136] More recently, another estimate was that the wraparound process was available via nearly 1,000 initiatives in nearly every one of the states in the United States, with the number of them taking implementation statewide increasing every year.[137]

Several studies have shown successful outcomes being achieved with wraparound approaches. A recent meta-analysis identified seven outcome studies comparing wraparound and control groups for students with emotional and behavioural disorders. The researchers found effect sizes as follows: living situations (0.44), mental health outcomes (0.31), overall youth functioning (0.25), school functioning (0.27) and juvenile justice-related outcomes (0.21).[138] Positive results were also reported in a multiple-baseline study of four adolescents with serious mental health issues. Evidence was presented showing that the wraparound process resulted in substantial changes that persisted over time.[139] Another study found that improved emotional and behavioural functioning, as well as academic performance, was obtained with students with emotional and behavioural needs receiving services through a wraparound approach.[140] A matched comparison study of youths in child welfare custody compared the outcomes for 33 in wraparound with 32 receiving usual mental health services. After 18 months, 27 of the 33 youths who received wraparound moved to less restrictive environments, compared with only 12 of the 32 comparison group youth. More positive outcomes were also found for the wraparound cohort on school attendance, school disciplinary action and grade point averages. No significant differences were found in favour of the comparison group.[141] Another study also reported positive findings in favour of wraparound approaches. This was a matched comparison study of youths involved in juvenile justice and receiving mental health services: 110 in wraparound vs 98 in conventional mental heath services. Youths in the comparison group were three times more likely to commit felony offences than youths in the wraparound group. Youths in the latter group also took three times longer to recidivate than those in the comparison group.[142] Finally, a UK study found that school exclusions were reduced by 25% through the work of home-school support social workers in secondary schools.[143]

In contrast to the above, somewhat less positive findings were reported in a study of outcomes for children needing mental heath services. In a comparison of a wraparound group and a 'treatment as usual' group, the researchers found that while the former received greater continuity of care, there were no differences between the two groups on such measures as their functioning, symptoms and life satisfaction. Possible reasons for the apparent failure of the wraparound approach to affect clinical outcomes were advanced. First, it was possible that the 'logic chain between the types of services introduced in wraparound and clinical outcomes is too long'; second, 'the ability to assign youth to appropriate services is not sufficiently well developed'; third, the 'services delivered to families [within the wraparound model] may not have been effective'.[144] Elsewhere, other writers put forward a fourth explanation why research on wraparound is producing mixed findings. They noted that wraparound is difficult to study in a controlled way because intervention plans are individualized for each person.[145]

6.28 *Explore Full-Service Schools*

See section 3.24 in Chapter 3.

6.29 *Provide appropriate teacher education programmes*

In the emerging era of inclusive education, every teacher is being expected to teach children with disabilities, as well as other categories of diversity covered in this book. Most of the topics in this chapter have implications for the design and delivery of teacher education programmes that take account of the challenges of educating students with disabilities and special educational needs.

Issues that arise include: (a) should there be categorical or a non-categorical programmes for teachers of children with disabilities? (b) what relationship should there be between initial teacher education programmes for special education teachers and general education teachers? (c) should special education teachers be trained as general education teachers before being trained as special education teachers? (d) what specialist qualifications should there be for professionals working in an advisory or consultancy capacity? (e) should there be a prescribed set of professional development expectations for the various professional groups? (f) who should design and deliver such professional development, in what locations? and (g) what should be the content of such training courses?

It is beyond the scope of this chapter to answer all of these questions and how they have been addressed in various jurisdictions around the world. Instead, I will outline a set of values, knowledge and skills that I believe educators should acquire before and during their professional careers if they are to be successful in their work with students with special educational needs (SWSEN).[146] These comprise 24 values, knowledge and skills sets, which should be developed at three levels – basic, intermediate and advanced – depending on the level of expertise that is expected of the various professionals. Respectively, 'basic' refers to the application of values, knowledge and skills to individual students with special educational needs by teachers and other professionals at the classroom level, 'intermediate' refers to the provision of appropriate advice and guidance by advisers and consultants to professionals working at the classroom level, while 'advanced' refers to the training of professionals working at the basic and intermediate levels, as well to advancing knowledge through relevant research. The following comprise the 24 sets:

- Adapt the curriculum for SWSEN
- Employ curriculum-based assessment
- Adapt assessment and develop alternate assessment and report results for SWSEN
- Diagnose difficulties in learning and behaviour, including functional assessment and curriculum-based assessment
- Understand broad concepts of diversity
- Understand legal and ethical issues in inclusive education
- Evaluate and use evidence-based teaching strategies and underlying learning theories
- Engage in collaborative teaching and interdisciplinary practices
- Support family and community involvement

- Demonstrate respect for cultural differences, especially in the main minority groups
- Understand the principles of equity, social justice and non-discrimination
- Understand issues in defining and identifying SWSEN
- Address barriers to learning
- Articulate a philosophy of inclusive education, including the rights of SWSEN
- Cooperate with other relevant agencies
- Provide appropriate resourcing for SWSEN
- Provide appropriate professional development for school personnel
- Provide leadership in educating SWSEN
- Utilize appropriate assistive technology
- Engage in transition planning for SWSEN
- Ensure that classrooms have optimal physical features
- Demonstrate skills in collecting and analyzing data on SWSEN, including responses to intervention
- Employ relevant disability-specific teaching
- Understand relevant research; design and carry out research.

II School-level accommodations

6.30 Provide School-wide Positive Behaviour Support programmes

As I pointed out in my recent book, since the early 2000s or so, attention has increasingly been paid to how the school as an organization impacts on the behaviour and achievement of its students, and in particular how school-based universal interventions can be harnessed.[147] One such intervention is School-wide Positive Behaviour Support (S-WPBS). This is a behaviourally based, proactive approach to building a school's capacity to deal with the wide array of behavioural challenges. It emphasizes (a) the prevention and reduction of chronic problem behaviours, (b) active instruction of adaptive skills, (c) a continuum of consequences for problem behaviours, and (d) interventions for learners with the most intractable problem behaviours.[148] It comprises a cluster of effective strategies, centring on the school as an organization, and aimed at enhancing the quality of life of all its members.[149] Such an approach recognizes that a school has its own unique culture and is a complex organization comprising (a) people of varying ages, abilities and authority, (b) environments ranging from classrooms to cafeterias, (c) policies, (d) routines, and (e) procedures, all of which must function as a coordinated whole.[150] S-WPBS has four main elements: a team-based systems approach, a proactive focus on prevention, evidence-based intervention and social skills instruction.

There is a growing body of evidence that by developing a proactive, school-wide system that incorporates these strategies, S-WPBS can be effective in decreasing the level of problem behaviour. S-WPBS is increasingly being used. For example, according to a 2009 estimate, it was being implemented in more than 9,000 schools in at least 44 states in the United States.[151] As well, it is used in a range of other countries, including Australia, Canada, Finland, New Zealand and Norway. The foregoing description refers particularly to the writings of its American developers. I turn now to brief descriptions of its deployment in three other countries: Finland, Norway and New Zealand.

Finland

Hannu Savolainen and his colleagues are engaged in a nation-wide implementation of S-WPBS.[152] In one component of it they reported on the effects of a two-month pilot study on the impact of a class-wide intervention involving multiple teachers in Finnish middle schools. The intervention was based on teachers having clear behavioural expectations for students, providing positive behaviour support and making rapid responses to any disruptive behaviour. The results showed large reductions in disruptive behaviours, in the time needed to maintain positive learning climates, and in the strain experienced by teachers. It was estimated that these improvements led to teachers having two hours more time per week to devote to teaching instead of behavioural control.

Norway

Mari-Anne Sørlie and Terje Ogden have described how an adapted version of S-WPBS (referred to as N-PALS) was implemented in 28 Norwegian intervention schools over a period of three years, the results being compared with 20 control schools.[153] Multilevel analyses revealed significant positive intervention effects on student problem behaviours and classroom learning climates. Moreover, the number of segregated students decreased in the intervention group, while it increased in the control group. The authors also noted that the model also increased schools' ability to reach out to all students, reducing the number who needed individual intervention. Implementation quality moderated the outcomes.

New Zealand

Since 2009, the New Zealand Ministry of Education has been implementing a programme, Positive Behaviour for Learning (PB4L). It comprises three tiers of support for students, including PB4L School-Wide, which looks at behaviour and learning from a whole-school as well as an individual student perspective. Its focus is on changing the school environment and putting systems in place to support students to make positive behaviour choices.[154] As of 2015, there were 415 primary schools and 182 secondary schools actively engaged in PB4L School-Wide. Preliminary findings on its effectiveness indicated that it is valued by many staff because it helped to create a more respectful, safe and inclusive school environment and increased students' on-task behaviour and engagement.

6.31 Ensure that the built environment is conducive to learning

As I have pointed out elsewhere, it is important to ensure that all the elements of the indoor physical environment that may affect students' ability to learn are optimal.[155] Simply put, learners who spend time in well-designed, well-maintained classrooms that are comfortable, well lit, reasonably quiet and properly ventilated with healthy air, will learn more efficiently and enjoy their educational experiences. In such environments, teachers too, will be healthier, happier and more effective as educators.

Four major aspects of the indoor physical environment should be attended to: physical space and equipment; temperature; humidity and ventilation; lighting; and acoustics. Briefly, here is a sample of recommendations:

Physical space

Arrange learners' workspaces to facilitate flexible grouping and differentiated instruction by allowing for whole class, small-group and individual instruction. Some learners with autism may need access to personal space, with calm, ordered, low-stimulus spaces, no confusing large spaces and safe indoor and outdoor places for withdrawal and to calm down.

Temperature, humidity and ventilation

Several studies attest to the importance of attending to the air quality in classrooms. For example, a 1999 US study found that ventilation was rated as unsatisfactory by 26% of schools.[156] A Swedish study investigated the impact of air quality on absenteeism in two day-care centres. It found that the introduction of electrostatic air cleaning technology reduced the level of absenteeism from 8.31% to 3.75%.[157] A recent Danish study in two classes of 10-year-old learners investigated the effects of classroom temperatures and the supply of outdoor air on schoolwork.[158] Average air temperatures were reduced from 23.6C to 20.0C and the supply of outdoor air was increased from 5.2 to 9.6 litres per person. Singly and in combination, the experiment resulted in improved performances in reading and mathematics.

Lighting

A UK review of the effects of lighting in classrooms made the following points:

- the visual environment affects learners' ability to perceive visual stimuli and affects their mental attitudes and, therefore, their performances;
- day-lighting has the most positive effects on learners' achievement;
- since day-lighting as a sole source of lighting is not feasible, it should be supplemented by automatically controlled electric lighting that dims in response to daylight levels;
- lighting should be as glare-free and flicker-free as possible, especially when computers are being used.[159]

Acoustics

Since much classroom learning takes place through listening and speaking (estimates vary from 50-90%, according to one study[160]), it is essential that students can hear educators' speech clearly. Unfortunately, this is not always the case, with typical classrooms in many developed countries providing inadequate acoustical environments. In a New Zealand study of 106 classrooms, for example, it was found that only 4% had acceptable noise levels for instruction.[161] This situation, which is by no means limited to New Zealand, has a major impact on the students' opportunities to learn, especially for those with mild or fluctuating hearing loss, learning disabilities, attention disorders and language disabilities. One way of improving the acoustic environment is to introduce sound field amplification (SFA). For example, a New Zealand study examined the effects of SFA for four children with Down syndrome aged six to seven years.[162] The results showed that they perceived significantly more speech when the SFA system amplified the investigator's voice by 10dB.

Recent research has highlighted the importance of considering the complex interactions and additive effects among various aspects of indoor environmental quality on student achievement. In a recent UK study, for example, researchers found the following classroom characteristics related positively to achievement: (a) light: e.g., classrooms receive natural light from more than one orientation and they have high quality and quantity of electric lighting; (b) choice: e.g., classrooms have high quality and purpose-designed furniture, fixtures and equipment, including ergonomic tables and chairs; (c) flexibility: various zones can allow varied learning activities at the same time, and teachers can easily change the space configuration; (d) connection: wide corridors can ease movement, and pathways have clear way-finding features; (e) complexity: classrooms are designed with quiet visual environments balanced with a certain level of complexity; and (f) colour: warm colours in senior grades' classrooms and bright, cool colours in junior grades' classrooms.[163]

NB. As with many of the recommendations made in this chapter, what constitutes good design of indoor physical environments for students with disabilities is also good design for all learners.

6.32 *Provide professional development for staff*

It is incumbent upon school leadership to provide school staff with appropriate professional development to work effectively with students with disabilities. See section 6.29 for a range of values, knowledge and skills that could form the basis of a programme, depending on the backgrounds, responsibilities and needs of the staff. In my experience, professional development should be school-based and involve all members of staff.

III *Classroom-level accommodations*

6.33 *Prefer mixed ability grouping of students*

In summarizing the research on ability grouping, two Dutch writers put forward a range of arguments as to why it is detrimental to low-achieving learners:

- being assigned to low-ability groups communicates low expectations to students, which might be self-fulfilling;
- because ability groups often parallel social class and ethnic groupings, they may increase divisions along class and ethnic lines;
- between-class ability grouping reduces students' opportunities to move between groups;

- low-achieving students tend to receive less instruction when placed in ability groups than when placed in mixed ability groups;
- ability groups composed of low-achieving students do not provide a stimulating learning environment and lack positive role models.[164]

6.34 Employ evidence-based pedagogy[165]

There is a growing expectation around the world that teachers should employ teaching strategies that have a sound evidential base. Thus, in the United States, for example, the No Child Left Behind law required teachers to use 'scientific, research-based programs', defined as being '(1) grounded in theory, (2) evaluated by third parties, (3) published in peer-reviewed journals, (4) sustainable, (5) replicable in schools with diverse settings, and (6) able to demonstrate evidence of effectiveness'.

A key question here is do students with disabilities require distinctive teaching strategies? The answer to this question is both 'Yes' and 'No'.[166] First, 'Yes': for many such students do require specific strategies that take account of their special needs. For example, many students with visual impairments rely on their tactile and auditory senses for learning and require specialized techniques such as Braille and orientation and mobility training. Similarly, many students with hearing impairments will require such adaptations as total communication (including signing), FM listening systems and assistance with maintaining hearing aids. Many students with physical disabilities will require assistance with positioning and mobility, normally provided by physiotherapists or occupational therapists. Second, 'No': for the most part, students with disabilities simply require good teaching. All learners benefit from a common set of strategies. What is required is the systematic, explicit and intensive application of a wide range of evidence-based teaching strategies.

The following is a brief summary of teaching strategies that have been found to be effective in teaching students with disabilities and special educational needs (as well as other students). They are grouped under four broad headings.

Behavioural approaches

These strategies focus mainly on changes in a learner's observable behaviours and emphasize the role of external stimuli, particularly the role of reinforcement and the role of the teacher in transmitting knowledge. They focus on how events that occur either before (antecedents) or after (consequences) learners engage in a verbal or physical act affects their subsequent behaviour. Behavioural approaches include:

- *functional behavioural assessment*: the procedures used to determine the function or purpose of a learner's repeated undesirable behaviour and what leads to it being maintained;
- *review and practice*: planning and supervising opportunities for learners to encounter the same skills or concepts on several occasions;
- *direct instruction*: a multi-component instructional strategy centring on teacher-directed, explicit, systematic teaching based on scripted lesson plans and frequent assessment;

- *formative assessment and feedback*: a combined strategy in which teachers (a) probe for knowledge within lessons, (b) give frequent feedback to learners (sometimes referred to as corrective feedback), and (c) adjust their teaching strategies, where necessary, to improve learners' performances;

Social approaches

These strategies emphasize the importance of social contexts – families, peer groups and classrooms – in facilitating learning. The following strategies fall into this category.

- *cooperative group teaching*: based on two main ideas about learning: (a) when learners collaborate, it has a synergistic effect and (b) much knowledge is socially constructed;
- *peer tutoring*: peers play multiple roles in supporting and teaching each other – a 'natural' social relationship that teachers should capitalize on;
- *social skills training*: helping learners establish and maintain positive interactions with others;
- *classroom climate*: a multi-component strategy comprising the psychological features of the classroom, as distinct from its physical features.

Cognitive approaches

Cognitive approaches focus on how we collect, store, interpret, understand, remember and use information. These strategies typically emphasize the role of learners in actively constructing their own understanding. They include:

- *cognitive strategy instruction*: focuses on ways of assisting learners to acquire cognitive skills, or strategies by helping them to (a) organize information so that its complexity is reduced, and/or (b) integrate information into their existing knowledge;
- *self-regulated learning*: aims at helping learners to define goals for themselves, to monitor their own behaviour, and to make decisions and choices of actions that lead to the achievement of their goals;
- *memory strategies*: focus on ways of enhancing primary memory, short-term memory, long-term memory and the executive system;
- *reciprocal teaching*: involves teaching learners, by means of guided practice, how to improve their reading comprehension, in all subject areas, by predicting, clarifying, questioning and summarizing what is in a text;
- *cognitive behavioural therapy*: is an active process of changing a student's negative thinking patterns, which in turn leads to changes in behaviour and, ultimately, to a reduction or elimination of feelings of anxiety or depression.

Mixed approaches

Some strategies do not fall readily into one of the above three approaches. Three in particular are worthy of mention:

- *assistive technology*: employing any item, piece of equipment, or product system, whether acquired commercially off the shelf, modified, or customized, that is used to increase, maintain, or improve functional capabilities of children with disabilities;

- *augmentative and alternative communication*: the former is used to supplement whatever existing methods of communication a learner has, while the latter represents an attempt to replace the lost means of communication;
- *phonological awareness*: is an oral language skill that involves the ability to notice, reflect upon and manipulate (move, combine and delete) the individual sounds in words.

6.35 *Provide individualized support for students*

Article 24 of the UN *Convention on the Rights of Disabled Persons* includes the clause that states should ensure that 'Effective individualized support measures are provided in environments that maximize academic and social development, consistent with the goal of full inclusion.' This requirement found expression in the *World Report on Disability*, which noted that education systems should move away from more traditional pedagogies and adopt more learner-centred approaches. This means that 'the curricula, teaching methods and materials, assessment and examination systems, and the management of classes all need to be accessible and flexible to support differences in learning patterns'.[167]

In turn, this draws our attention to individualized education plans (IEPs). These involve planning an individual child's education programme and do not necessarily mean one-to-one teaching. They are developed through a multidisciplinary process, which includes parents and often the child. They focus on identifying needs, learning goals and objectives, appropriate teaching strategies, and required accommodations and supports. IEPs had their origins in the United States in the 1975 Education for All Handicapped Children Act (PL94-142) and have been reaffirmed in IDEA legislation ever since. They are ubiquitous, virtually every country including them, or their equivalent, as a key element in their special education provisions.

In a 2010 review of the literature on IEPs, my colleagues and I made the following points, *inter alia*:[168]

- IEPs suffer from having multiple purposes ascribed to them, the same document frequently being expected to serve educational, legal, planning, accountability, placement and resource allocation purposes;
- when the majority-culture views and practices of the school take little or no account of the cultural values of students' home cultures, there can be a breakdown in home-school communication;
- all teachers should be provided with training and support in designing and implementing IEPs; and
- studies indicate limitations in both the quantity and quality of parents' participation in the process.

Underlying individualization is the principle of differentiation. This process involves 'varying content, activities, teaching, learning, methods and resources to take into account the range of interests, needs and experience of individual students'.[169] It is based on the premise that one size does not fit all and that teachers should adapt the curriculum and instruction to student differences. Perhaps the best-known advocate of differentiation is Carol Ann Tomlinson, who asserted that teachers should differentiate three aspects of the curriculum: content, process and products:[170]

- Content refers to the concepts, principles and skills that teachers want students to learn. All students should be given access to the same core content, teachers addressing the same concepts with all students but adjusting the degree of complexity. Content also refers to the means teachers use to give students access to skills and knowledge, such as texts, lectures, demonstrations and field trips, which can be varied as well.
- Process refers to the activities that help students make sense of the ideas and skills being taught. Teachers can modify these activities, Tomlinson advises, to provide some students with more complexity and others with more scaffolding, depending on their readiness levels. Like content, process can be varied by student interest and learning preferences as well.
- Products refer to projects that allow students to demonstrate and extend what they have learned. They reveal whether students can apply learning beyond the classroom to solve problems and take action. Different students can create different products, Tomlinson suggests, based on their readiness levels, interests and learning preferences.

6.36 *Implement universal design for learning*

See section 6.21.

E Conclusions

Ten conclusions may be drawn from this chapter.

First, disability is part of the human condition, with almost everyone facing the prospect of becoming temporarily or permanently impaired at some point in their lives.

Second, responses to disability have changed since the 1970s, prompted largely by the self-organization of people with disabilities and by the growing tendency to see disability as a human rights issue.

Third, persons with disabilities are diverse, with differences being influenced by gender, age, socio-economic status, sexuality, ethnicity or cultural heritage. A related point is the clear evidence of disproportional representation in special education of boys, children from low socio-economic homes, and children from ethnic minorities.

Fourth, while disability correlates with disadvantage, not all people with disabilities are disadvantaged.

Fifth, since 2006, countries' approaches to disability have been influenced by the United Nations *Convention on the Rights of Persons with Disabilities*. Article 24, which focuses on education, is of particular relevance to the theme of this book.

Sixth, three different paradigms dominate approaches to educating students with disabilities: the psycho-medical paradigm, the socio-political paradigm and the organizational paradigm. Rather than viewing disability solely according to one of these perspectives, a balanced approach is needed.

Seventh, given this variation of paradigms, it is not surprising that there is no universal agreement as to how students with disabilities should be referred to, how they should be defined and what, if any, categories they should be divided into. Other factors influencing this diversity of approach include differences in (a) the histories of organizations/systems, (b) local

Table 6.1 Summary of actions to accommodate to disabilities

Society and education system	Schools	Classrooms
• Sign, ratify and abide by the UN Convention on the Rights of People with Disabilities. • Recognize the economic benefits of accommodating to children with disabilities. • Ensure that all children with disabilities receive education. • Develop early prevention and intervention programmes. • Adopt and implement inclusivist policies in education. • Ensure that students with disabilities and special educational needs have access to the general curriculum. • Ensure that students with disabilities and special educational needs have access to the national or state assessments. • Protect the rights of children with disabilities at times of disasters and conflicts. • Develop policies on transition from school to post-school situations for children with disabilities. • Develop equitable funding and resourcing models. • Develop wraparound services. • Explore Full-Service Schools. • Provide appropriate teacher education programmes.	• Provide School-wide Positive Behaviour Support programmes. • Ensure that the built environment is conducive to learning. • Provide professional development for staff. • Encourage interactions between the school and its community.	• Engage parents in their children's education. • Prefer mixed ability grouping of students. • Employ evidence-based pedagogy. • Provide individualized support for students. • Implement universal design for learning.

traditions, (c) legal foundations and (d) fiscal policies and constraints. As countries change their approaches to ability differences, this remains a very fluid situation.

Eighth, cultural perspectives on disability differ, helping us understand how disability and issues such as inclusive education are interpreted in different societies.

Ninth, disabilities arise from multiple causes that can be broadly classified into two groups: endogenous factors originating from within the individual and exogenous factors originating from outside of the individual.

Tenth, the question of how best to educate children with different abilities is one of the most dominant and controversial issues confronting educators around the world today. It is a complex and dynamic issue that requires accommodations at three levels: (a) society and system-level, (b) school-level and (c) classroom-level. Table 6.1 summarizes the range of actions at these three levels to mitigate the effects of disabilities as presented in this chapter.

Notes

1 World Health Organization & World Bank (2011). *World report on disability*. Geneva: World Health Organization.
2 Ibid., p. xxi.
3 Ibid., p. 8.
4 Ibid., p. 10
5 In December 2012, a vote in the US Senate fell six votes short of the two-thirds majority required for ratification.
6 For an overview of the UNCRPD and its precursors, see Mittler, P. (2015). 'Working for inclusive education by 2030.' In F. Kiuppis & R.S. Haustatter (eds), *Inclusive education twenty years after Salamanca*. New York, NY: Peter Lang, Chapter 21.
7 Baglieri, S. & Shapiro, A. (2012). *Disability studies and the inclusive classroom: Critical practices for creating least restrictive attitudes*. New York, NY: Routledge, p. 20.
8 Kuhn, T.S. (1962). *The structure of scientific revolutions*. Chicago and London: University of Chicago Press, p. 10.
9 Clark, C., Dyson, A., Millward, A. & Skidmore, D. (1995). 'Dialectical analysis, special needs and schools as organizations.' In C. Clark, A. Dyson & A Millward (eds), *Towards inclusive schools?* (pp. 78-95). London: David Fulton.
10 Ackerman, P., Jaeger, R. & Smith, A. (2002). 'Special education: current trends.' In *Encyclopedia of Education*. Farmington Hills, MI: Gale Group.
11 Christensen, C. (1996). 'Disabled, handicapped or disordered: What's in a name?' In C. Christensen and F. Rizvi (eds), *Disability and the dilemmas of education and justice* (pp. 63-78). Buckingham: Open University Press.
12 Christensen, op. cit.; Clark, et al., op. cit.; Skidmore, D. (2002). 'A theoretical model of pedagogical discourse.' *Disability, Culture and Education*, 1(2), 119-131; and Skrtic, T.M., Sailor, W. & Gee, K. (1996). 'Voice, collaboration, and inclusion: democratic themes in educational and social reform initiatives.' *Remedial and Special Education*, 17(3), 142-157.
13 Clark et al., op. cit.; Ainscow, M. (1995). 'Special needs through school improvement: school improvement through special needs.' In C. Clark, A. Dyson and A. Millward (eds), *Towards inclusive schools?* (pp. 63-77). London: David Fulton; and Lipsky, D.K. and Gartner, A. (1999). 'Inclusive education: a requirement of a democratic society.' In H. Daniels and P. Garner (eds), *World yearbook of education 1999: Inclusive education* (pp. 12-23). London: Kogan Page.
14 Lindsay, G. (2003). 'Inclusive education: A critical perspective.' *British Journal of Special Education*, 30(1), 3-12.
15 Weishaar, M.K & Borsa, J.C. (2001). *Inclusive educational administration: A case study approach*. New York: McGraw-Hill Higher Education.
16 UNESCO (2009). *Defining an inclusive education agenda: Reflections around the 48th session of the International Conference on Education*. Geneva: UNESCO IBE.

17 European Agency for Development in Special Needs Education (2003). *Special needs education in Europe: Thematic publication*. Middelfart, Denmark: Author. Available online at: http://www.europe-an-agency.org; OECD (2000). *Special educational needs: Statistics and indicators*. Paris: Author; and OECD (2005). *Students with disabilities, learning difficulties and disadvantages: statistics and indicators*. Paris: Author.

18 Evans, P. (2000). 'Equity indicators based on the provision of supplemental resources for disabled and disadvantaged students.' In W. Hutmacher, D. Cochrane & N. Bottani (eds), *In pursuit of equity in education: Using international indicators to compare equity policies* (pp. 253–266). Dordrecht: Kluwer Academic.

19 OECD (2005). *Students with disabilities, learning difficulties and disadvantages: Statistics and indicators*. Paris: Author.

20 Hjorne, E. & Saljo, R. (2004). '"There is something about Julia": Symptoms, categories and processes of invoking attention deficit hyperactive disorder in the Swedish school: A case study.' *Journal of Language, Identity and Education*, 3(1), 1–24.

21 President's Commission on Excellence in Special Education (2002). *A new era: Revitalizing special education for children and their families*. Jessup, MD: US Department of Education, p. 21.

22 Ibid.

23 Ibid., p. 22.

24 Farrell, M. (2010). *Debating special education*. London: Routledge.

25 American Psychiatric Association (2000). *Diagnostic and statistical manual of mental disorders fourth edition, text revision*. Washington, DC: Author.

26 Ibid.

27 Shaddock, A., MacDonald, N., Hook, J. Giorcelli, L. & Arthur-Kelly, M. (2009). *Disability, diversity and tides that lift all boats: Review of special education in the ACT*. Chiswick, NSW: Services Initiatives.

28 Ibid.

29 Batsche, G.M. (2006). *Problem-solving and response to intervention: Implications for state and district policies and practices*. Presentation to C.A.S.E., January 25 2006.

30 Yell, M., Katsiyannis, A. & Bradley, M.R. (2011). 'The Individuals with Disabilities Education Act.' In J.M. Kauffman & D.P. Hallahan (eds), *Handbook of special education* (pp. 61–76). New York, NY: Routledge, p. 74.

31 Gallego, M.A. & Cole, M. (2001). 'Classroom cultures and cultures in the classroom.' In V. Richardson (ed.), *Handbook of research on teaching*. Fourth edition (pp. 355–390). New York, NY: Macmillan, p. 367. For a detailed analysis of the cultural dimension in inclusive education, see Artiles, A. & Dyson, A. (2005). 'Inclusive education in the globalization age: The promise of comparative cultural-historical analysis.' In D. Mitchell (ed.), *Contextualizing inclusive education: Evaluating old and new international perspectives* (pp. 37–62). London: Routledge.

32 Mitchell, D.R. (2001). 'Japanese schools' accommodation to student diversity.' *Journal of School Education*, 14, 159–178.

33 Here I draw upon the following studies: Lewis, C.C. (1998). 'Fostering social and intellectual development: the roots of Japanese educational success.' In T. Rohlen & G. LeTendre (eds), *Teaching and learning in Japan* (pp. 79–97). Cambridge: Cambridge University Press; Okano, K. & Tsuchiya, M. (1999). *Education in contemporary Japan: Inequality and diversity*. Cambridge: Cambridge University Press; Rohlen, T.P. & LeTendre, G.K. (1998). 'Conclusion: themes in the Japanese culture of learning.' In T. Rohlen & G. LeTendre (eds), *Teaching and learning in Japan* (pp. 369–376). Cambridge: Cambridge University Press; Sato, N. (1998). 'Honoring the individual.' In T. Rohlen & G. LeTendre (eds), *Teaching and learning in Japan* (pp. 119–153). Cambridge: Cambridge University Press; Shimizu, H. (1998). 'Individual differences and the Japanese education system.' In R.W. Riley, T. Takai, & J.C. Conaty (eds), *The educational system in Japan: Case study findings* (pp. 79–134). Washington, DC: National Institute on Student Achievement, Curriculum, and Assessment, Office of Educational Research and Improvement, US Department of Education; Walsh, D.J. (2000). 'Space and early schooling: From culture to pedagogy.' *Journal of School Education*, 12, 123–137; and White, M. (1987). *The Japanese educational challenge: A commitment to students*. New York, NY: The Free Press.

34 Brown, R.C. (2005). 'Inclusive education in Middle Eastern cultures.' In Mitchell (2005), op. cit. (pp. 253–278).

35 Macfarlane, A.H. (2012). 'Inclusive education and Māori communities in Aotearoa New Zealand.' In S. Carrington & J. MacArthur (eds), *Teaching in inclusive school communities* (pp. 163–186). Milton,

Qld: John Wiley and Sons; and Macfarlane, S. (2015). 'In pursuit of culturally responsive evidence-based special education pathways for Māori: Whaia kit e ara tika.' In J. Bevan-Brown, M. Berryman, H. Hickey, S. Macfarlane, K. Smiler and T. Walker (eds), *Working with Māori children with special needs* (pp. 30–51), Wellington, NZ: NZCER Press.

36 Ritchie, J.E. (1992). *Becoming bicultural.* Wellington, New Zealand: Huia Publishers, p. 75.

37 See also my description of the project, *Te Kotahitanga,* in section 4.36 of Chapter 4.

38 UNESCO Institute for Statistics and UNICEF (2015). *Fixing the broken promise of Education for All: Findings from the Global Initiative on Out-of-School children.* Montreal: Author. URL: http://dx.doi.org/10.15220/978-92-9189-161-0-en (accessed 3 February 2015).

39 World Health Organization and World Bank (2011). *World report on disability.* Geneva: World Health Organization. URL: http://www.who.int/disabilities/world_report/2011/en/ (accessed 10 February 2015).

40 United Nations (2006). *United Nations Convention on the Rights of Persons with Disabilities.* New York, NY: Author.

41 World Health Organization (2001). *International classification of functioning, disability and health (ICF).* Geneva: Author.

42 World Health Organization (2007). *International classification of functioning, disability and health for children and youth (ICF-CY).* Geneva: Author.

43 World Heath Organization & World Bank, op. cit.

44 McLaughlin, M.J., Miceli, M. & Hoffman, A.Y. (2009). 'Closing the achievement gap and students with disabilities: The new meaning of a "Free and Appropriate Public Education".' In M. Rebell, A.S. Wells & J. Wolff (eds), *NCLB at the Crossroads* (pp. 106–133). New York, NY: Teachers College Press.

45 Lamb Inquiry (2009). *Special educational needs and parental confidence.* Annesley, Nottingham: DCSF Publications, p. 2. URL: http://www.dyslexiaaction.org.uk/files/dyslexiaaction/the_lamb_inquiry.pdf (accessed 26 February 2016).

46 Office for Disability Issues, Department for Work & Pensions (2014). *Disability facts and figures.* URL: https://www.gov.uk/government/publications/disability-facts-and-figures/disability-facts-and-figures#fn (accessed 28 February 2016).

47 See http://www.2010disabilitysurveys.org/indexold.html

48 Hendey, N. & Pascall, G. (2001). *Disability and the transition to adulthood: Achieving independent living.* Brighton, East Sussex: Joseph Rowntree Foundation.

49 ILO, op cit..

50 Gravois, T.A. & Rosenfield, S. (2006). 'Impact of instructional consultation teams on the disproportionate referral and placement of minority students in special education.' *Remedial and Special Education*, 27, 42–52, p. 42.

51 MacMillan, D.L. & Rechsley, D.J. (1998). 'Overrepresentation of minority students: the case for greater specificity or reconsideration of the variables examined.' *Journal of Special Education*, 32(1), 15–24.

52 Fiedler, C.R., Chiang, B., Haren, B.V., Jorgensen, J., Halberg, S. & Boreson, L. (2008). 'Culturally responsive practices in schools: A checklist to address disproportionality in special education.' *Teaching Exceptional Children*, 40(5), 50–59; Garcia, S.B. & Ortiz, A.A. (2006). *Preventing disproportionate representation: Culturally and linguistically responsive prereferral interventions.* National Center for Culturally Responsive Educational Systems; and Skiba, R.J., Poloni-Staudinger, L., Simmons, A.B., Feggins-Azziz, R. & Chung, C.-G. (2005). 'Unproven links: can poverty explain ethnic disproportionality in special education?' *Journal of Special Education*, 39(3), 130–144.

53 Dyson, A. & Gallannaugh, F. (2008). 'Disproportionality in special needs education in England.' *Journal of Special Education*, 42(1), 36–46; and Strand, S. & Lindsay, G. (2009). 'Evidence of ethnic disproportionality in special education in an English population.' *Journal of Special Education*, 43(3), 174–190.

54 Department of Education (2001). *Education White Paper 6. Special needs education: Building an inclusive education and training system.* Pretoria: Republic of South Africa Department of Education.

55 Elementary and Middle Schools Technical Assistance Center, op. cit.; Fiedler et al., op. cit.; Gabel, S.L., Curcic, S., Powell, J.J.W., Khader, K. & Albee, L. (2009). 'Migration and ethnic group disproportion in special education: An exploratory study.' *Disability in Society*, 24(5), 625–639; Losen, D. J. & Orfield, G. (2002). *Racial inequality in special education.* Cambridge, MA: Harvard Education Press; and Skiba et al. op. cit.

56 See Chapter 3 for a more detailed analysis.

57 Skiba et al., op. cit.

58 Ibid., p. 131.

59 Crnic, K., Hoffman, C., Gaze, C. & Edelbrock, C. (2004). 'Understanding the emergence of be-havior problems in young children with developmental delays.' *Infants and Young Children*,17(3), 223–235.

60 Ibid.

61 Katz, G. & Lazcano-Ponce, E. (2008). 'Intellectual disability: definition, etiological factors, classifica-tion, diagnosis, treatment and prognosis.' *Salud de pública México*, 50, suppl. 2. URL: http://dx.doi.org/10.1590/S0036-36342008000800005 (accessed 29 February 2016).

62 Ibid.

63 Lajiness-O'Neill, R. & Erdodi, L.A. (2011). 'Traumatic brain injury'. In J.M. Kauffman & D.P. Hallahan (eds), *Handbook of special education* (pp. 262–276). London: Routledge.

64 Pullen, P.C., Lane, H.B., Ashworth, K.E. & Lovelace, S.P. (2011). 'Learning disabilities'. In Kauffman & Hallahan, op. cit. (pp. 187–197).

65 Rooney, K.J. (2011). 'Attention deficit/hyperactivity disorder.' In Kauffman & Hallahan, op. cit. (pp. 198–208).

66 Kauffman, J.M. & Landrum, T.J. (2009). *Characteristics of emotional and behavioral disorders*. Upper Saddle River, NJ: Merrill.

67 Mitchell, D. & Karr, V. (eds) (2014). *Conflict, disaster and disability. Ensuring equality*. London: Routledge.

68 United Nations Development Programme (UNDP) (2004). *Reducing disaster risk: A challenge for development*. New York: Author. URL: http://www.undp.org/content/dam/undp/library/crisis%20prevention/disaster/asia_pacific/Reducing%20Disaster%20risk%20a%20Challenge%20for%20development.pdf (accessed 31 August 2013).

69 International Committee of the Red Cross (2008). *How is the term 'Armed Conflict' defined in inter-national humanitarian law?* Geneva: Author. URL: https://www.icrc.org/eng/resources/documents/article/other/armed-conflict-article-170308.htm (accessed 31 August 2013).

70 UNDP, op. cit.

71 Reinhardt, J.D., Li, J., Gosney, J., Rathore, F.A., Hauq, A.J., Marx, M. & DeLisa, J.A. (2011). 'Dis-ability and health-related rehabilitation in international disaster relief.' *Global Health Action*, 4, 71–91.

72 Quigley, B. (2006) 'Six months after Katrina: Who was left behind – Then and now.' *Counterpunch*, February, 2006.

73 Reilly, R. (2010). 'A shared vision.' *Forced Migration Review*, 35, 8–10.

74 World Health Organization & World Bank, op. cit., p. 44.

75 Ibid., p. 207.

76 UNICEF (2013). *Children with disabilities: The state of the world's children 2013*. New York, NY: Author.

77 Social and Rural Research Institute of IMRB International (2009). *All India survey of out-of-school children of age 5 and in 6-13 years age group*. Noida, Uttar Pradesh: Educational Consultants India.

78 World Health Organization & World Bank, op. cit.

79 European Agency for Development in Special Needs Education (2005). *Early childhood intervention: Analysis of situations in Europe*. Middlefart, Denmark: Author.

80 The term 'parent' encompasses a range of people, including natural parents, adoptive or foster parents, guardians, extended family, carers and caregivers. Here 'parent' will be used to cover all categories of such relationships.

81 Hornby, G. (2000). *Improving parental involvement*. London: Cassell.

82 Dybwad, G. (1982). 'The re-discovery of the family.' *Mental Retardation*, 21(6), 234–239.

83 Singer, G. (2011). 'Parent and family issues in special education.' In J.M. Kauffman & D.P. Hallahan (eds), *Handbook of special education* (pp. 637–638). New York: Routledge.

84 Stalker, K.O., Brunner, R., Maguire, R. & Mitchell, J. (2011). 'Tackling the barriers to disabled parents' involvement in their children's education.' *Educational Review*, 63(2), 233–250.

85 See Mitchell, D. (2014a). *What really works in special and inclusive education: Using evidence-based teaching strategies*. Second edition. London: Routledge, Chapter 7.

86 Ibid.

87 Webster-Stratton, C. & Reid, M.J. (2004). 'Strengthening social and emotional competence in young children: The foundation for early school readiness and success: Incredible Years classroom social skills and problem-solving curriculum.' *Infants and Young Children*, 17(2), 96–113.

88 Webster-Stratton, C., Reid, M.J. & Hammond, M. (2001). 'Preventing conduct problems, promoting social competence: A parent and teacher training partnership in Head Start.' *Journal of Clinical Child and Adolescent Psychology*, 30(3), 283–302.

89 Reid, R., Gonzalez, J.E., Nordness, P.D., Trout, A. & Epstein, M.H, (2004). 'A meta-analysis of the academic status of students with emotional/behavioral disturbance.' *Journal of Special Education*, 38(3), 130–143.

90 Mitchell, D., Morton, M. & Hornby, G. (2010). *Review of the literature on individual education plans: Report to the Ministry of Education, New Zealand*. Christchurch: College of Education, University of Canterbury.

91 UNESCO (2008). *Inclusive education: the way of the future: Conclusions and recommendations of the 48th session of the International Conference on Education (ICE)*. Geneva: IBE and UNESCO.

92 Mitchell, D. (2014a) (Chapter 22).

93 Mitchell (2010), op. cit.

94 Hegarty, S. (2001). 'Inclusive education: A case to answer.' *Journal of Moral Education*, 30(3), 243–249.

95 These arguments are similar to those advanced by UNESCO: see UNESCO (2001). *Understanding and responding to children's needs in inclusive classrooms*. Paris, Author URL: http://unesdoc.unesco.org/images/0012/001243/124394e.pdf (accessed 5 March 2016).

96 See Mitchell (2014a), op. cit., Chapter 27.

97 Lindsay (2003), op. cit.

98 Kavale, K.A. & Mostert, M.P. (2003). 'River of ideology, islands of evidence.' *Exceptionality*, 11(4), 191–208.

99 Fuchs, D. & Fuchs, L.S. (1994). 'Inclusive schools movement and the radicalization of special education reform.' *Exceptional Children*, 60(4), 294–309, p. 295.

100 Kauffman, J.M. (1999). 'Commentary: today's special education and its message for tomorrow.' *Journal of Special Education*, 32(4), 244–254, p. 246.

101 European Agency for Development in Special Needs Education (2003). *Special needs education in Europe: Thematic publication*. Middelfart, Denmark: Author.

102 Department of Education (2001). *Education White Paper 6. Special needs education: Building an inclusive education and training system*. Pretoria: Republic of South Africa Department of Education.

103 Marcal, G. (2003). *Impact of armed conflict on children: A review of progress since 1996*. United Nations Report on the Impact of Armed Conflict on Children. New York: UNICEF.

104 Roth, M. (2014). 'GETTING REAL: Promising practices in disability-inclusive emergency management for the whole community: A case study for the United States.' In Mitchell & Karr, op. cit., pp. 105–123.

105 Aldrich, P. (2013). *Social capital in post-disaster recovery*. Chicago: University of Chicago Press.

106 This section draws upon Mitchell, D. (2015). 'What's next? Standards and guidelines for strengthening school-to-post-school transition programmes for students with disabilities.' In D.L. Cameron & R. Thygesen (eds), *Transitions in the field of special education* (pp. 273–299). Munster, Germany: Waxman.

107 International Labour Office (1998). *Education, employment and training policies and programmes for youth with disabilities in four European countries*. Geneva: Author, pp. 5–6.

108 Kessler Foundation and National Organization for Disability (2010). URL: http://www.2010disabilitysurveys.org/octsurvey/pdfs/surveyresults.pdf (accessed 3 March 2016).

109 Hendey, N. & Pascall, G. (2001). *Disability and the transition to adulthood: Achieving independent living*. Brighton, East Sussex: Joseph Rowntree Foundation.

110 Kohler, P.D. & Field, S. (2003). 'Transition-focused education: Foundations for the future.' *Journal for Special Education*, 37(3), 174–183.

111 International Labour Organisation (1998). *Education, employment and training policies and programmes for youth with disabilities in four European countries*. Geneva: Author.

112 Aston, J., Dewson, S., Loukas, G. & Dyson, A. (2005). *Post-16 transitions: A longitudinal study of young people with special educational needs (Wave Three)*. Brighton, UK: Institute for Employment Studies.

113   OECD (1997). *Post-compulsory education for disabled people*. Paris: Author.

114   Cleland, G. & Smith, A. (2010). *Journey to work: Creating pathways for young disabled people in New Zealand*. Discussion document prepared for CCS Disability Action and Workbridge New Zealand.

115   United Nations (2008). *Convention on the Rights of People with Disabilities*. New York, NY: Author.

116   Ibid.

117   Ferrier, F., Long, M., Moore, D., Sharpley, C. & Sigafoos, J. (2007). *Investigating the feasibility of portable funding for students with disabilities*. Melbourne, Australia: Monash University; and Moore-Brown, B. (2001). 'Case in point: The administrative predicament of special education funding.' *Journal of Special Education Leadership*, 14, 42–43.

118   Ferrier et al., op. cit.

119   Shaddock et al., op. cit.

120   Hattie, J. (2005). 'What is the nature of evidence that makes a difference to learning?' Paper presented at the ACER Conference, Melbourne.

121   Shaddock et al., op cit., p. 91.

122   Mitchell (2014a), op. cit., p. 224.

123   Chambers, J.G., Shkolnik, J. & P rez, M. (2003). *Total expenditures for students with disabilities, 1999-2000: Spending variation by disability*. Report 5. Special Education Expenditure Project. Submitted to: United States Department of Education, Office of Special Education Programs.

124   Ibid., p. 30.

125   Evans, P. (2004). 'Educating students with special needs: a comparison of inclusion practices in OECD countries'. *Education Canada*, 44(1), 32-35.

126   Drawing upon the work of Beek, C. (2002). 'The distribution of resources to support inclusive learning.' *Support for Learning*, 17, 9-14; Ferrier et al., op. cit., Fletcher-Campbell, F. (2002). 'The financing of special education: Lessons from Europe.' *Support for Learning*. 17, 19-22; Meijer, C. (ed.) (1999). *Financing of special needs education: A seventeen-country study of the relationship between financing of special needs education and inclusion*. Middlefart, Denmark: European Agency for Development in Special Needs Education; Naylor, N. (2001). The Ontario special education funding model. *Journal of Special Education Leadership*, 14, 21-26; Pijl, S.J. & Dyson, A. (1998). 'Funding special education: A three-country study of demand-oriented models.' *Comparative Education*, 34(3), 261-279; Reynolds, M.C., Wang, M.C., & Walberg, H.J. (1987). 'The necessary restructuring of special and regular education.' *Exceptional Children*, 53, 391-398; Riddell, S., Tisdall, K., Kane, J. & Mulderrig, J. (2006) *Literature review of educational provision for pupils with additional support needs: Final report to the Scottish Executive Education Department*, Edinburgh: University of Edinburgh. URL: http://www.gov.scot/resource/doc/152146/0040954.pdf (accessed 19 May 2016); and Shaddock et al., op.cit.

127   Evans et al., op. cit.

128   Parrish, op. cit.

129   Evans, op. cit.

130   Parrish, op. cit.

131   Fletcher-Campbell, op. cit., p. 20.

132   Shaddock, et al., op.cit.

133   Synthesized from Beek, op. cit.; Ferrier, et al., op. cit.; Gallagher, J.J. (2006). *Driving change in special education*. Baltimore, MD: Paul H. Brookes Publishing Co.; Itkonen, T. & Jahnukainen, M. (2007). 'An analysis of accountability policies in Finland and the United States.' *International Journal of Disability, Development and Education*, 54, 5-23; Harr, J.J., Parrish, T. & Chambers, J. (2008). 'Special education.' In H.F. Ladd & E.B. Fiske (eds), *Handbook of research in education finance and policy* (pp. 573-589). New York, NY: Routledge; Meijer et al., op. cit.; Shaddock et al., op. cit.; and Weishaar, M.K & Borsa, J.C. (2001). *Inclusive educational administration: A case study approach*. New York: McGraw-Hill Higher Education.

134   Shaddock, et al., op. cit.

135   Landrum, T.J. (2011). 'Emotional and behavioral disorders.' In J.M. Kauffman & D.P. Hallahan (eds), *Handbook of special education* (pp. 209-220). New York: Routledge.

136   Bickman, L., Smith, C.M., Lambert, E.W. & Andrade, A.R. (2003). 'Evaluation of a Congressionally mandated wraparound demonstration.' *Journal of Child and Family Studies*, 12(2), 135-156.

137   Bruns, E.J., Sather, A., Pullmann, M.D. & Stambaugh, L.F. (2011). 'National trends in implementing wraparound: Results from the state wraparound survey.' *Journal of Child and Family Studies*, 20, 726-735.

138 Suter, J.C. & Bruns, E.J. (2009). 'Effectiveness of the wraparound process for children with emotional and behavioural disorders: A meta-analysis.' *Clinical Child and Family Psychology Review*, 12, 336-351.

139 Myaard, M.J., Crawford, C., Jackson, M. & Alessi, G. (2000). 'Applying behavior analysis within the wraparound process: A multiple baseline study.' *Journal of Emotional and Behavioral Disorders*, 8, 216-229.

140 Eber, L. & Nelson, C.M. (1997). 'School-based wraparound planning: Integrating services for students with emotional and behavioral needs.' *American Journal of Orthopsychiatry*, 67, 385-395.

141 Bruns, E.J., Rast, J., Peterson, C., Walker, J. & Bosworth, J. (2006). 'Spreadsheets, service providers, and the Statehouse: Using data and the wraparound process to reform systems for children and families.' *American Journal of Community Psychology*, 38, 201-212.

142 Pullman, M. D., Kerbs, J., Koroloff, N., Veach-White, E., Gaylor, R. & Sieler, D. (2006). 'Juvenile offenders with mental health needs: Reducing recidivism using wraparound.' *Crime and Delinquency*, 52, 375-397.

143 Webb, R. & Vulliamy, G. (2004). *A Multi-agency approach to reducing disaffection and exclusions from school*. DfES Research Report 568. London: DfES.

144 Bickman, L., Smith, C.M., Lambert, E.W. & Andrade, A.R. (2003). 'Evaluation of a Congressionally mandated wraparound demonstration.' *Journal of Child and Family Studies*, 12(2), 135-156, p. 152.

145 Stambaugh, L.F., Mustillo, S.A., Burns, B.J., Stephens, B.B., Edwards, D. & Dekraai, M. (2007). 'Outcomes from wraparound and multisystemic therapy in a center for mental health services system-of-care demonstration site.' *Journal of Emotional and Behavioral Disorders*, 15(3), 143-155.

146 Mitchell, D. (2013). 'Proposed values, knowledge and skill sets for educators working in inclusive settings with learners with diverse educational needs.' *Baltic Journal of Special Education*, 2(29), 145-157.

147 Mitchell (2014a), op. cit.

148 Horner, R.H., Sugai, G., Todd, A.W. & Lewis-Palmer, T. (2005). 'School-wide positive behavior support: An alternative approach to discipline in schools'. In L. Bambara and L. Kern (eds), *Individualized supports for students with problem behavior: Designing positive behavior plans* (pp. 359-390). New York: Guilford Press.

149 Carr, E. G., Dunlap, G., Horner, R. H., Koegel, R. L., Turnbull, A. P., Sailor, W., Anderson, J., Albin, R. W., Koegel, L. K. & Fox, L. (2002). 'Positive behavior support: Evolution of an applied science.' *Journal of Positive Behavior Interventions*, 4(1), 4-16.

150 Sprague, J., Walker, H., Golly, A., White, A., Myers, D. R. & Shannon, T. (2001). 'Translating research into effective practice: The effects of a universal staff and student intervention on indicators of discipline and school safety.' *Education and Treatment of Children*, 24(4), 495-511.

151 Horner, R. (2009). 'Extending the science, values and vision of positive behavior support.' Presentation at Sixth International Conference on Positive Behavior Support, Jacksonville, Florida.

152 Narhi, V., Kiiski, T., Peitso, S. & Savolainen, H. (2014). 'Reducing disruptive behaviours and improving learning climates with class-wide positive behaviour support in middle schools.' *European Journal of Special Needs Education*, 30(2), 274-285.

153 Sørlie, M.-A. & Ogden, T. (2015). 'School-wide positive behavior support - Norway: Impacts on problem behavior and classroom climate.' *International Journal of School and Educational Psychology*, 3(3), 202-217.

154 For information on PB4L School-Wide, see http://pb4l.tki.org.nz/PB4L-School-Wide (accessed 24 May 2016).

155 Mitchell (2014a), op cit.

156 National Center for Educational Statistics (1999). *Condition of America's public school facilities*. URL: http://nces.ed.gov/surveys/frss/publications/2000032/index.asp?sectionID=5 (accessed 2 January 2013).

157 Rosen, K.G. & Richardson, G. (1999). 'Would removing indoor air particulates in children's environments reduce rate of absenteeism: A hypothesis.' *Science of the Total Environment*, 234(3), 87-93.

158 Wargocki, P., Wyon, D.P., Matysiak, B. & Irgens, S. (2005). *The effects of classroom air temperature and outdoor supply rate on the performance of schoolwork by children*. URL: http://www.ie.dtu.dk/ (accessed 2 January 2013).

159   Higgins, S., Hall, E., Wall, K., Woolner, P. & McCaughey, C. (2005). *The impact of school environ-ments: A literature review.* Produced for the Design Council. Newcastle, UK: The Centre for Learning and Teaching, University of Newcastle.

160   Schmidt, C., Andrews, M. & McCutcheon, J. (1998). 'An acoustical and perceptual analysis of the vocal behaviour of classroom teachers.' *Journal of Voice,* 12(4), 434-443.

161   Blake, P. & Busby, S. (1994). 'Noise levels in New Zealand junior classrooms: Their impact on hearing and teaching.' *New Zealand Medical Journal,* 107(985), 357-358.

162   Bennetts, L.K. & Flynn, M.C. (2002). 'Improving the classroom listening skills of children with Down syndrome by using sound-field amplification.' *Down Syndrome Research and Practice,* 8(1), 19-24.

163   Barrett, P., Zhang, Y., Moffat, J. & Kobbacy, K. (2013). 'A holistic, multi-level analysis identifying the impact of classroom design on pupils' learning.' *Building and Environment,* 59, 678-689.

164   Houtveen & Van de Grift, op. cit.

165   See Mitchell (2014a), op. cit.; and Mitchell, D. (2014b). 'Twenty evidence-based strategies for en-hancing learning.' *Erdelyi Pszichologiai Szemle (Transylvanian Journal of Psychology),* Special Is-sue 2013, 13-32.

166   Mitchell (2014a) op. cit.

167   World Health Organization & World Bank, op. cit., p. 220.

168   Mitchell, D., Morton, M. & Hornby, G. (2010). *Literature review of Individual Education Plans,* Wel-lington, New Zealand: Ministry of Education. Available on NZ Ministry of Education website: http://www.educationcounts.govt.nz/__data/assets/pdf_file/0012/102216/Literature-Review-Use-of-the-IEP.pdf (accessed 24 May 2016).

169   National Council for Curriculum and Assessment (2007). *Guidelines for teachers of students with general learning disabilities. Introduction.* Dublin: Author. URL: http://www.ncca.ie/uploadedfiles/Publications/SEN_Introduction.pdf (accessed 19 May 2016).

170   Tomlinson, C.A. (2014). *The differentiated classroom: Responding to the needs of all learners.* Sec-ond edn. Alexandria, VA: ASCD.

7 Conclusions

WE WERE ALL HUMANS
UNTIL
RACE DISCONNECTED US,
RELIGION SEPARATED US,
POLITICS DIVIDED US,
AND WEALTH CLASSIFIED US.
(Banksy)

Human history becomes more and more a race between education and catastrophe.
(H.G. Wells)

I begin this chapter with Banksy's succinct definition of the problem and H.G. Wells's hopeful optimism regarding its solution. In writing this book, I regretfully come to the conclusion that most countries' education systems are losing Wells's race; they are failing significant numbers of their children who are disadvantaged by one or more aspects of their backgrounds. In some cases, it is girls who are excluded from education (Chapter 2); in others, it is boys who trail girls in achievement (Chapter 2) and, in still others, it is those whose different religions or beliefs lead to discrimination (Chapter 5). In many cases, it is children from low socio-economic status backgrounds whose performances lag those from higher socio-economic homes (Chapter 3), or children from ethnic minorities (Chapter 4), or those who have disabilities (Chapter 6), who are disadvantaged. In yet other cases, it is the combination of two or more of these markers of identity that leads to discrimination or low achievement. In all cases, segregation of children by reason of their diversity is a major cause for concern.

This need not happen! It is an indictment on politicians and educators that underachievement and discrimination among diverse learners has been tolerated for so long. It need not be the case. We know enough about its causes and about the remedies, yet we continue not to take effective action. Such dereliction of our duties towards the most vulnerable of our children must cease. Would we accept doctors having similarly low success rates with their patients? Would we accept engineers designing faulty buildings? What about aircraft designers creating aeroplanes with a proclivity for crashing? Would farmers stay in business when their crops or animals fail to thrive? Would we accept lawyers who consistently give poor legal advice? Why should the same standard of professionalism not be expected of our educational policy-makers and those responsible for delivering those policies? Ultimately, these are moral questions that challenge our commitment to the rights of people who are disadvantaged. Answers to them help define the nature of our societies and our view of ourselves as individuals and as a species.

But perhaps these are the wrong analogies, for I have drawn attention to professions that have a low tolerance of error. Maybe justice systems or mental health systems are more appropriate comparisons. Given the gravity of the problems manifested by their clients, these systems seem to have a high tolerance of errors, even if they try valiantly to reduce them. No, I don't think they should constitute a model for our education systems for, by and large, these deal with children who have the potential to succeed, even if they come from diverse backgrounds. So I come to the question, why has underachievement and discrimination among diverse learners been tolerated for so long? Why have evidence-based analyses of causes and attendant remedies not been more extensively put in place? These are moral questions that demand attention from educational policy-makers and those responsible for actioning them. Moreover, they are urgent questions that require addressing at all levels of our education systems. As I hope I have shown in this book, around the world there are many examples of successful programmes that accommodate to student diversity. The challenge is twofold – how to bring those programmes to scale and how to dispense with those that are failing. This will require enlightened leadership to bring about changes that equate with nothing less than a revolutionary transformation of education rather than evolutionary tinkering.[1]

In this final chapter, I will bring together the major findings presented in the substantive chapters, referring where appropriate to relevant sections of the chapters as summarized in Table 7.1 at the end of this chapter.

7.1 Most countries are becoming increasingly diverse

At least in western countries, populations are becoming increasingly diverse, leading to the notion of 'superdiversity'. This trend reflects a range of factors, including the impact of globalization with the attendant mobility of labour; the upsurge of refugees fleeing conflict or the consequences of global warming, or seeking better economic futures; changes in people's belief systems; changes in demographic profiles resulting from such factors as differential fertility rates among various groups; and independent choices of identity exercised by free citizens.

While it may be tempting to focus attention on the most pressing area of diversity at any one time – such as the refugee crisis confronting many countries at the time of writing – I believe it is imperative to address inequalities in all areas and their interactions.

7.2 Diversity often leads to prejudice and conflict

Unfortunately, diversity – and superdiversity – often creates intolerance and conflict at macro (societal) and micro (individual) levels, creating vulnerabilities in children. There is evidence that problems such as violence and drug abuse are worse in more unequal societies. Wilkinson and Pickett explain this by arguing that inequalities erode the cohesion of a society, the degree to which individual citizens are involved in their society, the strength of the social networks within it, and the degree of trust and empathy between citizens. Often, these inequalities have their origins in historical imbalances of power and marginalization, such as occurred in slavery and colonialism. Sometimes, they reflect the unintended consequences of social policies as seen, for example, in the implementation of some forms of multiculturalism. Sometimes, too, prejudice and conflict arise from state-sponsored or state-tolerated segregation of children based on various identity markers.

7.3 Schools have a major role to play in ensuring social cohesion

By addressing issues to do with diversity, schools can and should do much to create more peaceful societies and a world order based on mutual respect and tolerance. Education plays a major role in creating centripetal forces to counteract centrifugal forces that threaten societal cohesion. If centrifugal forces are stronger than centripetal forces, there may be fragmentation, instability, internal discord and challenges to the state's authority – to the extent that its very existence may be threatened. The education system should play a major centripetal role but, at the same time allowing for divergence of views and the creativity that can often ensue from this. The challenge to educators is to strike a balance between unity and diversity.

7.4 Finding the right balance between sameness and diversity is a challenge

Striking a balance between recognizing the rights of diverse peoples and the need to establish social cohesion constitutes a major challenge to societies around the globe. Inevitably, this challenge falls to a significant extent upon educators. When does tolerating or encouraging diversity threaten the fabric of a cohesive society? Conversely, does the aspiration for social cohesion have the intended or unintended consequence of marginalizing those who are different? To what extent should educators seek to achieve homogeneity of values, achievement and behaviour among students? To what extent should they attempt to assimilate those who are perceived to differ from the mainstream of society? What differences should they celebrate and enhance? Which ones should they seek to reduce, even eliminate? I recognize that the answers to these questions very much depend on the context of those who pose them. They are, nevertheless, important questions to consider.

7.5 Education systems should respect and enhance the human rights of diverse people

Consideration of society's responsibilities towards children who are disadvantaged for whatever reason must be predicated on the broad concept of human rights, as first articulated in the 1948 United Nations' *Universal Declaration of Human Rights*. This Declaration subsequently formed the basis of a wide range of Conventions or other instruments relating to the rights of women, children, indigenous people, people with mental illness, national or ethnic minorities, religious minorities, linguistic minorities, migrant workers and their families, refugees and, recently, people with disabilities.

These rights inform us as to what we may, must, and must not do to others and what we may expect of others in their behaviours towards us. Unfortunately, these rights are not always honoured; we must ensure that all decisions and actions in education respect and advance the human rights of the children we teach.

7.6 Theories of distributive justice should underpin our approach to diversity

In understanding the basis of human rights, we must also consider arguments about which economic framework and which resulting distribution of wealth is morally preferable. Deciding on the principles of distributive justice that should apply is extremely significant for determining how societies respond to differences among its citizens, particularly how they behave towards those who are disadvantaged – and especially towards children.

I believe that John Rawls's theory forms a substantial basis for determining our obligations towards children who are disadvantaged by their socio-economic status or cultural backgrounds, level of ability and, in some circumstances, by their gender or religion. In his 'difference principle', Rawls argued that divergence from strict equality is permitted so long as the inequalities in question would make the least advantaged in society materially better off than they would be under strict equality.

7.7 Developing inclusive societies and global community is both a means and an end

Inclusive education may be defined as education that fits the abilities, interests, values and experiences of learners – and their needs to relate to their peers in all their diversity. It is a multi-faceted concept that requires educators at all levels of a system to attend to vision, placement, curriculum, assessment, teaching, acceptance, access, support, resources and leadership.

A major theme of this book is that inclusive education should encompass *all* learners, not just those with disabilities. Around the world, however, there are many instances of children being segregated on the grounds of their gender, religion, ethnicity, socio-economic status, as well as their ability. At its most extreme, some groups of children are totally excluded from education, as in the case of girls in some Islamic societies or disabled children in many developing countries. Sometimes segregation occurs as a matter of policy, for example through allowing parents to choose their children's place of schooling or through governments deciding that special schools are legitimate places to educate children with disabilities. At other times it is (presumably) an unintended consequence of other policies, for example housing policies that lead to stratification of communities on the grounds of income. Whatever the circumstance, segregation occurs despite evidence that it at best bestows no advantages and, at worst, does harm to children.

Advocacy for inclusive education revolves around five main arguments. First, segregation of students with special needs is a violation of their human rights and represents an unfair distribution of educational resources. Second, inclusive education contributes significantly to a democratic society. Third, contact between members of different groups can work to reduce prejudice and intergroup conflict. Fourth, there is the related argument that inclusive education enhances social interconnectivity. Fifth, reliance on segregated special schools is economically non-viable.

7.8 There are multiple causes of diversities

In all of the chapters in this book, I drew attention to low achievement and social problems experienced by various groups of children. To what or whom should we attribute these occurrences? The child? The parents/caregivers? The school? Society? Globalization? Often, the debate hinges on efforts to determine the relative influence of schools vs societal structural features such as socio-economic constraints.

The position I take in this book is that there are multiple causes of differences among human beings. These include, singly and in combination, such factors as: evolution, globalization, poverty, geographic location, genetics, neuroscience, environmental degradation, cultural values, conflict, disasters, socialization, politics, neo-liberalism, technology, resources, parenting, diet, xenophobia – and education itself.

7.9 Diversities must be seen from an ecological perspective

The diversities outlined in this book were considered from an ecological perspective by focusing on how children are influenced by complex interactions among their societal, community, family, school and classroom contexts. In turn, this provides a framework for designing appropriate education for all children.

Thus, children are embedded in families, which, in turn, interact with a series of other systems – classrooms, schools, communities and the broader society. Family factors include interaction patterns, language, cultural capital and perceptions of the value of education. Classroom factors include the curriculum, assessment, pedagogy, peer group influences and classroom climate. School factors include policies, leadership, school culture and the deployment of human and capital resources. Community factors include demographic features, economic resources and cultural values. Societal factors include educational policies, resourcing and accountability mechanisms. Ideally, such systems should be 'joined up', which involves both horizontal and vertical integration. Horizontal integration requires linking systems at the same level to ensure consistency and compatibility of approach (e.g., among teachers in a school). Vertical integration requires linking more immediate, or proximal, systems with the more distal systems in which they are embedded (e.g., schools, communities and the wider society). Influences between systems should be seen as bi-directional. Just as families influence children, so too do children influence their families and just as schools influence families, so too do families influence schools, and so on. Children should be seen as active participants in their own development and not mere clay being shaped by forces around them.

7.10 Perceptions of diversity vary across time and space

Differences are perceived differently in different countries and at different times in their histories. Contexts of time and space matter. They determine how various domains of difference are or have been socially constructed and the nature of the competing social forces that may operate in such struggles. I am mindful, too, that while I have endeavoured to take an international perspective in writing this book, I will not have done justice to many countries' circumstances. As I asserted elsewhere, I believe that 'while every country can and should,

learn from other countries' experiences, it is important that each one gives due consideration to its own social-economic-political-cultural-historical singularities'.[2]

7.11 Interest convergence helps to explain shifts in behaviour and policies

Derek Bell explained the principle of interest convergence in 1980. He argued that the interest of Blacks in achieving racial equality will be accommodated only when it converges with
the interests of Whites. In this book, I presented a range of other circumstances when interest
convergence has or could take place to bring about shifts in policies and behaviours relating
to various disadvantaged groups.

7.12 Diversities intersect with each other

While I dealt with five major diversities in this book, it is essential to note that each one
interacts with several others. This means that individuals' identities are composed of various
combinations and permutations of these major categories, a situation which becomes even
more complex when we throw other diversities such as age, family background, location and
so on into the mix. For example, there is clear evidence of intersections between ethnicity,
gender and class in influencing achievement (see Chapter 3). Similarly, abilities/disabilities
interact with gender, class and ethnicity (Chapters 2, 3, 4 and 6), and so it goes on ... As Margaret Mead put it, 'Always remember that you are absolutely unique. Just like everyone else.'

In designing and evaluating educational programmes, decision-makers should be careful to disaggregate data on student performances when making judgments. This means
not only giving consideration to the five major categories of diversity explored in this
book, but also to the subcategories of each and the intersections among them, all the
while remembering that each individual learner is a unique person. It is important for
educators to disaggregate data so that patterns that may be masked by larger, aggregate
data can be revealed - and acted on. For example, some decisions can be guided by examining gender difference such as performance in STEM subjects. Other decisions might
require drilling down into broader categories, as in in the case of ethnicity, for example,
where Chinese students appear to have higher achievement than other ethnic groups.
Similarly, young boys are more likely than older boys to be referred to special education,
and White British girls are more educationally successful than White British boys. Looking specifically at sub-populations such as these can help to ensure that resources are
directed at students who most need them. A word of caution: disaggregation is probably
best undertaken at a system or school level, rather than at a classroom level where there
is low statistical power related to small sample sizes.

7.13 Human beings are genetically similar across major identity markers, but individually are genetically divergent

Genetic variation across the human population is surprisingly small. For example, some
estimates claim that only 6-15% of genetic variation can be accounted for by race. Thus,
if the total variation in the human species is partitioned into between-race and within-race

components, the former is a very small fraction of the total. Even though we may differ in trivial, superficial features, these may be conspicuous enough to serve as discrimination fodder, not just in mate choice but also in choice of enemies and leading to individuals becoming victims of xenophobic or religious prejudice.

Notwithstanding these points regarding broad genetic similarities, individuals are genetically divergent. For example, estimates suggest that around 40% of the variance in educational attainment is explained by genetic factors. Future studies may well see improvements in the predictive power of polygenic factors.

7.14 Consideration should be given to evolutionary perspectives on diversity

Evolutionary psychology argues that much human behaviour is the result of psychological adaptations that evolved to solve recurrent problems in past environments and to ensure survival and reproduction. Evolutionary processes have influenced not merely the body, but also the brain, the psychological mechanisms it houses, and the behaviour it produces. According to some writers, the notion that psychological mechanisms have adaptive functions is a necessary, not an optional, ingredient for a comprehensive psychological science.

7.15 Many differences are quite small, even if statistically significant

While many of the findings I presented in this book refer to statistically significant differences within various categories, it is important that we bear in mind that many of them are quite small and may not have great practical significance. For example, there is more variability *within* the two genders than there is *between* them.

7.16 Economics play a major role in catering for diversities

There are distinct economic benefits in achieving greater equality for disadvantaged groups. In pure cost-benefit analyses, there is an economic payoff in investing extra resources in such groups. These benefits accrue not only to the individuals, but also to society more broadly. In making decisions regarding such investments, various weighted funding models aimed at redressing various perceived disadvantages have been developed. Such models should meet the criteria of transparency, adequacy, efficiency, equity, robustness and freedom from unintended consequences. Not surprisingly, given the difficulty of simultaneously meeting these criteria, the various funding models that have been developed to take account of socio-economic status, ethnicity and ability differences are extraordinarily complex – and often controversial.

7.17 Education is multi-level and multi-faceted

The ultimate purposes of education are to enhance the quality of life of individual students and to enhance democracy, harmony and peace. To achieve these goals, education must be considered at multiple levels: national and district systems, schools and classrooms. As well, education is multi-faceted, comprising such features as curricula, assessment and pedagogy. For policies to be successfully designed and implemented, it is important that they be integrated vertically – both up and down various levels of government and the whole community – and horizontally – across jurisdictions.[3] Education systems are complex entities that reflect a host of different influences, both historically and contemporaneously: economic, philosophical, cultural and political. As a consequence, one approach to education cannot possibly fit all contexts.

7.18 There can be mismatches of cultural and social capital

Children who come from class, gender, cultural and religious backgrounds that differ from the prevailing norms and expectations of schools can be seriously disadvantaged. This disjunction leads us to consider Bourdieu's concept of cultural capital, Gramsci's idea of hegemony and Freire's critical pedagogy. Children come to school with worldviews – frameworks of ideas and attitudes about the world and themselves, with the beginnings of belief systems. These may be at variance with those held by some or many of their peers and their teachers. It is a challenge to educators to understand the parameters of these worldviews and to determine how far it is morally justified to support them or to challenge them.

7.19 Reason and evidence should determine educational policies and practices

As I have pointed out in my recent book, *What Really Works in Special and Inclusive Education*,[4] increasingly around the world, educators are being expected to draw upon credible data and research-based evidence in planning, implementing and evaluating their teaching. There is a wealth of evidence available to assist educators in their work with diverse students. Strategies that been found to be effective in teaching learners with a range of special educational needs may be summarized under four broad headings, according to their overarching theories of learning: social (e.g., cooperative group teaching, peer tutoring, social skills training, collaborative teaching, parent involvement,); behavioural (e.g., functional behavioural assessment, review and practice, direct instruction, and formative assessment and feedback); cognitive (e.g., cognitive strategy instruction, self-regulated learning, memory strategies, reciprocal teaching, and cognitive behavioural therapy); and mixed approaches (e.g., assistive technology, augmentative and alternative communication, and phonological awareness).

A related theme is the importance of gathering and utilizing data on students' performances. With regular stories in the news of massive thefts of people's private information and the fears associated with the newly coined term, 'metadata', 'data' are in danger of becoming discredited. With proper safeguards, however, students with disabilities could be the beneficiaries of recent technological developments that have made it possible to acquire, combine, store, analyze, interpret and report information on individuals during any phase of data management and to make decisions based on such information. Certainly, if there is a commitment to evidence-based decision-making in educating diverse students, it is essential to obtain, analyze and act upon outcome data. Data should be sought throughout the education system, nationally,[5] regionally and at the school and classroom levels. Depending on the purposes to which they will be put, data should meet a range of criteria: right to privacy, right to control information about oneself, validity, reliability, completeness, relevance, timeliness, availability and comparability.

7.20 Account should be taken of the impact of disruptive technologies

Given that high proportions of children who are the focus of this book leave school with minimal or no qualifications, consideration should be given to their future job prospects. Advances in computerization and other technology areas mean that, at best, some jobs will continue to be available but will undergo significant transformations, whereas, at worst, some will disappear altogether. On the plus side, technological change also brings direct and indirect job creation as machines require building and maintenance, more wealth is created and new markets are opened. Educators have a responsibility to prepare their students for a future where technology and its applications will become increasingly sophisticated in all spheres of life.

7.21 Technology has the potential to transform education

As we have seen, not all children are in a position to benefit from information and communications technology. Many children are on the wrong side of the 'digital divide', whether it is because their families or schools cannot afford modern technologies or their parents and teachers are unfamiliar with its use.

The time has come to change this situation, not only for the benefit of disadvantaged children, but also for all children. One of the clearest, most forceful and comprehensive advocacies in this direction was put forward in a US Department of Education's report *Transforming American education: Learning powered by technology*. In brief, it argued that technology-based learning and assessment should be 'pivotal in improving student learning and in generating data that can be used to continuously improve the education system at all levels'.[6] Further, technology enables collaborative teaching and professional learning that can enhance teachers' competencies. As noted in this report,

> The model of twenty-first-century learning described in this plan calls for engaging and empowering learning experiences for all learners. The model asks that we focus what and how we teach to match what people need to know, how they learn, where and when they will learn, and who needs to learn. It brings state-of-the art technology into learning to enable, motivate, and inspire all students, regardless of background, languages, or disabilities, to achieve. It leverages the power of technology to provide personalized learning instead of a one-size-fits-all curriculum, pace of teaching, and instructional practices.[7]

7.22 The focus should be on the uniqueness of individuals

Throughout this book, I have emphasized the importance of looking at diversity in terms of individual differences rather than exclusively in terms of group membership. This perspective extends from taking account of individual rights to the individualization of teaching and learning. As I mentioned earlier, this process involves 'varying content, activities, teaching, learning, methods and resources to take into account the range of interests, needs and experience of individual students'.[8] Given the heterogeneity of children who fit within the categories of diversity, I suggest that rather than trying to accommodate education programmes to such broad categories, the best way forward is individualization or, as some put it, 'personalization'. Such an approach is not only educationally necessary, but also with the advances in technology, it is increasingly feasible to put into operation – and urgent.

7.23 Universal design for learning provides fair opportunities for learning

In most of the chapters, I either explicitly or by inference advocated the importance of implementing the principles of universal design for learning. This involves planning and delivering programmes with the needs of *all* students in mind and applies to all facets of education: from curriculum, assessment and pedagogy to classroom and school design. It means that schools should provide multiple and flexible methods of presentation of information and knowledge, expression with alternatives for students to demonstrate what they have learned, and engagement to tap into diverse learners' interests.

7.24 Early prevention and intervention programmes should be developed

In four of the five substantive chapters (gender, socio-economic status, ethnicity and abilities), I emphasized the importance of the early prevention of underachievement and behaviour problems. Preferably intervention programmes should commence in the pre-school years, but certainly as soon as difficulties start to become apparent.

7.25 Educators and those who prepare them for their responsibilities play critical roles in educating diverse learners

There can be little doubt that teachers and school leaders play a critical role in improving the outcomes of students who are, for one or more reasons, disadvantaged. The challenges I have laid down in this book require educators who are sensitive to and welcoming of diversity among their students, who are willing and able to understand and accept different worldviews, who are able to develop and implement curricula based on the principles of universal design for learning, and who are able to adapt their pedagogy to take account of the diverse needs of their students. This means that teachers and school leaders must be educated to discharge these responsibilities, both in their initial teacher education programmes and in their ongoing professional development. In turn, this draws attention to the important role played by teacher educators and their accountability for preparing teachers to work with diverse learners. It also emphasizes the need for diversity content to be embedded in all components in initial teacher education programmes, instead of relying on stand-alone courses.[9] It is important, too, to conduct empirical evaluations of the effectiveness of diversity content in teacher education programmes.[10]

Just as I emphasized individualization with regard to teaching diverse students, so, too, is that approach needed with teachers. In an OECD Teaching and Learning International Survey (TALIS) carried out in 2009 across 23 countries, data were obtained from 90,000 teachers.[11] On average, 47% of them reported a high or moderate need for professional development for teaching in a multicultural setting. This level of need varied within schools, but not as a function of school types or different categories of teachers. Accordingly, the authors recommended that professional development programmes should focus on the needs of individual teachers rather than on schools or regions. While this study focused on ethnicity, I believe its findings apply equally to the other diversities discussed in this book.

7.26 A final word

Let me end by returning to H.G. Wells's claim that human history becomes more and more a race between education and catastrophe. While I believe that education has a major responsibility, the situation facing the world calls for a wider response. As recently expressed by Ban Ki Moon, the UN Secretary General:

> Today's world is a troubled world; one in turmoil and turbulence, with no shortage of painful political upheavals. Societies are under serious strain, stemming from the erosion of our common values, climate change and growing inequalities, to migration pressures and borderless pandemics … The nature and scope of this daunting array of enormous challenges necessitate that both inaction and business-as-usual must be dismissed as options … Simply put, this generation is charged with a duty to transform our societies.[12]

Finally, let me, with hope, quote a Māori saying:

> *Kia mau koe kit e kupu,*
> *Kia mau koe kit e mahi.*
>
> *Lay hold of the words,*
> *The deeds will follow.*

Notes

1   US Department of Education, Office of Educational Technology (2010). *Transforming American education: Learning powered by technology. National Technology Plan 2010*. Washington, DC: Author.
2   Mitchell, D. (2014). *What really works in special and inclusive education*. Second edition. London: Routledge, p. 12.
3   FEMA (2010). *Developing and maintaining emergency operations plans. Comprehensive preparedness guide*. URL: https://www.fema.gov/media-library-data/20130726-1828-25045-0014/cpg_101_comprehensive_preparedness_guide_developing_and_maintaining_emergency_operations_plans_2010.pdf (accessed 14 February 2016).
4   Mitchell, op. cit.
5   Australia's programme of Nationally Consistent Data Collection on School Students with Disability is a nationally consistent model for collecting information about the support ('adjustments') provided to students with various disabilities. See PricewaterhouseCoopers (2013). *2012 trial of the nationally consistent collection of data on school students with disability: Final report*. Sydney: Author.
6   US Department of Education, Office of Educational Technology, op. cit., p. ix.
7   Ibid., p. vi.
8   National Council for Curriculum and Assessment (2007). *Guidelines for teachers of students with general learning disabilities: Introduction*. Dublin: Author. URL: http://www.ncca.ie/uploadedfiles/Publications/SEN_Introduction.pdf (accessed 19 May 2016).
9   Essomba, M.A. (2010). 'Teacher education for diversity in Spain: Moving from theory to practice.' In *OECD, Educating teachers for diversity: Meeting the challenge* (pp. 219–236). Paris: OECD.
10 Burns, T. & Shadoian-Gersing, V. (2010). 'The importance of effective teacher education for diversity.' In *OECD, Educating teachers for diversity: Meeting the challenge* (pp. 19–40). Paris: OECD.

Table 7.1 Perspectives on diversity, by chapter

Perspective	Ch 1 Introduction	Ch 2 Gender	Ch 3 SES	Ch 4 Ethnicity	Ch 5 Religion	Ch 6 Ability	Ch 7 Conclusions
Most countries are becoming increasingly diverse	1.1	2.1	3.10	4.2, 4.4	5.2, 5.3, 5.7	6.5	7.1
Diversity often leads to prejudice and conflict	1.1, 1.4, 1.7, 1.8	2.8, 2.15	3.10	4.11, 4.12, 4.23, 4.29, 4.35	B, 5.12	6.24	7.2
Schools have a major role to play in ensuring social cohesion	1.12		3.10	4.12, 4.13			7.3
Education systems should respect and enhance the human rights of diverse people	1.7	2.56, 2.57, 2.58 2.65	3.2	4.12, 4.20, 4.21	5.9, 5.11	6.3, 6.23	7.4
Theories of distributive justice should underpin our approach to diversity	1.9		3.2, 3.5, 3.10, 3.33	4.18, 4.30		6.3	7.5
Developing inclusivist societies and global community is both a means and an end	1.8	2.51, 2.59, 2.60	3.29, 3.31	4.13, 4.14, 4.15, 4.16, 4.17, 4.23	C, 5.13, 5.16	6.6, 6.22, 6.32	7.6
Diversities must be seen from an ecological perspective	1.10	B, D	3.9, 3.19, 3.24	4.18		6.6	7.7
Perceptions of diversity vary across time and space	1.11	2.5, 2.6, 2.7, 2.8	3.10	4.3, 4.4, 4.8, 4.11, 4.35	5.2, 5.3, 5.5, 5.6, 5.7, 5.9, 5.12, 5.16	6.6	7.8
Finding the right balance between sameness and diversity is a challenge	1.12		3.10	4.12	5.13		7.9
Interest convergence helps explain shifts in policies and behaviour	1.13	2.7	3.4, 3.10	4.23, 4.24	5.15		7.10
Diversities intersect with each other	1.14	2.8, 2.33, 2.40, 2.54	3.7, 3.36	4.5, 4.6	5.4, 5.5	6.2, 6.10	7.11
There are multiple causes of diversities	1.15	B	C	C		C	7.12
Human beings are genetically similar across major identity markers, but genetically divergent individually	1.16	2.29, 2.31, 2.62		4.1		6.12	7.13

Consideration should be given to evolutionary perspectives	1.17	2.52	3.20	4.1	5.8	7.14
Many differences are quite small, even if statistically significant	1.18	2.4, 2.9, 2.10, 2.53				7.15
Economics play a major role in catering for diversities	1.19	2.7, 2.58	3.4, 3.10, 3.20, 3.22	4.24	5.8	6.16, 6.22	7.16
Education is multi-level and multi-faceted	1.20	D	D	D	C	D	7.17
There can be mismatches of cultural & social capital	1.21	2.57, 2.63	3.11	4.42	5.13	6.10, 6.23	7.18
Reason and evidence should determine policies and practices	1.22	2.39	3.27, 3.44	4.34, 4.40	5.1, 5.13, 5.14, C	6.33	7.19
Account should be taken of impact of disruptive technologies	1.23	2.5, 2.11, 2.51	3.18, 3.40	4.24	5.13	6.24	7.20
Technology has the potential to transform education	1.24	2.11, 2.51	3.18	4.42	5.13	6.33	7.21
The focus should be on the uniqueness of individuals	1.7, 1.25	2.6, 2.69, Conc	3.6	4.12	5.9, 5.11	6.34	7.22
Universal design for learning provides fair opportunities for learning	1.26	2.70	3.41	4.39		6.20	7.23
Early prevention and intervention programmes should be developed	1.27		3.26	4.25, 4.28, 4.31. 4.34		6.18	7.24

11 Jensen, B. (2010). 'The OECD Teaching and Learning International Survey (TALIS) and teacher education for diversity.' In *OECD, Educating teachers for diversity: Meeting the challenge* (pp. 63–91). Paris: OECD.

12 Ban Ki Moon (2014). *The road to dignity by 2030: Ending poverty, transforming all lives and protecting the planet. Synthesis report of the Secretary-General on the post-2015 agenda, 4 December 2014.* New York, NY: United Nations, p. 157.

Index

Note: For multiple-authored sources, only the first-named author is included.